UNDERSTANDING BONSAI

UNDERSTANDING BONSAI

Pieter Loubser

DELTA BOOKS

ACKNOWLEDGEMENTS

DELTA BOOKS (PTY) LTD
A division of Jonathan Ball
Publishers (Pty) Ltd
P O Box 2105
Parklands 2121

© Pieter Loubser 1993

All rights reserved. No part of this publication may be reproduced, stored in a retrieval system, or transmitted in any form or by any means, electronic, mechanical, photocopying, recording or otherwise, without the prior permission of the publisher.

First published 1993

ISBN 0 908387 65 2

Cover design by
Michael Barnett
Typesetting and reproduction by
Effective Reproductions
Printed and bound by National
Book Printers, Goodwood, Cape

Not only did my wife Magriet type this book several times, she had the arduous task of typing the first draft on a small portable typewriter. She also had to decipher my scribblings on a subject which she did not understand. I would not have been able to produce this book without her help and influence. Suzanne Jooste always believed I should do it; Steyn van Riet introduced me to bonsai; my bonsai friends kept me going. Thanks to them. Above all I thank and praise the Lord who created the trees and gave us the ability to appreciate their beauty in all its variety.

FRONT COVER
Ligustrum
English privet
Height: 75 cm
Owner: Eddie van der Westhuizen

FRONTISPIECE
Ficus craterostoma
Forest fig
Height: 50 cm
Owner: Pieter Loubser

CONTENTS

1   **GENERAL INTRODUCTION TO BONSAI**   1

What is a bonsai? 1, Saikei 3, Haiku 3, Questions and answers 4, History: beginning and development of bonsai 5, Period before China 5, In China 5, Bonsai in Japan 6, Bonsai in present-day China 9

2   **GUIDELINES TO SHAPING A BONSAI**   11

General principles 11, The trunk 15, The branches 15, Position of branches 16, Inclination of branches 17, The leaves 20, General shape 20, Forming smaller leaves 21, The roots 24, Groundcovers 25, General faults and problems 27, Roots 27, Improving faulty root systems 28, Trunks 30, Improving faulty trunks 30, Branches and leaves 34, Improving faulty branches and leaves 34, Grafting 35, General notes 35, Grafting branches and trunks 36, Bud grafting 38,

3   **SHAPING TECHNIQUES**   39

General 39, The lingnan technique 40, The reduction method 42, Shaping through pruning 43, The purpose of pruning 43, General rules 44, Pruning thick branches 45, Prevention of pruning scars 45, The effect of hormones 46, The effect of pruning at different times in the year 48, Defoliation 49, Methods of trimming 52, Pines 52, Broad-leaf varieties 56, Tufted growth 58, Cored growth 58, Scale-like growth 58, Flowering and fruiting varieties 58, Shaping through bending 59, Introduction 59, Time to wire 61, General pointers 62, Techniques to bend thicker branches 64, Removal of wires 66,

4   **CLASSIFICATION**   67

According to size 67, According to the inclination of the trunk 67, According to the base of the tree 67, According to the shape of the crown 68, According to the condition of the trunk 68, According to the number of trees 68, According to the number of trunks 68, South African styles 69, The influence of Zen Buddhism 69

5   **BONSAI STYLES**   71

Formal upright style — *Chokkan* 72, Informal upright style — *Moyo-gi* 73, Slanted style — *Shakan* 74, Semi-cascade style —

Han-kengai 76, FULL CASCADE STYLE — *Kengai* 78, ROOT OVER ROCK STYLE — *Seki-joju* 80, ROCK-CLINGING STYLE — *Ishi-zuke* 82, ROCK CONTAINER — *Ishi-uye* 84, EXPOSED ROOTS STYLE — *Ne-agari* 84, RAFT AND SINUOUS STYLES — *Ikada-buki* and *Netsuranari* 86, CLUMP OR SPROUT STYLE — *Kabudachi* 89, BROOM STYLE — *Hoki-zukuri* 90, BALL OR SPHERE SHAPE — *Tama-zukuri* 92, FLAME SHAPE — *Rosoku-zukuri* 92, UMBRELLA STYLE — *Kasa-zukuri* 92, WEEPING BRANCHES STYLE — *Shidare-zukuri* 92, OCTOPUS STYLE — *Tako-zukuri* 93, SPIDER STYLE — *Kumo* 93, LITERATI STYLE — *Bunjin* 93, WINDSWEPT STYLE — *Fuki-nagashi* 94, GROUP PLANTING — *Yose-uye* 95, TWO TREES AND DOUBLE TRUNK STYLES — *Soju* and *Sokan* 98, TRADITIONAL PINE SHAPE — *Matsu-zukuri* 100, BAOBAB STYLE 100, PIERNEEF STYLE 101, FLAT-CROWN STYLE 102

6 SPECIAL TECHNIQUES TO ENHANCE APPEARANCE OF BONSAI — 103

HOLLOW TRUNK — *Saba-miki* or *Sabakan* 103, JIN AND SHARI 104, PLAITED TRUNK — *Pien-tshu* 107, TWISTED AND COILED TRUNK — *Horai* 108, DRIFTWOOD — *Sharimiki* 109

7 MAINTENANCE AND DAILY CARE — 111

BONSAI CALENDAR 111, THE BONSAI-EN 115, WATERING BONSAI 117, PESTS AND DISEASES 119, FERTILISING 120, SOIL 125, ROOTS 129, PRACTICAL TIPS 130, HOW PLANTS LIVE 133, TOOLS AND THEIR CARE 136

8 POTS, POTTING AND REPOTTING — 139

HISTORY OF CERAMICS AND POTS 139, CHOICE OF POT 141, THE ANATOMY OF A BONSAI POT 143, HANDLING A POT 144, MATCHING POTS WITH TREES 144, PLACEMENT OF POT 145, PLACEMENT OF BONSAI IN POT 145, ROOT-PRUNING AND REPOTTING 146

9 DISPLAYING BONSAI — 149

PLACES TO EXHIBIT BONSAI 149, COMPLEMENTARY ITEMS 150, SUISEKI 151, INHERENT MOVEMENT IN A DISPLAY 152, POSITION OF PIECES ON DISPLAY 154, STANDS 154, BACKGROUND 155, JUDGING BONSAI 155

10 SOURCES OF BONSAI — 157

FROM SEED 158, FROM CUTTINGS 158, FROM LAYERING 160, FROM NATURE OR THE GARDEN 164, FROM NURSERY STOCK 167

GLOSSARY — 171

JAPANESE TERMINOLOGY AND TRANSLATIONS — 174

BIBLIOGRAPHY — 176

INDEX — 177

PREFACE

There is no wealth equal to knowledge,
and no poverty equal to ignorance,
and no support equal to sound advice.
CALIPH ALI

I was introduced to bonsai in 1981. I received basic training from Rudy Adam, but due to distance I had to rely on books to give me more information, and through trial and error I struggled on. The books I had to rely on were not satisfactory, to my mind, and I felt I virtually needed a library on bonsai to get the fundamental information. It happened that I moved to a more remote part of the country, and to my surprise I met people who wanted to start a bonsai club. I was asked to help with training the novices and this led to me putting my thoughts together in an orderly fashion. After a while I put together a small training manual, but this developed into a far more comprehensive book, which I think covers all aspects of bonsai growing. The book is based on my own experience and frustrations, plus many hours of literature research.

The photographs shown are of bonsai that have been in training for only a few years (six to ten). The drawings are all my own and vary from very simple line drawings to explain a principle, to more artistic dream trees, through which I hope readers will be able to understand the principles of the art and build into their own trees their own interpretations and artistic leanings. The act of putting everything together in one book, has helped me a lot to understand and appreciate bonsai.

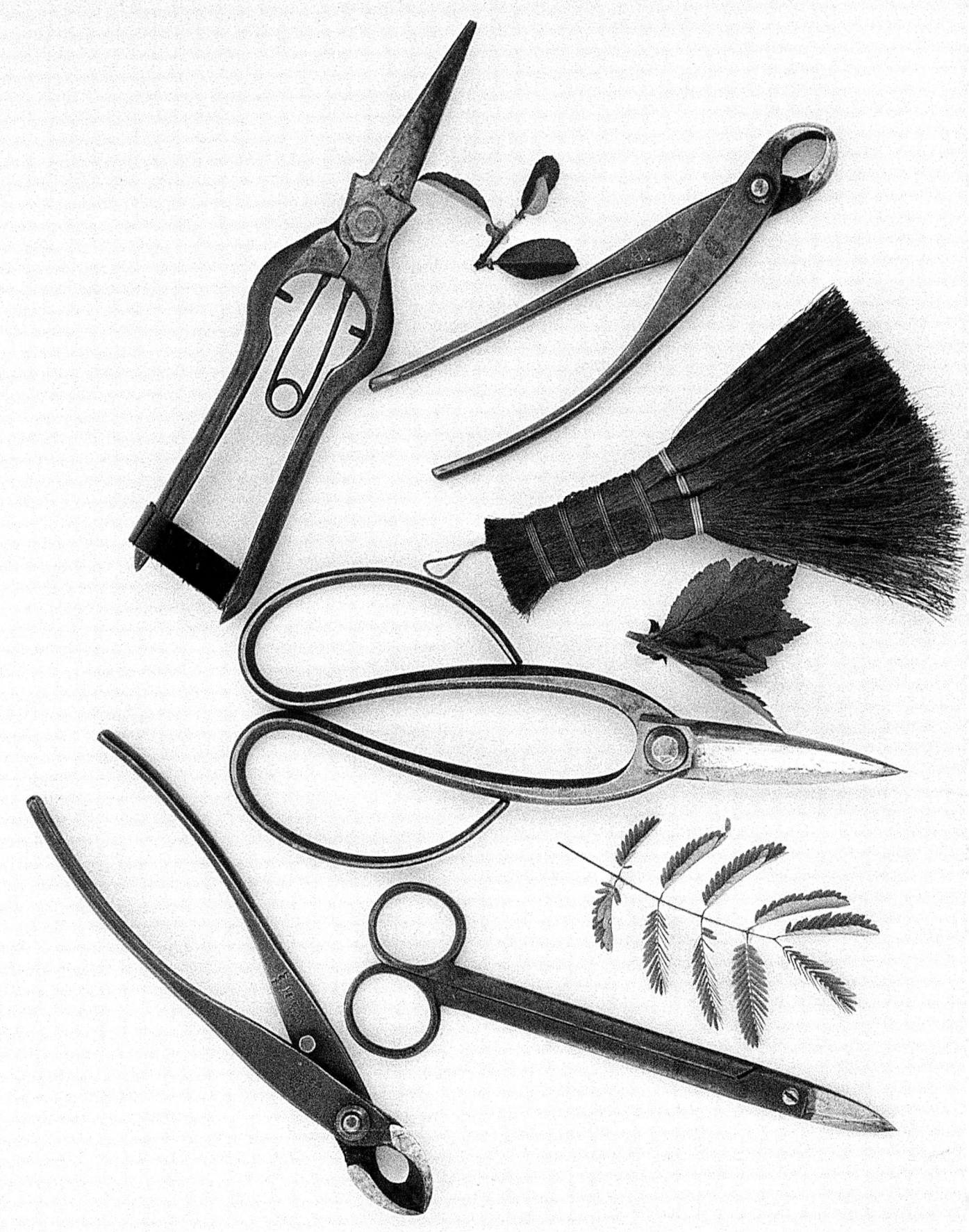

GENERAL INTRODUCTION TO BONSAI

WHAT IS A BONSAI?

There are three parts to this definition. First, a bonsai is a miniature replica of the tree in nature. Second, the tree must be planted in a container, preferably ceramic, and the container may not visually overwhelm the tree. In some instances the tree may be grown very successfully on a rock or piece of slate instead of in a ceramic container. Third, the tree *must* be trained correctly into a recognised bonsai style. One cannot, for example, call a potted *Monstera deliciosa*, or a *Ficus benjamina* or *Fuchsia* species bonsai. Neither are the trees in pots or other containers, displayed on sidewalks or patios, even though they are smaller versions of the naturally growing trees. So what is a bonsai? Continuing the third point above, the rest of the definition of a bonsai is contained in Chapter 5 on bonsai styles, and is probably the longest definition I know.

To grow a tree and train it strictly according to somebody else's prescription would show a lack of initiative, creativity and artistry. Stunting the growth of a tree which would otherwise grow to a considerable size, does not mean that a bonsai has been created. To my mind the answer lies in creating a bonsai within the framework of rules regarding each style and governed by the three points mentioned at the start of the chapter.

These so-called rules are flexible and are there to give a general idea of at least the outline of the tree, the general position of the branches and many more facets. No artist would allow himself to be absolutely restricted by rules, as this would stifle his *creative* spirit. Art cannot be contained or limited by constricting regulations. Also, in the case of bonsai, the tree will develop in its own individual way. Bending the tree to one's own will may not be only be impossible, but — and this is of extreme importance — highly undesirable, as such manipulation would prevent the natural development of the tree, according to its own genetic pattern, into a unique and remarkable specimen. This is especially true for trees that have already been growing for some years, and have formed a lot of wood in their trunks and branches.

The bonsai is not an exact replica of the natural tree, but should symbolise it in a simplified way. Where a tree in nature might have twenty or more primary and secondary branches with masses of leaves, the bonsai would have approximately six or seven main branches. It is like comparing an impressionist painting to a photograph of the same scene — an illusion is created, and the bonsai must in all its simplicity tell you the same story as the natural tree, which has withstood the onslaught of nature for some years.

Because a bonsai should be giving you a vision of nature, it is clear that one can learn a lot by taking note of the way in which trees grow in nature and how particular circumstances influence their growth. No two trees are the same! You

Art! Who comprehends her? With whom can one consult concerning this great goddess?

LUDWIG VON BEETHOVEN

will seldom find a tree in nature which is perfect according to bonsai standards, but the eye should be trained to see bonsai potential in nature.

The actual age of a tree is not as important as its apparent age. It is the bonsai grower who creates the illusion of age. This enables a grower, using a young tree, to create a bonsai of a reasonable standard within a few years, and places the art of bonsai within the reach of the average person.

To improve one's knowledge, perception and judgement, trees should be studied in nature and compared with photographs and examples of bonsai. Stealing with the eyes is no crime!

The style of the tree and the influence of the pot will be described in Chapters 5 and 8.

The purpose of bonsai is to reproduce an aged, beautiful tree which should in all respects resemble its counterpart in nature — it may for example portray the effects of a harsh environment — simply for the enjoyment of its owner and other viewers. Trees may be called bonsai generally, but depending on *who* cared for these trees they will become either masterpieces or trees of little value. Here is a list of points to consider when viewing and evaluating a tree:

- the condition of the rootage at the base of the trunk (called *nebari*)
- the base of the trunk itself
- the curvature of the trunk
- the appearance of the bark
- the artistic appearance of the branches
- the appearance of the leaves, paying attention to their relative size, colour and health
- the flowers and fruit, when in season
- the position and shape of the crown of the tree (the foliage canopy)
- the appearance of the surface soil and its covering
- the suitability of the container
- the suitability of the stand

The potential bonsai grower may be daunted by the seemingly complicated and wide-reaching prerequisites for a tree to be called a bonsai, but all will become clear as you progress through this book. It could be compared to learning how to drive a car, which seems complicated when one starts to master all the intricacies and technicalities that later become formalities. The same happens when you grow bonsai; in time you learn to notice all the different aspects and how to attend to them. Venture forth into this incredibly fascinating world of living art; learn, apply your knowledge, create and enjoy bonsai.

One can imagine that the first dwarfed trees were found in nature, in adverse conditions such as clefts in rocks, against cliffs, on wind-ravaged mountain peaks, in shallow soil and similar situations. In these circumstances, the small amount of soil surrounding the roots would soon be exhausted of nutrients, stunting the growth of the tree. The tree somehow stays alive by receiving enough water via dew and rain. The root system deteriorates, with resultant deterioration of the trunk, branches and leaves. At times the tree would receive nourishment from bird droppings or soil washed down from elsewhere, leaves falling and decomposing, as well as from trace elements contained in rain and dust. Some roots decay and die and new ones are formed. In this way the tree survives, albeit precariously, and because of these hardships it cannot grow to its normal size.

What happens to a bonsai is analogous to the above description, the main difference being that the changes in the life of a bonsai tree are all carefully controlled. The soil is replaced regularly and fertilising supplies the required additional nutrients. Dead twigs and leaves are removed and pests and injuries are

There never was any yet that wholly could escape love, and never shall there be any, never so long as beauty shall be, never so long as eyes can see

LONGUS
(third century AD)

controlled. This is also the reason why a bonsai could live longer than its equivalent in nature.

The technical explanation for the dwarfing lies in the balance between the quantity of minerals absorbed by the root system and the quantity of carbohydrates (starches and sugars) the leaves can produce through photosynthesis.

Whenever a tree's roots are reduced, the remaining roots absorb less minerals. Because these are used in the production of the carbohydrates, the leaves produce less carbohydrates than are needed for the normal functioning of the tree. The leaves which form are then smaller in size and number. The same process takes place when leaves are reduced in size or number, through pinching back or defoliation. In this instance the leaves — the carbohydrate factories — do not produce enough carbohydrates, and this stunts the overall growth, but in particular the roots, as they are dependent on a continuous supply of sugars for their cellular processes. There is no sense in the tree absorbing a large quantity of minerals if there is no such demand from the leaves. In time, if left unheeded, the tree will form more leaves and as the quantity of leaves increases the mineral absorption will increase proportionally. If it should happen that the root system recovers, a corresponding recovery in the leaves will be noticed. This is clearly seen in the increased growth after a tree has been repotted and should be kept in mind when a tree has reached its required size and shape. If the soil is replaced too often and without other restricting measures your bonsai will keep on increasing in size, until it is no longer a bonsai. Remember that no tree stays small of its own accord. The bonsai grower is responsible for the bonsai's stunted growth, which he achieves by using the above-mentioned knowledge, along with knowledge of how hormones affect growth.

SAIKEI

A *saikei* is a grouping of trees and other items to simulate a landscape. In general the art is similar to bonsai, but the tree (or trees) play a minor role, as the other elements of the landscape scene are also important. The additional elements include mosses, miniature grasses, rocks, gravel and water as needed to create the scene. The trees used are generally smaller and less mature than in bonsai group plantings, but as in group plantings, you may use trees which, due to unwanted properties, cannot be used on their own. Choose trees with naturally small leaves. The pots used are shallow and should preferably be of a subdued colour. Gravel can be used to form beaches or rivers, while rocks are used to create ravines, cliffs and mountains.

The *saikei* may be used as a temporary training stage for a tree or trees, until they have developed well enough to be used as bonsai. This will require the usual wiring and pruning.

HAIKU

Haiku are short verses with a specific form. The Japanese have been writing haiku for many centuries, and they have served as inspiration for poetic descriptions and for bringing about awareness of and expressing feelings about the wonderful world around us.

The classical *haiku* consists of three lines, with five syllables in the first, seven in the second and five in the third line. One need not abide strictly by this ruling as even the Japanese *haiku* poets used other forms, for instance using four lines but retaining approximately seventeen syllables. The one important fact is that the *haiku* must speak to the reader about inner feelings related to what is seen in nature.

Haiku should tell a little story and refer to nature in plant or animal form, or to natural phenomena like rain, winter and clouds.

---

*H*AIKU
A rough sea!
Stretched out over Sado
The Milky Way

MATSUO BASHO

In this book, *haiku* will be used on occasion, with the hope of inspiring the reader to strive towards creating and enjoying ideal bonsai.

QUESTIONS AND ANSWERS

These are some of the questions commonly asked about bonsai, along with their answers:

Question: How long does it take to create a bonsai?
Answer: A quick-growing species would reach a reasonable appearance within three to five years.
Question: How long do bonsai trees live?
Answer: A bonsai lives longer than its equivalent in nature and with the necessary care may even live a few hundred years.
Question: How often must bonsai be repotted?
Answer: Bonsai are repotted anywhere from every six months to ten years, in the case of pines. This depends on the particular species and on whether growth must be encouraged or not.
Question: Must a Japanese pot be used?
Answer: The Japanese have, over centuries, developed the art of producing pots with the right shape, size and appearance. Their pots are made of the best clay available, to enable them to protect the roots against the heat of the sun, for instance. Locally made pots are of a reasonable quality.
Question: Do all bonsai come from Japan?
Answer: No, all bonsai do not come from Japan. Since the introduction of this form of botanical art to the Western world, many species of trees other than those found in Japan have been grown as bonsai with great success. New varitions in style have been created, of which the baobab style is but one example.
Question: Aren't bonsai a lot of trouble?
Answer: Growing a beautiful tree which complies with bonsai requirements definitely requires a lot of attention — more than a tree or shrub in the garden. The pleasure it gives, however, surpasses the difficulties experienced.
Question: Why are bonsai trees so expensive?
Answer: Both Japanese and locally made pots tend to be expensive. An ordinary flower bouquet which lasts only a few days, costs a lot of money. Compare the short lived pleasure of a bouquet to the longevity of a bonsai as well as the time and effort involved in growing a bonsai, and it becomes apparent why bonsai cost as much as they do.
Question: Isn't it cruel to the trees?
Answer: Is it cruel to mow a lawn and keep it in a perfect condition? Also, as shown before, a bonsai lives longer than its counterpart in nature, which proves that the tree actually benefits from the treatment.
Question: Did the art originate in Japan?
Answer: As will be explained later, the Chinese practised a similar art form, many years before the Japanese did.
Question: Are there any special or magical chemicals used to dwarf the trees?
Answer: It is simply through timely pruning of roots and leaves that growth is restricted.
Question: How are bonsai trees started?
Answer: As with any other tree a bonsai can be grown from seed, cuttings, nursery trees or taken from nature.
Question: What are the elements and conditions required for growing bonsai?
Answer: Conditions are: an outdoor growing area, two to six hours of daily sunshine, regular watering, fertilising (especially during the summer months),

---

*'The sun strokes softly.
Shining lies the morning dew;
bonsai grows green'*

Japanese poetry has as its subject matter the human heart. It may seem to be of no practical use and just as well left uncomposed, but when one knows poetry well, one understands also without explanation the reasons governing order and disorder in the world.

KAMO MABUCHI
From: Writings

pruning and repotting as required. Elements are: suitable tree material, a shallow container, soilmixture, water, sunlight and fresh air.

HISTORY: BEGINNING AND DEVELOPMENT OF BONSAI

Period before China

Contrary to popular belief, the ancient art of bonsai does not originate in Japan. In fact history shows that other civilisations grew miniature trees in various containers many centuries before the Japanese did.

In ancient Egypt trees were grown in containers hewn out of rock. Drawings on the temple walls of Neb-hepet Re'Mentuhopte (2110–2061 BC) and Hatshepsut (1520–1479 BC) at Deir-el-Bahri close to Thebes, depict this. The Pharaoh Rameses II gave five hundred and fouteen so-called gardens to the temples as gifts. These gardens consisted of olive trees, dates, lilies, grasses and other plants in containers and they were used for their fruit and herbs, as well as for their medicinal value. Whereas modern bonsai are kept for purely ornamental or aesthetic reasons, it is obvious that those ancient gardens were functional.

The Ayurvedic physicians in ancient India practised the science of dwarfing enormous trees for medicinal purposes. The art or science was called 'Vaamantanu Vrikshaadi Vidya'. Because the physicians could not readily get hold of those parts of the tree necessary for their medications, they learnt how to miniaturise giant trees like the banyan, acacia and others, and kept them conveniently at hand.

There is also proof that other ancient civilisations, for instance the Romans, Greeks, Babylonians, Persians, Hindus and peoples of Europe, grew trees in containers.

TRAINED TREES
A bush cut into shape and looked after carefully, is not a bonsai – this is the art of topiary. A tree trained to look like a bonsai, but grown in the garden, no matter how small the tree may be, is not a bonsai – it is a niwa-gi!

In China

Chinese dynasties:

Fu Hsi (Animal tamer)	4754–3495 BC	Ch'in	256–207
Shen Nung (Divine farmer)	3494–2674	Han	206 BC–AD 221
Huang Ti (Yellow emperor)	2674–2575	The Three Kingdoms	222–265
Shao Hao	2574	The Six Dynasties	265–580
Chuan Hsu	2490	Sui	580–618
Ti Ku	2412	T'ang	618–907
Ti Chih	2366	The Five Dynasties	907–960
Yao and Shun	2333–2184	Sung	960–1276
Hsia Dynasty	2183–1752	Yuan	1276–1368
Shang (before migration)	1752	Ming	1368–1644
Yin (after migration)	–1028	Ch'ing	1644–1911
Chou	1028–257	The Chinese Republic	1911–

In China, the art of gardening evolved over centuries from as early as 2205 BC when it was merely the artistic planning of gardens, through a stage during which trees were pruned into various shapes comparable to western topiary, to the T'ang dynasty (618–907). During the latter period miniature landscapes were created to fit into containers. A wall painting in the tomb of Prince Chang Huai in Chien Ling depicts some of these plantings.

During the Sung dynasty (960–1276) the art of dwarfed rock and tree landscapes (*penjing*) became popular again. In the Yuan dynasty (1280–1368) these potted plants were called *shea tzu ching*. The art was also quite popular during the Ch'ing dynasty (1644–1911), when porcelain figurines were used alongside the trees. In a botany book published in 1688, *Pi-chuan Huasching*, the art was referred to as *pentsuai* — 'to plant in a pot'. By then trees were being trained into different styles in different parts of China, depending on the influences of current traditions at the

Every age has its pleasures, its style of wit, and its own ways.

NICOLAS BOILEAU DESPRAUX

time and how the trees were affected by their natural surroundings. Examples of these are the pagoda style from the Yangchow area, the earthworm style from Szechuen and the flat top style from Hunan and Hupeh, as well as others.

There followed a period in which it was fashionable to shape trees into bizarre Chinese characters, but gradually these unusual, artificial styles became unpopular and virtually disappeared. Towards 1900 monks in a monastery in the Kwangtung province began training trees according to the clip and grow method, also known as the *Lingnan* method. This development modified the bizarre creations in other centres, but the ancient themes are still evident in the modern Szechuen, Yangchow and Anhui styles amongst others.

What has been described above may not be true bonsai as we know it today, but certainly laid the foundation from which bonsai has developed into the present art form.

It should be noted that due to the great expanse of mainland China, and the resulting different climatic conditions, a larger variety of trees is utilised in China than in Japan.

The Western world is only now becoming acquainted with the development of the art of bonsai in China due to the Chinese government relaxing restrictions on visitors to their country. Since 1978 China has staged an annual bonsai exhibition in Canton (Guangzhou).

> PERSPECTIVE OF JAPAN
> We Orientals ... find beauty not only in the thing itself but in the pattern of shadows, the light and the darkness, which that thing produces.
>
> TANIZAKI JUNICHIRO

Bonsai in Japan

Japanese periods and eras:

Heian period	794–1185 AD
Kamakura period	1185–1333
Muromachi period	1333–1568
Momoyama period	1568–1603
Tokugawa (Edo) period	1603–1868
Meiji period	1868–1912
Taisho period	1912–1926
Showa period	1926 to present time

The Edo period is subdivided into:
the Genroku era   1688–1704
the Temo era   1830–1844

The sixth century marks the advent of Ch'an or Zen Buddhism in Japan, which came to full flower in the 12th century due to the work of two monks, Eisai and Dogen. Eisai was a Tendai monk, who wished to restore pure Buddhism in Japan and with that purpose visited China. Eisai also taught that Zen should defend the state and that its followers should observe ceremonial rules and offer prayers and incantations.

Zen influence can be seen in the *Nō* plays, in poetry, flower arrangement and the tea ceremony; all of which stress grace and spontaneity — the hallmarks of a good bonsai!

It is thought that some of the Buddhist monks were masters of the bonsai art and brought their knowledge to Japan.

Zen Buddhism was introduced to the Western world by Dr Daisetz Suzuki in 1908. To the Westerner the importance of Zen doctrines lies in the focus on simplicity, tolerance and acquiring a sense of freedom and personal peace through meditation. As one's knowledge of bonsai increases, the influence of Zen Buddhism on bonsai training becomes apparent. This influence will be discussed a little later.

During the Kamakura period in Japan (1180–1333) the art of Japanese gardening was well established, however the trees were grotesque and unnatural. The first known and authentic record of bonsai is in *Kasuga Gongen Kenki Emaki*, a picture scroll (*emakimono*) by Takashina (1309). In another picture scroll on the life of Saint Horen (1133–1212), there are pictures of dwarfed trees in ceramic containers which had obviously been made for the purpose.

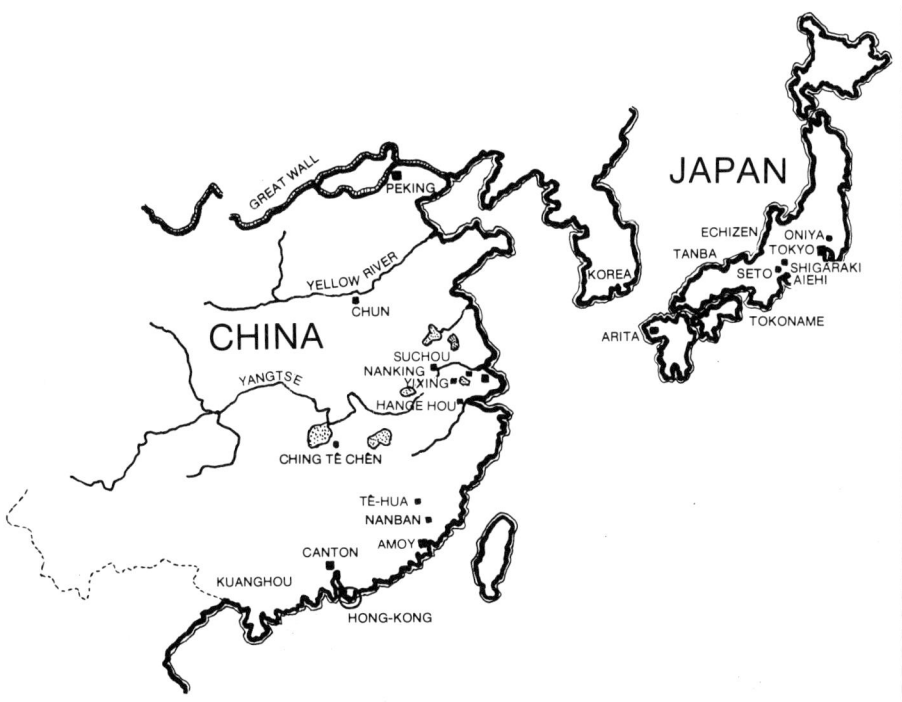

'To appreciate and find pleasure in curiously curved, potted trees, is to love deformity,' Kenko Yoshida (1283–1351) wrote in his satirical manner, in his famous *Tsurezure-gusa* (Essays in Idleness), around 1330. This essay tells the story of a man taking shelter from rain under the pylon of the Toji temple in Kyoto. While there, he notices a group of crippled beggars, their legs and arms twisted and deformed. Once home he looks at his potted trees and in them sees a resemblance to the poor beggars. In disgust he throws away his whole collection and longs for trees with normal shapes. Dwarfed and grossly twisted potted trees were indeed fashionable among the upper classes of the time. Other scrolls on which bonsai can be seen are the *Saigyo Monogatari Emaki* (1250–1270), the *Ippen Shohin Eden* (1299) and the *Honen Shohin Eden* (1317).

Somewhat later bonsai plays a part in the 'Hachi-no-ki', a *Nō* play, written by Seami (1363–1444). Tokiyori (1227–1263), a retired Regent of the Kamakura Shogunate and the poor yeoman Tsuneyo are the main characters in the play. Tokiyori, disguised as an itinerant priest, comes to the hamlet of Sano while he is on a pilgrimage through the provinces. Initially the priest, caught in a snowstorm, is not allowed into the house. Later when he is allowed in, Tsuneyo burns three bonsai trees, a pine, an apricot and a cherry — prized possessions — to keep the unexpected guest warm. As a token of appreciation, the Regent Tokiyori presents the family with three country estates!

The Muromachi period followed the Kamakura, and lasted about 260 years, during which time the development in arts and crafts was remarkable. The well-known tea ceremony is but one example. The collection of dwarfed trees in containers became popular, although knowledge of pruning and training was rudimentary. In the early years of the Muromachi period, bonsai were placed on display shelves in the home, and not only on verandas or near the house, as in earlier times.

The bonsai style of *tako* (the octopus) was in vogue. In fact, it was the only styling technique of any note, until the twentieth century. The *tako*-trained pine tree is rather like the upper half of the *horai*-trained pine, which in turn is similar to the *hankan* (gnarled trunk). The trunk is curled several times, in tiers, with an equal distance between them, but narrowing gradually upwards to form a pyramid shape. The *horai* style was a later modification. The Enshu school of floral arrangement at that period followed this style and was very skilled in curving shoots and branches.

Then came the Tokugawa period (1603–1867) which was a long and peaceful era under feudal government. In the latter half of the seventeenth century gardening and landscape gardening reached the highest degree of artistry in Japan's history. Ibei Ito, the most famous nurseryman and author, lived during this time. Details of his nursery can be seen on a large printed sheet painted by Kiyoharu. On it, different styles of bonsai can be discerned — but no *tako*-styled trees! The containers were deep, unlike the shallow containers presently in use, but the training techniques were advanced. *Kinsei-jufu*, published in 1830, contains illustrations of containers of various shapes and depths. During this time (the early nineteenth century) a group of Japanese masters of Chinese literature, as well as some poets and artists, met in Hami City, near Osaka, to discuss the various styles of potted trees. It is presumed that they decided to call the art 'bonsai', although the word '*hachi-ue*' remained in use for some time. '*Hachi-ue*' means 'a tree in a tray'.

Japan was exposed to Western influence only after feudal government ended in 1867. Western visitors to Japan then became interested in bonsai. Bonsai nurseries sprang up to supply a growing export market. There were two main groups, namely the *tako-zukuri* group in Edo (the present Tokyo) and the *Literati* group in the regions of Kyoto and Osaka. After continued criticism from the *Literati* group, the *Tako-zukuri* group simplified their distorted style.

During the early part of the twentieth century the Japanese became a prosperous nation and this resulted, among other things, in a burst of enthusiasm for bonsai growing. Japan has been overpopulated since earliest times, and now there was an opportunity for people living in dwellings with no gardens to 'garden' and experience the spirit of nature by growing bonsai.

Previously, the containers had been relatively deep. In the Meiji era (1868–1912) shallower pots were introduced. Due to the influence of Regent Meiji, 'bonsai' became the official name for these miniature potted trees.

In June 1912 the Bonsai Promotion Group was founded by Seian Shimuzu and others. They met during monthly meetings and published a magazine, *Bonsai*.

The bonsai collections withstood a terrible flood and, in 1923, a destructive earthquake. The Bonsai Promotion Group did not survive. However, various exhibitions were held and the art became established and grew in status and recognition.

Some of the earliest bonsai in the West came from Japan. It seems clear that Japan acted as a bridge between China and the Western World, to establish bonsai in the West. Introduced during the Third Universal Exhibition in Paris in 1878, and later displayed at the 1889 and 1900 exhibitions, the miniature trees aroused much curiosity and were eventually sold at auctions, fetching very high prices for those times. At about the same time various bonsai were imported into England and displayed by the Japanese at the London Exhibition of 1909. It is said that King Edward VII had a collection in which he took a keen personal interest. The general public however was then, as some are even today, under the impression that secret methods and agents were used to control the size of the diminutive trees.

Yuji Yoshimure and Toshio Kawamoto, two modern masters, realised that Westerners needed to be taught how to master the art, but that it could not be done via the Oriental method of 'looking and learning'. Oriental students picked up the knowledge as it was passed on from generation to generation, as well as by watching masters at work. It is obvious that only a few acquired the knowledge and had the artistic ability to continue the work of the truly gifted. As this method was generally speaking unavailable to Western students of the art, another method of teaching had to be devised in keeping with their educational approach.

Yuji Yoshimura then put together the first practical English manual, in which he catalogued some of the well-known bonsai in Japan, grouping them according to trunk and branch positions. This suited the occidental analytical approach and, following these 'primitive' rules, a start was made. Toshio Kawamoto favoured a different method because he realised that aged tree material was difficult to come by. He came up with the idea of *saikei* (miniature landscapes), enabling a person to use young trees. As the trees aged, so they could be removed from the landscape and used as individual trees.

Bonsai has drawn public interest in recent years through exhibitions in Japan, but also from four paramount exhibitions in the West which are open to the public: the U.S. National Bonsai Collection in Washington D.C., the Jardin Botanique de Montreal in Canada, the Bonsai Museum of Heidelberg in Germany and the Brooklyn Botanical Garden in New York.

It will be helpful to bear in mind that the so-called 'rules' for bonsai are flexible. The bonsai grower should always be led by a particular tree and the possibility of growing it into a particular shape, within a *framework* of rules, to produce a unique work of art. A telling example of violation of the 'rules' is found in the *bunjin* style. It is also called the Literati style, referring to a cultural movement, the Southern School of Chinese Landscape Painting, called '*nanga*' in Japan. These painters were not professionals but in fact a group of scholars in art, painting, philosophy and religion. They were called the *literati*. The *literati* did not want to be restricted by the rules of the community and they became hermits or wanderers, devoting their time to meditation, Buddhism, calligraphy, poetry, painting, sculpture and similar arts. In their paintings, the shapes of the trees were different and exceptional. The lines were stark, with sudden and unexpected changes in direction and branches that crossed one another. However, the general impact was one of simplicity, without masses of branches or leaves overwhelming the tree.

It now becomes apparent that to grow an acceptable bonsai does not only entail the technical application of botanical principles, but also depends to a great extent on artistic talent, with a strong oriental influence.

Bonsai in present-day China

The undermentioned five schools of *penjing* are all located to the south of the Yangtze River in China, in the Jiangnan area, which has a rich cultural heritage dating back to the end of the 12th century.

- The Lingnan school, with its main centre at Canton (Guangzhou) on the Pearl River, still persists with the 'clip and grow' method, which results in a natural, angular growth. In a way one could say that, although this style is influenced by cutting away excess or unwanted growth, it actually 'happens', instead of being artificially created. The unnatural neatness, which one would initially appreciate, is replaced by the unexpected, the bareness and simplicity of natural development. 'Lingnan' is translated as meaning 'south of the five ridges' and refers to the area of the Guangdon and Guangxi provinces.
- The Shanghai school. These growers of *penjing* believe in growing miniature trees into a natural style, but they do not only prune, they also apply mechanical means of bending branches through the use of wire, twine and raffia. The Shanghai school as an entity only dates back to the 1970s.
- The Szechuen school in the Szechuen province has Chengdu as its main centre. These trees are severely styled and forced into shape. They are coiled upwards as though around a post or pillar, similar to a snake coiled around a branch. There

During his lifetime, an individual should devote his efforts to creating happiness and to enjoying it and also keeping it in store in society so that individuals of the future may also enjoy it

CH'EN TU-HSIU

Genius is nothing but a greater aptitude for patience

GEORGES LOUIS DE CLERC DE BUFFON

are set patterns for the number of coils and also for the number of branches.
- The Yangchow school is situated in the city of Yangchow, renowned for the construction of the Grand Canal, the world's largest manmade waterway linking China's northern and southern regions. The city also boasts beautiful garden villas, built by rich salt merchants in the Ch'ing Dynasty (1644–1911). The *penjing* growers in this area contort the trees into shapes using twine from palm fibres. The main contortions or coils are in the trunks of the trees. Thereafter, the branches and then the branchlets are coiled to form a latticework-like structure. The foliage on these trees resembles 'discs of clouds'. There can be up to nine discs.
- The Suchou school in the city of Suchou present their trees with thick, gnarled, knobby trunks, but the tender green foliage on smaller branches softens the harshness of the trunk, and creates an image of vigour. Some enthusiasts in this school of *penjing*, grow their trees with slightly taller trunks and with the branches to the left, right and back forming the so-called 'cloud discs'. The branches are parallel to each other. A bird's eye view resembles a flower with nine petals (three to the left, three to the right and three to the back, with a central core — the apex).

In all the above-mentioned styles there is also variation in the angles of the trunks. A recent trend has been to allow the trees to take on a more natural shape, unlike the traditional styles.

Penjing also refers to or includes miniature landscaping, in which rocks play the central part. This is similar to the Japanese *san-sui-seki* and is characterised by rocks in water or on gravel (sand), or a combination of the gravel and water.

As is the case even today, where some individuals own bonsai (and *penjing*, for that matter) only to be recognised or fashionable, *penjing* became a measure of one's degree of culture or sophistication during the latter part of the Ming and early Ch'ing Dynasties, when the *penjing* schools were developed. This unfortunately and inevitably led to a decline in the artistic quality of the trees. This is unquestionably happening today, with people buying so-called 'bonsai' at rediculous prices, solely for the purpose of being able to exhibit them. In China the rich even hired artisans to develop trees with very intricate artificial designs. As always the hardcore fundamentalists persisted with the simplicity and objectivity of the Chinese art and culture. Their trees projected only the essence of nature, as seen and interpreted by the artist. As in painting, these artists would not let themselves be regulated by strict rules and prescriptions. They believed that art could not be taught through textbooks, and could only be handed down by the masters to their pupils by word of mouth and practical experience. This explains why far greater value is attached to trees which have a natural appearance.

GUIDELINES TO SHAPING A BONSAI

2

Every man that striveth for the mastery, is temperate in all things

I CORINTHIANS 9:25

GENERAL PRINCIPLES

There are many different styles according to which a bonsai could be grown, but I will use the *moyogi* (the informal upright) style as a basis to work from. Once this style has been mastered, the principles involved can then be applied to other styles. This is because the basic principles of using a triangular shape, branches in three dimensions and others, remain the same, whether the style is *han-kengai* (semi-cascade), *chokkan* (formal upright) or any other. The different styles are described in Chapter 5.

The growth of a tree must be planned with its future shape in mind, even though this might mean planning for years in advance. It is appropriate to remember this Chinese proverb, freely translated as follows:

Don't be afraid to move slowly;
be afraid not to move at all.

Bonsai is an art, is an art, is an art. Bonsai enthusiasts would all agree on this statement. I will not try and describe what art is, but one may well wonder, if this statement is true, whether the growing of bonsai is limited only to those who have artistic ability. Having said that, artistic ability also needs defining. One word which immediately enters the mind is creativity, because art without creativity is an impossibility. Betty Edwards, in her book *Drawing on the Artist Within*, describes the qualities of the right and left halves of the brain, with the right half (right hemisphere) in most individuals being the half which handles visual, spatial and relational thinking, whilst the left half controls the linear, logical, language-based thinking. Betty Edwards writes: 'What about so-called naturally talented persons? I believe that these are individuals who somehow "catch on" to ways of shifting to brain modes appropriate for particular skills.' Vincent van Gogh is reported to have said about his own creativity: 'Such a man often doesn't know himself what he might do, but he feels instinctively: yet am I good for something, yet am I aware of some reason for existing!... something is alive in me: what can it be!' (quoted in Brewster Ghiselin, ed. *The Creative Process*, 1952).

Take a tree which has the potential to become a bonsai — perhaps because of its roots, good trunk base, tapering trunk, enough branches to select correctly placed ones — and ask the question: 'What is inside this tree, or, where is the bonsai inside this tree?' Two people looking at a tree, will not necessarily see the same thing. It appears that there is a difference between 'looking' and 'seeing'. Frederick Franck says in *The Zen of Seeing* (1973): 'Looking and seeing both start with the sense of perception, but there the similarity ends. When I "look" at the world and label its phenomena, I make immediate choices, instant appraisal, I like or dislike, I accept or reject what I look at, according to its usefulness to "ME". The purpose of "looking" is to survive, to cope, to manipulate ... this we are trained to do from our first day. When, on the other hand, I SEE, suddenly I am all eyes, I forget this ME,

---

CONCERNING THE SIX PRINCIPLES OF PAINTING

The first is that through a vitalising spirit a painting should possess the movement of life.

The second is that by means of the brush the structural basis should be established.

The third is that the representation should so conform with the objects as to give their likeness.

The fourth is that the colouring should be applied according to their characteristics.

The fifth is that through organisation place and position should be determined.

The sixth is that by copying the ancient models should be perpetuated.

From: *The Spirit of the Brush*
HSIEH HO (500 AD)

> *Resemblance reproduces the formal aspect of objects, but neglects their spirit; truth shows the spirit and substance in like perfection. He who tries to transmit the spirit by means of the formal aspect and ends by merely obtaining the outward appearance, will produce a dead thing.*
>
> CHING HAO

am liberated from it and dive into the reality that confronts me.'

For example, to simply take a potential bonsai and develop the tree with all its branches in exactly the correct positions and order, would be a mechanical, robot-like procedure. You are showing no creativity. Why create an ordinary tree? You are allowing the left half of your brain to control the right, and although this may give you a feeling of security, you will have lost the feeling of challenge and the sparkle of 'art' will be missing. Georges Braque says: 'the more one probes, the more one deepens the mystery: it's always out of reach. Mysteries have to be respected if they are to retain their power. Art disturbs: science reassures.' Bonsai is an art!

It is not enough to describe a bonsai as beautiful. There are a complexity of ideals to strive for when growing a bonsai: lush foliage, striking dead wood, an impressive trunk, to name but a few. No bonsai will be perfect in design, according to the so-called rules, with every branch correctly placed and all the small details just right. Yet in the eyes of the creator and the many bonsai enthusiasts, it may be considered a masterpiece. It is thus important to know what attributes a bonsai must have to be considered beautiful.

What is most apparent is the *individuality* of a particular bonsai. No two bonsai are alike. However, whilst each bonsai remains unique, it should nevertheless conform to the norms and parameters of its particular style. This is not to suggest that it should be copied mechanically or mathematically, as this would result in trees that all look virtually alike. Since the very nature of bonsai art is the creation of a tree that is unusual and different from the norm, it is clear that in comparing different bonsai trees, the fact that a tree is unique is not enough to make a bonsai masterpiece. Much more is asked of the bonsai grower.

This brings us to the next feature to consider, namely the *harmony* of the bonsai as a unit. Harmony is the combination of parts of related items to form a well-ordered whole which is appealing to the eye. These different parts include the roots, the trunk, the branches, the foliage, the apex, the slant of the bonsai, the degree of asymmetry, the shape of the asymmetry, the container, the position of the bonsai in the container, and the stand. In order to achieve an overall harmony, one needs to consider factors such as the size and position of the roots, the taper of the trunk, the size of the leaves, and the distance between branches. Each one of these details should be unique to the individual tree, in harmony with its style, size and the aura which that particular tree radiates. When the whole bonsai is harmonious it means that no single aspect of the unit will either distract or dominate.

The third quality which is closely linked to the notion of harmony can be described as the *aura*, the character, or the mood of the bonsai. The tree could be a tree with dignity, elegance or charm, and could portray either the masculine or feminine aspects of these qualities, depending on the line of the branches, the appearance of the trunk and the container. The bonsai with the masculine appearance will have branches with more angular curves, a thicker trunk with more sharply pronounced curves and trunk with rough bark, rough scarring and a more angular and straight-edged container. One finds dignity in an older bonsai, or at least one that appears older, showing a thicker trunk, aged bark, perhaps some *jin* and *shari*, and a natural, serene presence. The more natural the style the more dignified the tree will appear, unlike a tree whose style seems artificial or forced. Younger bonsai and those with more slender trunks will appear elegant. For instance, the more elegant bonsai would be found in the *literati* (*bunjin*) style, where the line of the slender trunks and sparse foliage are the dominant features. A forced, unnatural style could in a way be described as charming or quaint, being more of an oddity than something which one expects to find in nature. One might also find a

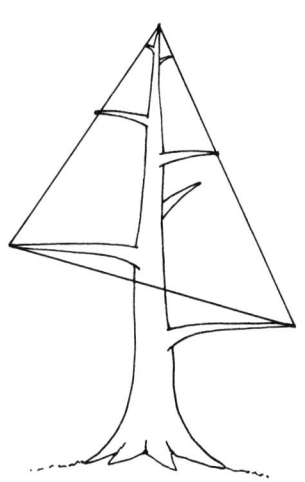

FIGURE 1 Note the triangle, with sides of unequal length and corners at different levels. The same triangle concept can also be seen in Figures 87, 88, 91, 98, 99 and others.

bonsai which combines these characteristics — for example an old tree which appears dignified but where the lines of the trunk and branches are elegant and probably more feminine.

A bonsai will not start out with many of the above-mentioned characteristics, but will in time be moulded into its personality, I dare say according to its owner's personality and psyche. Being a living, growing organism the bonsai is not going to stay the same all its life and due to age, disease, accidents or change of owner, its character will change. One must however be aware of the bonsai having its own personality, over and above its physical needs, and continuously try and shape it to maintain its individuality, harmony and aura.

Bonsai is an art form which requires a great deal of patience. In cultivating the tree you should at all times bear in mind its eventual size and appearance, a process which may take several years. In this book the bonsai shown are generally not older than eight to ten years in training.

A *bonsai unit* consists of three parts:
- the container
- the growing medium in which the tree is planted, covered with moss or gravel
- the tree

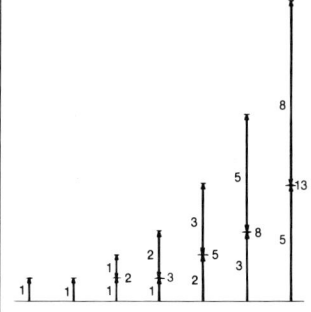

FIGURE 2 The Fibonacci series (or sequence) 1, 1, 2, 3, 5, 8, 13, 21, 34, 55 etc is arrived at by always adding the two preceding numbers. This results in a very even, logarithmic increase.

Together the three have a total aesthetic impact, although the tree is the important partner. The pot and the groundcover should never be eye-catching components — they must never dominate. For the same reason, rocks and figurines should not be used. However rocks or miniature grasses are sometimes used to disguise faults at the base of the tree. Rocks, ornaments, ornamental grasses and reeds are used as complementary exhibits when bonsai are displayed. These exhibits are presented in detail in Chapter 9 on 'Displaying bonsai'.

A *bonsai tree* is divided into three parts:
- roots — surface roots present strength and stability
- trunk — it is the soul of the tree
- branches and leaves — they represent growth and vitality.

The bonsai tree is a *unit*, made up of individual parts: roots, trunk, branches and leaves. You look at the tree as a whole but the individual parts need the utmost detailed attention to enable them to make their rightful contribution to the complete unit! Neglecting any one of these members will detrimentally affect the artistic value of the bonsai.

When viewed from *any* side, the overall shape of the crown of the tree must be roughly triangular. (For exceptions see Chapter 5 on 'Styles'.) The triangle may not be equilateral. The three different corners must be on different levels and the sides may not be the same length. The top corner (apex) represents heaven, the middle corner represents man and the lowest corner is the earth. These three points are united by the lines of the triangle.

There must be nothing symmetrical in bonsai. When using trunks, branches or trees, they must always be uneven in number, the so-called prime numbers (i.e. 1, 3, 5, 7, 11 etc). Curves of the trunk or branches must be uneven or irregular. There is a particular ruling as to the position of branches, or the order in which they sprout from the trunk. See page 12. There must at all times be a feeling of balance. Balance here means a sense of equality on both sides of an imaginary midline, although the two halves are not identical in shape, size or weight in an aesthetic sense. There is the belief that the devil takes pleasure in all perfect things. That is why a piece of art may not be absolutely perfect — it should have some flaws, albeit minor, to ward off the devil.

I grant, however, that if we adhere strictly to this rule, we would have a monotonous set of trees, with no originality to be seen. We would be practising a

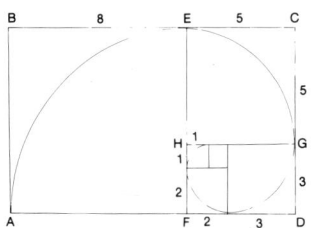

FIGURE 3. In this case FD/AF = AF/AD, which represents the Divine Proportion. If each smaller rectangle is subdivided according to the Divine Proportion, you would continue to get even, smaller rectangles. If the corners (e.g. A to E and E to G) are joined in an arc, you get a logarithmic spiral.

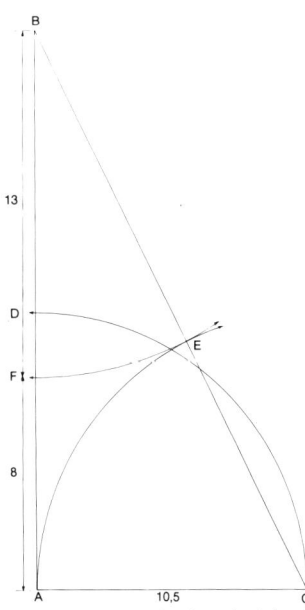

FIGURE 4 To apply the principle of the 'Fibonacci series' to bonsai growing, you first have to relate it to the 'Golden Section of Division', which works as follows: a line AB (which represents the height of the tree) is halved at point D. With point A as centre, draw an arc with AD as diameter; then draw line AC perpendicular to AB. Join B and C and with C as centre, draw another arc with the same diameter as AD. Where the arc intersects line BC, point E is marked. Now with B as centre, draw another arc with the diameter of BE. Where this arc intersects line AB, mark point F. Line AB has been divided at the Golden Section of Division. If the line AB is 21 cm in length, it would be divided into 8 cm and 13 cm sections. Similarly 34 cm would give 13 cm and 21 cm.

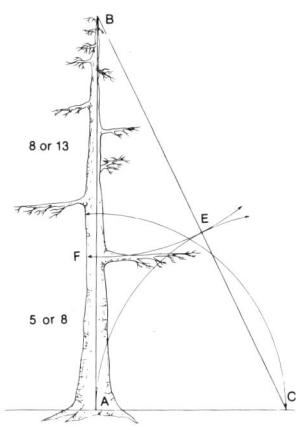

FIGURE 5 The Golden Section of Division applied to a tree.

science, not an art. It is in this respect that bonsai is unique, for we have to apply scientific, and more specifically, horticultural laws to an art form. I cannot stress this fact enough — it is a science and art combined. The mere mechanical application of bonsai styling rules, strictly 'according to the book', results in uninteresting trees.

Symmetry refers to an object being similar on the two sides of its midline, like for instance the human body, on the surface, that is. This is a very monotonous or unimaginative setting for bonsai, albeit perhaps easier for the novice to understand, until experience in the more aesthetically complicated design has been gained. When you look at a triangle with the two sides of equal length (ignoring the base), the impression is that of total balance, but the moment one side is longer than the other you have imbalance and thus movement!

One of the few European mathematicians of the Middle Ages outstanding enough to be remembered even today was Leonardo of Pisa. He lived from about 1175 to 1230. He is better known today by the name of Fibonacci, which was his family name and comes from the Latin *Filius Bonacci* meaning 'son of Bonacci'. He wrote a book in 1202, *Liber Abaci*, which could be translated as 'A book on counting'.

Fibonacci lived with his father in North Africa, where he studied mathematics with the Moors. He was confronted with the following problem: 'how many pairs of rabbits can be produced from a single pair in one year, if it is assumed that every month each pair begets a new pair, which from the second month becomes productive?'

The answer is as follows:

Month	1	2	3	4	5	6	7	8	9	10	11	12
Number of pairs	1	1	2	3	5	8	13	21	34	55	89	144

This sequence has a logical pattern of development, which from about the fifth month, is quite obvious. The sequence, the 'Fibonacci series or sequence', was so named in his honour.

The Fibonacci numbers are exemplified by the botanical phenomenon known as *phyllotaxis*, which refers to the way leaves are arranged on a branch or stem.

Thus the arrangement of the whorls on a pine-cone or pineapple, of the petals on a sunflower, and of branches from some stems, follows the same sequence as the Fibonacci numbers or the series of fractions $\frac{1}{1}$ $\frac{1}{2}$ $\frac{2}{3}$ $\frac{3}{5}$ $\frac{5}{8}$ $\frac{8}{13}$ etc.

In the case of the pineapple the bumps on the outside are arranged in two spirals — some going clockwise and some counter-clockwise in the ratio of 8:13, with 8 in one direction and 13 in the other. On the pine-cone the ratio is 5:8 and in the sunflower it is 34:55.

In the 15th century Lucas Pacioli, an Italian mathematician, devised the so-called *Divine Proportion*, namely:

$$\frac{a}{b} = \frac{b}{(a+b)}$$

This means that dividing a segment into two parts, in mean and extreme proportion, so that the smaller part is to the larger part as the larger is to the entire segment, yields the *Golden Section of Division*, an important concept in modern artistic and architectural design. These relationships form the basis of the theory of dynamic symmetry that has been applied to the fine arts as well as to living forms.

Both Fibonacci's and Pacioli's concepts are related to the proportions one strives to realise in bonsai, and this is depicted in Figures 2, 3, 4 and 5.

Another feeling that should be imparted by the bonsai, is one of proportional balance. Proportional balance refers to the relationship between one part and another, for instance the thickness of the first branch to the thickness of the trunk at the level from which the branch sprouts. In this context the 'Golden Section of Division' should be mentioned. According to this rule, there is a continuous ratio of increase or decrease in size. If this relationship or ratio is recreated in a tree, referring to position and diameter of trunk and branches, it has a pleasing effect.

The so-called 'Golden rectangle' also shows exactly the same relationship. When one side of a rectangle has a dimension of one unit, the other must then have a length of 1,618 units. Related to a bonsai it means that if a tree is 1,618 units in height the first branch must be at a height which is one unit from the apex or alternatively if the first branch is one unit up from the base of the tree the rest of the tree should be 1,618 units in length.

The Trunk

In general, when seen from the front, the trunk should be visible for approximately the first two thirds of its length. Only the top third is usually completely covered with branches and leaves. No branches may cross the lower part of the trunk. (Note Figures 7 and 8.) To help create depth perspective the first two or more primary branches may partially overlap the front of the trunk with their more proximal secondary branches, that is those closest to the trunk. (Compare Figures 7 and 8 with Figure 86.)

The trunk must be devoid of pruning scars unless they can be used to imitate places where branches have broken off or shaped to form a hollow trunk. Where branches have been cut off, no protruding stumps may be left. This is explained under in Chapter 3 on 'Shaping techniques'. Unavoidable scars should, where possible, be kept at the back of the tree.

The trunk must lean slightly forwards as if in obedience to its creator. The very tip of the trunk, the apex, must be directed upwards to prevent giving the impression that the whole tree is falling forwards. If the whole tree is leaning backwards, it is likened to a trunk person losing balance.

With the informal upright style, when the first branch grows either to the left or the right of the trunk, the direction of the trunk leading up to the branch must be made to flow in approximately the same direction as the branch. Thereafter it is angled away from the first branch in the direction of the next branch up to where this branch originates, repeating the process for every branch. This is a golden rule in bonsai design — the trunk leading into a branch and then changing direction to lead into the next branch. This allows sunlight to reach every individual branch, ensuring healthy foliage.

The Branches

It is rare to find a potential bonsai tree with all its branches in the right positions. It should however be the bonsai grower's ideal to have the branches correctly placed. If this is not possible you have to try and compensate for the flaw in some manner, for instance by bending a branch acutely downwards to the required level and then growing it sideways at that level.

Ideally the first branch should be located at a height which is one third of the total length of the tree. (Refer to Golden Section of Division on page 14) The second branch is located at a third of the height of the remaining two thirds of the tree. This same ratio is repeated almost to the apex of the tree. It is only close to the apex, where there are more branches, that this rule does not apply. It is obvious that a mass of branches is undesirable, no matter how tall the tree may be — for the sake of simplicity (in an aesthetic sense) as well as to allow sunlight to reach each individual branch.

When designing a tree, especially when you have many branches to choose from, the selection of the first branch is the first and most important step. This

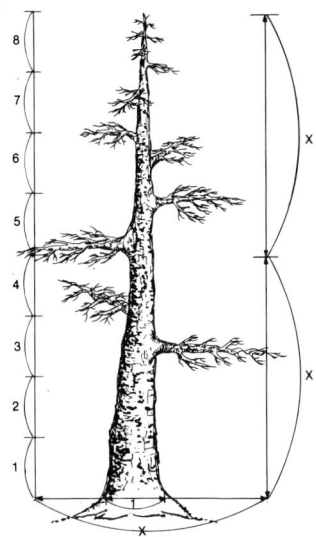

FIGURE 6 The tree is eight times as tall as its base is wide, which tends to give an impression of a tall tree. Note that all the branches grow sideways at the same angle — in this case perpendicular to the trunk. The total side to side width of the widest reaching branches is half the tree's height. There is a gradual tapering of the trunk towards its apex, with no widening anywhere along the length of the trunk.

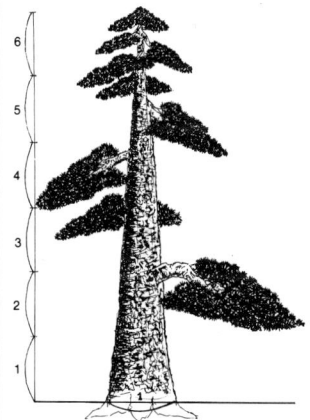

FIGURE 7 Virtually the same as the tree in Figure 6, but now the trunk is six times as tall as the base is wide and the branches are all in a downward slant. The tree with a thicker trunk looks better with the branches close together.

choice is influenced by factors like the curves in the trunk, the thickness of the trunk, the total height you aim to grow the tree, whether you want a shorter, squatter appearance or a taller tree and the visibility of scars and dead wood. As soon as the first branch has been selected it determines the position of the following branches as described in the previous paragraph. The first branch is not necessarily the longest or thickest, that is, the most striking one! The branch growing closest to the roots is called *ichi-no-eda* and the most important branch is called *sashi-eda*. The first branch (*ichi-no-eda*) may thus also be the most important one (*sashi-eda*) or it may not. It is also possible for the first branch to temporarily be of less importance than another one until it has developed further, although this on its own may present problems in that if the thicker and longer branch (*sashi-eda*) is located above the first branch it may rob the first branch of the nutrients it requires to develop into the *sashi-eda!*

Of importance in the later stages of development (after the trunk has reached a satisfactory diameter and possibly also taper), is the ramification of the branches. A bonsai is not considered to be mature until it has at least tertiary and preferably quarternary branches. The branch which sprouts from the trunk is a primary branch and this gives rise to a secondary branch which in turn gives rise to a tertiary and this to a quaternary branch. The techniques to develop better ramification involve pruning back the growing tips and defoliation. (See Chapter 3.)

Each branch must have its diameter, at its base, equal to about one third the diameter of the trunk at the level where the branch sprouts. A branch may never be as thick as the trunk, as one would not know which one is the continuation of the trunk. A branch may not be thicker than any branch below it, with the exception of the ballshaped styles, or sometimes the so-called 'natural' style. (See Figures 165 and 166.) It is only logical that the lower branches are the first to develop and, consequently, that they are thicker and better developed. In time, however, because of the development of branches above, a branch may be retarded in growth and thus be smaller than the ones higher up.

No branch may cross the lower two thirds of the trunk and branches should not cross one another. A branch in the lower two thirds of the trunk may not point directly at the viewer — if it does, it is called an eye-poker. (A list of unwanted branch characteristics is presented on page 34).

POSITION OF THE BRANCHES The branches, in many instances, determine which side of a tree should face forwards. If you experience difficulty in deciding which side is the front, you may well find a side which definitely belongs at the back (due to a variety of reasons). It then follows that the opposite side must face forwards, towards the viewer. Remember that the roots and trunk also have to be taken into consideration when deciding on which side of the tree faces forwards. (See Figure 28 for the position of the roots.) This means that, if you find a tree with the branches in such a position and number that any side of the tree may face the viewer, either the roots or the condition of trunk will determine the front. The position of branches and roots can be manoeuvred to a greater degree than the curves and the appearance of the trunk. One has to decide which aspect is the most desirable one and *that* must then determine the front of the tree. Do not always take the easiest route.

The first branch is usually directed to the left or right of the trunk at an angle of about 35 degrees forwards from the facing plane, as seen in Figure 13. The second branch must grow either to the opposite side of the first branch (if the first is to the left, then the second must be to the right and vice versa) or towards the back. The first branch may never grow straight towards the viewer and it should rarely be directed backwards. It is not recommended that this last position be tried by the inexperienced person, but if this is deemed necessary, it should grow backwards *and* to a side, to have it visible from the front and to have it serve the function of a false first side branch, otherwise the space between the soil and the first side branch will be too great.

If the second branch grows to a side (left or right) of the trunk, the third branch must grow towards the back of the tree; however if the second branch is growing towards the back, the third branch must grow to the opposite side of the first branch. (See Figures 13 and 19) The initial sequence is repeated, with the branches becoming shorter the closer they are to the top of the tree. The result is a tapering spiral. The second turn of the spiral must have three branches, which do not grow exactly above their counterparts in the first turn of the spiral. This would then have branch number four slightly more to the front or back than branch number one, as seen in Figure 13. When seen from above the result is not only that all the branches can be seen, but also that the individual branches are all exposed to the sun. Only in the upper third of the tree may any branches grow directly forwards, blocking the view of the trunk.

In general the branches growing to the back project slightly further backwards than the branches growing to the side project forwards. This is to create better depth perception — if this is not done, the tree gives a flat impression, due to foreshortening, as shown in Figure 15. Also, the back branches should have their foliage in a slightly more rounded triangle than the side branches, because they are not viewed from the side but in their length.

If a trunk has any curves, and it usually has in all the styles, excepting the formal upright and broom styles, no branches may grow from the concave (hollow) side of a curve. (See Figure 16.) When a branch grows from the inside of a curve, it is in the shade of the trunk above it. Nature would not allow this to happen normally. However, if the trunk is straight, the branches are also straight and if the trunk is curved the branches should also be.

INCLINATION OF THE BRANCHES The upward or downward inclination of the branches is an indication of the age of the tree, but it can also suggest the apparent age of the tree, which is usually quite different from the actual age. (See Figures 17 A and B.) Branches growing upwards indicate a young tree, while branches hanging down are those of a tree which is old, where the branches are either pulled down by their own weight, or the tree has lost its youthful vigour. This being a general rule it seems contradictory to have a tree with its lower branches drooping, the middle branches growing horizontally, and the top branches growing upwards. However, such a tree indicates that it is not yet fully grown and retains some vigour in the top section. Nature allows for the seemingly disharmonious, but it is wrong to cultivate a tree with one or two branches inclined in a totally different

FIGURE 8 The general construction of a bonsai.

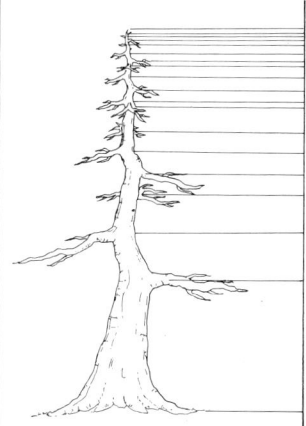

FIGURE 9 The spacing of the branches gradually decreases as the eye travels upwards, although in an irregular fashion so as not to have a monotonous appearance.

FIGURE 10 If you have a tree which has too large a space between two consecutive branches, it is preferable to lower the branch above the space, rather than lift the branch underneath it, as this will enable you to compact the tree.

FIGURE 11 Where the lower branch is too low down on the trunk, it may be bent to appear higher. It may however look better if the lower branch were removed. In time the other branches should also be curved so that all will have the same character and so as to prevent contradiction in lines of movement.

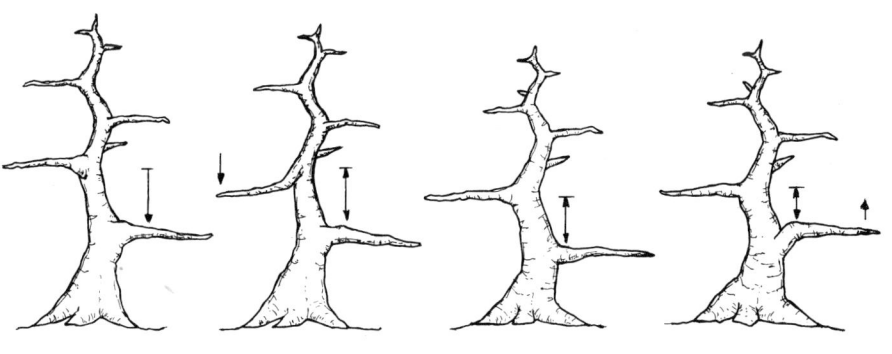

FIGURE 10   FIGURE 11

FIGURE 12 The trunk may also be bent to bring branches closer together, thus actually compressing the tree.

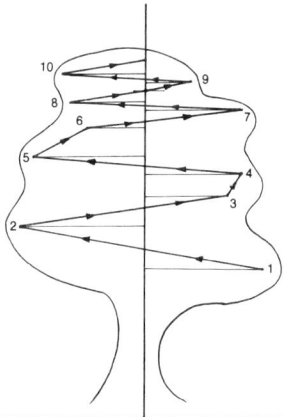

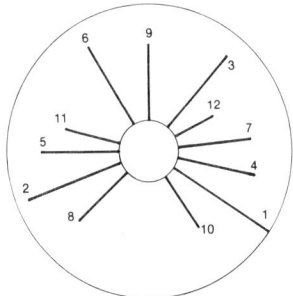

FIGURE 13 A diagram (aerial view), to show the position of the branches in the spiral around the trunk, with no branch above any other one.

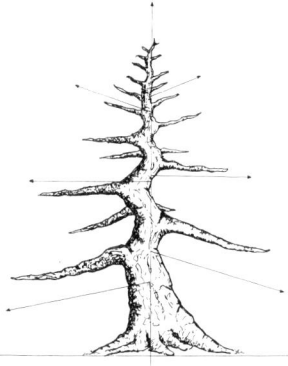

FIGURE 14 A young tree with the lower branches angled downwards, the middle branches horizontal and upper branches pointing upwards. This creates an impression of movement because, as the eye follows the trunk from the base upwards, the branches also start pointing upwards — indicating that the tree is youthful and growing at the apex.

FIGURE 12

direction from the rest, as shown in Figure 18: it not only confuses the viewer as to the age of the tree, but it is also visually disturbing and is not in keeping with the general growth pattern of the tree, or the general direction in which the other branches are growing.

Having too many long branches on a formally upright tree restricts the potential of the tree to appreciation of its outline only. It prevents the viewer from looking into the heart of the tree (the trunk!) and is also confusing. Keep in mind the principle of simplicity. Regarding the number of branches on a tree it is worth mentioning that the more branches a tree has, the younger it appears and vice versa. Less foliage gives the impression of an older tree.

Whether it is more important to focus on the detail of the trunk and branches or on the outline of a tree, is debatable. Some species and individual trees are grown better with accent on the detail of the separate branches, whilst others look better with a lot of foliage and thus more accent on the outline or general shape. You may find that a young tree falls in the second category, but as it matures it will fall in the first category. It is recognised that there are three groups of bonsai trees, depending on this approach, as follows: the first group showing the detail of trunk and individual branches, with the foliage in definite separate units; the second group embraces the trees which, due to the mass of foliage or the larger size of the leaves, are grown to display the volume of foliage in a particular shape; the third group is seldom seen, and is frowned upon by some bonsai purists (as is the case with the second group, but to a lesser degree), because it leans towards topiary, and rightly so due to the fact that these trees, with their small leaves, are clipped into shape with disregard to detail of branches. My own experience shows that it is extremely difficult, if not impossible, to grow trees with larger leaves in the first method, unless the trees are grown to a fairly large size. I base this view on my experience with a variety of *Ficus* species, as well as some other trees, including *Galpinia transvaalica* (a wild privet) and *Erythrophyllum* species. The leaves of these trees are large and tend to obliterate the branches, making it impossible, or esthetically unsatisfactory, to create 'discs of clouds'. It is still possible to discern the general position of the branches, but the overall shape is now more important. I do think that in this manner of growing, the tree should show at least a good trunk base (*nebari*), as well as the first one quarter of the trunk, otherwise it would look like a section of clipped hedge. An alternative, if you insist on showing separate branches and leaf canopies, is to grow these bonsai to a large size, in which case the leaves and branches would be small in relation to the size of the whole tree.

Taking a popular bonsai magazine and a book (the book containing only photographs of bonsai from Japan), I sorted the trees according to whether they (in my opinion) belonged in either the first or second group. I was rather surprised to find that out of 1013 trees, 631 were grown in the manner of the second category (accent on silhouette), and 382 in the first category (separate branches). I even saw trees that started off in group one but are presently in group two, due to their development over many years. It is true that photographs are only a two dimensional image, but they still show you the general shape of the tree and the branches. By no means does this mean that the one grouping is superior to the other: it is a matter of choosing the right one for a particular tree.

Bonsai can be grouped into a first category in which the trees are grown to imitate trees as they grow in nature, and then a second category in which I place trees which are more like works of art, although they still portray the nature of the tree. The dividing line is fine, and in the end is a matter of artistic disposition. I dare say that the second group is more for the advanced bonsai enthusiast, but this does not mean that the more natural appearance is of less value. It also does not mean that, when you grow a tree to appear more natural, you can disregard the 'rules' of bonsai styling. Some people simply dislike the artistic styling, like cases of driftwood, *bunjin* and some extremely aged trunks, and prefer to have trees which are shaped similar to what they normally see in nature, like the broom and umbrella styles. Not many of us have the artistic abilities which enable the more creative people to compose their masterpieces, and we are thus forced to grow our bonsai in a less intricate, more natural design. Knowledge of bonsai techniques also places a restriction on what you can do with a tree, for instance the ability to bend branches and reposition them. It may mean that you have to restrict yourself to reasonably straight branches (trunks, for that matter) and to the position from which they originate on the trunk. The part of the world in which you live has an effect on the way in which trees grow there, and this may have an effect on the way in which you see your ideal tree. Where I live, trees tend to grow in umbrella, flat top and broom

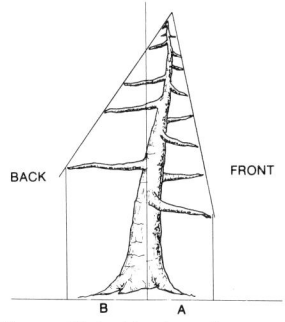

FIGURE 15 A side-view of a tree. The tree leans towards the viewer, with the apex growing upright to balance the tree. Seen from the side the tree is also a triangular shape. The side branches which grow to the front, project forwards less than the back branches project backwards. A is shorter than B.

FIGURE 16 The trunk shows a very even S-curve, which is monotonous. Some branches grow from the inside of curves — this is unnatural. This S-curve should not be confused with the exaggerated curves of the *ô-moyogi*.

FIGURE 17

FIGURE 17
A. An older looking appearance.
B. A younger looking appearance.

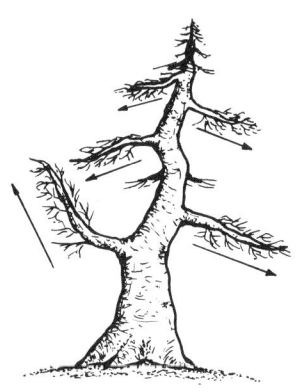

FIGURE 18 One branch is growing in a contrasting direction to the rest of the branches, causing visual disharmony.

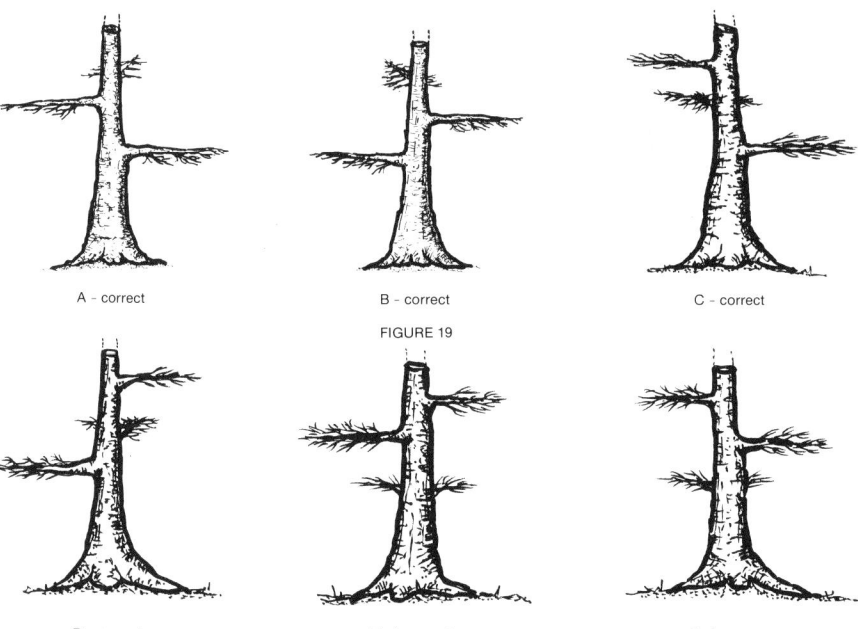

FIGURE 19

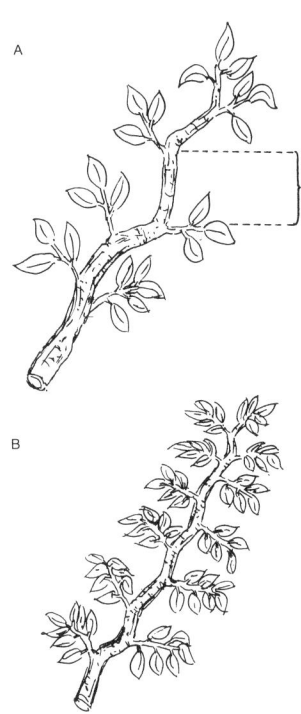

FIGURE 20
A. A branch with long internodal distance, thus less compact.
B. A more compact branch.

shapes in many cases, because it is their natural tendency. It is rather difficult to try and grow the acacia trees in anything but a form of umbrella style and this is the approach I have to follow when I use the species of tree which commonly grows around here. Do be open-minded and try whatever you like, keeping the previous paragraphs in mind.

The Leaves

The leaves are an indication of the vitality of the tree and should have a healthy appearance. In fact the leaves act as the tree's mouthpiece, accurately indicating its state of health; for instance yellow leaves would point to a magnesium shortage or too little sunshine.

Unlike flowers and fruits, leaves are capable of being dwarfed to a considerable degree. They must be grown very compactly, that is, the internodal or leaf-to-leaf distance must be short.

There are various means of achieving this, one of which is the regular nipping back (cutting) of the young growing tips. If the nipping back is delayed or postponed, the distance between the tip, where the growth is taking place, and the last leaf directly behind it, is elongated (stretched), resulting in a particular length of branch with less leaves to that length. This technique requires patience, because some trees only produce new leaves once or twice a year, for instance, pines, spruces and firs. If nipping back is delayed you may lose a year in time, because the branch will grow too long and you may have to cut off the whole year's growth to compact the branch again.

Another method of compacting the leaves is to employ spartan training, whereby the trees are given reduced amounts of water and nutrients (especially those with a higher concentration of nitrogen). This technique is discussed in Chapter 7 on page 118, as well as the section on creating smaller leaves which follows below.

GENERAL SHAPE The overall shape (outline) of the branch, branchlets and leaves should form either a triangle or a diamond, whether viewed from above or from the side. The side-view has a *flattened* diamond or triangular shape as seen in Figures 21 & 22. The flattening is due to the absence of vertically growing branches, which would prevent one from achieving a sense of width (see Figure 23.) It would also mean that the branches would have to be far apart to allow for the greater mass of leaves, so that leaves of different branches would not become entangled. The result of the flattened triangle or diamond shape, in a *side-view*, means that the tree now has layers of leaves and not a mass of foliage — or perhaps these layers could be described more poetically as 'discs of cloud'. However, to create a triangle, even though it may be flattened, does necessitate some vertical growth of the secondary and tertiary branches closest to the trunk and to a lesser degree towards the end of the main branch to allow for tapering off.

In the initial stages of a tree's development, one should aim at creating these layers of branches, but in time as described earlier, the tree may well be developed with the leaves of the branches touching and thus forming a larger entity.

FORMING SMALLER LEAVES The very first principle you have to understand is that the leaves are a tree's factory for producing carbohydrates (sugars and starches) through the action of photosynthesis. This is explained in detail in the section on 'How plants live' in Chapter 7. By interfering with this function, you can retard the tree's growth and control the size of the trunk, branches and leaves to a degree. It is like keeping the tree on a diet. Keeping this in mind, it follows that you should not practise leaf-size reduction on trees that are not absolutely healthy. Neither should it be done on very young trees that have not reached their adult shape. On very old trees the results may also be catastrophic due to the inability of the tree to produce new leaves or to survive the shock of the treatment. There are however means to overcome this problem and they are mentioned a little further on.

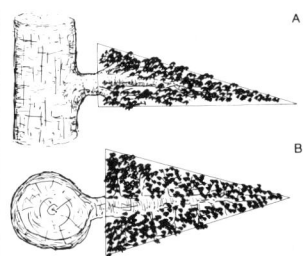

FIGURE 21
A. The side-view of a triangle shape.
B. The triangle shape seen from above.

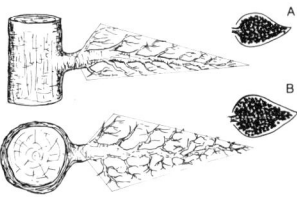

FIGURE 22
A. The side-view of a diamond (or flame) shape.
B. The diamond (or flame) shape seen from above.

The reason why the leaves should be small is simply a matter of proportion: a small bonsai of say 15 cm tall, having leaves of 4 cm in length would be quite out of proportion and not aesthetically pleasing. For this reason, trees with naturally smaller leaves are preferable, or, for that matter, trees with needles as leaves, although if the needles are of a long type (*longifolia*) they will also present reduction problems. Examples of trees which respond nicely by forming smaller leaves are: *Ulmus, Acer, Acacia, Juniper, Pinus, Cedrus, Celtis* and *Olea*. Should you have trees with larger leaves, like *Ficus ingens, Fraxinus americana* or *Quercus rubor*, you must then grow these trees to form larger bonsai so as to have a better leaf size–tree size ratio.

An additional benefit of smaller leaves is that there is less water loss through the leaves during the hottest hours of the day, preventing the trees from drying out.

Remember that you will not be able to reduce the size of flowers or fruit to a noticeable degree by any method!

There are at least seven ways in which you can influence the size of the leaves:
- amount of sunlight
- spartan watering
- leaf cutting
- root size.
- fertilisers
- nipping of buds
- defoliation

FIGURE 23 If the triangles are too high they overlap.

Sunlight It is a well-known fact that large leaves are a sign of a plant receiving less sunlight. The reverse is also true: a plant will form smaller leaves when it is subjected to a lot of direct sunshine. This is due to the fact that more photosynthesis is now taking place and a larger total leaf surface would be unnecessary. At the same time the smaller leaves also reduce water-vapour loss.

Fertilisers Nitrogen increases leaf size, especially when the leaf is in its early formation. If the bonsai were to receive nitrogen fertiliser in spring it would cause the new leaves to grow too large. This is more pertinent in the case of deciduous trees where a complete new set of leaves has to be formed at the beginning of the growing season. It is better to use fertilisers with a higher potassium and phosphate content in earlier summer. The potassium will also reduce the effect of nitrogen present and

FIGURE 24 Exactly the same trunk and branches as in Figure 23 but the triangles are now flatter. A completely different atmosphere is created by changing the height of the triangles. Whichever shape is used depends on the trunk and overall age which the tree must appear to have.

will give the bonsai a higher resistance to disease. The phosphates will improve the root system. The effect of the root system on leaf size is described a little further on.

Spartan watering 'Spartan' refers to being without luxuries and thus being strong and hardy. In the case of bonsai, spartan training refers to a reduction in the frequency of watering but not in the quantity given in a session. Applied during spring when the new leaves are being formed, this technique will produce smaller leaves. It can be applied to younger as well as older trees. An additional result is a better 'crop' of flowers and fruit — this is due to the fact that the tree has the impression that it is experiencing conditions close to drought and to survive it has to produce flowers and seed (i.e. fruit) to ensure posterity. A tree producing flowers too early in the year may be indicative of drought conditions.

The right that you have to do something does not mean that you are going to do it right!

The spartan technique entails watering the tree only when the soil in the container is virtually dry. When the tree is watered it should be done thoroughly, so that the water flows out through the drainage holes. The water is then withheld till the soil is dry again. Obviously it is a risky treatment, and should only be followed when the bonsai can receive the necessary attention.

Bud nipping The reasons why the nipping of buds is successful are multiple and interrelated. Firstly, nipping the buds removes the dominant hormone, auxin, from the growing tips. This results in cytokinin taking over and, in so doing, spreads the growth over the whole tree, while sharing the same amount of available nutrients. There are now many growth points instead of only a few. The new leaves and finer branching which follow are smaller.

Auxin is the hormone present in the growing tips of branches and the main trunk, and is responsible for the growth in length of branches and the trunk. Cytokinin is responsible for secondary and finer branching, as well as leaf development. Auxin, however, dominates when a tree is younger and needs to increase in size. As mentioned, the process of bud-nipping removes the influence of auxin. It is useful to know that fertilisers made from seaweed, such as Kelp or Seagrow, contain cytokinin and, if included in the fertilising program, will help to form finer branching and smaller leaves.

When a branch is sending out its new growth in spring (and in the case of some trees throughout most of the summer) the first leaves that form are the smaller ones. As the branch stretches in length, the leaves that follow grow larger. If the buds are nipped early, you leave the smaller leaves behind, removing the larger ones. You also prevent the branch from stretching between the leaves and forming longer internodal distances, which would result in a leggy, less compact tree. The nipping must be done early in spring, as soon as the first leaves have formed. Do not be afraid to nip back quite severely, as you have most of the summer left to allow for further growth with less severe nipping.

If nipping in the later part of summer is severe, you will force the tree to utilise nutrients which would otherwise have been stored away for the coming winter and following spring. The sap-flow will also have been reduced, and this would be detrimental to the tree's ability to recover, and could inhibit new growth. Although this reduced sap-flow may be just what you need to force the tree to form smaller leaves, it becomes a risk late in the season.

Leaf cutting Leaf cutting means a reduction of the total leaf surface by cutting off half to two thirds of the actual leaf with a sharp pair of scissors (Figure 26). Do not attempt this technique on a weak or ill tree, and if a particular branch is not in prime health do not cut the leaves on this branch, as the procedure is a drastic one and the result may be traumatic. Do not shock the tree if it is not in a condition to recover easily. In the case of trees with larger leaves, a larger section of the leaf can be cut off without too much difficulty. However where the leaves are smaller and corres-

FIGURE 25 A yew-tree with discs of clouds, from the Suzhou style in China.

pondingly more numerous as for example on an elm tree, it would be a very tedious task to cut every single small leaf. In this instance, a light pruning of all unnecessary branch tips will considerably lessen the number of leaves on the tree. A week or two before the leaf cutting is attempted, the tree should be given some fertiliser to prepare it for the formation of new leaves. When the new leaves have formed you can remove the cut ones or leave them to drop off during winter.

To lessen the trauma or shock to the tree, you can do the leaf cutting in two stages, by cutting about half the leaves at random around the tree, and two weeks later cutting the rest.

Defoliation Defoliation boils down to having the tree experience two growing seasons in one summer (or causing it to go through two spring periods). The second spring is enforced during the period when the sap-flow has started diminishing and the growth which then follows is smaller — exactly what you want. Furthermore, it reduces the tree's ability to store nutrients for the coming winter, which will influence the following year's spring growth.

Defoliation is practised on deciduous trees and large-leafed evergreens. The best results are achieved using young and always healthy trees. It is not applied to trees which are meant to bear flowers or fruit, nor to conifers.

The advantages of defoliation are:
- it forces the trees to form smaller leaves
- it removes damaged leaves and these are replaced by numerous healthy smaller ones
- it improves autumn colours
- foliage and twigs will be more compact while the twigs will also be finer
- if only a section of the tree is defoliated, the tree's energies will be directed towards healing that particular section, resulting in less growth in the rest of the tree

Defoliation is described in detail on page 49.

Root size: If the roots are finely branched, the twigs tend to follow suit and the leaves are also smaller. It is standard procedure to see that your bonsai has a root system consisting of three, five or seven larger main roots, but underground these roots must be branched into countless small rootlets to enable them to absorb the sparse water and nutrients from the restricted amount of soil. To induce finer branching of roots, the soil should contain sand which has sharp (rough) particles. The sand is usually found in the upper regions of rivers, where the particles have not weathered down to smooth spheres. Whenever a growing root-hair is opposed by a sharp sand-particle, it splits in two to pass the particle, instead of sliding around it as it would do with a smooth sand-particle. The sand-particles should also be small. The small, finely divided roots are reflected in the foliage as smaller and more numerous leaves.

The natural tendency of a bonsai tree is always to grow to its normal size (as if in nature) and if it were planted in the garden and left to grow without further interference, it would do just that. Should the bonsai not receive regular attention, it would be impossible to really reduce the leaf size. If bud nipping is neglected, you may well lose a whole year's opportunity in spring. As a last thought, remember that there is no sense in having extremely dwarfed leaves if they are not healthy. Always keep your bonsai in prime condition and, in return, it will smile through its healthy leaves and flowers.

A few words about evergreen trees: because evergreens have a more placid existence you will find that if you prune them just before spring they will respond by forming smaller leaves than deciduous trees. The explanation for this lies in the fact that they do not need to build up as many nutrients for the next winter, because they

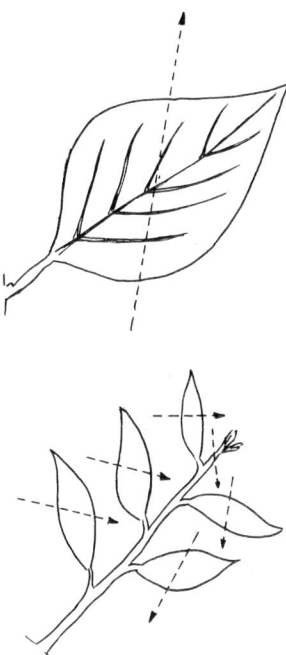

FIGURE 26 Leaf cutting.

retain their leaves. The deciduous trees have to start off in spring forming as large a foliage surface as possible, to produce enough carbohydrates during summer to survive the following winter.

Trees which naturally have smaller leaves or needle-like leaves are preferred. Smaller leaves are more in proportion to the dwarfed trunk and do not appear grotesque. A bonus is their being less likely to transpire — that is to release water-vapour into the atmosphere — which makes them less liable to wilt during the heat of the day. Examples are Oleaceae, *Pyracantha*, *Celtis*, *Cotoneaster*, *Acer*, *Acer*, and *Pinus* species. If a large-leafed tree is grown, each leaf has virtually got to be regarded as a branchlet, which means the loss of a 'branchlet' every time the tree drops a leaf — as all trees, including evergreens, tend to do. When slightly larger-leafed trees are grown, like the large-leafed privet or the *Ficus ingens*, you need to grow the tree to a larger size — for instance 60 to 90 cm tall — to ensure the leaves are in correct proportion to the size of the trunk.

An interesting fact is that some trees, like acacias, have the ability to move the leaflets, via a small joint at the base of every leaflet, which enables the tree to fold the leaves into a 'closed' position at night, but also, and this is important, whenever the temperature increases to a certain level, thus preventing the tree from overheating and drying out.

It is a pleasure to have trees of some variety, especially ones which excel in autumn shades, for instance *Acer palmatum*, although even the *Celtis africana* with its yellow leaves, or the *Ulmus parvifolia* with its brown leaves during autumn, are picturesque in their own right. Some trees, grown into styles like the broom or ball shapes, are at their best when they are without leaves — for the sheer beauty of their branches and twigs. When trees shed their leaves and stand in their stark winter nakedness, it is a good time to study the shape, position and development of the branches, and to attend to wiring, a job done more efficiently without the hindrance of leaves, and moreover, without running the risk of damaging them.

It is easier to handle trees that grow slowly, because fast-growing trees might even need two soil changes in one year and their massive leaf production needs constant attention — a very time-consuming affair.

The Roots

The roots give the tree its stability — they anchor it in the earth. Without roots, the tree would be like a post planted in the ground — easily uprooted. The roots close to the trunk (*nebari*) are extremely important visually, so much so, that they may be the reason why a certain side of a tree is chosen as the front. The roots have to be visible on the soil surface, at the base of the trunk, and they must project outwards for some distance before they disappear into the soil. They may not simply lie on top of the soil, neither may there be any opening between root and soil. The only exception to this rule is in the exposed root style (*ne-agari*). Even in the case of the rock-clinging style (*seki-jojo*), the roots must have intimate contact with the rock surface. The roots in all cases must not be allowed to grow into the soil and then reappear on the surface to dip into the soil a little further on. Roots should only be visible reasonably close to the trunk. The roots (*nebari*) flow into the trunk and form a unit, which leads up into the rest of the tree. The section of trunk between the roots and the first branch must taper upwards and be of sufficient thickness to seem to be able (along with the *nebari*) to support the rest of the tree. This first section of trunk is called the *tachi-agari*. The importance of well-developed *nebari* and *tachi-agari* must be stressed, as this is the foundation of a visually pleasing bonsai.

A bonsai may only have three, five or seven roots, an uneven number, and they should be approximately the same size. Place the tree so that one root is facing forwards to the right or left of centre. (See Figure 28)

Some trees, like the Oleaceae (wild olive), tend to have their roots fused close to the trunk, instead of individual roots, so that a wide base for the trunk is formed. This creates a good, overall impression of stability.

The swamp cypress has the curious tendency to form so-called 'knees': the roots form knee-like bulges which protrude above the water in which they are standing. However, roots bulding up like that, some distance from the trunk, would be distracting.

Some *Ficus* trees send out aerial roots from the branches and higher up on the trunk, especially when they are in a moist area. This natural tendency can and should be encouraged by keeping the area around the tree moist — whether this is soil or a rock. One simple method of achieving this, is to support a plastic bottle above the tree, fill it with water and puncture it at the bottom and top. This will ensure a constant dripping of the water onto the tree trunk or rock. Where the waterdrops fall, they break up in a spray, moistening quite a large area. The bottle needs a hole at both top and bottom to ensure that a vacuum does not develop inside the bottle. A screwtop should be kept closed, to prevent mosquitoes breeding in the water, but may be lightly screwed on to allow air into the bottle. It also helps to keep an open container with water close to the fig tree, to keep the air moist through vaporisation. A micro-climate or micro-ecosystem is thus formed around the tree.

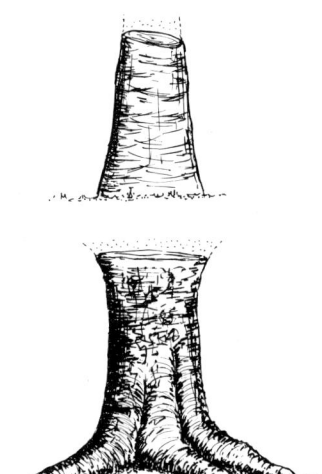

FIGURE 27 Roots show stability.

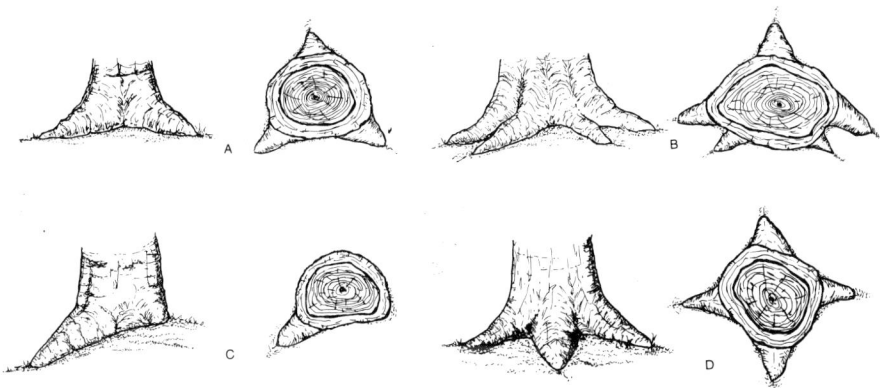

FIGURE 28
A. Correct
B. Correct
C. Incorrect
D. Incorrect

Groundcovers

The groundcover rounds off the bonsai planting. If there is no groundcover the tree gives the impression that it is standing in barren soil. The groundcover adds to the overall impact a bonsai has on the viewer. Some moss growing up against the base of the trunk will give an impression of age. Different groundcovers can be used, for instance moss, gravel, sand or lichen. The most popular is a combination of moss and gravel. Usually only one kind of moss is used, but there are different kinds, with different colours and textures, which when grown in patches have a beautiful visual impact. There are a few thousand varieties of mosses, but those with a velvet appearance are preferred.

ADVANTAGES OF MOSS
- Moss prevents loose soil from washing out of the pot, because the rhizoids, which are the moss's root system, hold the superficial soil particles together. The moss prevents waterdrops falling directly onto the soil particles
- Moss helps to prevent the soil drying out, by retaining water
- Moss imparts the feeling of age

  DISADVANTAGES OF MOSS
- A thick layer of moss can act like plastic sheeting and prevent water from entering the soil

- With total coverage of the soil, the moss will prevent you from seeing whether the soil is dry or not
- A dense moss coverage reduces the exchange of gases (oxygen and carbon-dioxide) between the soil and the atmosphere.

Moss should not be used with every bonsai, as it should suit the scene that you are trying to create; in some cases gravel or a rough textured sand would be better. Do not cover the whole soil surface with moss, as it prevents water reaching the soil and also appears unnatural. Moss grows in the shade of a tree, which means that moss should be planted close to the trunk and the rest of the surface covered with a suitable colour gravel.

Because moss is a very primitive plant and does not have real leaves or roots, it reacts quickly when it receives water and dry moss turns green within a very short time.

Moss carries special reproductive cells at different places on the stems. These cells produce a special tiny stem which has on its tip a little sachet containing spores. Spores are minute seeds which can be distributed over a wide area with ease, through wind and rain. Apart from this, moss is also able to reproduce vegetatively, which means that pieces broken off simply grow again and multiply. This ensures an everlasting presence of moss spores and, if your bonsai garden is kept moist, you will always have moss.

This same characteristic enables you to gather moss and replant it. Look for moss on the shady side of a building, under trees and rocks, or between buildings. Try to scrape off the moss without taking soil along. If soil is also scraped off, it might contain unwanted insect eggs or weeds. The moss is then rolled flat and placed on the soil surface. The edges of the moss tend to curl up, but it can be pinned to the soil with small wire staples, until it takes hold. The edges can also be covered with a layer of gravel or soil to hold them down.

Instead of planting the moss directly, it can be dried out, which causes it to form many spores. The dried moss is then ground finely, passed through a fine screen and then kept in a sealed bottle. When it is needed, it is strewn over the soil surface and kept wet with a fine spray, until it starts growing. It helps to wet the moss with a mixture of buttermilk and water in a 1:4 ratio. When drying out moss, it is best to do it in the open air, otherwise it will rot. Some moss varieties will not grow with the drying-out method, and you will have to experiment with whichever kind you have available.

The best time to plant moss in the winter-rainfall area is during autumn because the falling temperature and humidity encourages growth. In the summer-rainfall area, plant during spring because the time for frost is over and the rain brings about a higher humidity which is necessary for the growth of moss. Moss dislikes both freezing temperatures and the extreme heat of summer, as well as drought.

A type of groundcover which should be avoided is liverwort. It has fan-shaped leaves which form an impenetrable layer. Liverwort is fine as long as it is restricted to a small area, but it tends to spread easily. Remove the 'leaves' by picking them from the soil with a tweezer, or rubbing vinegar into the leaf. If this is not done in time, the liverwort will invate the pot and completely cover the soil.

A warning when using sand or gravel: see to it that the colour does not clash with the colour of the pot, or detract from the beauty of the tree.

Other groundcovers like 'Baby's tears' or 'Happiness in the home' seldom look good because it is difficult to have them in the right size ratio to the tree. There are miniature grasses available, but you should beware of cluttering the soil surface. One instance where a pod of grass has its use is against a trunk, to disguise the absence of roots, or a scar.

Mistakes should be like a light to show you the way ahead and not like a well from which you cannot get out.

A problem experienced in a constantly damp area is that algae form in the moss, or on the soil surface. These algae can be controlled by using Jeyes fluid at a concentration of 5 ml to 5 litres of water. It helps to use a soil which has very good drainage, and also not to overwater the soil and allow it to dry out between waterings.

GENERAL FAULTS AND PROBLEMS

Roots

An even number of roots, like two or four, or the complete absence of visible roots is unacceptable. Even seeing only one root is not right. This problem can be solved by stimulating the tree to form roots where they are required. There are various ways of doing this:

- Cross cuts are made in the trunk, in the area where roots are missing. Cover the area in sand. (Figure 29A)
- Drill holes into the trunk and stick the unburned ends of matches or dry sections of twigs into the holes. Cover the area in sand. (Figure 29B)
- Make horizontal cuts in the trunk and lift the flaps up by placing small stones under them. Cover in sand. (Figure 29C) You could use a sorghum seed instead of or along with the pebble, as this promotes root-formation.
- By grafting a small tree of the same kind to the trunk, where the roots are required. The small tree can be cut off when the graft has taken, and the grafted tree's roots then become the roots of the larger tree (Figure 29D).

In the cases where cuts or holes are made in the trunk, application of a root-forming hormone on the wounds is beneficial. Using willow water for a few weeks also promotes root-formation. If small flaps are cut, and a sorghum seed is forced in under the flap, this also stimulates new root-formation.

A root growing upwards and then entering the soil (thereby leaving a space between the root and the soil) is wrong, and should be pinned down, by means of wire staples, even if it means taking the wire through a drainage hole and tying it there. Protect the tender root with a rubber or paper pad between the wire and the root. (Figure 30)

Roots must not be tangled before they enter the soil — they should appear to grow away from the trunk and into the soil individually.

The size of the roots must be in an acceptable proportion to the size of the trunk. Extremely large roots do not appear natural (See Figure 31). Do not have a root which is larger than about 1/3 of the diameter of the base of the trunk.

It is unsightly to have too long a root running on the soil surface, or dipping into the soil to reappear again. This is often the problem with a tree with one large taproot, which has been kept in a container for a long time. The root has no choice but to circle around the trunk base in the container and it is very difficult to get it to stay underground when you remove it from the original container and plant it in a shallow pot.

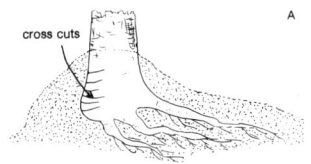
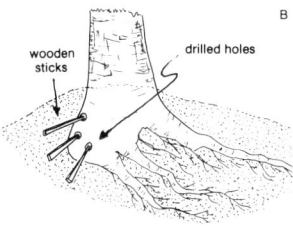
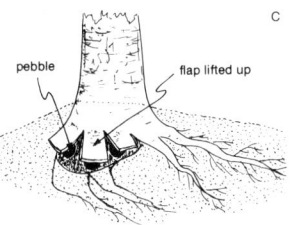
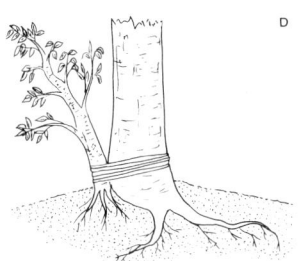

FIGURE 29
A. Cross-cuts to stimulate rooting, covered with soil.
B. Drilled holes, filled with sticks and covered with soil.
C. Flaps of bark, cut and kept open with pebbles.
D. A tree with its own roots grafted onto the rootless area of another tree.

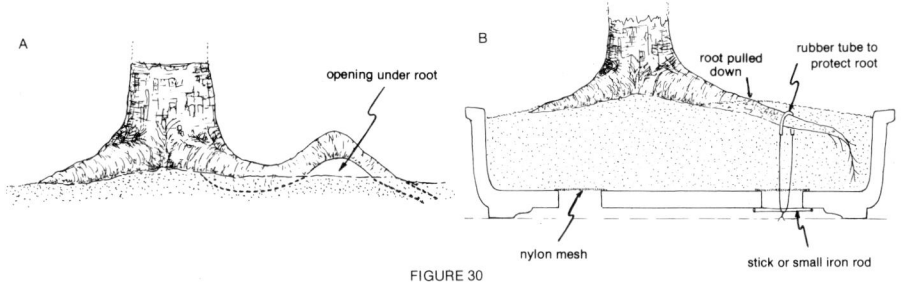

FIGURE 30

FIGURE 30
A. No opening is allowed between a major root and the soil.
B. Tie the root down into the soil.

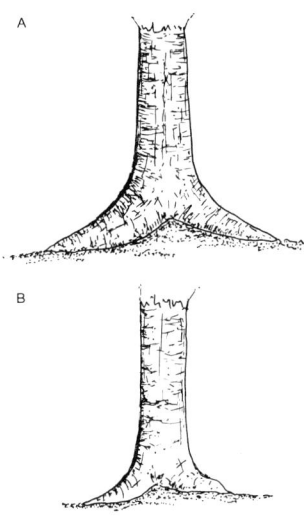

FIGURE 31
A. These roots are far too large in relation to the trunk diameter.
B. These roots are in better proportion to the size of the trunk.

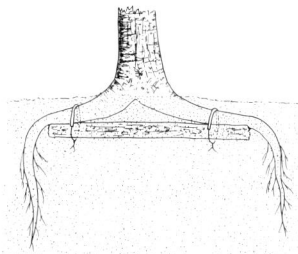

FIGURE 32 The roots are spread out over a wooden block.

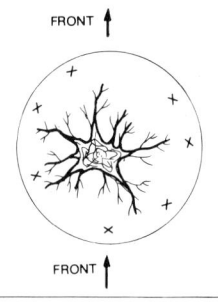

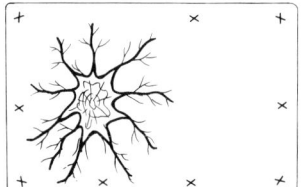

FIGURE 33 Fertiliser should be placed at the points marked with crosses far from the base of the trunk, to stimulate root growth in that direction.

When roots start appearing on the soil surface, it means that either the soil is too soggy, or the space is cramped. Remember that a root also exchanges gases, and it cannot do so in soggy soil — it 'suffocates'.

Roots form bark in the same way the trunk does, but because roots are underground, the bark is absorbed. To hasten the thickening of roots they should be exposed to sunlight and air. On the other hand new roots are formed more easily in the dark or on the shady side of the tree. For roots to grow better it helps to plant the tree in the garden for a while, or in a very large container. If fertiliser is applied some distance away from the trunk, the roots will also spread better, in order to reach the fertiliser. If roots are weakly developed on one side of the tree, that side of the tree should be turned towards the direction in which it will receive the most shade, for instance facing a wall.

It is essential to have roots which grow horizontally away from the trunk, before they disappear into the soil. This can be assured by one of the following methods (applied to a young tree with a reasonable distribution of roots around the trunk):
(a) With a very young tree the roots should be teased out of the soil and spread horizontally over a flat piece of slate, or a flat stone, which is small enough to fit into the training pot. The roots can be tied to the stone to keep them flat. The tree is planted in a large container, or in the garden, with the roots completely covered. Roots grow better in the moist darkness. The stone is removed after about a year.
(b) Exactly the same process as above is used, but the tree is planted on a hardboard plate or a piece of wood. (Figure 32)
(c) A young sapling or cutting can be placed in a hole in a thin tile or piece of wood. The hole should have a diameter of not more than about six millimetres. When the sapling or cutting grows, it soon reaches the same diameter as the opening through which it is growing, and the wood or tile acts like a tourniquet causing swelling above it. If the wood or tile is kept under the ground, roots will also develop out of the swelling in time, and they will grow horizontally over the wood or tile. Later, the roots under the obstruction are cut off (using a chisel or rootcutter), and the tree on top of the tile or wood is pushed through the opening and planted in the usual way — with a well developed base, a thick trunk and a good root system in a very short time.

When a tree in a container receives fertiliser of whatever kind, it must be applied as far away as possible from the trunk, to encourage the roots to grow towards the fertiliser; in so doing they will stretch horizontally. This method is applied when you use fertiliser of a more solid nature. When liquid fertiliser is used, also drip or spray it near the edges of the container, although this is not as effective as in the case of solid cakes or bars of fertiliser.

IMPROVING FAULTY ROOT SYSTEMS

(a) If it is a one-sided root system and the tree is upright, the possibility exists that, if the tree is tilted towards the side which has roots, the smaller or finer roots on the other side (which are not visible in the upright position) would be exposed, and would then develop into larger roots. The tree could subsequently be grown in the slanted or windswept style. (Figure 34) One-sided roots can also be disguised by turning the tree, to hide the weak-rooted side at the back. Although the slant of the trunk or position of the branches will now be changed, it may be adapted into another style, with either a slant, as mentioned above, or simply a change in the direction of the trunk. A branch that is aesthetically displeasing may require removing altogether, or should at least be wired to grow at a different angle or in a different direction.
(b) Use rocks to disguise the fault, by either placing the rock against the area where the roots are lacking (Figure 35), or under a root which is above soil-level. See

sketch of tree in rock container (Figure 146), for growing the tree close to the side of the container, with the side lacking roots close to the edge.

(c) By elevating the tree above the soil, the trunk may well be elongated, but there are bound to be roots at a lower level which will develop well in time. Be sure to anchor the tree well, using wire or a rod as prop, until the roots have grown strong and are able to support the tree on their own. (Figure 36)

(d) It may be that too few roots are exposed in the present situation, but when the tree is elevated — lifted out of the soil — the exposure of the new roots could be treated as an exposed root style. (Figure 37)

(e) Where roots are missing on a particular side of the trunk, you could make it look natural by having a dead portion of the trunk like *saba-miki* or driftwood above this area (Figure 38). If this has not occurred naturally, it can be created by removing the bark above the area where roots are lacking. It is especially effective if the trunk is hollowed out in this area. Do not take the dead wood area down to a level where the dampness of the soil will cause rotting of the wood.

(f) By grafting the same species of tree to the area where the roots are needed, it can either be kept as the smaller trunk of a twin trunk combination, or when the graft has taken, the trunk portion can be severed to retain only the newly acquired roots. (See Figure 39.) A seedling can be kept in position by tacking it to the trunk with a very thin tack (nail), or tying it to the trunk as described under 'Grafting techniques' on page 37.

(g) A particularly thick or heavy root could be split. The two thinner roots will be easier to bend and wire into place. A piece of wood or a pebble can be used to keep the two split sections apart. (Figure 40)

(h) By air-layering at a position just above the present roots, or by tying a piece of wire tightly around the trunk below soil-level (as described in the next section), roots may be stimulated to develop in the circumference of the trunk. The tree must be turned in relation to the sun, as roots develop better on the shady side.

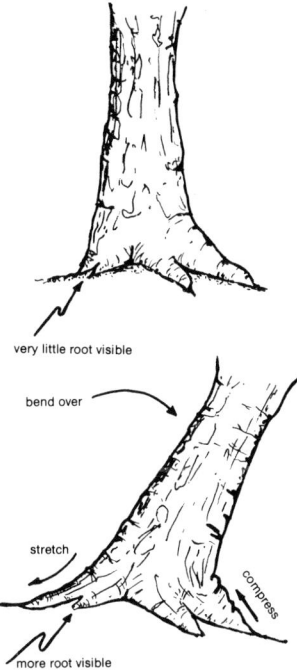

FIGURE 34 By tilting the tree, the unexposed roots will become exposed and will develop better.

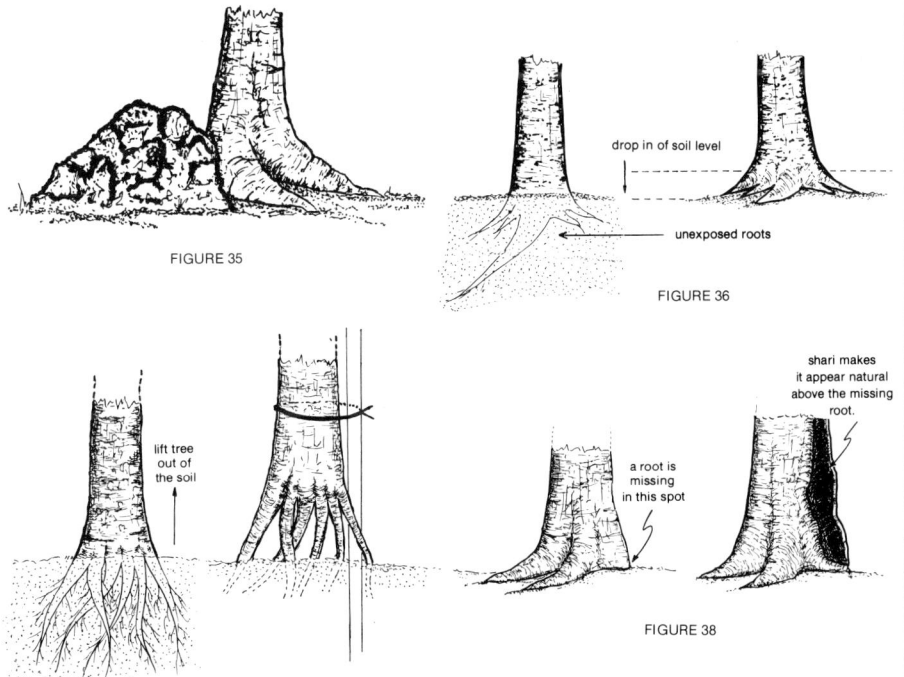

FIGURE 35

FIGURE 36

FIGURE 37

FIGURE 38

FIGURE 35 A small rock used to disguise the absence of roots.

FIGURE 36 By dropping the soil-level more roots are exposed.

FIGURE 37 These roots are below soil-level and are not spreading well. By lifting the tree higher above the soil, an exposed root style (*ne-agari*) is created. In time the roots will thicken to have a more natural appearance.

FIGURE 38 Above the area with no root, a dead strip of bark can be created. It is usual to find no roots under such a dead strip or *saba-miki*.

FIGURE 39 Grafting of a tree to use its roots on an old tree. The scion can be tacked in place or tied to the mother tree.

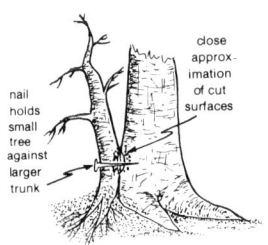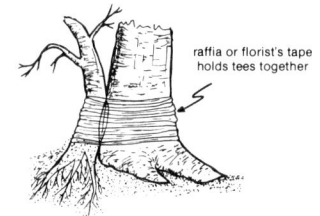

FIGURE 39

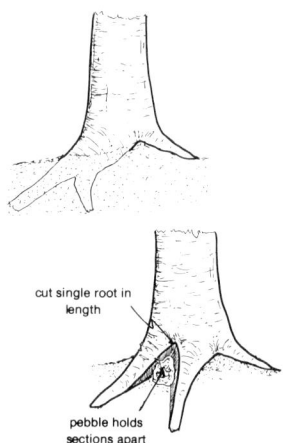

FIGURE 40 A large root split into two and forced apart with a pebble.

FIGURE 41
A. Trunk without taper.
B. Repeated S-curves.
C. A pot-belly thickening.
D. A very even curve.
E. A repeated zig-zag curve.
F. A trunk split into two very even trunks, with two apices.
G. Unnatural, ugly scars.
H. A tree leaning backwards, away from the viewer, as well as having a 'pigeon crop' bulging forwards.
I. The texture of the base of the trunk and the rest of the trunk are contrasting.

Trunks

The following appearances of a trunk are unwanted:
- cylindric trunk
- pot-belly thickening above soil surface
- zig-zag or repeated S-curve
- trunk leaning backwards
- twin-trunk which splits at a level somewhere above its base;
- ugly pruning wounds
- a rough-textured base with an otherwise smooth trunk
- sharp forward-directed bend just above soil-level (pigeon breast).

IMPROVING FAULTY TRUNKS Any bonsai needs to have a trunk with a broad base and a gradual, even taper in the length of the trunk. Very often the material we are working with has defects in this respect, for instance a reverse taper or unusual thickening in the trunk, and this could be corrected by judicious use of selected techniques. A trunk can be increased in size by two basic methods only, although in each group there are a number of different techniques based on the same underlying principles. The two methods are either injuring the cambium, which stimulates reparative growth, or increasing the movement of sap through a trunk or branch, which also increases growth.

To enlarge a trunk, the following methods can be tried:

(a) Flexing the trunk. The flexing (bending) should always be in the same direction, for instance forwards and backwards, because if it is done in all directions, the cambium is broken or torn loose right around the circumference of the trunk, and the tree could die. Do not apply this to conifers, as the bark could tear loose and the tree will die (this applies to all resinous trees). (Fig 42)

(b) Vertical incisions are made to a depth through the cambium, or tiny holes are punched into the trunk through the cambium, using a thin pin or a small diameter drill. This forces the cambium to repair the injuries and in so doing the trunk thickens. The vertical incisions can be made by using a sharp knife or using a rootcutter sideways. (Figures 43 and 44)

(c) The tree is planted in the garden or in a very large container. In the garden, the tree should have a wooden board or piece of slate underneath it, to prevent the roots growing too far downwards (see also page 28 for a more detailed

FIGURE 41
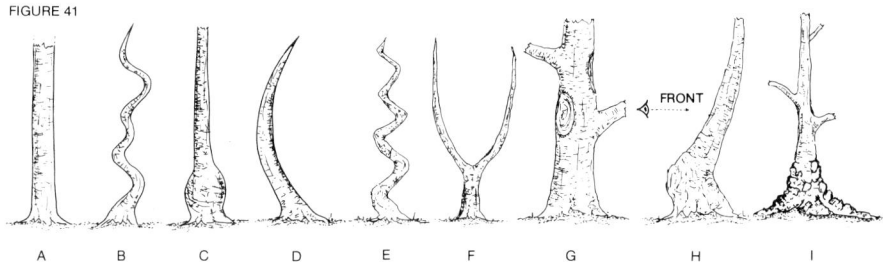

description). Because of the availability of more nutrients, there will be rapid growth in all dimensions. This can be controlled by nipping out new growth in areas where it is not desired, which allows selective thickening of the trunk and branches. Once again, the excessive growth can be cut back every year, to minimise pruning scars or, alternatively, it could be *jinned*.

(d) The apex of the tree is allowed to grow wild and is then cut off every year until the trunk has reached the required diameter. Be sure to have the cut surface facing towards the back of the tree, so as not to show an ugly wound, or else, when the trunk is thick enough, shape the tip into a *jin*. This method will increase the girth of the trunk over its entire length, without having any influence on the already established shape of the tree.

(e) If only a lower portion of the trunk needs to be thickened, allow the branch above that portion of the trunk to grow wild, after cutting off this branch in front of a bud which will then develop into a leader. Alternatively, the branch apex (growing tip) is allowed to lengthen excessively. This method allows the whole branch to thicken, and will also allow you to attend to the shaping of the rest of the branch, as there will be some development in that area as well. The apex could be cut off every winter and a new leader allowed to develop in spring, as this will cause less obvious scarring. The new growth is trained upwards, higher than the existing apex as if to form a new one. The tree is then under the impression that this new apex requires large quantities of nutrients to get it to grow higher. The trunk and branch thus thicken, at the expense of the rest of the tree. This same method is used to thicken a branch. The new branch or section thereof is removed when the trunk is thick enough.

Sacrificial branches are very effective in creating large fat trunks especially in the case of deciduous trees and some pine trees. The method involves letting a branch develop, which is accompanied by a thickening of the trunk below that branch. This branch is later sacrificed, either by cutting it off, or first air-layering it and then removing it. The time to remove the branch is when its diameter is approximately half of the mother trunk's.

A robust and luxuriantly growing tree will quickly erase the pruning wounds even if they are quite large. That is why you can allow a young tree to grow well, without pruning off the unwanted branches. These can be removed at a later date by creating the proper pruning wound. In the case of an older tree, it is better to under-fertilise, as quick growth here will cause an ugly scar to develop.

(f) Tie a wire tourniquet tightly around the trunk. (Figure 46) The carbohydrates moving down to the roots then pool above the tourniquet. The portion of the trunk involved is covered with sand. When the trunk thickens, it also forms new roots above the tourniquet. As soon as enough roots have formed, and the trunk has thickened to the required diameter, the old trunk and roots below the tourniquet are cut off and the tree replanted.

(g) If the base of the trunk is too small in diameter, the trunk can be slit from below with a sharp knife and a stone or wooden wedge forced into the cut to open it outwards. (Figure 47) The tree should be planted deeper into the soil to cover the cut. The cut surface can be treated with root-forming hormone compound, to cause roots to develop from the cut, creating an interesting *nebari* and contributing to the thickening of the trunk base.

To make young smooth bark look older, you can lightly tap on the bark with a hammer to injure the cambium, supporting the trunk with your hand. It heals in a knobby way and thickens the trunk. The trunk can be protected by covering it with rubber, which then lessens the injury to the soft bark, and only causes some thickening.

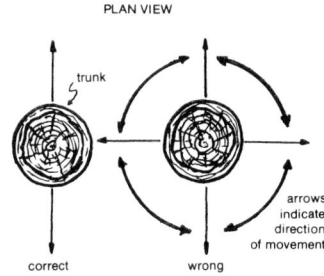

FIGURE 42 Direction in which to flex a trunk to thicken it.

FIGURE 43 Making vertical cuts into the trunk.

FIGURE 44 Punching tiny holes through the cambium results in thickening of the trunk through scar-tissue formation.

FIGURE 45 Supporting a lower branch which is allowed to lengthen to increase the trunk diameter.

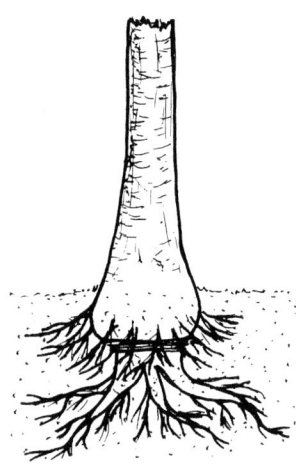

FIGURE 46 Tying a wire tourniquet thickens the trunk above the tourniquet.

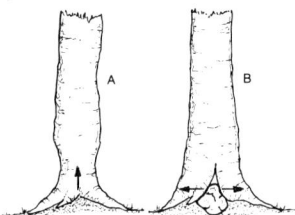

FIGURE 47 Splitting a trunk in two and keeping it open with a pebble. Roots may even form out of the wounded surface.

A remark about watering: regular and adequate watering encourages growth of the cambium, which leads to thickening of the trunk. Combine this with balanced fertilising to obtain the best results. Excessive water will cause longer internodes on branches, larger leaves, and weaker plants.

When a bonsai, or a potential bonsai, is in a container and growing well, the girth of the trunk will not increase at a noticeable rate. Neither will the character of the trunk change to any discernable degree. If, for instance, you have a tree with a trunk diameter of say 3 cm, at its base, you will perhaps have a tree with a base of 5 cm after ten years. If this particular tree has a straight trunk with no blemishes or scarring, ten years will make little difference to the appearance. If the first branch is located at a height of 10 cm above soil-level, this will still be the case in ten years' time. A trunk with a bend at about 6 cm above soil level (or at any other height) will have a bend at exactly the same height above the ground in ten years' time, although the trunk will have fattened somewhat, making the bend less obvious. The growth potential of a tree growing in a small container is, therefore, severely restricted, as is the likelihood of potentially interesting characteristics on the trunk.

So what do you do about those spindly trees in your collection? They certainly bear little resemblance to the beautiful examples with thick interesting trunks in bonsai books and magazines, or the 'unfair' trees used during demonstrations. Where do bonsai growers get these ideal trees on which to demonstrate their techniques, or to simply grow and enjoy? Do they have a secret and exclusive source? From your own experience, you probably know that it is nearly impossible to acquire a potential bonsai tree with a well-developed trunk from ordinary nurseries. Trees in nurseries are all grown in containers, are also restricted in their growth and their lower branches have usually been removed, making them look like poles planted in the ground. If you remove a beautiful specimen from nature, you run the risk of killing the tree and at the same time, you will probably find that the tree has some large roots with few, if any, fibrous roots near the trunk (see page 166).

These problems can all be solved quite easily, and with little waste of time. As I will again have occasion to point out, the answer is to replant your tree in the garden to accelerate growth. To be sure, it means foregoing the sheer enjoyment of seeing your bonsai standing in its beautiful pot, but the bonsai will be back in the pot in a few years, and will have improved immensely. The essentials of the technique are as follows:

The tree has to be planted in such a way as to force the developing thick roots in a horizontal direction, as this ensures a trunk with a thick base from which the roots can radiate outwards. This can be achieved by planting the tree on a piece of slate or wood (as described on page 28), and is a good method if the tree is not being grown in a bonsai pot, for instance when you take it out of its nursery container for the first time. However, if your tree is growing in a shallow container that you don't mind burying underground for a while, such as an asbestos or plastic one, you should plant the tree in the ground while still in the pot! Cover the pot with soil to a depth about equal to the depth of the pot. To allow the existing roots directly under the trunk to develop as well, be sure to have the drainage holes in the containers enlarged, as this will permit the roots to grow through these holes. When the tree is removed from the soil, and lifted out of the container, the roots close to the trunk will have many small fibrous roots filling the space in the container. This method of planting the tree in the garden whilst still in a container can also be done with a tree that has not previously grown in a pot, by simply taking it out of the present container and planting it in a pot before burying it.

After the tree has been planted in the garden it should be allowed to grow wild,

FAR LEFT
Juniperus
Height: 33 cm
Owner: Eddie van der Westhuizen

LEFT
Ficus natalensis
Natal fig
Height: 86 cm
Owner: Pieter Loubser

BELOW LEFT
Ficus natalensis
Natal fig
Height: 60 cm
Owner: Pieter Loubser

RIGHT
Acer palmatum
Japanese maple
Height: 20 cm
Owner: Derry Ralph

BELOW RIGHT
Olea europaea
subsp. *africana*
Wild olive
Height: 75 cm
Owner: Alf Jones

BELOW
Buddleja saligna
White olive
Height: 90 cm
Owner: Eddie van der Westhuizen

and in no time at all the trunk will develop beautifully. The soil in which the tree is planted should be ordinary, good garden soil, with good drainage. If drainage is a problem, a hole should be prepared and a gravel base used under the soil mixture. Be sure to work compost and some bonemeal or superphosphate into the soil before planting the tree or trees. Even though this also encourages weeds, they should not be too much of a problem if the trees are planted far enough apart, or in rows to enable you to walk between them and do the weeding. If you have an automatic spray system this could be extended to your 'wild bonsai patch' to ensure a daily watering.

Pruning your bonsai in the garden is not a time-consuming endeavour at all. If the basic shape of the trunk is correct, or at least acceptable, you need only trim away branches that develop in unwanted places. Do not attempt fine pruning as this would defeat the purpose of the soil planting. Allow the tree to grow! If your tree has a slender, straight trunk, wire it and shape some curves into the appropriate positions before you let it grow. Be sure to keep an eye on the wiring as it will very soon cut into the trunk due to the faster growth rate. Do not remove all unwanted branches at this point in time, as they might be used as *jin* later on, creating an aged appearance sooner than usual. These same branches will in the meantime cause a more rapid thickening of the trunk.

A technique for the more daring enthusiast is the following one, which has the additional benefit of creating a trunk with great character: allow the trunk to develop to a considerable thickness and then cut it off at a height which is about twice the diameter of the trunk. Slant the cut from the measured height downwards, to end at about the same level as the diameter of the trunk.

If possible, start the cut above an eyelet on the trunk, because the trunk should start growing from that particular end when it starts to lengthen again. Allow the trunk to grow quite thick again, for at least a year, as this will enable the cut wound to close neatly and will give a gradual taper into the newly developed trunk. When the new section of trunk is thick enough, the same procedure is repeated at a higher level, slanting the cut in a different direction. If, in the meantime, branches have developed, allow them to grow, as this also helps to thicken the trunk. These branches, or at least some of them, will be sacrificed later when they are not needed any more. (For the technique of sacrificing branches see page 31) The whole process of repeated cutting off at a slant and growing, results in a tapered trunk full of interesting knobs and bulges. The process will not even take very long — about three to four years in a fast-growing species. The wounds where cuts were made may not be completely closed in a year's time, but they will close as growth continues. It is true that, especially in fast-growing species, wounds that heal cause ugly scars when trees receive fertiliser, therefore, one should not be fertilising these trees too much. On the other hand one wants quicker growth, and these scars will contribute to the aged appearance of the tree.

Another advantage of using this technique is that the tree needs very little attention during this period of growth. You only need to cut the trunk once or perhaps twice during the growing season.

A variation of this technique, or perhaps more aptly the original version, is the *Lingnan* technique. (See page 40)

The wounds created when cutting off the trunk may be sealed off, to prevent unwanted dying back, or ingress of disease-forming bacteria. The scars will add character to the trunk and they may be reshaped and hollowed out when refining is done at a later stage. In the case of conifers, especially (but not only them), it is better to leave a short stub of branch, to allow the tree to form a bypass for the sap, while the stub dries out. The dead stub can be removed later or turned into a *jin*. By

'If a tree dies, plant another in its place'
LINNAEUS

that time the stub will have been sealed off from the rest of the trunk and no damage through sap withdrawal could have taken place.

The above-mentioned technique will ensure an attractive interesting trunk — essential to the design of your bonsai. The trunk is the soul of the tree from which all the rest springs, and cannot be mediocre or neglected.

Once the trunk has been allowed to reach the right stage of development, the whole tree is removed from the ground and the container will most probably come out along with the roots and soil, especially if roots have grown through the drainage holes. The unwanted roots are now cut off (the cuts facing downwards) and the tree removed from the temporary pot, which shouldn't present a problem. After trimming the roots, repot the tree in its new container and treat it once again as a bonsai. Usually you will find that the tree has now grown thick roots from its trunk, and they are spread out horizontally over the edges of the pot or slab or slate. Also, the tree will have a base of considerable girth, tapering nicely upwards.

You can, if you are inclined to do so, lift the tree out of the soil every year, do some root pruning and replace it in the soil. This will slow down the root development to a degree, but is still an improvement on keeping the tree in the pot continuously. Also, it will allow more fibrous roots to develop, and make the final removal from the soil much easier, as the root system will not have been allowed to spread too far or too deep.

Branches and Leaves

Every tree must have an apex. Never have the tree splitting into two even branches at the top. This does not mean that the tree must necessarily have a pointed apex, indicative of a younger tree. Older trees will in many cases have rounded apexes, because they have stopped growing in height, and the branches have spread out. This may be created by bending the apex over, with one of the small branches from this section now forming the new, flatter apex.

IMPROVING FAULTY BRANCHES AND LEAVES The faults mentioned in Figure 48 can all be corrected by judicious pruning and training. It is somewhat more difficult to correct a branch that is too thin, or absent.

To enlarge a branch, a secondary branch, which can be done away with, is allowed to grow, and is trained to grow higher than the apex of the tree. This allows the main branch to thicken, and the overgrown branch is simply cut off when the main branch has acquired the desired diameter.

In the case of a tree which has been dug out of a garden or somewhere in nature, it will need a few years to establish itself in the temporary container and start growing strongly. As explained, you do not need to remove the thicker branches initially, as the wounds will heal well if the tree is growing strongly. The old branches are seldom used as they are. New branches are developed instead, and the thicker ones are formed into *jin* or driftwood. The older branches are usually not compact enough, in terms of side-branching and leaves, whereas new branches can be grown compactly.

In the case of, for instance, needle junipers and oleas, new branches are readily developed from trunk buds.

Where a branch is lacking, there are different ways of grafting branches to the trunk:

- A secondary branch, preferably a lower one, is allowed to grow longer, and thicker When it has reached the required thickness, the bark of the trunk is cut away through the cambium in an oval shape, where the new branch is required. A similar wound is made in the branch in such a position that these two wounds can be approximated. The branch is tied against the trunk with the two wounds pressed tightly together. Cover this with tree-seal. Within some months, the

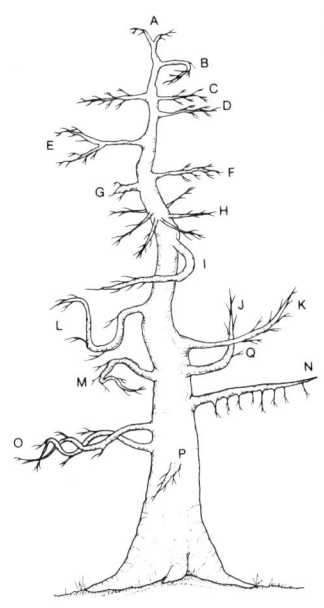

FIGURE 48 Combination of branch faults.

A No apex   *Shinnashi*
B Ingrowing branch   *Gyaku-eda*
C Branches at same level
                       Kannuki-eda
D parallel branches   *Kasane-eda*
E Y-shaped branch   *Futamata-eda*
F Pocket branch   *Fotukoro-eda*
G Stubby branch   *Shinkire-eda*
H Wheel spokes   *Kuruma-eda*
I Branch crossing trunk
                       Miki kiri-eda
J Upward growing branch
                       Tachi-eda
K Evenly bow-shaped branch
                       Han-en-eda
L U-shaped branch *Kaerumata-eda*
M Sharply bent, backwards
   growing branch   *Hiji tsuki-eda*
N Drooping secondary
   branches   *Sagari-eda*
O Tangled branches   *Karami-eda*
P Eye-poking branch *Metsuki-eda*
Q Crossed branches   *Kosa-eda*

branch can be cut underneath the grafting to allow the grafted section to continue on its own, receiving its nourishment from the trunk.
- Another tree of the same kind, or a branch of another tree of the same kind can be grafted.

For details of the techniques, see the following section.

When a branch is too thick in relation to the other branches, the development of the thick branch may be held back by nipping out its growing tips while the rest of the tree is allowed to grow. This method, however, requires considerable time to produce the desired effect.

It is possible to get a latent bud to develop into a branch by making a cut through the bark into the cambium below the bud. The downwards-moving carbohydrates will heap up in the bud and force it to develop.

GRAFTING

Grafting — an age-old technique — can be used to improve the branches on a tree.

It is also possible to graft the trunk of one tree onto another, where the properties of the graft are preferable to those of the trunk onto which it is grafted, as is done in the cases of different fruit trees or vines, such as apricots and grapes.

Grafting is a standard horticultural technique, and is covered in detail in horticultural books dealing with the subject. As a bonsai grower, you will find a basic knowledge of grafting most helpful, if confronted, for example, with a tree lacking roots or branches.

General Notes

It goes without saying that grafting generally occurs between trees of the same species, unless you particularly wish to combine the qualities of two different types of bonsai.

Try and match the scion and understock in size. If you do not, the cambium layers will not match and you will have little chance of success. Because the cambium is alive, and is responsible for healing the newly created wounds, it starts growing. For the graft to take, the two 'growing' cambiums must meet and unite. This will not be possible if the two layers of opposing cambium are not in close contact.

The two different parts of the match — scion and understock — must be stable, and if one keeps moving, the graft will not take. This means you have to secure the two parts tightly, using grafting tape if possible. You must also tie the long branch or grafted trunk to some form of support, to prevent anything at all, even a breeze, from moving it.

Remember that sap-flow is taking place in scion and understock. If you graft a scion onto the understock with the sap flowing in opposite directions, the graft will fail.

After having secured the scion and understock, the union must be sealed off, to

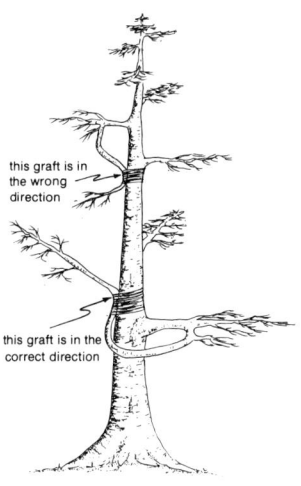

FIGURE 49 Grafting a branch from the same tree. Remember to keep the sap-flow in the same direction.

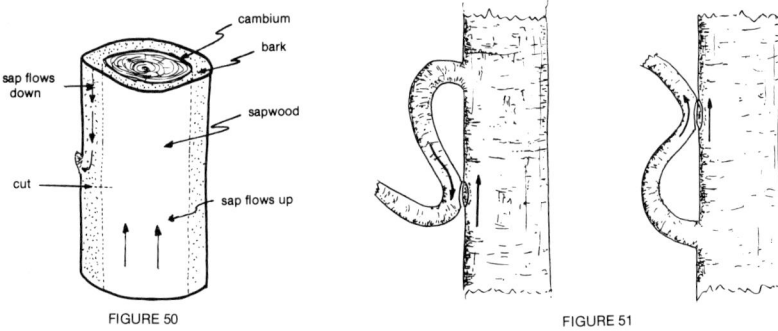

FIGURE 50 Direction of sap-flow.

FIGURE 51 Direction of sap-flow in scion and mother tree.

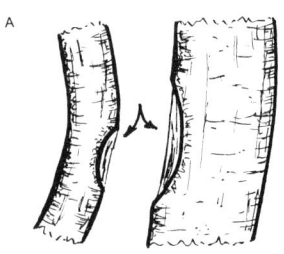

FIGURE 52B shows a better size match in the two wounds that have to be joined.

prevent moisture loss on the one hand and ingress of disease-forming organisms on the other.

Grafting results in a scar at the union, but if the tree is allowed to grow vigorously after grafting, the scar will virtually disappear and only add character to the trunk.

Grafting should be done when the understock is experiencing a high sap-flow — thus in spring. If the graft takes, the branch will have the summer months to develop.

Note: The understock is the tree onto which the scion is grafted.

Grafting Roots

This works best with deciduous trees. It can be used to reduce the length of a branchless trunk. On the understock, small flaps are cut into the trunk where roots are required. Root pieces are then taken and bevelled from two sides, to form a wedge, which is then inserted under the flap. The flap must be deep enough to allow the scion to contact the sap-wood. The flap is tied over the roots securely, if possible with grafting tape. The grafting area is covered with a wet mixture of 1/2 peat moss, 1/2 sand, as with an air-layering.

There is a second method of grafting roots onto a trunk, but as it is the same as branch-grafting, which is called inarching or approach-grafting, it will be described along with the branch grafts.

Grafting Branches or Trunks

It is not uncommon to find a tree which lacks a branch just where you would like it to have one. The problem can be solved by grafting a branch of the same tree into the right position, or using a branch of another tree of the same species, or even a whole, smaller tree as scion.

A branch is bent into position and a portion of the branch, as well as a portion of the trunk, is sliced off with a sharp knife in the area where the graft is to take place. Be sure to cut deep enough to enter the sap-wood — that means cutting through the cambium. The cambium is the live tissue in the trunk and will do the joining. Keep the two wounds the same size, and when the branch is in position, the direction of sap-flow must correspond in the scion and understock (branch and tree). The latter is not easy to accomplish when a branch of the same tree is used, because the branch must be long enough to be able to be bent in the right direction. This sometimes requires at least one full season of growing. You can do this by training a branchlet to grow upwards, till it is long enough to bend into position. It is also clear why a lower branch is best (you don't need to bend it acutely).

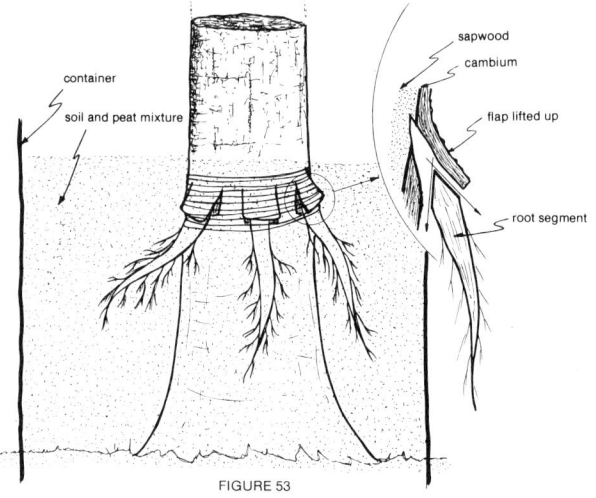

FIGURE 53 Grafting roots to the trunk.

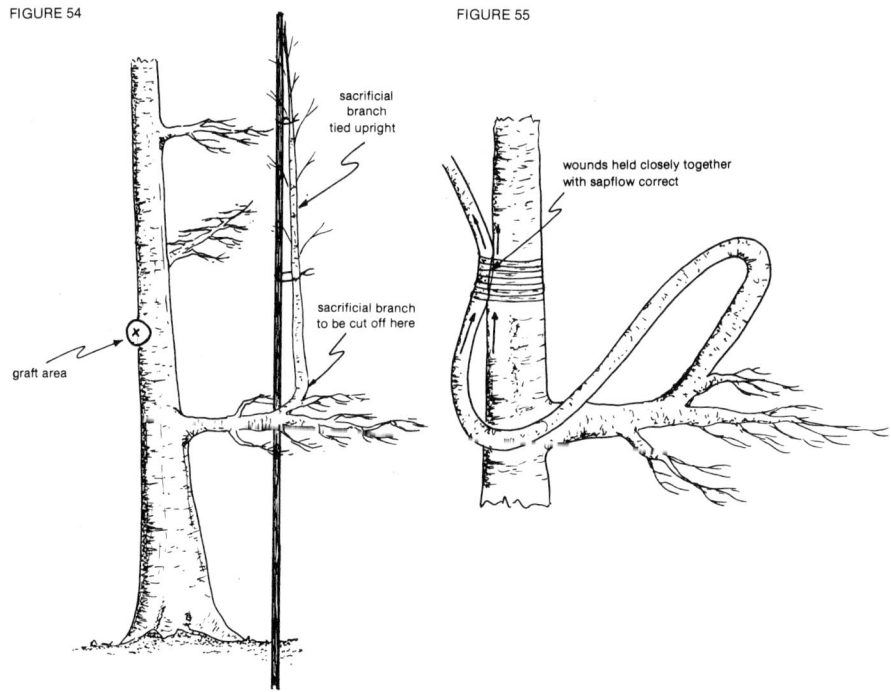

FIGURE 54
1. The first step is to grow one branch very tall — even if it takes a few years.
2. Grow the branch from an area where the wound, when cut off, will not be obvious.

FIGURE 55 The long branch is bent around to the area where the graft must take place, appositioned and sealed.

The same procedure is used to graft a smaller tree of the same species onto the trunk. The scion tree is kept in its own container — it just needs to be supported in some manner, for instance by having its container tied to a post or standing on some prop. (Figure 56)

When the two wounds have been approximated, they are tied together with grafting tape and the wound is sealed. Remember not to allow any accidental movement. I have used some shavings from the branches, mixed with sealing compound and packed around the grafting site, to protect the trunk against the tight wires used to hold the scion in position. Florist's tape also works well, because it can stretch to allow for growth.

When the scion is placed under the flap that has been cut, it will not always be possible to match the two opposing cambium layers. If this is the case, see to it that the cambium layers are exactly in contact on at least one side otherwise no union will take place. The same rule appears when two trees or a tree and a branch are being grafted.

The enormous advantage of the above technique is that the scion stays alive in its own container, or is supplied by the parent tree till the graft has taken. There is no chance of the scion drying out through a deficiency of nutrients or moisture.

As mentioned under root-grafting, when a whole tree is grafted onto the parent tree you can, instead of cutting the roots, sever the main trunk of the scion above the graft. Now your parent tree can have its trunk cut off below the graft, and it will continue living with a shorter trunk, but with a new set of roots gleaned from another tree.

With any of the above techniques you can expect the graft to take, and in about a year or even less, you can start cutting the branch or tree from the scion in stages, cutting deeper every month until the branch has been completely severed. This gives the new branch a chance to develop a sound water transport system in the sapwood.

A variation of the grafting techniques can be used to create a thick trunk with an aged appearance, or one in the baobab style. A few trunks are tied together and

THE KIMONO EFFECT
It is theoretically wrong to have a branch growing from the inside of a curve of a trunk, as this particular branch would then be in the shadow of the trunk above it – something you would not usually find in nature, because the trunk would try to grow away from the branch to allow it to receive its allotted share of sunlight. This is called a pocket-branch – as though growing from a pocket of clothing. In Japanese the branch is called a futokoro-eda *(eda = branch).* Futokoro *is the front of a* kimono *where the two sides overlap. Because the* kimono *is held in place by a sash or* obi, *the overlap can be used as a pocket! To alleviate the problem, the branch can be bent forwards, out of the curve and then grown in front of the trunk like the spread of the sleeve of the* kimono *as it spreads out on a dancing girl (the* kimono *has very wide sleeves). Another solution is to direct the branch upwards to make it look as though it is growing from the trunk at a higher point.*

FIGURE 56 A whole tree in its own container can be grafted to another.

FIGURE 57 The principle of grafting one tree to another. By cutting off the one tree's tip and the other's roots and trunk base you create a completely different tree.

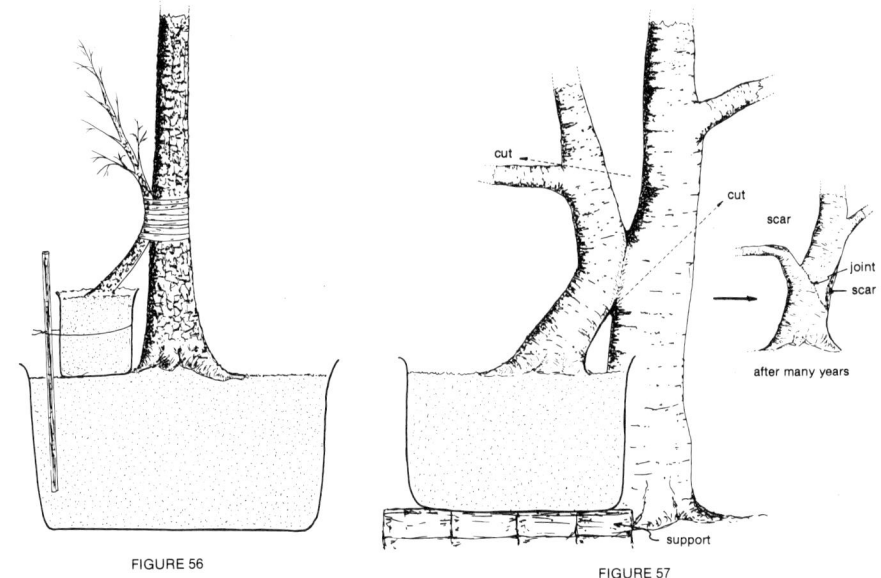

allowed to grow wild. They must all be in the same container. You can strip some of the bark in the areas where the trunks touch each other. When this is done, the wound-edges must be sealed. After a few years you will have a beautiful trunk consisting of a number of smaller trunks fused together.

Bud Grafting

It is possible to graft a bud onto the parent tree. A slit in the form of a T is made into the trunk to a depth just deeper than the cambium. The slit is opened and the bud is slipped in and tied down securely. Do not expose the tree to direct sunlight until the bud shows definite growth.

FIGURE 58 Bud grafting.

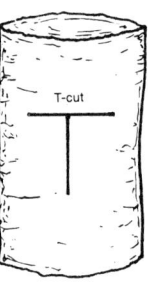 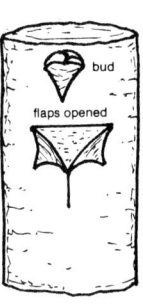 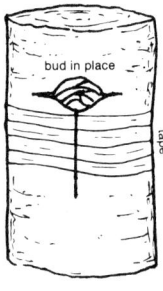

SHAPING TECHNIQUES 3

English proverb:
'Better to bend than to break.'

GENERAL

A bonsai tree cannot be allowed to grow into an obscure, indefinite shape. According to my own definition of a bonsai, and as can be seen from examples, every bonsai must be grown in a particular style. This being the case, it follows that a potential bonsai must be guided in order to grow into the shape (style) one has decided on. One may be fortunate to come across a *potensai* (potential bonsai) which virtually has the correct shape for a certain style and needs little alteration, but as the tree grows, it will have to be corrected at times, or its growth will have to be stunted. The usual case is, however, a tree which only has the potential of becoming a bonsai after the trunk, and more often the branches, have been changed in shape, position and direction (angle). This chapter describes how to manage this shaping or moulding process. Bear in mind that every tree places some constraint on the grower, simply due to the fact that it is an individual tree growing in the way it 'wants' to, and in most cases having done so for quite some time! The grower of bonsai will want to direct a tree into growing in some manner or direction and will apply the techniques popularly used, but in the end the tree is going to grow in the way that its genetic pattern allows it. It is therefore essential to know the growth pattern of the particular tree you intend developing into a bonsai.

There are only two ways of controlling the direction in which you want the tree trunk or branches to grow, namely:

- By physically bending the trunk or branch, using wrenches, wire, wedges and other means. The branch or trunk is then kept in this new position until it is able to remain there without help.
- By pruning, so as to allow a specific portion of the tree to grow in a particular direction. This is the so-called 'clip and grow' or *Lingnan* technique, when practised in its pure form.

The usual method however is to combine the two techniques.

One uses either young, immature bonsai material or older, developed trees. It is clear that one cannot use the same method for these two very different kinds of raw material. The two different methods are:

- The modelling method: the 'positive technique' of building up the younger tree, which can be compared to the way an artist would build up a statue by adding amounts of clay, until the required shape has been reached.
- The sculptural method: the 'negative method' of reducing a larger tree, comparable to the way a sculptor would chip away (reduce) a block of marble or wood to the required shape.

With the modelling technique you start with a younger tree which has the potential of being grown into a bonsai. First cut off everything you don't need, and then let the tree grow. When it is sufficiently developed, once again trim away the unwanted branches or sections of branches. Repeat this process till the tree has reached the

'We all find the time to do what we really want to do.'
WILLIAM FEATHER

FIGURE 59 The Lingnan technique in steps.

FIGURE 59

How can you profess to love an art if you don't attempt to understand it?

stage where it is only trimmed to maintain its shape. In this way you will have allowed the tree to develop step by step, only trimming unwanted growth. The accent here is on allowing the tree to *grow* into the required shape with only a *little trimming*.

With the sculptural method a well-developed tree is pruned to remove unwanted branches, and this pruning is usually quite severe. Thereafter the pruning is used to keep the tree in shape, while allowing some growth to fill in spaces as required. The accent in this instance is on removing existing branches that are not required. You would be very fortunate to come across a tree which enables you to shape it entirely in this manner.

Again, in practice the two methods are more or less combined.

THE LINGNAN TECHNIQUE

Lingnan is a very old way of shaping a bonsai, and one which has stood the test of time. The name is derived from the Lingnan monastery in China, where the monks practised the technique. Given such a background, it is not surprising that the time factor was of no importance and, indeed, it takes many years to complete the development of angular bends and radical changes in trunk or branch lines when following this particular method.

The *Lingnan* method does not mean that you have to grow the tree into a *bunjin* (or *literati*) style; you can use it to train the tree into virtually any style you wish.

As earlier indicated, the Lingnan method is the repetition of a twofold procedure, the first entailing severe pruning and the second waiting for the tree to reach a certain stage of development. This second step may take a few years, but is

'Delay is preferable to error'.

THOMAS JEFFERSON

much quicker if the tree is grown in a very large container or in the garden for a while.

You may use either young or older trees, but choose a tree of which the lower portion of the trunk is to your liking. The trunk is then severed just beyond a branch, at the required position. If the trunk is well developed to a point past two or three branches, it can be cut off at the height where it ceases to be pleasing, and if preferred, the one, two or three branches are then left to develop until they have reached an adequate size. The branches and the trunk are then cut back drastically. Usually, the cut is made just beyond a bud which will grow in the right direction.

Once again a waiting period follows and the process is repeated. Keep a watch on the taper of the trunk and branches! If a short section of branch is left, instead of cutting it off flush with the bud, this short piece will act as an obstruction and force the new growth to a side, with a resultant zig-zag development. The stump is removed at a later stage.

The result is a dramatic, angular style, giving the illusion of a tree shaped by forceful winds or, perhaps, recovering after lightning has destroyed some of its branches; whatever one is trying to portray, it is not the kind of tree one would find growing in a sheltered environment — the tree will show movement, excitement, effect.

The technique makes use of the properties of the growth hormones auxin and giberillin, which are contained in the terminal bud. These hormones stimulate the cambium cells to divide rapidly, and thus thicken the trunk or branches. When the terminal bud is removed, the effect of the hormones is lost, and the thickening will slow down or even stop. The message is thus *not* to cut the terminal bud off before the trunk or branch has reached the required thickness! Growing the tree in a large container, or in the garden to encourage root growth, will also help to thicken the trunk and branches. Always supply sufficient water and nutrients at the correct times.

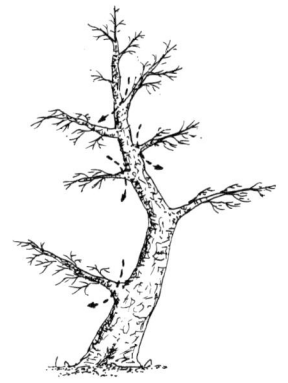

FIGURE 60 If more branches are needed, the same principle as for a *bunjin* is applied. Now the only difference lies in the fact that certain branches are not removed.

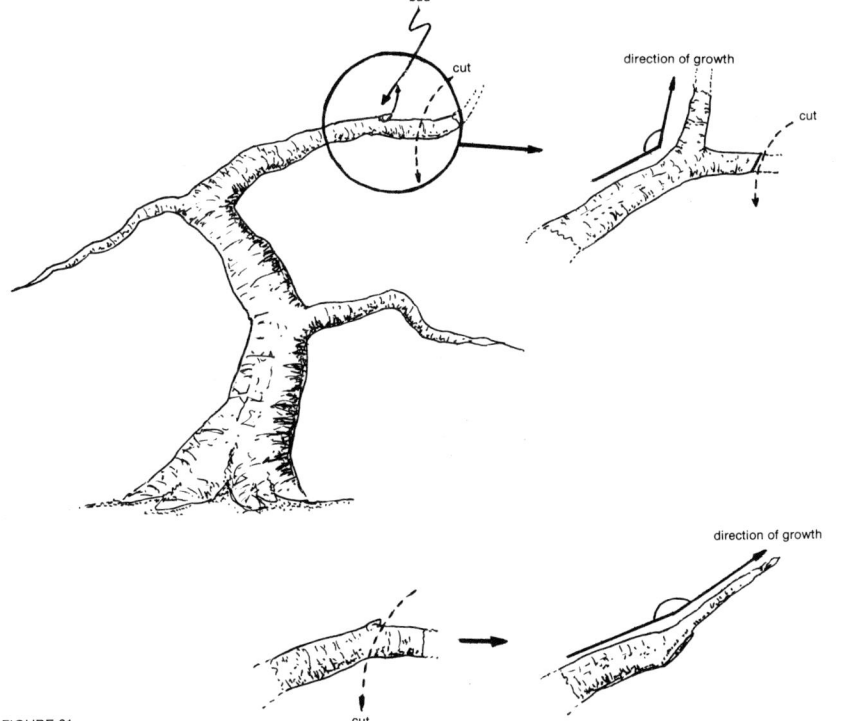

FIGURE 61

FIGURE 61 Stimulating growth and changing the direction of growth, as is necessary in the Lingnan technique.

FIGURE 62 Pruning of opposite leaves to influence direction of new growth.

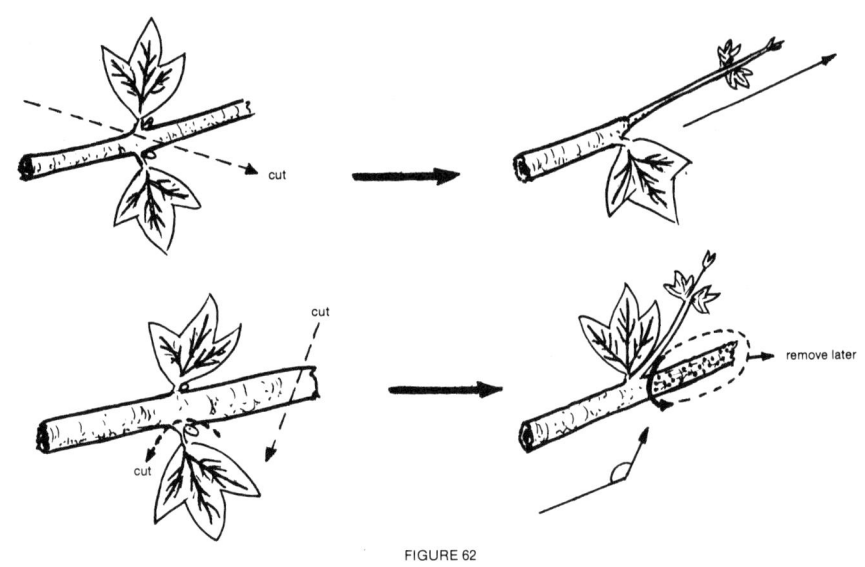

FIGURE 62

THE REDUCTION METHOD

This is also called the sculptural method, for which you need a well-developed tree with branches more or less where you want them to be.

Study the tree carefully before deciding which branches to keep, and which ones to cut off. Remember one thing, however — do not cut off an unwanted branch unless there is an obviously better-placed one available. A branch somewhat out of place is better than no branch at all, and other techniques (as described in Chapter

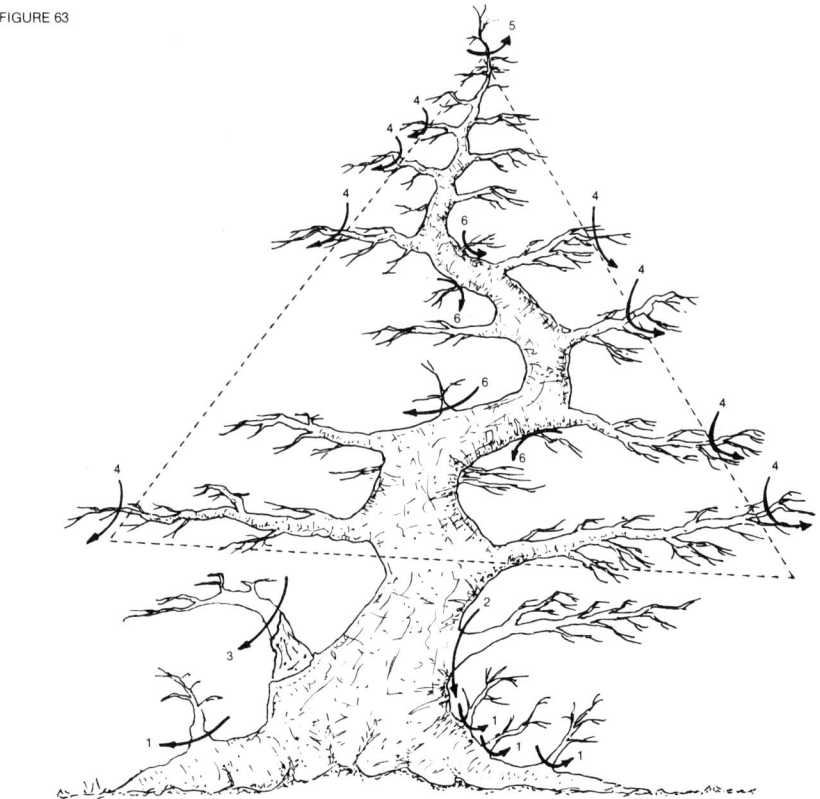

FIGURE 63

FIGURE 63 The basic technique of reducing a tree
1 Remove all suckers
2 Remove branches in the convexity of the trunk
3 Make *jins* from unwanted branches
4 Shorten branches that are too long
5 Shorten apex
6 Cut off small unwanted branches from the trunk.

2) can be used to correct its appearance. In any case, it is safe to cut off the branch while leaving some length, which can be shaped into a *jin*, if this is to your liking, and if not, the stump can be completely removed as soon as you are sure of your design. Always keep Chapter 2's styling principles in mind, even when other subjects are being dealt with, as in the following section on pruning.

The branches or even the trunks are wired and bent and will eventually grow into their positions. Wiring techniques are discussed under 'Shaping through bending' on page 59.

After the initial pruning and possibly wiring, the tree's growth is directed by trimming back and removing buds until it reaches its so-called 'final' size and stage. From then on, it is treated exactly like a mature Lingnan-grown bonsai. One must always remember that the tree is alive, with a natural tendency to grow and form new branches and leaves — it is never static, and will always need care in the form of trimming (apart from watering, fertilising, etc). It may even, due to either growth or disease, require drastic re-shaping. The tree does not stay small because it wants to; it does so due to the treatment it receives! A bonsai will never reach a stage where it can simply be kept alive whilst it stays in that particular shape and size.

SHAPING THROUGH PRUNING

The Purpose of Pruning

It may seem silly to ask why a tree needs pruning, as the obvious answer is to shape the tree — but that is not the only reason! When a tree is pruned, it affects the growth of the tree and this repair growth is determined by:
- which part of the tree is pruned
- to what extent the tree is pruned and
- when the tree is pruned.

If these three factors are not kept in mind, the pruning will not have the desired effect. Late or faulty pruning will result in parts of the tree growing to the wrong length or in the wrong direction. You may lose a whole season, or at least part of a season in the tree's development!

The important question of when to prune a particular tree could be answered by detailing every species of tree, but this answer would have to take into consideration the effects of different climates, different soils, different places where bonsai are grown and many more variables. This would be an impossible task.

Essential for the timing of pruning procedures, is an understanding of the climatic growth cycle, regardless of whether it is an evergreen or deciduous tree. Every tree goes through a cycle of building and storing reserve nutrients during its active growing period, and then surviving on these reserves after it has lost its leaves or growth has slowed down. The reserves are stored in the trunk and when they are needed to form new leaves and restart the cycle, they are moved back out of the trunk and roots, and into the developing leafbuds. This process of renewal is initiated by rising temperatures and lengthening days. One could compare the reserves in the trunk and root to a fully charged battery. As the nutrients are moved into the branches and leaves during the start of the new growing season, the 'battery' becomes depleted. To recharge this 'battery', the leaves unfold and through photosynthesis trap solar energy and form starches which will later be stored in the trunk and roots.

If the leaves are removed before they have unfolded completely and started 'recharging the battery', the tree will have to call on its remaining reserves to develop new leaves. The ability of the tree to form new leaves will vary, depending on how long and harsh the winter was, how healthy the tree is and the quality of the preceding summer. Should these new leaves once again be prematurely removed,

Before most people start boasting about their family tree, they usually do a good pruning job.

O. BATTISTA

To think too long about doing a thing often becomes its undoing.

EVA YOUNG

the tree may well lack the reserves to form another set of leaves and will die. This comparison shows that pruning should be done either before the new leaves have started unfolding, or after they have had a chance to replenish the reserves.

The above knowledge can be applied when you wish a tree to develop smaller leaves and also in defoliation techniques. If you are willing to run the risk of pruning after the leaves have started forming, the second set of leaves may well be smaller due to the depleted reserves. It can also be seen that each tree should be handled individually and any generalisation should be avoided.

The bonsai grower prunes for the following reasons:
- To create the right shape by removing unwanted parts of the tree.
- To create a more compact growth with more ramification and leaves closer together.
- To keep the tree small by restricting and regulating growth.
- To keep the tree healthy.
- To direct the growth in a particular direction.

General Rules

A few general rules should be kept in mind:
- Always use a sharp branch cutter or secateur (scissors).
- Disinfect any cutting instruments after use, to prevent the transmission of disease.
- Always seal off larger pruning wounds.
- Never leave a stump protruding after smaller branches have been cut off. Always try to ensure a hollowed-out cut, as it will heal more quickly without leaving a scar. Cut preferably in the shape of an upside-down teardrop or make an oval cut in the length of the trunk or branch. At the worst leave a flat cut surface.
- Ensure a cleanly cut wound, as torn bark will heal with difficulty and, moreover, will be vulnerable to infection.

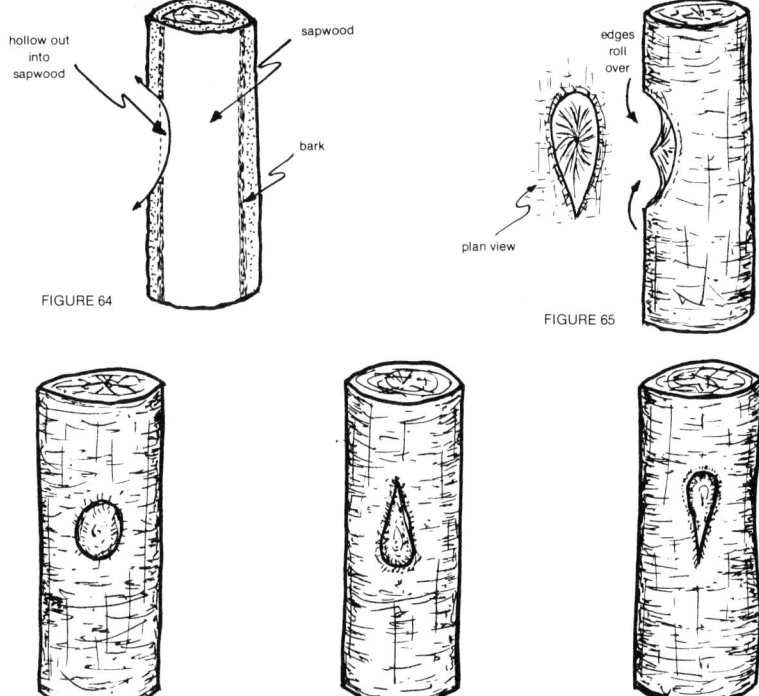

FIGURE 64 Making a hollow pruning wound.

FIGURE 65 Leaving a cone in the middle of the wound makes for better healing.

FIGURE 66 Wounds in different shapes. The upside down teardrop will heal the best.

Pruning Thick Branches

Usually leave a concave (hollow) wound, and be sure that the hollow reaches into the hardwood, as it is the cambium which has to heal the cut, without producing an unsightly bulge. If you are lucky enough to have a branch directly above the cut, the healing process will be faster, as it will benefit from the sugars (carbohydrates) which are fed into the wound edge.

An improvement on the above-mentioned method is to hollow out the wound, and to leave a little cone of wood in the middle.

If it seems as though the healing of a wound has stopped, without complete closure, the margins of the wound can be re-injured by scratching with a knife. This stimulates healing. The process can be repeated till the wound has closed completely.

With trees that do not send out growth from old wood easily, and trees that have a lot of sap (pine, spruce, fig), it is better to leave a short stub for a few months. It enables the tree to seal off the stub, or to form a natural bypass for the sap. The stub is later cut to form a hollow, which will heal over, or it can be shaped into a short *jin*. The problem with a tree that produces large quantities of sap, is that it drips out of the wound onto the trunk or leaves, and, as with figs, this sticky white material stains the leaves. The so-called bleeding of a fig can be stopped by applying water to the cut end.

If a branch is so thick that it has to be sawn through, it should be given a cut from underneath first, before the sawing from above starts, as this will prevent the branch from tearing off. Finally, you should seal the wound with a tree-seal or at least rub in a mixture of saliva and clay. This is a practical measure to prevent further loss of sap, to prevent disease organisms from entering the wound, and to discourage die-back due to the fact that the cells on the wound surface do not dry out.

When cutting a large branch you could leave a 'heel' of bark on the lower edge of the wound. This can be done by cutting into the branch on its lower surface where it joins the trunk. (See Figure 68) The length of the heel must be equal to the diameter of the branch being cut. The heel is then taped or tied onto the wound and sealed. This grafting of the bark should be done in winter, to prevent the pitch from separating the bark from the cambium.

The Prevention of Pruning Scars

All bonsai undergo pruning to varying degrees throughout their existence. The pruning leaves a wound, which has to heal in order for the tree to survive. Small wounds present no problems because they heal over with no scarring. This is not the case with large wounds. What constitutes a large wound is a matter of opinion, but certainly it depends on the relation between the size of the wound and the diameter of the trunk or branch. You will find that in the case of a young tree which still has a relatively thin trunk, the branches, even though still thin, are thicker as measured against the trunk. Removal of these branches results in ugly scarring. When the tree has a thicker trunk, and branches up to a diameter of approximately one third of the trunk are cut off, the wounds heal better.

Thus, when cutting off thick branches, you have to decide whether the tree is going to look better with or without a scar. A bonsai should appear natural, and the influence of man should not be apparent, which means that pruning wounds should not be seen to be the result of pruning. These wounds have either got to heal, to make them invisible, or they have to be carved and moulded so as to appear as if they are the result of some natural accident.

When a tree is injured, as in the case of a pruning wound, the cambium layer is stimulated to start forming cells, which is seen as growth at the wound edges. If at all possible, this growth will continue till the wound surface has been completely

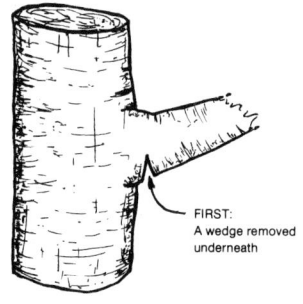
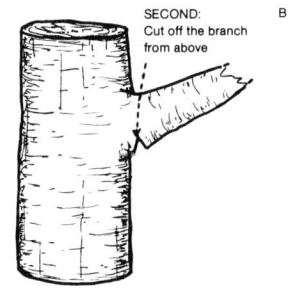

FIGURE 67 This is the order in which to saw through a branch to prevent it tearing off.

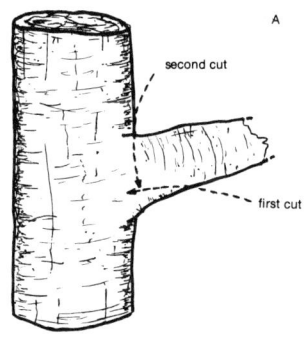
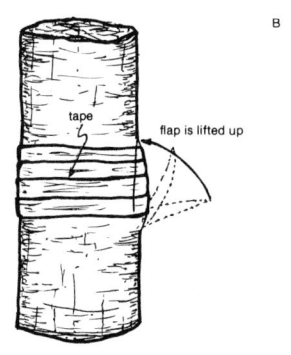

FIGURE 68 The wound could be closed with a flap of bark.

covered. This happens to prevent bacteria and other injurious agents from penetrating into the tree through the wound, as the tree has to have an intact outer covering. In cases where the wound is too large to be closed completely, the wood that is exposed will dry out and may rot when exposed to wet conditions. Different circumstances affect the healing process: healing is slow during winter and summer, due to the cold and heat respectively; a young or healthy tree heals more easily than an older tree; an older tree heals more predictably; a tree heals better when not exposed to either very dry or very wet weather. The use of sealing paste is recommended, because it prevents the wound drying out, it keeps micro-organisms and excessive moisture out and protects the wound against temperature extremes.

It becomes obvious why pruning wounds should be hollow or concave. If a stub is left after pruning, the healing tissue cannot close over it, and when the wound is level with the surface of the trunk, the healing tissue (called callus) will form a bulge as it grows over the wound. Leaving a stub of branch does have merit, especially in the case of conifers, because it allows the tree to form new paths for the sap-flow whilst the stub is drying out. The stub is removed at a later stage. This is not the only factor that should be kept in mind when removal of a branch is considered. Other factors are the presence of the right fertilisers (phosphorus and potassium) and the flow of sap in the area where the branch is going to be removed. Pruning should thus be done during the correct season, under the right circumstances and after having followed a fertiliser programme rich in phosphorus and potassium.

The tree consists of two 'tubular' systems: one transporting dissolved nutrients from the roots up towards the leaves, and the other distributing the products of photosynthesis from the leaves to the rest of the tree. The upwards moving stream is on the inside of the cambium layer, in the centre of the trunk or branch, while the downwards moving stream is on the outside of the cambium, just under the bark, if any exists. Any injury to the tree causes an interruption in the sap-flow. Should a pruning wound be located directly underneath another branch, there will be a continuous flow of sap from the branch above the wound, past the wound, and quicker healing will result. This is even better in the case of a mature tree because of better established sap-paths or tubes.

The tree tries to protect itself by so-called sap-withdrawal, which means a drying out of the wood in a direction back towards the roots, away from the site of injury (in a descending fashion). This can happen to quite a degree, with a large section of tree dying in the process. However, if a branch of reasonable size exists below the wound, the sap-flow taking place in that branch will prevent the process of sap-withdrawal from moving further down. In the same way, a branch opposite the wound will also help to form good callus over the wound. In the case of a rapidly growing tree, the sap-flow is very active, and this may well result in the callus forming an ugly knob. This can be prevented, only in this instance, by simultaneously partially defoliating the branch above the wound.

THE EFFECT OF HORMONES In general, drastic pruning has the effect of stimulating growth, because the tree wants to regain its shape and size. When repeated trimming and bud pinching are done, they restrict growth, as will be explained.

In nature the young tree grows rapidly in length, leaving a considerable distance between branches, and between leaves. As the tree grows older, the branches and leaves become more compact — the tree has more side growth. The leaves also tend to be smaller when the tree is old. The growth in length is due to the influence of a hormone called auxin, which promotes apical growth. (The apex refers to the tip of the tree but can also mean the ends of branches.) Another set of hormones called cytokinins does the opposite and promotes side-branching. Auxin is dominant, however. The further the leaves and branches are from the apex (i.e. the closer they are to the trunk), the more the effect of cytokinins becomes apparent in the form of more branches and leaves. To promote the formation of shorter internodal distances, more compact and finer branching and smaller leaves, trimming of terminal (apical) buds must be done regularly. This removes the influence of auxin and in consequence slows down the overall growth of the tree, but allows redistribution of growth and vigour. The tree still has the same nutrient supply, but this is now shared by many growth points, resulting in smaller branches and leaves. The same principle is applied when timing the pruning and is discussed under that heading on page 48.

Trees placed in a very sunny area form smaller leaves and are more compact. This is due to the fact that enough sun is reaching the leaves and although the leaves are smaller, adequate photosynthesis takes place. In addition, the smaller total leaf surface restricts the loss of moisture through transpiration, due to the hot conditions.

The leaf formation is also dependent on the root condition, which means that after root pruning has been carried out, and a lot of new roots are being formed, there is vigorous top-growth, but this is in the form of finer branching. In the same context, the repeated trimming of leaves reduces the rate of photosynthesis in the leaves, and this slows down overall growth, resulting in smaller leaves and less root growth, but better divided roots.

To develop a particular branch, you have to prune or pinch back the finer twigs to shorten their growing tips, while leaving a central leader to grow unhindered. This allows the general growth of the branch to continue in a healthy way and stimulates buds which will give side-branching. If the central leader continues to develop, the base of the branch against the trunk will also thicken and allow the branch to form a good taper towards the tip.

A note of warning is however necessary, because with repeated trimming the tree will grow very compact and dense, with the leaves covering the trunk and branches. As both trunk and leaves are of primary aesthetic importance, the leaves and branches will have to be thinned out again to show off the trunk, and to prevent the leaves from forming too big a mass, making the tree top-heavy. The problem also arises where, due to the compactness of the leaves, many leaves will be in the shadow of others and they will deteriorate through lack of sunshine. Thinning out will solve this problem. It is interesting to note that older trees will have less luxuriant foliage, while younger trees will carry more leaves.

After a few years the tree will have reached the adult shape and size at which it must be kept. This will require occasional renewal pruning especially on trees which readily form branches on old wood. Renewal pruning is more drastic than nipping out and pinching, and once applied, the tree is allowed to grow back to its old size. Sometimes a whole branch can be removed, *if* another young one is available to take its place, or a secondary branch, on a severely reduced primary branch, could be wired into position as the new leader.

Where trees do not easily form branches on old wood, the cutting back has to be done at a spot where new growth can be expected. For instance, from the axil of a leaf or from potential buds where a branch originates.

When developing the triangular shape of a bonsai, one must keep in mind the normal growth pattern of the tree of which the apical dominance, during the earlier years, is the most important factor. If the top corner of the triangle is allowed to be established too soon, the two bottom corners will be difficult to develop. In other words, you will start off with a triangle that is higher and narrower than it should be for achieving the flatter, wider shape at a later stage. In this case, the lower branches have to be lengthened to give the triangle a wider base, but because these two or three branches are so low down on the trunk, the tree will continuously try and develop at the top section. It is therefore going to take a long time to gain the growth in the lower branches. If, however, the apical growth is initially curtailed by pinching back the new growth at the top of the tree, whilst the lower branches are not held back, you will allow the base of the triangle to develop quickly. Once the approximate width has been achieved, growth at the top of the tree is once again allowed, and will be rapid, being the tree's natural tendency. The same procedure needs to be followed with the triangular shape of the branches themselves, where the base closer to the trunk should be developed first and then the length increased. In both instances a flatter triangle is first developed and allowed to become 'taller' at a later stage. *Do not grow the tree to its envisaged height in the early stages of its training.*

In the case of older trees, the apex of the tree should be more rounded than sharply triangular.

One has to consider whether it is possible to prune *any* tree to *any* style (shape). What the bonsai grower is doing to a tree is not exactly the same as what is happening in nature, and one cannot expect a tree to grow in a direction contrary to its nature. The direction in which tree trunks, or roots, grow is affected by sunlight, water, gravity and the tree's genetic structure. The roots tend to grow towards water, into the dark and towards the earth's centre of gravity. The branches and trunk have the opposite tendency, with the exception of some shrubs, which grow mainly horizontally although their smaller branches and their leaves are slightly upwards growing. It is thus possible to get a horizontally growing shrub to grow downwards with relative ease. It is not so easy to achieve the opposite, that is, to get an upright tree to grow as a cascade or even a semi-cascade, as this is absolutely against the tree's natural tendencies. It will always try to revert to its natural form, or if there is a head and a tail the head will tend to be dominant, with the tail gradually losing vigour.

> *Nature never did betray the heart that loved her.*
>
> WILLIAM WORDSWORTH

This problem can be overcome by selective pruning. During the early spring, the lowest portion of the cascade is trimmed, and as this occurs during the time of high sap-flow, it prompts the tree to form new buds (leaves). After about three weeks, the middle third of the tree is trimmed back and three weeks later the top third is pruned. Because the sap-flow has started decreasing, repair does not take place as readily. The process results in an even growth over the whole length of the cascade and its 'head'. Once this growth has finished 'repairing' the tree, the top may be lightly trimmed again to thin out the leaves and reduce the energy production in that portion. The untrimmed 'tail' will have more vigour to enable it to compete with the naturally more vigorous 'head', as it will have more energy factories in its more abundant leaves. It will help to place an open container with water underneath the end of the tail. The moisture attracts and invigorates the tail tip.

Exactly the same procedure of selective pruning can be applied to an upright tree if you need an overall even growth, or if you want to hold back the apical growth. When a lower branch is weak, do not prune it, but wire it upwards until it regains its strength.

Some growers even advocate applying selective foliage fertilising, for what it is worth. It means spraying only the portion of the tree which needs to have its growth speeded up.

The Effects of Pruning at Different Times of the Year

PINCHING IN THE GROWING SEASON If the new shoots are left untouched while young and soft, the ones higher up on the tree will become stronger than the lower ones, which will become weaker and produce even weaker growth the following year. The tree then becomes 'heavy-headed' and leggy as its lower branches die out.

LEFT
Pinus thunbergii
Black pine
Height: 16 cm
Owner: Derry Ralph

Pinus densiflora
Red pine
Height: 12 cm
Owner: Derry Ralph

BELOW LEFT
Acacia galpinii
Monkey thorn
Height: 57 cm
Owner: Pieter Loubser

ABOVE
Juniperus horizontalis
Creeping juniper
Height: 29 cm (above rim)
Width: 48 cm
Owner: Eddie van der Westhuizen

RIGHT
Ulmus nire
Japanese elm
Height: 35 cm
Width: 53 cm
Owner: Alf Jones

BELOW RIGHT
Ulmus parvifolia
Chinese elm
Height: 55 cm
Owner: Derry Ralph

Therefore the young shoots must be pinched out on the branches where growth must be held back. The earlier and harder the pinching back is done, the slower and smaller the new growth tends to be. If a tree produces new growth throughout the year or growing season, it should be pinched back all the time. Weak and old trees should not be pinched back too severely.

PRUNING IN THE RESTING PERIOD If you have done your pinching back well, there should be little or no need for pruning during winter.

Woody plants which produce flowers in the current season's wood, such as pomegranates, pyracanthas and tamarix, have the previous year's growth shortened in early spring. This will cause the new growth to be near the trunk, thus keeping the tree compact. Trees which flower on the new shoots on the tips of the previous year's growth, like persimmons, cannot flower after severe pruning. Here you should prune some shoots one year and the rest the following year, or prune after flowering.

WINTER Do not prune in early winter. The ability of a tree to heal its wounds during this time of the year is greatly reduced, and the danger of having further winter die-back still exists. Pruning could, therefore, have disastrous results.

In late winter the tree is getting ready to start sending its remaining stored nutrients into the new buds in preparation for the spring. Pruning during this period will not remove these nutrients and it will result in vigorous growth in the new growing season, as the same amount of nutrients will now feed fewer growth points. At the sme time, auxin is also removed, to be re-established only after spring so that the tree gives off better branching.

SPRING Now there is a vast flow of sap in the branches to get the nutrients into the growing leaves and new branches. The buds have swollen and start breaking out into leaves. All winter die-back can now be removed safely, but refrain from heavy pruning due to the active sap-flow. Where bigger cuts are necessary they should be sealed off. If pruning is undertaken during the season when trees are actively growing, and there is a high flow of sap, this moisture (sap) will leak out through the pruning wounds, not only causing a loss of moisture content, but also spoiling the appearance by dripping onto the leaves and branches. This is one of the reasons for sealing off the wounds immediately.

Judicious pruning after the first leaves have formed will have a very good branching result.

SUMMER Early summer pruning has one big advantage and that is the ability of the tree, because of the high sap-flow, to heal its wounds. Pruning in the second half of summer has the disadvantage of winter being close, and the young growth that follows will be subjected to adverse weather conditions with the possibility of damage. It does make for smaller growth, however, because the sap-flow is diminishing towards the end of summer and the tree has to use stored nutrients which are left over — autumn storage has not yet taken place. Defoliation is also done at this time for exactly the same reason.

AUTUMN Because this is the time when nutrients are being stored before the onset of winter, especially in deciduous trees, care must be taken to maintain the leaves on the trees. The storage of food causes a thickening of the trunk and branches, which contributes to the aged look of the tree. The effects of the coming winter are unknown and it is therefore wise to be conservative and only trim away absolutely unnecessary growth.

Defoliation

Defoliation entails the removal of the tree's leaves with the purpose of accelerating growth and reducing leaf size, by creating a 'second spring' in the second half of summer. It is like squeezing two seasons into one — a false autumn and an enforced

The terrible burden of having nothing to do.

NICOLAS BOILEAU DESPREAUX

The tints of autumn – a mighty flower garden blossoming under the spell of the enchanter, Frost.

From: Patucket Falls
WHITTIER

second spring.

The process is applied to deciduous and large-leaved evergreen trees. The best results are achieved on healthy, younger trees. As with pruning the former condition is most important. Defoliation should, moreover, not be carried out on flowering, fruiting or conifer trees.

Defoliation is done for the following reasons:
- It accelerates growth.
- It results in smaller leaves, because it occurs late in the growing season.
- It gets rid of damaged leaves and produces a healthy clear-coloured foliage crop.
- The autumn colours are better.
- If defoliation is done as soon as the first leaves have matured, the second growth may include finer branching as a bonus.
- If defoliation is combined with a root pruning it reduces the shock of the root pruning.
- Defoliation may be applied over only a section of the tree and this regulates growth distribution. The tree has to attend to the new leaf-formation, with the result that development in other areas is held back.

The best time for defoliation is between December and February (in the southern hemisphere) but also depends on the area you live in, and your own preferences (that is, whether you want to do it a little earlier or somewhat later). If it is done in early spring (October to November) the second growth of leaves will be larger than the first; if done too later in summer, the leaves may fail to sprout again. If the trees are old, they may also fail to form new leaves and may die. Do not fertilise a tree shortly before defoliation, as this causes the next set of leaves to be very large.

The leaves must be completely removed, down to the stub of the stem, as any remaining leaves will aid the growth of the branch, instead of allowing the tree to form new leaves. When the stems of the leaves are thick, as with figs, they must be almost completely removed, because enough photosynthesis may still occur in the stems to prevent new leaves forming. If leaves are removed early in the season, when the sap flow is high, it is best done in two sessions, about two weeks apart. In the first session, half the leaves can be removed at random over the tree and the rest two weeks later. This prevents sap building up in the top of the tree and bursting cells (comparable to high blood pressure). When the process has been completed, the tree should be kept in a shady place until sprouting starts (after about a month). Because of diminished water loss, through absence of leaves, the tree needs less water!

A similar method is leaf cutting. Here the leaves are not completely removed, but cut in half. It is effective on maples, zelkovas and elms. If a branch is in a weakened condition, either fewer leaves are cut, or the branch is left untouched. This is similar to needle trimming on pines. The cut leaves could be left on the tree to drop during winter or they may be removed a few weeks later, when the new leaves have started developing.

When pruning and removing leaves, keep in mind what the natural ability of the tree is. Remember that some trees lack adventitious buds and they may not send out new growth at all or do so unreliably from older branches and the trunk. Pines are renowned in this respect, and other conifers are also doubtful, especially when they are old. Deciduous trees are generally more easily cultivated and can be pruned drastically, because they will willingly send out vigorous new growth in spring, particularly when young.

The evergreen tree has a more placid existence as it does not undergo the drastic process of leaf-loss and the later formation of a new cloak of foliage. The evergreen tree does not have the need to store a mass of food to survive the leafless winter. If it is pruned just before the growth in spring, it does not respond with the same vigour as the deciduous tree. By the same token, the evergreen tree will respond quickly to the loss of leaves and resultant diminished photosynthesis later in the year, as it does not have many reserves to rely on. It cannot survive without its leaves for long. Some trees send out only one growth every year (e.g. pines, beeches) and require less attention to keep in shape. Most others, however, grow throughout the summer (e.g. elms, *Celtis*, maples) and they require regular trimming to keep them compact.

Growth-regulating Substances

There are many chemical substances that are known, through years of research, to influence the way in which plants grow, either stimulating or inhibiting their growth. Some of these substances are hormones (in fact phyto-hormones), for instance the naturally occurring plant growth chemicals. The naturally occurring plant growth chemical, IAA, is a natural auxin and is thus a plant hormone, but 2,4-D, which is synthetically prepared, is not a plant hormone, although it is a plant growth chemical as well as an auxin. It is interesting that, even though a particular plant growth chemical would normally be considered an auxin, it may also have cytokinin properties. Chemical substances which influence the growth of plants are subdivided as follows:

AUXINS These cause growth in the length of stems, especially by lengthening individual cells. Chemically they are related to indole-acetic acid (IAA). IAA is called heteroauxin.

Charles Darwin was probably the first person to have done experiments which show the existence of auxins. His work was followed up by Paal in 1919 and later by Went. They noticed that light caused a lengthening in cells and the agent carrying this information was IAA, the naturally occuring form of auxin. They also found that this auxin was present in most plants. There are other chemicals, like nitril of IAA, which cause similar reactions, but research has shown that these are turned into the naturally occurring IAA by the plants.

In 1935 Went and Thimann discovered that if they treated cuttings of stems with IAA, these cuttings produced roots sooner than the untreated control group. They also noticed that synthetic auxins like indolebutyric acid (IBA) and napthalene acetic acid (NAA) produced even better results at times. Most plants have either a well-developed or a rudimentary axillary bud in the axil of every leaf. These buds do not normally grow into secondary branches. However, when the stem's main bud is removed, one or more of these secondary buds will develop into branches. This means that the main bud dominates the secondary buds in the sense that it prevents them from developing. This effect is mainly due to the presence of auxins.

CYTOKININS These chemicals stimulate cell division. Normally auxins dominate over the effects of cytokinins. One kinin, called kinetine, is derived from DNA (deoxyribonucleic acid).

Steward and Skoog of the USA did some important research on cytokinins. Initially a synthetic cytokin, kinetine, was used. Thereafter more than eight natural cytokinins were discovered. One of these is zeatine.

DORMINS These chemicals cause plants to go from an actively growing condition to a dormant condition.

Warein and co-workers discovered that during autumn, when deciduous trees are becoming dormant, the trees' leaves become increasingly richer in a chemical known as abscisic acid (ABA), which opposes the effect of auxins. This same chemical inhibits the germination of seeds. It also promotes leaf abscission and fruit abscission.

GROWTH INHIBITING CHEMICALS They are responsible for dwarf varieties of plants. These chemicals do not cause plants to stop growing, in other words go into dormancy. They only slow down and restrict growth, making the plants appear dwarfed. Examples are AMO-1618 and CCC. They appear to influence growth by either preventing it or impeding it, mainly through opposition to the formation of gibberillins. A well-known growth inhibitor is maleic hydrazide. It checks growth without injury to the plant. It also prolongs the dormancy of perennial plants. An example, which kills weeds in lawns, without killing the grass, is 2.4-D (2,4-dichlorophenoxyacetic acid).

GIBBERILLINS Kurosawa and co-workers in Japan isolated gibberillin in crystalline form, from a fungus, *Gibberella fujikuroi*, which is a parasite on rice, and causes the rice stems to grow abnormally quickly and too long. Later gibberellic acid was isolated, and presently over 40 gibberillins are known, for instance GA and GA20. When a gibberillin stimulates the lengthening of a plant stem, it usually only causes the stem's internodal distance to increase. Giberillins usually have little influence on growth of roots and very little or no influence on leaf growth.

ETHILENE This affects plants in a variety of ways. Ethilene is a gas: $CH_2=CH_2$. It can advance the colouring of ripening fruits, as well as the ripening itself. Ethilene promotes the formation of root-hairs.

Some of the growth-stimulating substances, depending partly on their concentration, may actually inhibit growth. Thus auxin produced in the terminal buds is thought to move down the stem, through the phloem and parenchymatous tissues, to the lateral buds, inhibiting their development. Auxin is also reported to inhibit root growth in concentrations that stimulate stem growth.

HAIKU
Clear Cascades
Into the waves scatter
Blue pine needles

MATSUO BASHO

Methods of Trimming

Trees can be divided into two basic groups, depending on their leaf shapes, namely needle-like and broad-leaved trees, with some other varieties like tufted, cored and scale-like growth, which all need to be treated differently when pruning.

PINES Pine trees will be discussed here as an example of needle-carrying trees, but they are really an entity on their own and not even all pines are treated exactly the same. Pines are not indigenous in all countries and one may find that only a few varieties of pine may be available in your country. Also, they will probably not be the ones described in bonsai books. However, because I think that pines are the classic trees for bonsai, they will be considered in some detail here. It is possible however, to write a complete book on the subject of pines as bonsai alone.

Although a pine is considered an evergreen it still loses some of its needles throughout the year and especially in autumn, but it is never without needles to a remarkable degree. Most of the needles last for one to two years. Old needles become ugly and must be pulled out when they reach that stage. A complete defoliation must never be done on a pine, as it may never form needles again and will die. The older needles must not be cut, because their tips will become brown and they will die slowly. Needle trimming (shortening) must be done on young pines and definitely not on old established trees. Needle shortening is necessary when needles have grown too long and bushy, or when needles are so long that they curl up at the ends. It may be done at any time of the year. The needles can also be pulled out, but it is preferable to cut them off as the process of pulling out the needle may injure the bark and possibly needles nearby. If you do decide to pull out some needles they should be pulled out individually and not as pairs (or groups), because the sheath that contains them, along with the latent bud, will be damaged. After the needles have been pulled out, a small percentage of the remaining latent buds will develop, even exceptionally on some older wood, and this will give more compact growth. The needle pulling should be spread out over a period of about three weeks, directly after the new needles have hardened. Young needles must not be pulled out.

During needle shortening, the needles must be cut off at a length of 2,5 cm, unless they are very young, in which case they must be cut off completely. After the needles have been cut, the tree must receive overhead spraying for about a month to prevent them from turning brown. If brown tips do develop it isn't too serious, as they will only remain on the tree for two years at the most. It should only be a problem when the tree is prepared for an exhibition, in which case needle cutting should not be done for some two years preceding the exhibition. Actually needle pulling and cutting has as purpose the compacting and shortening of the needles, which is thus preparation of the tree for eventual better proportions and harmony between parts.

Needle cutting and pulling results in the formation of smaller needles. An immediate bonus is, however, that air circulation around the remaining needles is improved, as well as the fact that sunlight can now reach all of them. Do not cut needles back into the previous season's growth, and always leave a few of the present season's growing needles behind when the needles are cut in autumn, in case the old wood does not produce new growth. With the coming of spring, new candles may form from the previous year's needles. This process is repeated annually.

During autumn all yellow or brown needles must be removed, as well as those which spoil the tree's shape.

Needles will turn brown or yellow for any of the following reasons:
- Poor drainage: when this occurs the tree must be transplanted to a better draining soil mixture or into the garden, during autumn or spring, whichever

comes first.
- Too much heat: the heat which is causing the damage could be reflected heat from walls and windows during summer.
- Malnutrition: this is prevented by fertilising regularly, although in reduced concentrations, from October to April (in the southern hemisphere). If this does not work, ammonium sulphate (5 ml to 1,5 litres water) can be applied once every week till the needles have regained their normal colour. Do not continue applications after the leaves have recovered, because an excess will kill the tree.
- Poor quality soil: for instance too much clay or poor soil retained in the ball of growing medium when transplanting.

When needles are removed, be sure not to damage the growing tips of the branches, because of the pine's reluctance to form needles or branchlets closer to the trunk. An important tip is not to prune too drastically in one season to improve the shape. Rather do this over a few growth seasons. Another method is to cut a branch halfway through in the first season, whereupon the cut is kept open, by placing a flat plastic disc or pebble into the cut to prevent it from closing again. During the following season, the branch is cut completely. This causes the branch to die in the affected area first, and it does not put too much strain on the tree. This procedure must be accompanied by root pruning to keep the foliage alive.

The needles of a pine grow in a whorled fashion and the new buds as 'candles'. The whorled fashion of candle-forming is more common in young pines. Not all the candles must be nipped out every year as it weakens the tree considerably, but through judicious removal of the candles at different times in the year, different growth patterns can be obtained.

On older pines, candles tend to form singly, in pairs, threes, or groups of five, depending on the species. Always tend to the position of the candle which is retained, to assure the development of alternating branchlets.

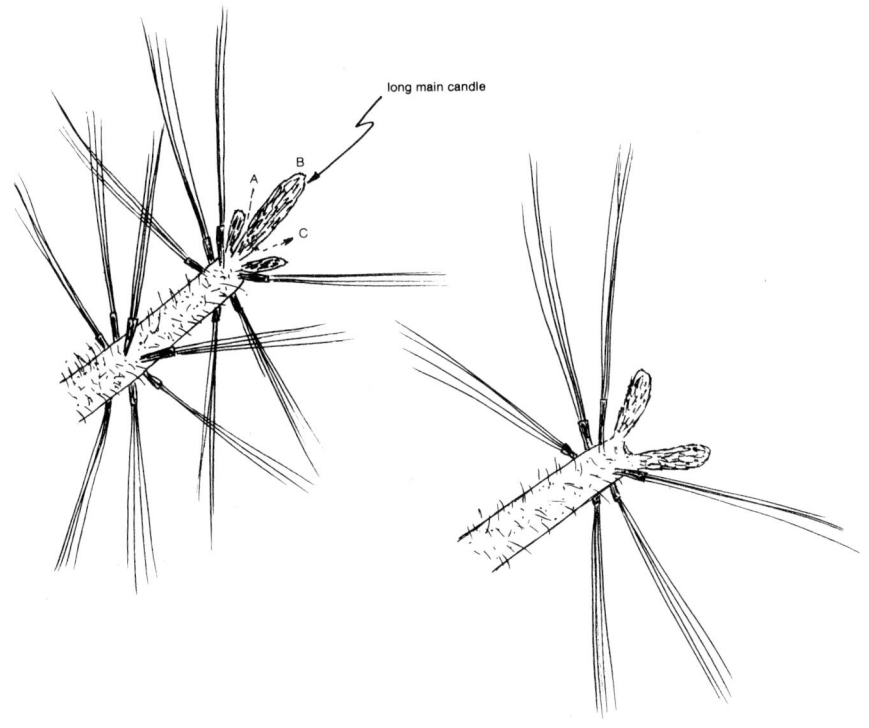

FIGURE 69

FIGURE 69 During autumn the remaining candles, A and C, may have developed sufficiently (longer than 2,5 cm). These candles can now be reduced.

There are three basic motivations for pruning pines (in fact it also applies to other trees), and these are:
- structural pruning
- refining
- regeneration pruning.

The normal growth pattern or tendency of pines is to produce an apical bud at the end of each branch, and at the tip of the leader trunk, plus two or three secondary buds nearby. This is the normal way pines grow in nature, but is not acceptable for bonsai purposes, because the internodal distances would be too large, giving so-called 'lollipops' at the end of branches. This refers to the branches being virtually bare of needles with the exception of their tips, where the needles are concentrated. Most pines have a rudimentary (potential) bud at the base of every pair of needles (note that not all pines have their needles in pairs). These rudimentary buds need to be stimulated to develop, or else they could be lost during the seasonal loss of needles, along with the dropping needles. This will happen naturally unless the tree (as a whole, or sections thereof — like a branch) experiences distress of some kind, like injury through a storm or — and this is important — pruning! Pruning is but an artificially induced injury, and the pine considers this to be a threat to its existence. It reacts by releasing auxin which stimulates the latent buds to develop at the ends of the branches, as well as in the length of branches, even those older than five years.

Applying this knowledge during different times in the annual growth cycle and on different parts of the tree will have varying results, such as more or less widespread development of latent buds. There is only slight variation in the different techniques, but with markedly different results. Different techniques can be used at the same time on different parts of the same tree. Generally, if a tree needs to increase in size along with better root development, new shoots should not be trimmed and the tree should be given plenty of nutrients and exposed to enough sun. This is in contrast to the tree which has reached the required size, which needs to be restricted in growth. In this last instance, the apical buds should be completely removed (they are the prominent buds at the end of the branches) as well as all other developing buds, with the exception of two side buds (lateral buds) at the end of the branch. This should be done before active growth has started. As soon as the two lateral buds have developed into 25 mm candles, they should be pinched back halfway. This method is best applied to older trees. These trees should not be fed extensively during the growing period in order to restrict the growth of the candles.

Leggy trees need compacting, and will also benefit by appearing neater and having better shaped 'clouds' of needles. To achieve this the candles should be shortened by about 2/3 during late spring, before the needles in the candles start lengthening. The trees should receive normal feeding and sunshine. The following year will show the development of average-sized candles. This should be practised on trees which have the correct basic structure and many secondary branches.

Pines may grow too strongly if feeding during the previous year was excessive. These trees respond to the feeding by growing long needles and lengthening their branches. To correct this, the apical and lateral candles should be pinched out entirely at their base when they have reached a length of about 25 mm — and this should be done early in the growth cycle. New adventitious buds will quickly form at the end of the branch, and even at the base of some needles. Some of these new buds will develop so quickly that they may even give you compact growth with short needles in the same growing season. Do not apply this technique for more than two consecutive seasons because it causes stress and will weaken the tree too much.

You may have a tree which is growing at a normal pace but it may not have enough finer branches and may thus not be compact. In this case, the new candles must be pinched out when their needles are about 10–12 mm in length and they have not hardened. This should take place in late spring or early summer. The multiple new buds that develop are usually small to average in size. Adventitious buds often develop on older wood. The next year's growth will be more compact with finer branches. Feeding should be normal.

If a tree needs to be compacted and have its trunk and branches thickened so as to appear aged, it should be allowed to grow normally for a full growing season. In early autumn the new shoots should be cut back up to their point of origin. In the next spring small buds will appear which should be allowed to develop. In this way, the long branches and their long needles have been removed, thus compacting the tree and in fact making it smaller, for a while at least.

As with other trees, the annual new growth on pines, in the shape of candles, forms during spring. Then is the time for the first pruning, always taking into account the direction in which growth must be guided. If the candles are left to grow freely, long spindly branches will form.

If the candle reaches a length of 2,5 cm during early summer, it must be cut off at its base, irrespective of there being more than one. If originally only one candle has grown to longer than 2,5 cm at a growing tip, it must be cut off. The chances are that more candles will develop before autumn.

When, somewhat later, new candles form, these will be ready for a second pruning during autumn. Should you notice more than two candles forming early on, cut out all but the two facing to the sides, and let them develop until autumn. If they grow to longer than 2,5 cm, they should be cut back by 1/3 to 1/2. If they don't grow to 2,5 cm in length, they must not be cut back.

A warning: do not remove or cut off the needles surrounding the cutback candles. Also, if there are no needles on a particular branch, the candle(s) should not be cut off, because the chances are remote that new candles will form on that branch.

Where the candles are shorter than 2,5 cm during spring, they are left until autumn, when they can be shortened. From this autumn pruning, new candles will develop in the following spring.

This procedure, as described, must be repeated annually until the required shape has been attained. To get a branch to grow longer, the candle or candles are not cut back in spring, but left to grow until autumn, when they are removed. During the next period of growth, new candles will develop closer to the trunk and they will be smaller in size.

Older pines do not readily form new candles, rather, they tend to lengthen the older cancles. The way to prune older pines is to cut them back to a secondary branch from where they will sprout again. Carefully choose the spot where the branch is to be severed to prevent the wrong shape developing. Prune during the period of active growth to enable the tree to seal off the wound. Always cut so that the wound is oval-shaped or the reverse teardrop shape. On the ends of branches, the cut must face upwards or sideways.

The theory behind this complicated pruning schedule is that when a pine has acquired the right size and shape, the middle, strong-growing candle is removed, whilst one or both sideways growing candles remain and are shortened by 1/3 to 1/2. If the middle candle is left to grow until late in the season, when the needles start opening, the side-candles develop with shorter needles. The explanation for this is that when the middle candle is removed early in the season, when the tree is still at its most vigorous, the growth will be concentrated in the side-candles, as they struggle for domination, resulting in healthier and larger needles. If the central candle is left to develop, it will concentrate much of the strength on itself and when it is removed later in the season, the overall vitality will be diminished and the side-candles deprived. If this technique is applied to older pines during late spring and early summer, growth will be minimal.

If the central candle is cut out in late summer, to leave only a few needles at the base, growth of a compact clump of needles follows, and they are generally smaller. When such pruning is deferred till growth has stopped, this form of compact growth is carried over to the next season.

In the case of a healthy pine, all the new buds can be removed in early spring, before they develop into candles, making it possible for buds to develop closer to the trunk. At the same time, buds can develop at the ends of branches and even at the base of needles or on older wood.

If a branch is required at a particular point, all the buds on the 'mother branch' can be nipped out, as well as all the needles, excepting a few in the vicinity of where the branch is needed.

At the end of November (May in the northern hemisphere) all the candles can be removed, in the case of a young quick-growing tree. Start with the lower portion of the tree, because it tends to weaken sooner and grows at a slower rate. Cut off the candles of the higher parts later so that they do not recover as quickly and grow at the expense of the lower portion.

BROAD-LEAFED VARIETIES It does not matter whether the broad-leafed tree is evergreen or deciduous, the technique stays the same. Pruning commences as soon as the new soft growth has matured sufficiently. This maturation means one of two things, namely:

- if you need to allow the tree to grow in size, the cut is made after two or three nodes have developed
- if the growth has to be restricted, the cut can be made as soon as the leaves have grown enough for you to discern the individual leaf on its stem. This is absolutely vital for trees which have paired leaves. Usually this underdeveloped leaf is pinched out instead of being cut off.

The pruning mentioned in the above two cases is not the same as the pruning done to correct shape or to renew growth; in these last-mentioned cases the pruning is far more drastic.

There are two groups of broad-leafed trees, according to the position in which the leaves develop. The first group has alternating leaves and the second group has paired leaves or buds. It must be stressed that to do this kind of fine pruning, very sharp pruning shears or scissors are needed. If the tree has alternating leaves, the branch is cut off above, or just after the leaf which faces the direction into which future growth must be guided. (See Figure 62)

If the tree has opposing (that is, paired) leaves, a cut can be made between the two leaves leaving the leaf facing the direction in which you want the branch to grow. If you don't have the courage to cut between the leaves, simply cut in front of the leaves, and then pinch off or rub off the unwanted leaf or bud. The second method is required if the tree has the tendency to die back to the closest node, even with alternating leaves, as in the case of *Celtis* and *Acer* species.

Try to have the cut facing upwards at a slant, as this heals quicker. The second best way is to cut the branch at a right angle, and the worst method is to have a slanting cut facing downwards.

Do not cut in front of a bud facing upwards, as it will be impossible to keep the future growth horizontal; the bud will grow upwards.

Always cut slightly away from the nearby bud or leaf for fear of possible damage

FIGURE 70

FIGURE 70 Positions and directions of cut wounds.

or die-back of the bud itself. Die-back of the tiny stump you have created will take place naturally, and can be removed with ease later, after the bud has developed into a branch.

When debudding paired buds do not remove lower buds. If only the upper buds remain, they grow vertically upwards, thus they are the ones that must be removed. Also remove buds that will grow into, or across other branches. Try to plan the debudding so as to have evenly spaced branches all over, but never allow the tree to have an unnatural 'made up' appearance.

A broad-leafed tree which needs special attention is the very vigorously growing fig. It forms alternating leaves for which the normal pruning procedure for broad-leafed trees is followed. The fig sends out its leaves in a different manner, however. It forms a rolled-up sheath at the end of the branch. This sheath is made up of a few leaves, with the proximal leaves (the ones closer to the trunk) which develop first, on the outside of the sheath. If these outer leaves are removed by gently twisting the sheath between the fingers, the inner (immature) leaves are exposed. This forces them to grow more quickly, but because of their immaturity, they remain smaller, with shorter internodal distances. In doing this, you allow the tree to grow, but end up with nice compact foliage. If you do not want the tree to grow in size, simply nip off the whole sheath. This method is not always possible, especially if the leaves have become smaller, and then the fig is handled like any other broad-leaf tree.

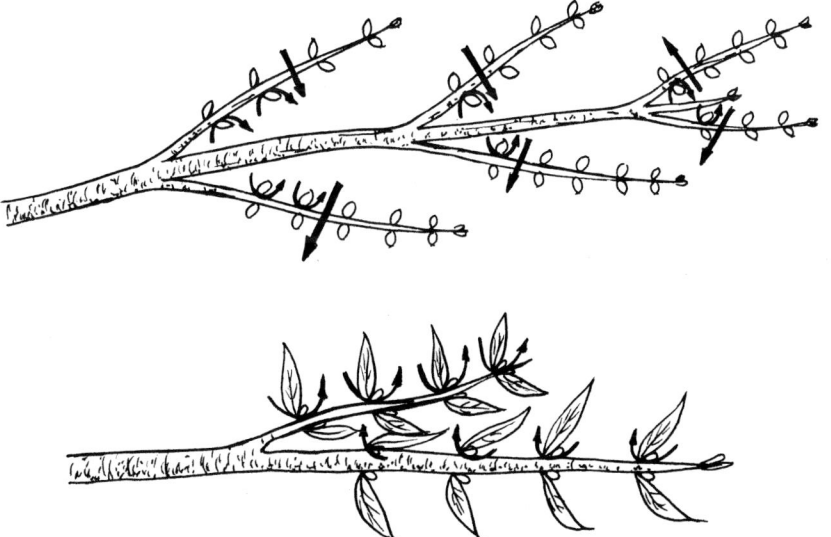

FIGURE 71

FIGURE 71 Debudding of inward and upward-growing buds.

FIGURE 72 Nipping off growing tips.

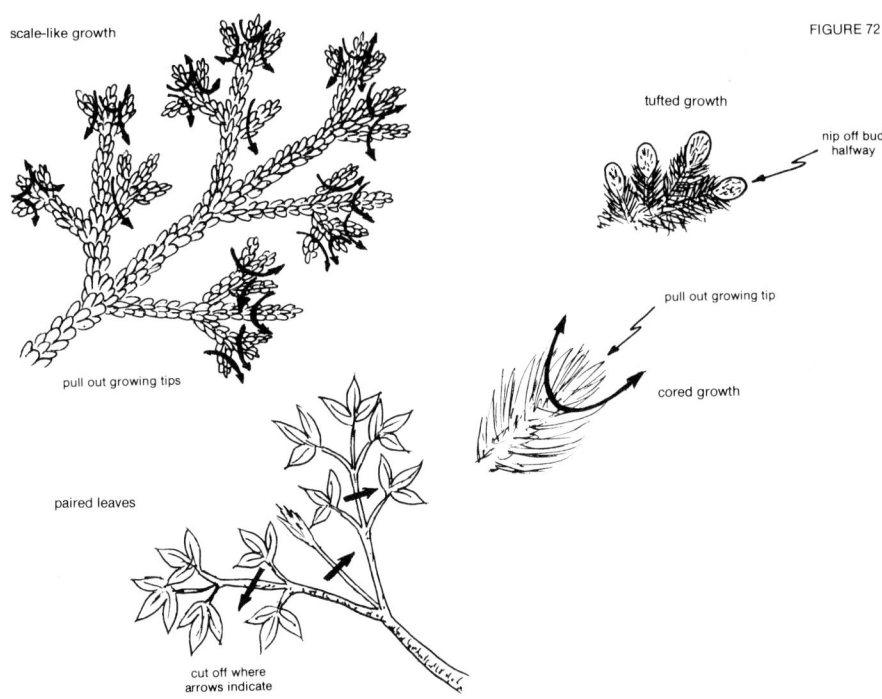

TUFTED GROWTH Some trees, like cypress, firs, spruces and junipers, send out their new growth in a tufted manner. The middle section of the tuft is gripped between the fingers and pulled out. Do not wait till the tuft has grown too long, as the new growth will then be spindly. Pulling out a portion of the tuft prevents the tips from turning brown, as with needle cutting.

CORED GROWTH This is seen in junipers with older foliage, or rather foliage which was formed while the tree was growing at a slower rate (for an unknown reason the tufted growth on junipers is called juvenile, and the cored growth adult foliage). Growing tips are pinched out, and individual branches are cut off with scissors. Don't cut off the foliage at random like a barber cutting hair; rather cut each branch at its base individually. The pinching should take place when the growing tips are still soft. Be sure to use a pulling action otherwise your fingernail will cut the 'leaves' and the ends of the tiny leaves will turn brown and die. This pulling out is accomplished by actually holding the leaves between the fingers of one hand and pulling with the other, because if you do not support the leaves you have no control over where they are going to pull out.

SCALE-LIKE GROWTH This appears in mature foliage of false cypress varieties. It is treated in the same way as corded growth.

FLOWERING AND FRUITING VARIETIES In general it should be known when the particular tree flowers, and whether the flowers (and fruit or berries) are formed on old or new branches.

Cotoneaster, privet, pyracantha, serissa and pomegranate are some examples of trees where, after a fairly drastic trimming in late winter or early spring, flowers will appear on the new growth. The pruning can also be deferred till flowering has taken place. Where flowers develop in the axil of the leaves or branches, they do not affect the shape as seriously as when they are carried on the ends of branches, and therefore they need not be interfered with. All dead flowers must be removed.

Wisteria, camellias and azaleas produce their flowers on the older branches. You must know where on the branch the flowers are carried. If the flowers are carried on the nodes further back on the branch (closer to the trunk), you only need

HAIKU
The white chrysanthemum
Even when lifted to the eye
Remains immaculate
MATSUO BASHO

to leave a few of these nodes, and the rest of the tree can be trimmed back at any time. If the flowers are carried on the tips of older branches, and the buds begin to form early in the previous season, you should only attempt pruning every second year, if you do not wish to sacrifice the flowers.

Remember, however, that the overall shape of the tree is of paramount importance, and must never be sacrificed for a show of flowers or fruit. When a tree is in bloom, or about to bloom, much of its energy is concentrated in the production of its flowers or fruit (particularly the latter), and if overburdened, for instance with pomegranates or Chinese quince, part of the tree could die. Try to have only a few fruits on the tree, and then only if the tree is healthy. Fertilise it well to ensure that fruit, or flowers, are also healthy.

If you have a flowering tree but no flowers, you may have used a fertiliser with a too high nitrogen content, or the tree may not have recovered from a severe pruning session. If the problem is due to the presence of too much nitrogen, it could take a few seasons before the nitrogen content in the soil has been reduced to an acceptable level to promote normal flowering. You can try to leach out the excess fertiliser, using copious amounts of running water, by placing the tree in its pot in a large container under an open tap for 24 hours. Alternatively you may replace the soil.

Azaleas need special mention. Unlike most trees they tend to grow strong branches in the lower section, while the top remains weak, and if this continues, the top may even die. Incidentally, the pomegranate, wild olive and pyracantha show the same trend. When suckers develop from the base it worsens the situation. If you let all the flowers in the lower portion of the azalea continue to bloom, while you partly debud the middle section (flowers and buds) and completely remove all buds from the top, you may find that no flowers at all will bloom in the top section. Because flowers exhaust a tree, the flowers in the lower portion will hold back the development of the lower branches. The top portion, being without flowers, will show new growth first and this will be quicker and stronger. When a stage is reached where the top portion is strong enough, you can allow the azaleas to flower all over. Azaleas produce branches easily from adventitious buds, but are low-growing and tend to be weaker at the crown than in the lower branches. The best time to prune azaleas is before new growth emerges, during spring and after the flowering period, and it is important to remove all the basal shoots, the downward pointing buds and excessive sidebuds. Azaleas have a tendency to form scars on the trunk when their thicker branches are pruned.

Kurume azaleas have smaller flowers and finer leaves than Satsuki azaleas, and are more resistant to cold weather.

SHAPING THROUGH BENDING

We have seen how trimming and pruning remove unwanted growth and influence not only the vigour, but also the direction of the new growth. However, this is by no means the alpha and omega of training — it is merely one method, albeit the principal one. The second method is to bend the branches and trunk mechanically into the desired shape and position.

One of the oldest techniques is to hang weights onto the branches. It has limited value for a variety of reasons. Although the method of tying branches to sticks anchored in the soil creates a better three-dimensionally curved tree, its difficult technique and unacceptable appearance have made it unpopular. You are compelled to use younger, more flexible trees, as older ones do not bend readily.

The more recently adopted technique of wiring the branches by means of a copper or aluminium wire, and bending them to the desired shape has made styling

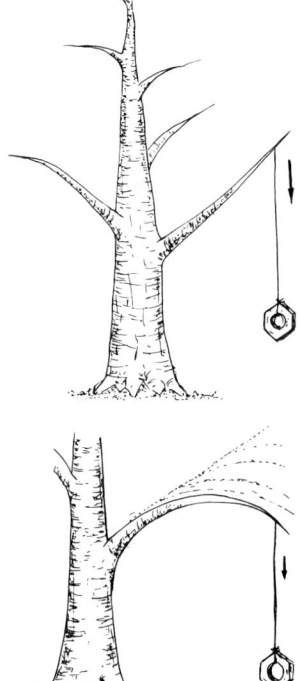

FIGURE 73 An even-shaped bow created by hanging a weight from the branch.

FIGURE 74 This is a chaotic picture while the bending is taking place, but results are quite good.

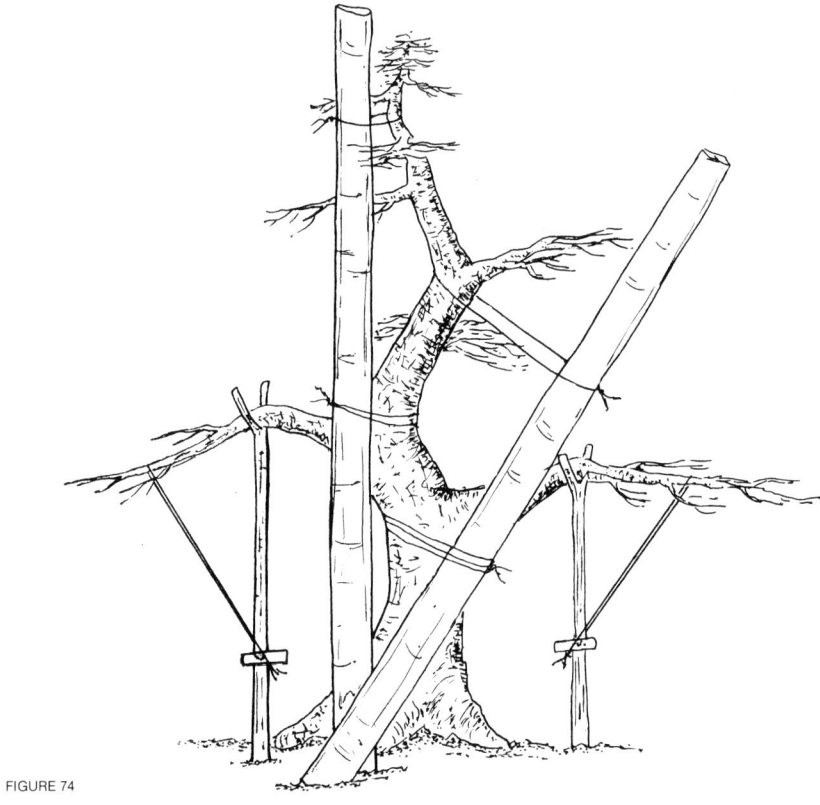

FIGURE 74

If you could learn the art of growing bonsai from looking at the masterpieces without knowing what happened to the grand old trees along the way, bonsai growing would not be an art at all. You cannot grow bonsai by observation only. You have to try your hand at it and, if you are privileged, you may be guided by an expert.

considerably easier. Probably the first book dealing with the subject of wiring dates back to 1910 and is titled *Sanyu-en bonsai-dan* meaning 'The history of bonsai in the Sanyu nursery'.

The wire used is either copper or aluminium. The aluminium wire is usually anodised. Sometimes trees are sensitive to copper or aluminium. Beware of using iron wire, as it will rust, and the rust will stain the branches. Also the oxide in the rust can damage trees. Aluminium wire is softer than copper, and while that may be of help when wiring, it needs to be a thicker gauge than copper wire to achieve the same results.

Copper wire is readily available from dealers in scrap metal, or where electrical wiring is used. That wire may be hard because it has not been annealed, but it is easy to anneal it to a more pliable condition by holding it in a gas or other flame till it becomes a dull red and then letting it cool slowly. The process entails annealing, then straightening and then annealing it again. In any case, if you are going to re-use the copper wire, it will become hard through bending and unbending, and this necessitates annealing it before using it again. On the other hand, this property of copper is an advantage, because the wire hardens when it is wound around a branch and it then holds its position better. Aluminium wire is softer, but this makes it easier to remove and it requires no annealing. Copper coloured anodised aluminium is available and is becoming very popular.

Deciding how thick the wire should be is an art learned through experience, but it is not very difficult. A too thin wire simply will not hold the branch in position and has to be wired too tightly. If a wire is too thin the problem can be solved by wrapping two wires lying next to each other (parallel) around the branch, without allowing them to cross. A wire that is too thick is not only unsightly, but one is liable to break the branch that is being bent, as you cannot 'feel' the elasticity of the branch due to the resistance of the thick wire. Never plait two or more wires together before applying them to the branch, as this will cause uneven pressure where the wires touch the bark, thereby cutting into it and leaving ugly marks. The advantage of using two parallel wires is that they spread pressure points evenly, but only as long as they are wound reasonably tightly and very close to each other.

The thickness of the wire used is not solely determined by the diameter of the branch (e.g.: wire used on a fig tree will not be successful on a wild olive with branches of the same diameter); the elasticity, or actually, the woodiness, of a tree also has to be taken into consideration.

If branches are well developed, they will not bend easily, so instead of running the risk of fracturing a branch while trying to bend it, or creating unnatural bends, it may be better to change the branch into a *jin*.

Use younger branches to develop the general shape of the tree.

The length of time it will take a branch to assume its permanent shape after wiring depends on various factors:
- The elasticity or pliability of the branches. The easier a branch bends, the longer it will take to set in position. This is seen in trees such as wild figs which have only a vague and short dormant period as compared to elms, maples or acacias which have definite and long dormant periods.
- If the tree is older, it will have lost its pliability due to the presence of more hardwood (that being the heartwood in the middle of the trunk or branch) or even dead wood, and the branch will take longer to set because of its inability to produce the necessary new cells.
- Thinner branches will set more quickly than thicker ones.

In any case, it is simple enough to remove the wire and check the tree for a week or two to see whether the new position is stable. If the branch is seen to move back, it is easily wired again and left for another few months. The tightness of the wire must always be checked, because if it starts cutting into the branch, it must be slackened or better still, unwound and rewired in a slightly different position.

If wire has cut into the tree you have a problem, because these unsightly marks are not easily removed. The first step is to be patient, and if the marks are not too deep, the thickening of the branch or trunk will slowly obliterate them. If this does not happen, the inside surfaces of the cuts can be scraped with a sharp blade to irritate the cambium and get it to grow and close the cut. This is not an easy procedure but you just might be lucky enough to end up with a trunk or branch that has a rugged appearance.

Time to Wire

Theoretically, wiring can be done at any time of the year, but it is somewhat easier when the trees are bare or just after pruning, when it is also easier to work without fear of damaging leaves.

WINTER Wiring deciduous trees in winter is a fairly simple procedure; you can see clearly what you are doing and do not risk damaging leaves. However, great care must be taken not to damage developing buds. Late winter wiring is even more advantageous, because there is no thickening of trunks or branches, and the sap-flow is at a low level. The branches may however be brittle.

SPRING Because of the accelerated growth and increased sap-flow the bark may be damaged. There is also thickening as well as lengthening of the branches, with the inherent danger of the wire cutting into the bark.

SUMMER The same cautions apply as for spring. By now some of the branches wired in winter may already have set. The main problem with applying wire in summer is the masses of foliage that complicate the technique.

AUTUMN During late summer and autumn the second session of growth is taking

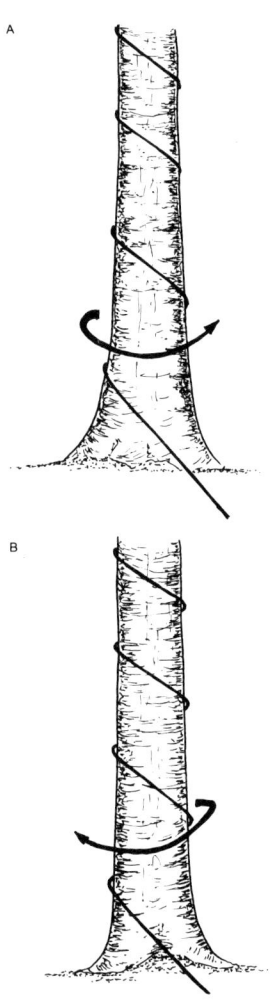

FIGURE 75
A. If the tree is twisted in the direction of the arrow it will unwind the wire.
B. If the tree is twisted in the direction of the arrow it will tighten the wire and the wire will damage the bark.

place, albeit now not in length. The trees are getting ready to survive the coming winter, and they are storing starches in the trunk and branches in tiny spaces (slits). This causes a rapid thickening of trunk and branches. Do not apply wire in autumn and be sure to prevent wire possibly cutting into branches.

Wiring is best done from early winter into spring, before the new buds have emerged. If it is done during summer while active water absorption and sap transport is taking place, the newly formed wood may be separated from the older wood, as the wire is being turned to force the branch. Be very careful when bending branches during summer.

General Pointers

Before wiring a tree, deny it water for up to three days so that it nearly wilts. If a tree is watered well before wiring, the cells are turgid (like a pumped tyre) and the branches are stiff, with the risk of them being broken.

Decide into which position a branch must be bent after wiring, and then bend it in one go. Do not bend it into different positions before finally finding the right one, as this loosens the cambium in the complete circumference of the branch or trunk and could cause it to die or form knobs.

When you have to wire a long length of branch or trunk, do not complete the wiring and then twist the branch or trunk, as you might then tighten the wire into the bark. Rather do the twisting gradually as you continue the wiring. The effect is shown in Figure 75.

Do the wiring before repotting or a few weeks after, because the wiring procedure might damage the roots that have not yet settled into the fresh soil.

The order of wiring is simply a matter of convenience. Start with the trunk first and move onto the thicker branches, doing the thin ones last. Always wire away from the trunk, which in many cases means that you have to anchor the wire onto the trunk. If this sequence of wiring is followed it means that you will use the thicker wire first, and gradually move to thinner wires.

Don't have loose ends of wire sticking out. Always tuck them in against the branch or trunk, or end them short of the branch tip.

When wiring the trunk, anchor the wire in the soil, even if it means threading the one end through a drainage hole and tying it to a thin rod underneath the pot. Anchorage of the wire is of extreme importance, for if it is not anchored it is useless. This simply has to do with the principle of leverage — if a lever is not anchored at one end, it will not have any effect. Using a too thin wire is also ineffective. The wire must be thick enough to hold the branch or trunk in position, given that it has sufficient anchorage. Only experience will teach you which thickness of wire is correct in a particular case.

If a tree has a tender bark, as is the case with *Celtis* or maples, the bark needs to be protected. This also applies to young trees. The wire could be wrapped with florist's tape. Do not use wire covered with insulation rubber, because such wire is usually too thin and lacks strength, not to mention the fact that the colour of the plastic will attract attention.

Be careful not to wind the wire too tightly, as it must allow the branch to grow while it is held in the new position. If the wire is too loose it will not be able to hold the branch in position. Wire at angles of 45° because if you wire at less than 45° the wire will not be able to hold the branch in its new position, and at more than 45° the wire acts like a spring.

When a branch is bent after the wiring has been done be sure that the wire passes over the convex (outer) part of the bend.

The windings must be evenly spaced. When more than one wire is used on one trunk, wind them in the same direction, in other words, do not cross wires. This will

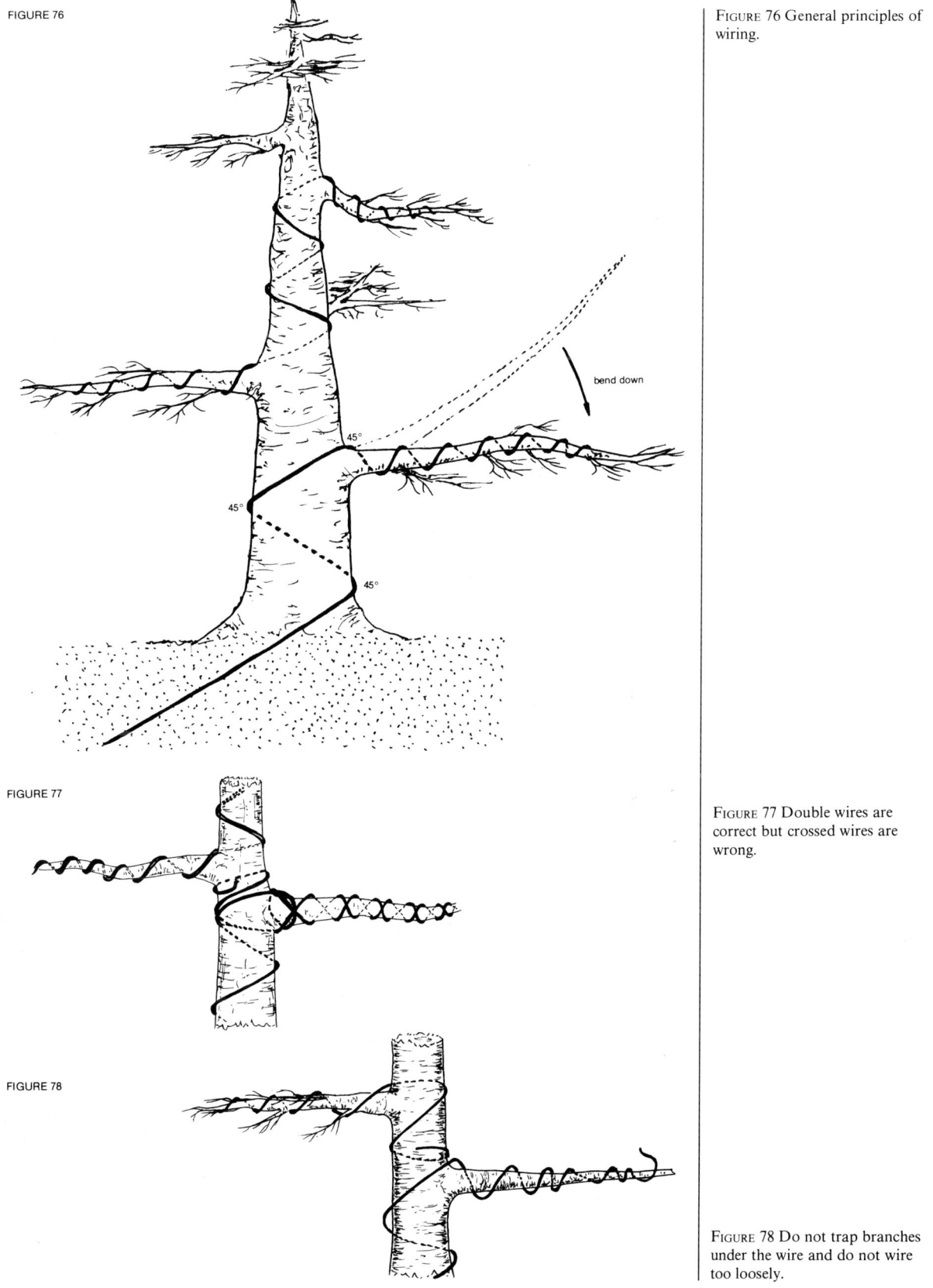

FIGURE 76 General principles of wiring.

FIGURE 77 Double wires are correct but crossed wires are wrong.

FIGURE 78 Do not trap branches under the wire and do not wire too loosely.

FIGURE 79 Wiring that is too tight leaves a permanent scar. Notice the position of the supporting wire where a branch is bent up or down.

FIGURE 80 The wire goes over the convex area where the branch must bend and the finger should support it underneath the bend.

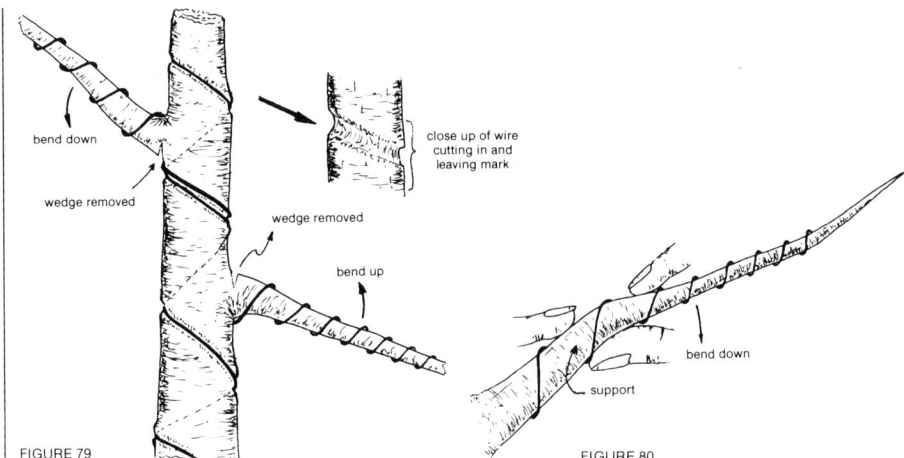

FIGURE 79

FIGURE 80

mean that any piece of wire can be unwound on its own, without disturbing any other piece.

When wiring a branch, be very careful not to trap leaves or needles under the wire, or to pass a wire over a bud which may still develop. Leaves or needles trapped under the wire may die. Do not bind a smaller branch up against the bigger one, i.e. do not trap a branch under the wire.

If a branch needs to be bent downwards from the trunk, the first winding of the wire must pass over the branch and not underneath it, to prevent it breaking when pressure is applied to bend it. The actual bending is done by supporting the branch between the fingers of both hands while applying pressure. If only one hand can be used, be sure to have the thumb on one side and the index finger on the other side of the bend.

Techniques to Bend Thicker Branches or Branches that will not Bend Easily

- Cut out a little wedge from the planned concave area of the curve, wire the branch and bend till the cut sides of the wedge approximate tightly. Seal the area of the wedge, but be sure that no sealant is pushed in between the opposing cut ends.

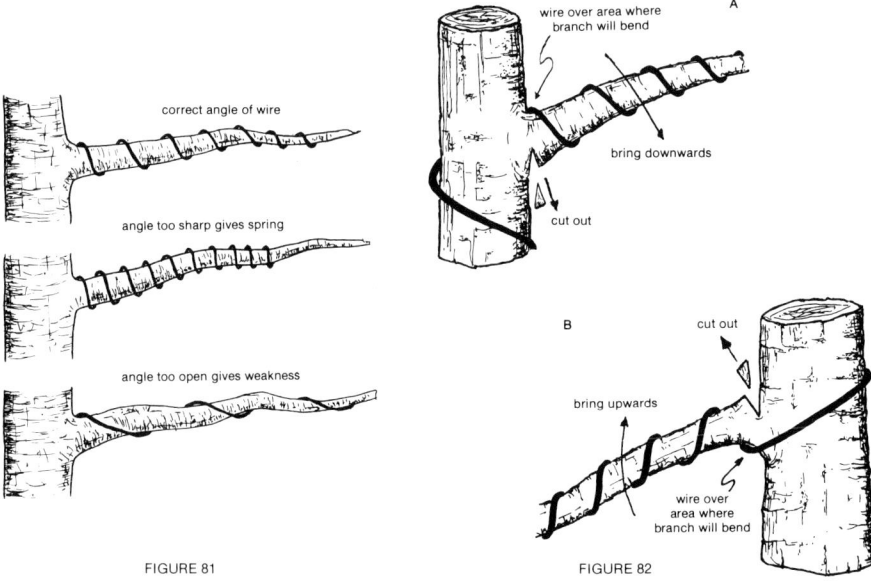

FIGURE 81 Correct and uncorrect angles of wiring.

FIGURE 82 The 'wedge technique' to bend a thicker branch.

FIGURE 81

FIGURE 82

- A little wedge can be cut out from the branch right up against the trunk and the branch is then bent upwards or downwards after wiring. It can even be bent forwards or backwards in the same way. If the branch must be bent downwards, the wedge is made on the under surface and the first winding of the wire must be over the branch, otherwise it will snap off when it is bent. The reverse is true when the branch needs to be bent upwards. If this method is not used, you will not be able to get a sharp, angular bend at the base of the trunk, but will end up with a branch that is bow-shaped (at least close to the trunk). A more advanced variation of this method is to drill a small hole through the branch or trunk, and then cut the wedge out towards the hole, so that the hole forms the tip of the wedge. The drilling must be done at a slow speed so as not to burn the wood.
- Slight cuts can be made into the bark, in the area of the bend, or in the length of the branch. Be very careful when you bend a branch, less it splits open lengthwise. The slight cuts could prevent this. If a branch should loosen its cambium when being bent, bandage it with florist's tape.
- You can try bending the branch in stages.
- In the case of pines and junipers the outside of the curve can be shaved off. This reduces the rigidity of the branch.
- A thick wire can be shaped into the exact curve that is required for the branch. Raffia is tied to the branch lengthwise, whereafter it is wrapped around the branch. This works like an ankle-guard and the tight wrapping prevents the branch from splitting. The thick wire (or wires) are then wired to the branch, and the whole construction is bent into the required shape, according to the shape of the thick guiding wire. A variation of this method is to position raffia lengthwise with, also lengthwise, a few lengths of thick copper wire, and this is held in place by raffia which is wrapped around the trunk (branch). The trunk or branch is then bent into position.
- The following is a safety method to be used with thicker branches if it is feared that they may break or split while being bent: the trunk or branch must be wrapped in string made from natural fibre before the wire is applied. You start at the base of the trunk or branch and wind the string around it with the string sides touching each other (thus no gaps, barring where a branch is given off). The wire is then applied as usual. The string will eventually disintegrate.

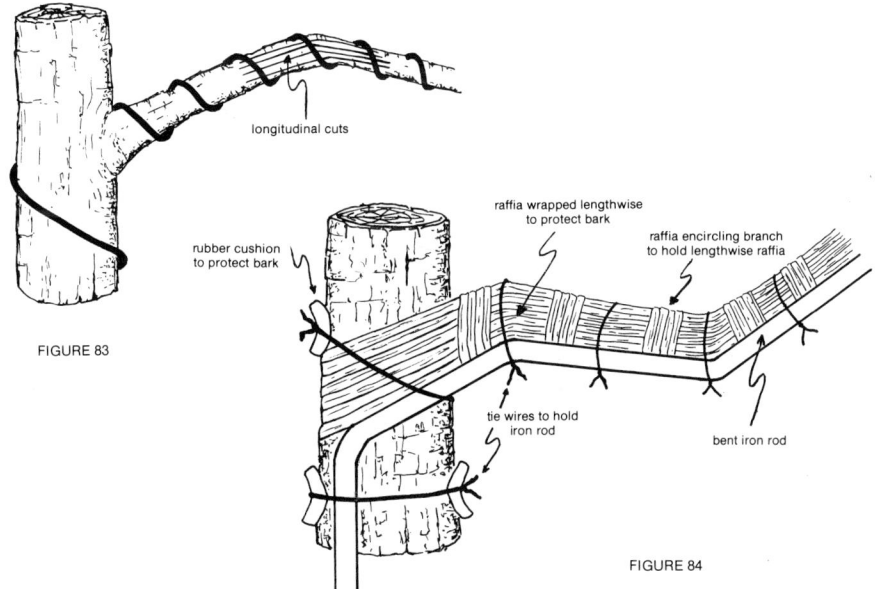

FIGURE 83 Cuts in the length of the branch make it more flexible.

FIGURE 84 Bending along a thick guide wire.

- One way in which to make a branch more flexible for the purpose of bending it, is to take a knife and make a horizontal cut through the branch over as long a length as needed to bend the branch. The cut will then leave you with two thinner halves, the one above the other, where the bend has to take place. When the cut heals it will leave a scar, but this will be in the length of the branch and will only add to the character of the branch. The edges of the cut will also unite in time, forming scar-tissue which will hold the branch in position sooner. Virtually the same process can be followed to have a branch set in position sooner than usual after bending, by making a vertical cut in the branch on the underside where it is going to be invisible. This last cut need not go all the way through the branch; it should only be through the cambium layer, to entice it to form scar-tissue.

Using wire is not the only method of shaping a tree through mechanical means. A variety of levers can be used to bend branches and trunks, especially the thicker ones. Wire or string can be used in different ways to correct certain faults in branches, somewhat similar to the peg and twine method. Any method which will correct the shape of a branch may be employed, from placing a pebble between two trunks to force them apart, through wooden wedges to lever systems. Just remember to protect the soft bark where the wire, string or levers touch it.

Removal of wires

Wires can be removed by cutting them off with a wirecutter into small pieces on every winding, or they can be unwound carefully so as not to damage any leaves or branches. If the branch springs back after a few hours the wire should be rewound, but in the opposite direction if any marks have been left. Unwinding wire has the inherent danger of damage being done to leaves and smaller branches.

CLASSIFICATION 4

One may well ask if it is necessary to complicate matters with an elaborate system of classification, but there are very sound reasons for this. A very important one is that it enables people to communicate about bonsai. For instance, if one has a system of classification, when talking about an informal upright tree, it is obvious what is meant. Classification would also be used to delineate the styles which one has to emulate. It also helps in training beginners. (See the influence of Yuji Yoshimura in Chapter 1 under 'History of bonsai in Japan'.)

Here are a few methods of grouping bonsai trees.

ACCORDING TO SIZE

- Large bonsai (*Omono bonsai*) 90 to 120 cm tall, not including the pot. (Also called *Dai bonsai*.)
- Medium bonsai (*Chumono bonsai*) 45 to 90 cm tall. (Also called *Chui bonsai*.)
- One-hand lifting size (*Katade mochi bonsai*) 20 to 45 cm tall. This is the popular size. (Also called *Ko bonsai*.)
- Small bonsai (*Komono bonsai*) 10 to 20 cm tall. (Also called *Shohin bonsai*.)
- Palm size (*Mame bonsai*) 7,5 to 10 cm tall. It is very difficult to reproduce the detail of large trees in this style. Sometimes it is called the pocket-size. Two or three should fit into one's hand.
- Fingertip size (*Shito bonsai*) smaller than 7,5 cm. It should be possible to carry the bonsai in its pot on the fingertip.

ACCORDING TO THE INCLINATION OF THE TRUNK

Formal upright (*Chokkan*)
Informal upright (*Moyo-gi or Tachiki*)
Slanted (*Shakan*)
    minimum slant (*Sho-shakan*)
    medium slant (*Chu-shakan*)
    extreme slant (*Dai-shakan*)

Cascading trunks

Semi-cascade (*Han-kengai*)
Full cascade (*Kengai*)
Waterfall cascade (*Taki-kengai*)
Hanging like a mass of strings (*Ito-kengai*)
Part of bonsai hanging over cliff (*Gaito-kengai*)
Vertical cascade (*Dai-kengai*)
More than two trunks cascading (*Takan-kengai*)

ACCORDING TO THE BASE OF THE TREE

Root-over-rock style (*Seki-joju*)

SMALL BONSAI
The smallest bonsai is the very minute keshitsubu, *or poppy seed size. It is so small that the seeds have to be sown directly into the miniature pots. Slightly larger is the pocket (*mame*) bonsai, of which two to four should fit into the palm of your hand. They are all very difficult to grow, due to their size and, consequently, branches with relatively smaller leaves. It means that everything must be simplified to have the miniature effect.* Mame bonsai are now called shohin *or* komono bonsai. *Literally translated this means 'small articles'. These tiny trees require special attention as to their soil needs, fertilising and watering.*

Rock-clinging style (*Ishi-zuke*)
Exposed root style (*Ne-agari*)
Raft style from fallen trunk (*Ikada-buki*)
Raft style from surface root (*Netsu-ranari*)
Stump style (*Korabuki*) (Multiple sprouts from a stump)
Sprout style (*Kabudachi*)
Sprouts from a fallen cone (*Yama-yori*)

ACCORDING TO THE SHAPE OF THE CROWN

Like a broom (*Hoki-zukuri*)
Like a ball or egg (*Tama-zukuri*)
Flame shaped (*Rosoku-zukuri*) (Also called *Honen*)
Umbrella shaped (*Kasa-zukuri*)
Weeping branches (*Shidare-zukuri*)
Octopus-like (*Tako-zukuri*)
Spider-like (*Kumo*)
Free style (*Bunjin* or *Literati*)
Natural shape (*Shizen-zukuri*)
Very traditional pine shape (*Matsu-zukuri*)
Windswept style (*Fukinagashi*)

ACCORDING TO THE CONDITION OF THE TRUNK

Hollow trunk (*Sabamiki* or *Sabakan*)
Struck by lightning (*Kaminari*)
Plaited trunk (*Pien-tshu*)
Twisted and coiled trunk (*Horai*)
Twisted trunk (*Nejikan*)
Split trunk (*Sogu-ki*)
Driftwood style (*Shari-miki*)
Gnarled trunk (*Bankan*)
Knobby trunk (*Kobukan*)
Peeled bark (*Sharikan*)
Entwined trunks (*Karame-miki*)

ACCORDING TO THE NUMBER OF TREES

Single tree (*Ippon-uye*)
Two trees (*Soju*)
Three trees (*Samon-yose*)
Five trees (*Gohan-yose*)
Seven trees (*Nanahan-yose*)
Nine trees (*Kyuhon-yose*)
Many trees (*Yose-uye*)
Natural grouping (*Yamahori*)
Clustered grouping or so-called fist planting (*Tsukami-yose*)
Scene with trees (*Saikei*)

ACCORDING TO THE NUMBER OF TRUNKS

One trunk (*Takan*)
Two trunks (*Sokan*)
Three trunks (*Sankan*)
Five trunks (*Crokan*)
Seven trunks (*Nanakan*)

Nine trunks (*Kyukan*)
Many trunks (*Kabudachi*)

SOUTH AFRICAN STYLES

Baobab style
Pierneef style
Flat crown style

I hesitate to call these South African styles as they are in my opinion only adaptations of recognised styles, like broom, umbrella and informal upright — almost like subspecies. However the baobab tree, found only in Africa, has a striking shape as do the acacias depicted in Pierneef's paintings.

All these variations in the styles are actually based on four styles, namely formal upright, informal upright, slanting and cascading, using the trunk as reference. The other 'styles' are but ways of copying nature, using one of the above-mentioned four styles as a basis. A so-called Pierneef style is simply an umbrella style on an informal upright trunk, with a tendency perhaps towards *bunjin*. The primary object of any bonsai is to show the viewer a tree in nature, albeit a simplified version. However despite its simplicity, it does not have less of a visual impact. Therein lies the art. All the Japanese terminology does not mean a thing, does not contribute to the beauty — *shibui* — of a bonsai, if the tree itself is not an object to admire. A tree *must* be *shibui*, a word used to describe simple beauty, which is subtle and unassuming. It should have a lingering effect. When you leave the tree it should remain in your mind and you should want to go back and enjoy its beauty again.

THE INFLUENCE OF ZEN BUDDHISM

Do you have to know all the Japanese terminology? If you see a beautiful painting, it is not necessary to know the name of the painter to appreciate the painting. However in my opinion when Japanese terminology is used it tends to orientate your mind to the Japanese background. And I think this is essential in one's approach, since, if one is British, South African, Australian or American and not Japanese, the art is not part of one's daily happenings. We are practising a Japanese art form and no matter which country we are living in, it remains essentially oriental in nature.

This is in my opinion the reason why the westerner, even though perhaps a Christian, would benefit by knowing something about Zen Buddhism and in particular about the way it influences bonsai craftsmanship and artistry.

Buddhism reached Japan via Korea as the Chinese *Ch'an* sect, and was first accepted by the powerful Soga clan, in the sixth century.

During the Nara period (710–784) Buddhism became the religion of the state. Only during the 13th century did *Ch'an* (*Zen*) Buddhism become popular through the teachings of the monk Eisai (1141-1215).

According to the teachings of Zen Buddhism a work of art should express certain feelings and concepts, which in bonsai are the branches of the three main trunks, called *wabi, sabi* and *kami*. *Sabi* refers to the absence of superfluous material possessions and a spiritual contentedness with the basic necessities. *Wabi* can be related to the Franciscan concept of life in the sense of inner harmony, spiritual health and satisfaction which could be experienced by contemplating the sublimity of natural manifestations. *Wabi* conveys the concept of humbleness when brought face to face with nature and the acceptance of natural occurrences. Such a concept does not place man in the centre of the universe but rather accepts that man is a part of a universal design which is entirely in harmony with itself. *Sabi*, on the other hand, refers to a form of loneliness and solitude in a graceful, perhaps old-fashioned

The truth is, the science of Nature has been already too long made only a work of the brain and the fancy: It is now high time that it should return to the plainness and soundness of observations on material and obvious things.

ROBERT HOOKE
From Micrographia (1665)

*Ancient simplicity is gone . . .
the people are satisfied with nothing but finery.*

IHARA SAIKAKU
From Millionare's Gospel Bk I

manner. *Sabi* has to do with the contentedness in possessing, loving and tending to things which have been moulded by nature, the passing of time and by the hand of man. *Sabi* is seen as having austerity, sedateness and straightforwardness.

Wabi and *sabi* along with *kami* form the triad which imbues the art of bonsai. Where bonsai is concerned, *kami* may be defined as the spirit of the inner dynamism of human artefacts, natural events and plants, inasmuch as these can be sources of almost devotional creativity.

Added to *wabi*, *sabi* and *kami* are the following characteristics that the branches of the three trunks need to display:
- simplicity — perhaps the most striking aspect of a bonsai;
- asymmetry — the absence of evenness and duplication;
- austerity — which refers to openness and honesty. The bonsai is not hiding anything. What you see is what there is;
- freedom from the conventional;
- subtlety to a profound degree. This is the ability of the tree to tell you a complete story by showing you the bare essentials and letting your mind read the rest;
- tranquillity — in a way this is coupled to *wabi*, but it is more: it is peace and calm although the design may suggest movement;
- naturalness — an unaffected scene, lacking any artificiality. The hand of nature resulted in the tree being what it is, not the hand of man.

The Western mind has difficulty in implementing Zen Buddhism, because it is a way of life, without fixed rules. It is not a religion. The Westerner is also caught up in a life of materialism and to a great degree, a life filled with artificial things. Man is removed from nature, living in a concrete and glass jungle. To implement the thought processes as mentioned above and recreate nature in miniature, means breaking away from what are now nearly instinctive patterns.

A little more about the advent of Buddhism in Japan is mentioned in Chapter 1, under the 'History of Bonsai' heading.

Nature does not proceed by leaps

LINNAEUS

BONSAI STYLES

5

*Do not seek to follow in the footsteps of
the men of old; seek what they sought.*

MATSUO BASHO

A bonsai is not simply any old miniature tree. (See page 1) It must be trained according to age-old rules, within the framework as laid down many years ago. When considering the styles, and more to the point, when looking at a bonsai, you should see the Zen influence and feel the Zen atmosphere. You should always be conscious of simplicity, austerity, the unconventional and the natural. The bonsai should be telling you a great deal, but it must do so with a minimum of tree material. *It must be rich in message, in intrinsic value, although apparently poor in quantity of material.*

No two trees are exact replicas of each other, in fact you can only copy a style in

No man ever yet became great through imitation

SAMUEL JOHNSON

I still find each day too short for all the thoughts I want to think, all the walks I want to take, all the books I want to read and all the friends I want to see.

JOHN BURROUGHS

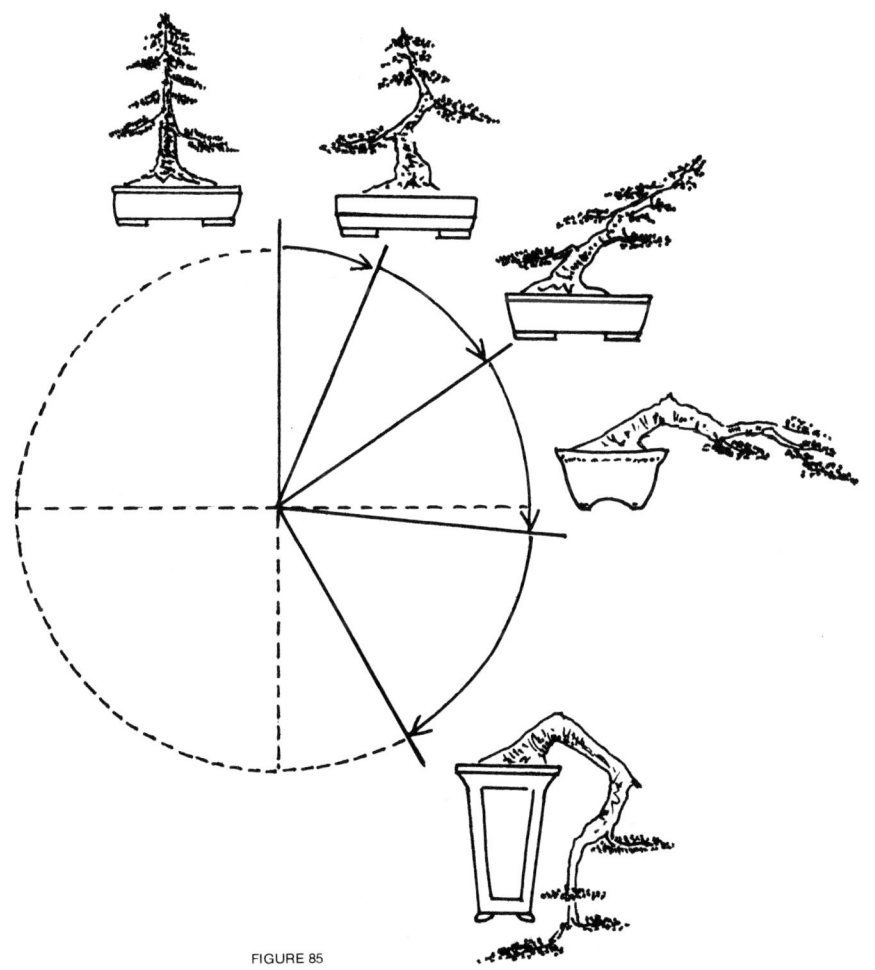

FIGURE 85

FIGURE 85 A graphic depiction of the different degrees of slant in the five basic styles.

FIGURE 86 A very formal upright tree.

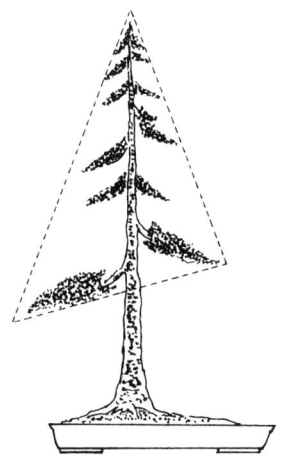

FIGURE 87 The branches point downwards, indicating an older tree.

FIGURE 88 These branches are pointing upwards indicating a younger tree.

FIGURE 89 These branches change inclination from downwards to upwards at the apex.

FIGURE 190 Even with *jin* and *saba-miki* the triangle principle still applies.

general and this *is* what you do, and what has been done through the ages. It is the way to learn. That is also why you need to know the different styles. It is only logical that the wise men of old will have tried every single natural style, that they know where the best place is to have branches to suit a particular style, how the trunk should slant, what the roots must look like, and all other aspects as described in Chapter 2 on 'Guidelines to styling'.

There are many combinations of styles, for instance a root-over-rock (*seki-joju*) which must have the crown (foliage) grown in a certain shape, like an umbrella style or informal upright. The 'style' may thus refer to the way the tree is grown as well as the shape of the tree. Also note that certain combinations will work and others won't, for example an informal upright tree growing on a rock will seem natural, but a formal upright in the same situation will not.

There are certain techniques which can be used to give the tree both beauty and character. These are discussed in Chapter 6 on 'Characterising' and include *kaminari* (struck-by-lightning), *shari-miki* (driftwood), *sogu-ki* (split trunk) and others.

The five first styles described are grouped according to the slant of the trunk. These styles are depicted graphically in Figure 85. All other styles are based on these trunk variations.

FORMAL UPRIGHT STYLE — CHOKKAN

This style is the closest any bonsai comes to a symmetrical arrangement, and it is precisely for this reason that it is a difficult style to accomplish. The trunk is absolutely straight. It might end in a *jin* and could be made interesting by adding *shari* or *saba-miki*. (For the description of *jin*, *shari* and *saba-miki*, see Chapter 6 on 'Characterising'.) The branches can be situated lower down or higher up, depending on whether you want to accent the height of the tree or not. The downward pointing branches indicate an old tree, where the weight of the branches pulls them down. Upward pointing branches are characteristic of a younger, strongly growing tree. A particular tree may even have the lower branches directed downwards and as you move higher up the tree, the branches become horizontal and then near the top grow upwards; however, they may not cross each other. This branch arrangement is indicative of a tree which is not young but is still growing actively. Always keep in mind that the tree must appear natural.

Remember to follow the general rules as described in Chapter 2. The one rule which *has* to be followed, is that the apex must be directly over the base of the trunk,

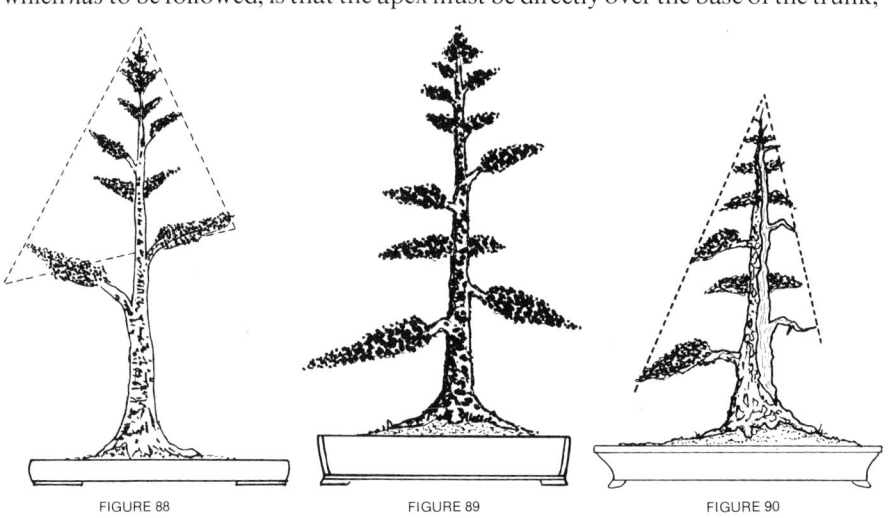

FIGURE 88   FIGURE 89   FIGURE 90

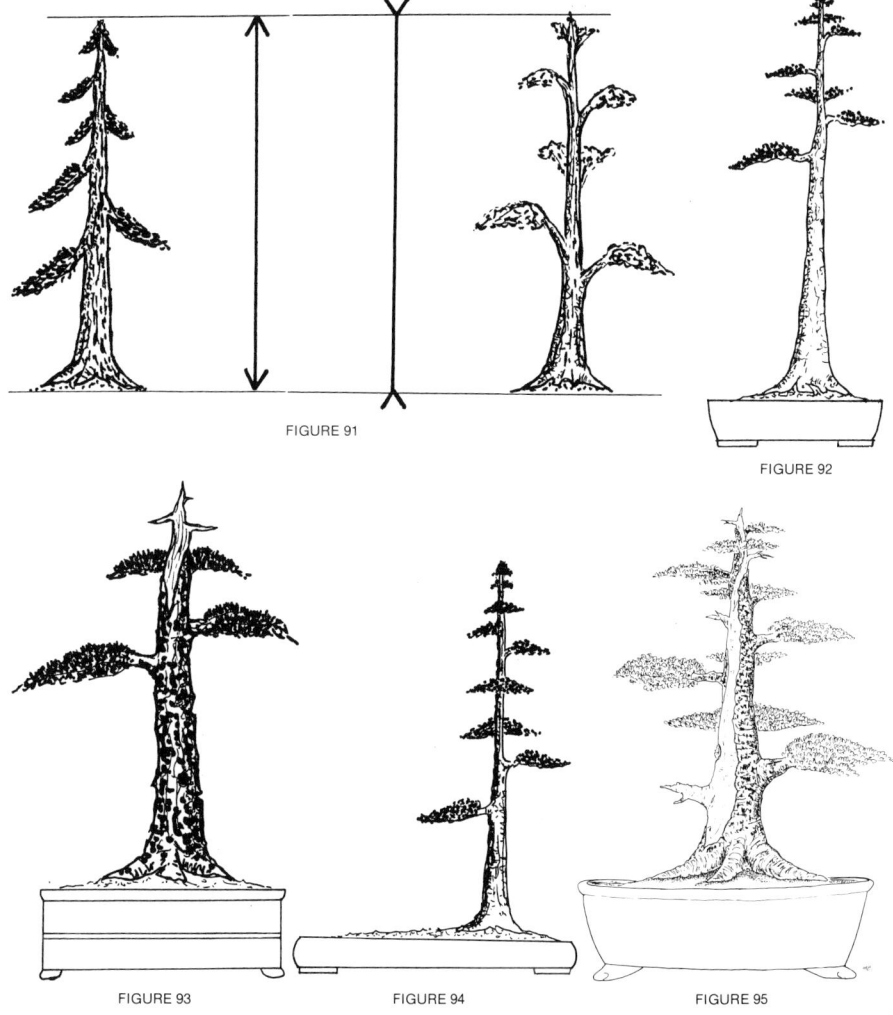

FIGURE 91 Which one is the longest? The length does not appear to be the same, although both lines are, and this shows what effect the direction of the branches may have.

FIGURE 92 To emphasise the height of the trunk, the branches are located near the top of the tree. This is done especially if the trunk has a remarkable texture.

FIGURE 93 Only three branches. This is an answer to the thick and tall trunk with no lower branches. The apex is a *jin* and there is a live branch behind the *jin*.

FIGURE 94 Note the very tall and narrow appearance.

FIGURE 95 *Jin* and *saba-miki* create the impression of old age.

in accordance with the formality of the style. The ball-shaped crown, as well as the flame- and broom-shaped crowns, all use a straight trunk, which would also group them with the formally upright bonsai. Their beauty is at its best when they are leafless. These variations of the formal upright style are best grown with deciduous trees, and are described as styles on their own because they are not the classical, very formal upright style with its triangular outline.

FIGURE 96 The ball-shape on a straight trunk.

INFORMAL UPRIGHT STYLE — MOYO-GI

In this style (a very popular one) the trunk is still upright, but now has some curves, and the tree need not be grown strictly according to the rules, making it far easier to cultivate, and an excellent style for beginners. It allows scope for variations, not only in trunk curves but also in crown shapes, more so than the formal upright. The apex of the tree still ends approximately above the base of the trunk.

The 'extras' like *jin*, *shari*, *saba-miki* and others are used with excellent effect. In Chapter 2 on 'Guidelines to Shaping Bonsai', the informal upright style is discussed in more detail as to the position of the branches, the shape of the foliage and other trunk and branch considerations.

The so-called natural shape *shizen-zukuri* is a form of informal upright, where the prescribed arrangement of branches is disregarded. The general outline of an

FIGURE 97 The flame-shape on a straight trunk.

FIGURE 98 A standard informal upright.

FIGURE 99 An informal upright tree with short trunk and wide-reaching branches to emphasise the shortness.

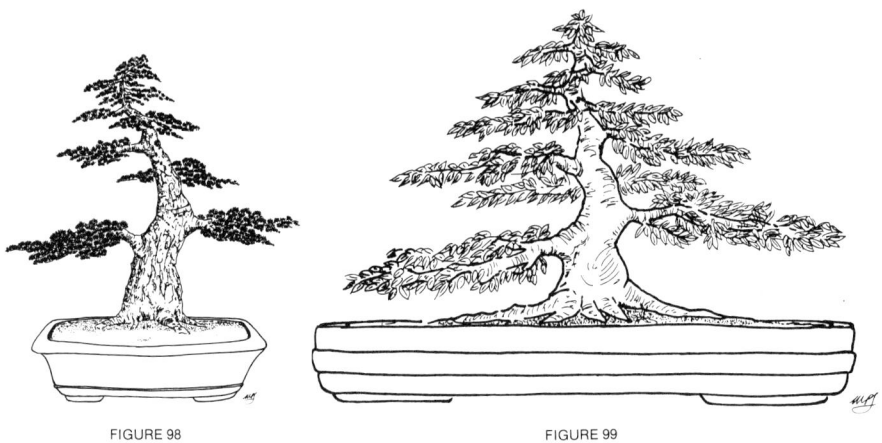

FIGURE 98

FIGURE 99

FIGURE 100 This is an informal upright tree which only has branches in the upper third of the trunk. The first branch to the right is necessary to balance the tree. The overall picture is of great age, brought about by the downwards pointing branches and angular bends in the trunk and branches, as well as the scarceness of foliage.

FIGURE 101 The first two branches are smaller than the branches above them, which is natural because they grow in the shadow of others.

informal upright tree is maintained and in particular the asymmetrical arrangement of branches and basic triangular form. The variation, however, contains more branches, and the flat triangular outline shape of the branches themselves is not necessarily adhered to. In this instance you may have shorter and smaller branches below larger branches.

In both the formal and informal upright styles, the branch and even root arrangements are very much the same. The foliage is also trimmed and grown to the same overall shape. There is a wider latitude, though, in the case of the informal style. You should still try and keep to the sequence of three groups or layers of branches in the upward spiral when growing an informal upright, but if this is not possible do not be too concerned.

In Chapter 2 on 'Guidelines to Shaping Bonsai', you will learn not to have the trunk in a repeated S-curve. However an interesting variation is the *Ō-Moyogi*, which has an exaggerated S-curve. When using a young tree it is called *bankan* (coiled snake). This style is shown in Figure 102.

SLANTED STYLE — SHAKAN

This is an informal style with the trunk leaning over to the side at varying degrees, from just off vertical to a few degrees above horizontal. The slight, medium and severe slants are called *sho*, *chu* and *dai-shakan*. The slant must be to one side, either to the left or right, and not directly towards or away from the viewer. The trunk can be reasonably straight, but curves in the trunk make it more interesting and give one a feeling that the tree is alive. Curves also impart a sense of movement, or resistance to forced movement. Thus, either the tree could be leaning over through the effect of wind or it could be trying to resist the force of the wind.

The tree must be placed to one side of the pot, with the slant over the rest of the pot. The tree should not be hanging over the edge of the pot. See Figures 103 and 104. With the tree positioned so that the trunk is projecting outwards, away from the pot, it seems unstable and ready to fall over.

The first branch is of special importance, especially where the slant is medium to severe, as it has to counterbalance the leaning trunk. This same branch may also be used to create the impression that it is pulling the tree over towards one side, but the second branch must then restore the balance.

You may view the tree as having been forced to one side by the wind; either a constantly blowing wind, or the occasional severe blast. The effect of a continuous wind would be to bend the whole trunk; the second effect aimed at conjures up a tree at the mercy of variable winds over a period of years: a strong wind blew the

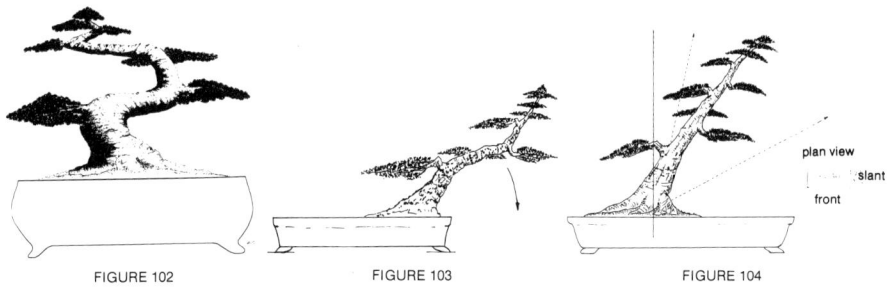

FIGURE 102   FIGURE 103   FIGURE 104

FIGURE 102 The severely curved Ō-Moyogi.

FIGURE 103 This tree is close to the edge of the pot and leaning away from the pot. It seems as though it is going to fall over. This is corrected by planting as shown in the next figure.

FIGURE 104 The slant must be between the broken lines. The tree is also leaning over the container and seems better balanced than in Figure 103.

tree over, the trunk grew upright again, only to have the process repeated some years later. The result would be a trunk bent or curved in stages (as shown in Figure 105) and it would be more like a windblown style.

When the wind is blowing against the tree, the first branch on the windside would be the one that tries to balance the falling tree. The actual reason why this branch and others on the same side of the tree (in fact, the opposite side towards which the tree is slanting) grow larger, is because they receive more sun, as opposed to those branches in the shade of the slanting trunk. A very interesting observation is that a tree may grow into a dry wind, because the wind retards the formation and growth on the windside of the tree. This results in the shrinking of the cells on that side, and the resultant bending of the tree in the same direction. Because, on the other hand, the branches on the protected side of the trunk are not influenced in the same way, they tend to be longer and better developed. The illusion is created that these branches have been lengthened by the wind, while the wind has compressed the branches on the other side in the manner of a concertina.

If a tree grows upright, with its branches horizontal, and a strong wind tips it over at an angle, the branches on the windside would initially grow upwards to a degree, with the branches on the other side pointing slightly downwards. After some time the branches will regain their horizontal direction, but not where they are closest to the trunk, as here they are too thick and contain too much mature wood. The effect is shown in Figure 108 and 109.

Apart from the fact that it *looks* natural to have a branch develop from the convex side (outside) of a curve, it is also practical, in the sense that the tree's natural inclination is to grow away from a strong branch, for balance, and also to allow sunlight to reach the branch. This results in a form compared to a spiral zigzag, growing smaller towards the apex. The rule is applied in nearly all styles of bonsai, (See Chapter 2: 'Guidelines to Shaping Bonsai')

Visualise a tree standing on a riverbank, leaning over the water. The roots and

FIGURE 105 The trunk is curved as the tree tried to right itself.

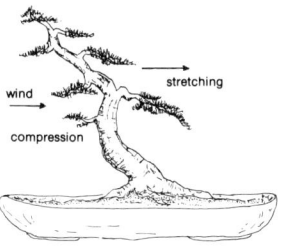

FIGURE 106 The compression and stretch action of the wind.

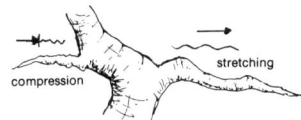

FIGURE 107 The concertina effect.

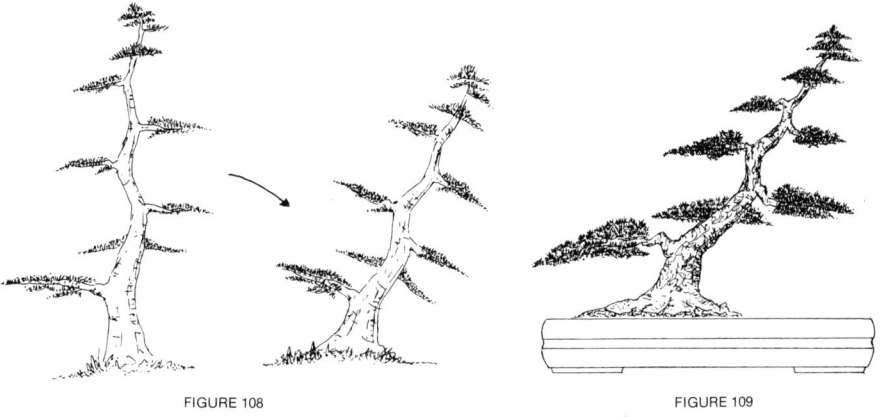

FIGURE 108   FIGURE 109

FIGURE 108 This tree is falling over and, as the branches have not corrected their horizontal positions, it looks unnatural. (Compare Figure 105)

FIGURE 109 What to plan for in the future.

FIGURE 110 A tree leaning over the water's edge.

FIGURE 111 A tree leaning from a cliffside.

FIGURE 112 The stretched and compressed roots.

FIGURE 113 A gnarled, weathered, slanting trunk.

FIGURE 114 The degree of slant in the semi-cascade.

therefore also the branches on the riverside will be better developed, giving the impression of a slanting tree. A gree growing on a steep mountainside, with the roots clinging for dear life, while the tree seems to be falling over, is balanced by the branches on the mountainside, and also because the roots on that side are better developed.

Because the tree in the slanting style is not standing upright, it depends on strong roots on the side opposite to the slant to keep it from falling over. These roots will be stretched out, compared to the roots under the trunk's slant which will appear crumpled. The roots impart a feeling of passive (isometric) movement, because if they were not there, the tree would fall over. It is due to their pulling back and support which cannot be seen as actual movement that the tree seems sturdy. Do not neglect this aspect. It also applies to the cascade styles.

Because one thinks of the slanting style as effected by the weather, *jin*, *shari* and *saba-miki* are perfectly suited to these trees.

The apex of the slanting tree cannot be ignored, and it must receive attention as to its inclination in two directions: (i) try to have the apex slightly inclined towards the viewer (approximately ten degrees). The tree as a whole must not be allowed to lean over backwards, even though it is slanted towards one side; (ii) in the second instance the apex may be seen as the tree's last effort to upright itself, and should therefore be growing in an upwards direction. It does not continue with the slant all the way into the apex.

SEMI-CASCADE STYLE — HAN-KENGAI

The semi-cascade is quite close to being a severely slanted tree. The degree to which the tree is slanted is between approximately ten degrees above a horizontal line through the upper rim of the pot to a few degrees below this line. Because a medium depth pot is used, compared to a deep upright pot in the case of the full cascade, you could say that the tip of the tail of the semi-cascade should not end below the bottom of the pot.

The placement of the trunk is very important, as is the direction it takes from its base to where it crosses the rim of the pot. In the case of the shallow pot, the trunk leans over sideways — not forwards — to cross the side rim of the pot, or perhaps the front rim near the corner. It may stretch so far that its tail-tip can end by crossing the rim. When a deeper pot is used, the base of the trunk is still positioned away from the side of the pot over which the trunk crosses it, but in this case, the trunk crosses the rim over the front half of the side rim, as seen in Fig. 117. If this is not done, the tree will seem unbalanced. See to it that the trunk does not touch the rim where it crosses it, as this may give the impression that the rim is supporting the tree.

In the semi- and full cascade the impression is usually created of a tree growing on the edge of a precipice, with the forces of nature having compelled it to grow horizontally or even vertically downwards. In many instances there are signs of the tree trying to recover its upward growth, thus presenting a step in the cascade. A semi-cascade may also be created by having an upright tree broken off, and a remaining downwards growing branch trained into a semi-cascade as shown in Figure 119.

The growing tip of the tail is far removed from the base of the trunk and the anchoring roots, in a horizontal direction. The effect is one of imbalance and can be counteracted by showing strong anchoring roots, a sturdy trunk and/or a balancing head of foliage, closer to the base of the trunk.

The roots should be the same as in the slanting style. The so-called *head*, as opposed to the *tail*, consists of a side branch with foliage, which forms the apex of

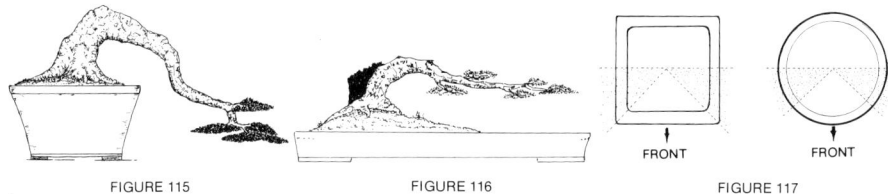

FIGURE 115   FIGURE 116   FIGURE 117

FIGURE 115 The semi-cascade in a deeper pot. The tail tip does not fall below the foot of the pot.

FIGURE 116 The semi-cascade in a shallow pot, but now standing on a mound of soil.

FIGURE 117 The trunk should cross the rim in the shaded areas.

the tree, and due to its size appears able to balance the rest of the tree. This is not as easy as it seems, because of the tree's tendency to grow horizontally and the scarcity of branches. The term balance does not refer to actual physical balance due to weight, but rather a visual impression. This is one of the problems of the cascade styles and is not easily overcome. The effect of the roots and trunk has been mentioned in its physical context, that is, in the way the roots grip the soil as well as the sturdiness of the trunk, which show that the tree cannot fall over. When using a 'head' and the branches for balance, the term 'balance' is used in an artistic sense and because of this, is open to criticism. General guidelines have to be outlined. First of all consider the position of the head or apex. It cannot be at the end of the growing tip (the tail). It has three possible positions: approximately a third of the way down the tail, approximately two thirds of the way down the tail, or directly over the base of the trunk. When the head is in this last position, care must be taken not to give it the appearance of an overdeveloped branch. This could perhaps create the impression that the trunk has divided in two, with the head representing the remainder of the upright growing tree, and the tail the part forced horizontally. Furthermore, the head should not be too large, because the tail would then give the impression of a branch that has grown too long. This could then be mistaken for the raincoat-hanger style (*mino-kake*). (See Figure 121)

With the first two positions, you must still remember that the head is the first large branch. (See Figures 122 and 123) The trunk is bare up to where this branch begins. You may encounter *jin* along the trunk before the branch that forms the head.

The direction in which the branches grow and the arrangement of the foliage also serve to balance the whole, and create a visually satisfying picture. The styling of the branches is somewhat more difficult to arrange than with upright trees. You cannot simply consider the cascade as an upright tree which has fallen on its side, for it would look ridiculous with branches growing from the, now, underside of the trunk, and others growing vertically upwards. It is very difficult to create the usual horizontal branch directions, as well as the grouping in threes to form a decreasing spiral. You must always try and style the branches in three dimensions. The vertical dimension is the easy one. The left and right dimensions are not easy, because you have to use branches which grow from the upper or lower surface, or even the front and back surfaces of the trunk, to create these 'side' branches. To help create the third dimension, the branches directed sideways must also point slightly forwards

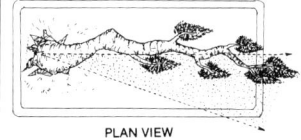

FIGURE 118 In the shallow pot the bonsai can even stretch over the pot edge, but always to the side and not forwards or backwards.

FIGURE 119 The upright tree broken off with a branch taking over the growth, but growing sideways.

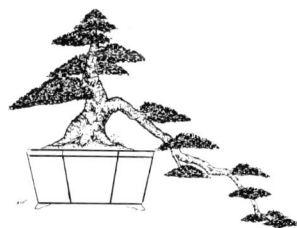

FIGURE 120 *Gaito-kengai*. Still a *han-kengai*, but with one large branch, which hangs over the rim of the pot as if hanging over a cliff edge.

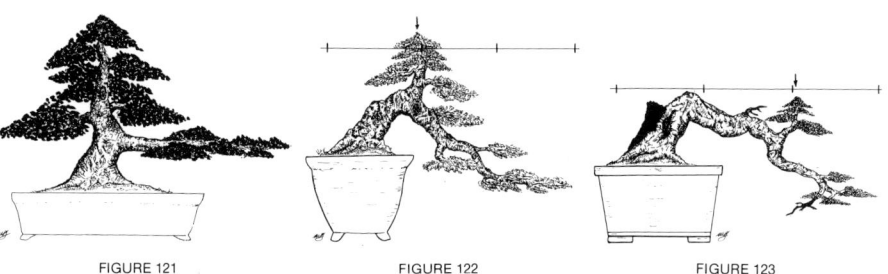

FIGURE 121   FIGURE 122   FIGURE 123

FIGURE 121 *Goza-kake* or *mino-kake*. It is the raincoat-hanger style with an extremely long first branch.

FIGURE 122 The head is located 1/3 along the length of the trunk.

FIGURE 123 The head is located 2/3 along the length of the trunk.

FIGURE 124 A semi-cascade with branches in all directions.

FIGURE 125 Branches cross the trunk to create depth.

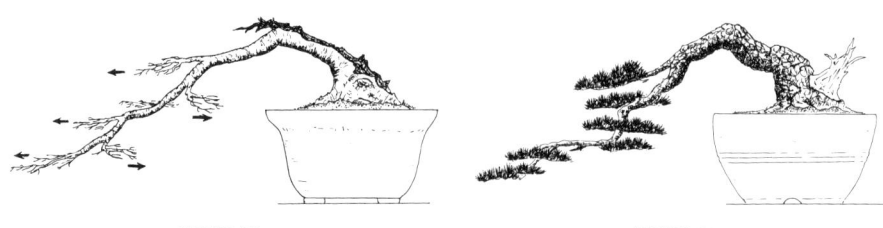

FIGURE 124

FIGURE 125

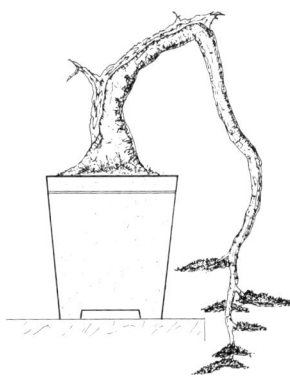

FIGURE 126 *Tachi-agari kengai* which means the upright cascade. See also in Figure 127.

FIGURE 127 The upright cascade in a shallow pot.

FIGURE 128 *Ito-kengai*. Strings of branches hanging over a cliff-edge into space ... The thick trunk acts as a buttress.

FIGURE 129 *Dai-kengai*. A vertical cascade without a balancing head, but the position of the tail compensates for the absent head. It is a formal cascade.

or backwards; and you *must* have branches growing to the back to some degree. If the cascade is, for instance, to the left, you will probably have most branches directed to the left, in accordance with the trunk, but there is nothing wrong in having one or two branches growing towards the right side.

When you have a trunk cascading downwards in a rugged, angular way, with sharp curves, the branches must show the same characteristics to harmonise with the trunk. And in the same way, when the cascade is more gradual with gentle curves, the branches should curve gently too. Try to train the curves not only in a downward direction, but also in a forward and backward direction for better perspective.

Beware of defining the "steps" in the downward bends too drastically, for fear of creating a full cascade instead of a semi-cascade. Should the trunk resist being bent in a forward-backward direction, you could create perspective by having one or two branches cross in front of the trunk, much in the *bunjin* manner.

From the foregoing you will realise that to set out to create a beautiful and balanced cascade — whether semi- or full — is a challenge and, if successful, must give one a most fulfilling sense of achievement.

FULL CASCADE STYLE — KENGAI

In this dramatic style the trunk rises from the soil, drastically changing direction to grow over the rim of the pot and then downwards as though over a cliff edge into a chasm. In the usual full cascade, the trunk is not allowed to grow vertically upwards to any significant height before it changes direction. An exception is an ordinary informal upright trunk, growing downwards to form the cascade. This interesting variation is called the upright cascade (*tachi-agari kengai*). It could be planted in the usual shallower pot if the cascading tail does not reach below the base of the pot.

Cascades can be in the form of one trunk or several trunks. The degree to which the trees cascade varies. Starting with the semi-cascade, which ends slightly under the horizontal line through the rim of the pot, you have the slight, medium and

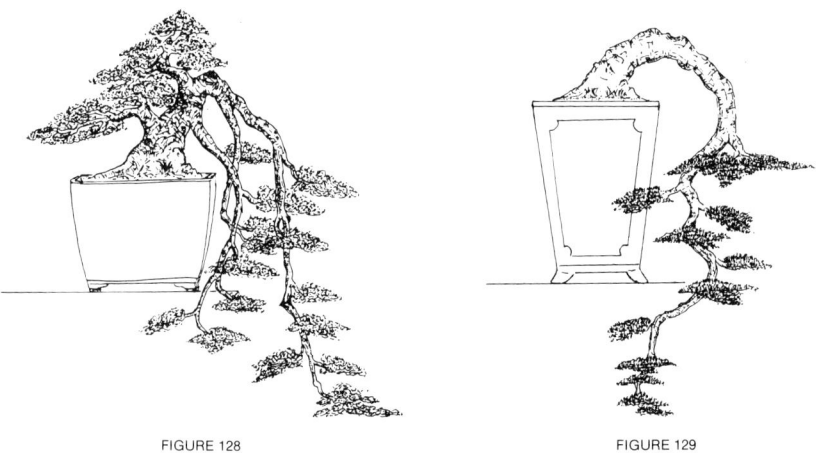

FIGURE 128

FIGURE 129

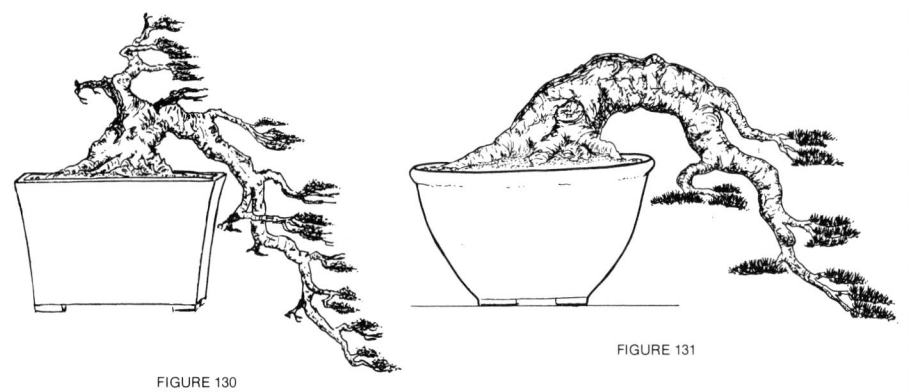

FIGURE 130

FIGURE 131

FIGURE 130 *Fuki-nagashi kengai*. A windswept cascade with the *jin* showing the effects of the wind, along with the windswept branches. The roots are exposed to emphasise the anchorage. The tree would seem in danger of falling over if it were in a tall upright container. This is an informal style of cascade.

FIGURE 131 *Yoko-nagashi kengai*. A side-sweeping cascade in this instance resembling a lizard.

severe cascades. The severe or nearly vertical cascade is called the *dai-kengai*. A striking picture can be created by training the cascade into a windswept style. Very similar to the windswept is the side-sweeping style, which looks like a side-view of a cascade, with no part of the trunk or any branches crossing in front of the pot.

The formal cascade usually has a head which balances the tail. The head is from the first branch, as with the semi-cascade, and is called *uke* (Japanese for 'to receive'). The tail is called *nagare* (which means 'flowing'). The apex of the crown (head) and the tip of the tail must be in line with the base of the trunk in the formal cascade.

The *gaito-kengai* represents a tree growing on a cliff-edge, with part of the tree hanging over the edge. This cascading part is the tail, but it is relatively smaller, and not the trunk, but a branch is growing down. Do not mistake this for the coat-hanger style. (See Figure 120 and 121)

The rules for creating a three-dimensional impression are identical to those for the semi-cascade. The trunk must cross the edge of the pot at the same place, the roots must be the same, the trunk must have the same curve, and the same arrangement of branches is used. The drastic bend in the trunk, which causes the trunk to cascade, must be a sharp bend and not a gradular change in direction, like a nice half-circle. The branches must sprout from the convex (outer) side of the bends. The tip of the tail may end above or at a point lower than the bottom of the container, but never on a level with it. (See Figures 134 and 135)

The watering of a bonsai grown as a cascade is not a simple matter, due to the depth of the container. When the soil surface is dry, the deeper part of the pot may still be very wet ... or vice versa. To overcome this problem, use soil with very good drainage properties in the deeper portion of the pot, to prevent waterlogging. Coarser or sandier soil over the whole depth of the pot, necessitating frequent watering, would be a practical solution.

The roots tend to fill the narrow deep pots more quickly than the shallow ones, because it is a natural tendency for a tree to grow its roots downwards. The condition of the tree must be watched constantly and it is usually necessary to repot cascade bonsai fairly often.

Jin, *shari* and *saba-miki* can be used with impressive results. In all cases of full cascade, barring the upright cascade, deep pots with different shapes must be used. The stands that are used may not be the same height as the pots *or* the cascade, to avoid a monotonous appearance.

The tree material used is the same as with semi-cascade, for instance *Cotoneaster horizontalis*. If you find that the tail tip is losing its vigour, remember that this is the natural tendency for an upright growing tree, now being forced to grow downwards. Encourage the tip to grow with the methods mentioned in Chapter 3

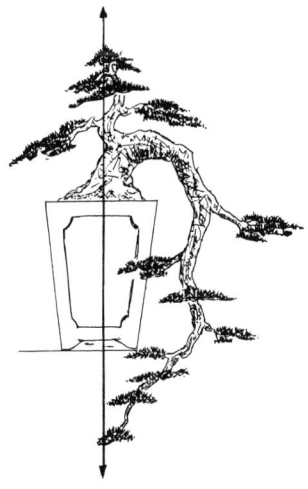

FIGURE 132 The formal cascade where a sense of balance is created by having the apex of the head (crown), the base of the trunk and the tip of the tail in line.

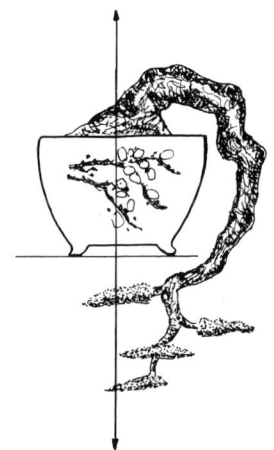

FIGURE 133 The formal cascade without a head.

FIGURE 134 *Jin* marks the apex of both the head and tail.

FIGURE 135 With the pot and the stand the same height, as well as the tail of the *kengai* ending at the same level as the legs of the pot, it creates a monotonous picture.

FIGURE 136 A *bunjin* cascade.

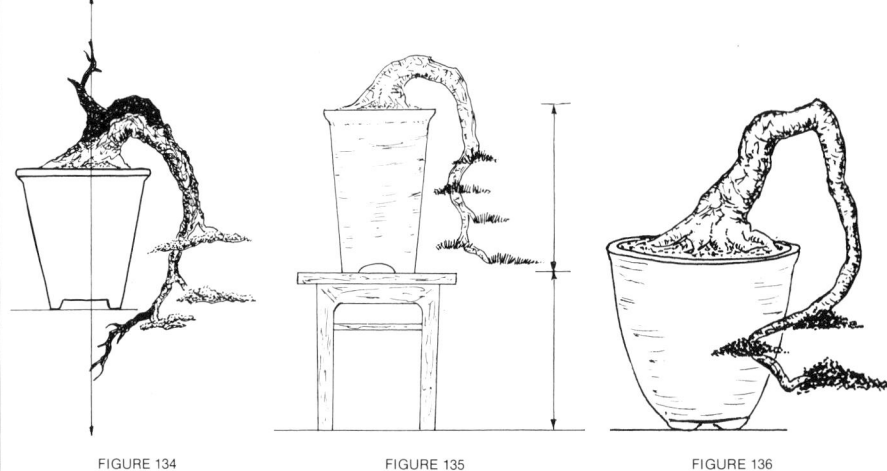

FIGURE 134   FIGURE 135   FIGURE 136

on page 48, even if it means growing the tree on its side for a while, before replacing it in the upright deep pot again. Keeping a container filled with water directly under the tip of the tail encourages its growth, as will the selective use of foliar fertiliser on the tail only.

ROOT-OVER-ROCK STYLE — SEKI-JOJU

In this style the tree is growing on a rock but has its roots embedded in the soil on which the rock is placed, and thus gets its nourishment from a reasonably large amount of soil in the pot. There is no problem when the time arrives to replace the soil. The tree must give the appearance of having germinated in a hollow in the rock, from where the roots were sent out in search of nourishment, while clinging to the rock. When choosing a rock for the purpose, bear in mind that the miniature landscape you are creating must look entirely natural. The rock must have some form of a hollow in which the seed might have germinated.

The choice of rock

A rock means much more to the Chinese than to a Westerner, and even more to the Japanese. This perception is described in more detail in Chapter 9 on 'Displaying bonsai', where *suiseki* is detailed. The rock which is used, for whichever purpose — *ishi-zuke*, *seki-joju*, *suiseki* or as *ishi-uye* — must be selected with care. When the tree is grown in a rock which is shaped like a container, somewhat saucer-shaped, it is called *ishi-uye*.

Rocks which have darker brown and grey colours are preferred. Use a very hard kind of rock, free of holes and not porous to prevent roots from entering and eventually splitting the rock. A vertical white line in the rock, perhaps formed by the presence of a quartz, can be used to symbolise a waterfall.

> HAIKU
> *Such stillness*
> *The cries of the cicadas*
> *Sink into the rocks*
>
> MATSUO BASHO
> From: The Narrow Road of Oku

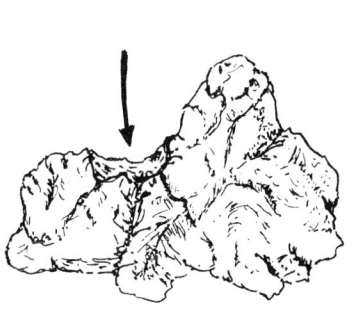 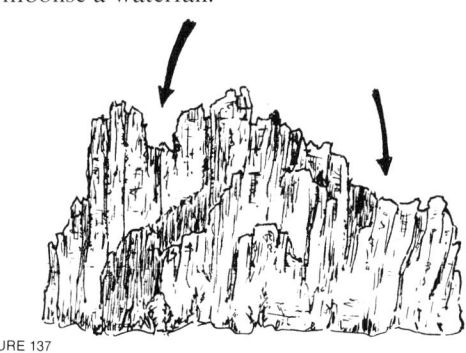

FIGURE 137

FIGURE 137 The arrows show where trees could be growing.

FAR LEFT
Species unknown
Height: 40 cm
Owner: Pieter Loubser

LEFT
Taxodium distichum
Swamp cypress
Height: 70 cm
Owner: Derry Ralph

BELOW LEFT
Cedrus deodara
Himalayan cedar or deodar cedar
Height: 53 cm
Owner: Eddie van der Westhuizen

RIGHT
Juniperus virginiana
Pencil cedar
Height: 60 cm
Owner: Eddie van der Westhuizen

FAR RIGHT
Ligustrum
English privet
Height: 42 cm
Owner: Eddie van der Westhuizen

BELOW RIGHT
Ulmus parvifolia
Chinese elm
Height: 80 cm
Owner: Eddie van der Westhuizen

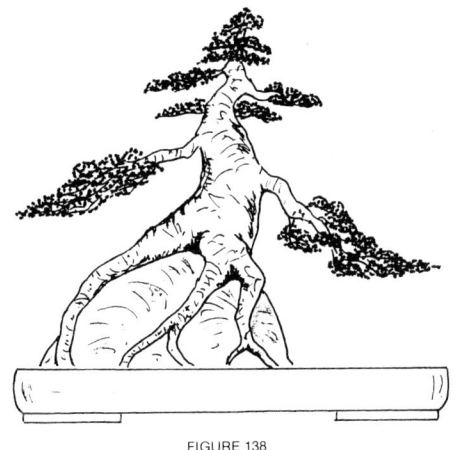
FIGURE 138

FIGURE 139

FIGURE 138 This is oversimplified, but it is done to stress the point that the tree must not overwhelm the small rock, nor may the rock be ball- or sphere-shaped. Note the shallow pot used.

FIGURE 139 The slats are gradually removed as the roots develop, thus exposing the whole rock with the roots growing over it.

The surface texture of the rock may vary from rough and craggy to smooth, depending on the scene you wish to create. Make sure the rock is neither too large nor too small, as it will then either dominate the scene or disappear underneath the tree. You must have a pretty good idea of the eventual size of the tree when choosing your rock. Do not use one with a side that has recently been broken off, unless this is the underside. The underside must be flat to prevent the rock from falling over: in other words stable enough to support the tree. The rock must have a front side. The front and top sides are of equal importance, because the front side is the one seen all the time and the top side carries the tree. Exceptionally the tree may be grown from the side of the rock. In the case of rocks that are flatter in shape, the tree should be growing on the top surface, whilst with rocks that are more vertical in nature, the tree should be growing from some tiny ledge on the side.

Occasionally you may find that the roots will not adapt to the rock-surface. It is then permissible to fill the gap with home-made tufa rock; merely assure that shade and texture are the same as those of the original rock.

Rock-settings are grown in shallow pots to accentuate the rocks with the roots developed over them.

Many species of trees are suitable for this style, including figs, trident maples, Chinese elms, *Celtis* and junipers.

There are different techniques to grow the root-over-rock style, two of which are described here.

(a) If the roots are long enough to reach over the rock and into the soil, you can make a box out of wooden slats which are placed horizontally to enable you to remove them layer by layer as the roots develop. Fill the box with the soil mixture, which must be on the sandy side to induce root-development.

The tree is placed on the rock with its roots spread out. Place rock and tree on the soil in the box and cover the loose root ends in the soil. These roots will then grow downwards into the soil in the box and thicken well, if the foliage is allowed to develop vigorously. To appear natural, the roots must be in close contact with the rock where they are above the surface of the soil; otherwise the tree would look like a spider standing spreadeagled over the rock. There are various ways to keep the roots against the rock, but perhaps the easiest one is to stick the roots to the rock with wet clay soil. The only problem with this method is that the clay must be kept wet. (See Chapter 7 on 'Soil') You can also tie the roots to the rock-surface by drilling small holes in the rock and cementing pins (nails) into the holes with epoxy glue (putty). Attach string to the pins and tighten the string, thereby pinning down the roots. Protect the roots by placing paper cushions (fold paper into small blocks)

FIGURE 140 Tie the roots to the rock with string, over a paper pad. The paper will eventually rot away, but by then the roots will be stabilised.

FIGURE 141 A root-over-rock bonsai in a shallow pot.

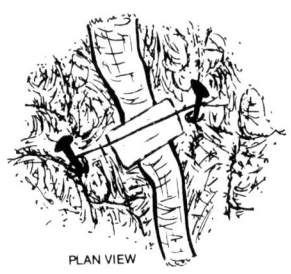

FIGURE 140

FIGURE 141

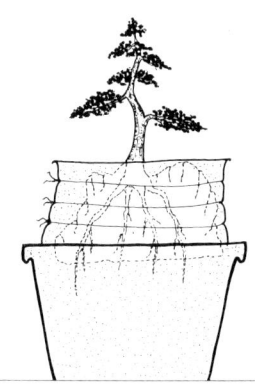

FIGURE 142 Around the rock is a foam-rubber or stocking cylinder filled with soil. Do not have a mass of small roots over the rock, because the growth will be shared by all, whereas if there are only a few they will develop into thick roots clasping the rock.

between string and root. Still another way to get the roots to develop against the rock initially, is to drape the young flexible roots over the rock and cover the roots and rock with a piece of tin foil (the kind used in the kitchen), then moulding the foil to the surface of the rock. The foil should be punctured with a sharp instrument at random over its whole surface to allow moisture to reach the roots inside the foil shell. The whole rock in the foil covering is then placed in a container or garden and completely covered with sandy growing medium. The weight of the growing medium keeps the tin foil tight enough against the rock to force the roots to develop in close contact with the rock. When enough roots have developed and to great enough length, the foil is removed and the roots could be tied to the rock with string or raffia, buried in the garden for a year or two and then exposed whilst the tree is developed further. Be sure to fold the roots in under the rock when they are long enough, to ensure that the roots will develop a permanent grip on the rock. Alternatively development could be continued in the wooden box.

After a few months the first layer of wooden slats is removed, exposing the roots and forcing them to grow deeper into the box. This is repeated till the roots have developed sufficiently, whereafter the tree is placed in the usual shallow container.

If the roots are too short to reach into the soil initially, simply place the rock and tree in the box, cover the roots and rock with soil, and proceed as described above.
(b) The second method entails making a foam-rubber cylinder to keep the soil in contact with the roots. After the roots have been fixed to the rock as in the first method, this foam cylinder is tied gently around the rock with string. Fill the cylinder with soil. Tie an old nylon stocking around the foam cylinder to prevent the soil from washing through the foam-rubber. Plant the whole contraption in a growing pot, covering the rock with soil. When you are satisfied that the roots have developed far enough, the stocking and foam cylinder are cut away starting at the top and gradually exposing the roots. Once the roots have thickened enough, the rock and tree are transferred to an ordinary pot. You may well find that the developed roots are now able to reach the soil and you will need to grow the tree as in method one for a while, before the tree is transferred to an ordinary pot.

THE ROCK-CLINGING STYLE — ISHI-ZUKE

Imagine a scene in nature where a tree (or trees) is growing against the side of a vertical rock or cliff. Transfer the scene to the bonsai world. This style is called *ishi-zuke*. It is reminiscent of the *saikei* art in that it represents a nature scene. The roots of the trees do not leave the rock, which means that the tree has to survive on such nutrition as it can glean from the soil in the little hollow or crevice in which it is growing.

The choice of rock is important, as is the case with *seki-joju*. The rock should resemble mountainous terrain. It must look old and craggy and it must have a vertical nature. The rock or rocks must have hollows or crevices which can contain some soil from which the tree can grow. A rock with horizontal markings looks

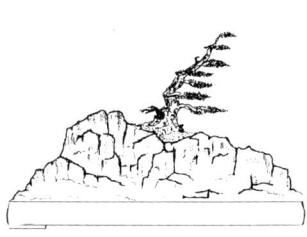

FIGURE 143 A windswept tree standing on a rocky outcrop.

shorter than a similar one with vertical lines or crevices. The purpose is to have the rock look like a cliff, and a rock with vertical markings enhances this appearance.

The trickiest hurdle to overcome, is to have the trees in the right proportion to the size of the rock(s). It must look like a normal tree in a particular scene. An enormous tree, or a few big ones, on relatively tiny rocks would be grossly out of proportion. If dwarf tree varieties are used, the problem will be easier to solve than trying to miniaturise normally growing trees.

Another problem is to prevent the trees from falling off the rock or coming loose from their position. You can drill small holes in the rock and fix wire loops into these holes with epoxy glue or putty. The trees are then tied into position using string of wire. Use string if you are sure that in time the tree will stabilise itself by means of its roots, because string decays. Use copper coloured aluminium wire because iron will rust and copper will oxidise. Also, certain trees react unfavourably to copper.

FIGURE 144 This rock, for *ishi-zuke* purposes, should give the impression of a landscape or mountain rather than a single large rock as in Figure 137, because in this case the whole tree has to grow on the rock as in Figure 145.

The rocks themselves may require fixing to the pot, in some way, to stabilise them. One way is to flatten the base of the rock. You can also support the rock with epoxy putty or smaller stones, or even tie the rock to the pot by means of aluminium wire through the drainage holes, making sure these wires are invisible. The rocks must not simply stand in the pot, they should rather be standing in gravel or perhaps even water to create an island effect. The gravel must be of a complementary colour to the rock.

Usually you would have the top part of the rock visible above the highest tree.

Because of the restricting conditions in which the trees grow, they need special soil. This soil must be sticky enough to prevent it simply being washed off the roots. It must have the ability to help hold the tree in position, must contain substantial nutrients and retain water. So-called 'muck' is made up to have just these properties. Mix either cattle manure or well-rotted compost with clay, in a 50/50 ratio. If cattle manure is used, some fermentation is likely and this process must be allowed to finish, without the muck drying out. Some slow release fertiliser and bonemeal can be kneaded into the muck, which can be stored for future use in sealed plastic bags to prevent it drying out. Another muck formula is equal parts of clay and humus kneaded together with water till it has the consistency of soft plasticine. You also get a reasonably sticky muck mixture by kneading peat humus (60%) and long fibre sphagnum moss (40%), together with water.

FIGURE 145 A few trees growing on a rocky mountain.

When you are ready to plant trees, the rocks must be soaked in water to get the muck to adhere to the rock. The trees are anchored to the rocks and the roots, especially the smaller ones, are literally stuck to the rock with the muck. Cover as much of the muck as possible with moss. The moss will help to prevent the muck drying out and also from being washed off the roots. Because of the high clay content of the muck it must not be allowed to dry out, as it will not wet easily again. By far the best method is to use a fine spray to keep moss and muck wet.

I have used another practical, albeit unsightly, method to keep a rock-planting wet. A large plastic container, like a 2 litre bottle, is filled with water, punctured above and below with a needle and positioned above the rock. The water then drips onto the rock, keeping it wet. The puncture on the top surface is necessary to prevent a vacuum forming inside the bottle as a result of keeping the screw-on cap in place, a necessary precaution against mosquitoes and other bugs. This method encourages moss to grow on the constantly damp rock.

The replacement of the soil, in the case of *ishi-zuke*, is a problem, as the tree cannot be removed without damaging the rootlets which have become embedded in the rock. The soil has to be replaced in the form of slices (wedges) or blocks, which are cut, lifted out and replaced.

FIGURE 146 The rock container could be used to disguise the weakly developed root-system on the left of this tree, instead of using individual rocks or grass. It gives the impression of the tree being held in the supporting hand of its creator.

FIGURE 147 A simple hollow rock used as container.

ROCK-CONTAINER — ISHI-UYE

A hollow rock can be used as a container, instead of a pot. This rock must be saucer-shaped and the tree is simply planted in the hollow, as in an ordinary pot. Any style of tree can be grown. The rock will not be as porous as a pot, and will not have drainage holes, although it is not impossible to drill holes through the rock. If you don't drill holes for drainage you must be very careful not to drown the tree; the soil, however, being shallow, does dry out quickly, reducing the risk. (See Figure 146 and 147)

EXPOSED ROOTS STYLE — NE-AGARI

This style must be understood well because it does not mean simply exposing the tree's roots above the soil surface. When the roots are exposed, it must be in an exaggerated way, even to the extent that they appear to be part of the trunk.

The roots can be plaited or bent into severe curves. You must imagine that the tree is standing in an area where the soil has been washed away from the roots to expose them. The trunk and roots must appear as one unit, and not as though the trunk has been positioned on top of some other tree's roots, where it does not belong.

When the roots are plaited together, in time they will fuse to form one thick root. Fig trees do this with ease. Even if roots are close against each other, or where one roots crosses another, they will fuse together.

The branches can be arranged into any style, as long as it suits the character of the exposed roots. You would not like rough-textured, curled roots growing under a smooth, evenly tapering trunk.

There are two methods of growing these trees to expose the roots artificially:
(a) Plant a young tree in a deep container, such as a wooden box, which contains a sandy soil to promote quicker root-development. In the following spring the roots are inspected and the unwanted ones are removed. The tree is once again repotted in the same container, with a new soil mixture, but this time only the lower half of the roots which obviously include the root-tips, are covered with soil. The rest of the root-system which is closest to the base of the trunk, is left exposed. The tree itself will need some form of prop, because the roots will not be able to support it, and this can be done by tying it to a stake, or by supporting it with a wooden block

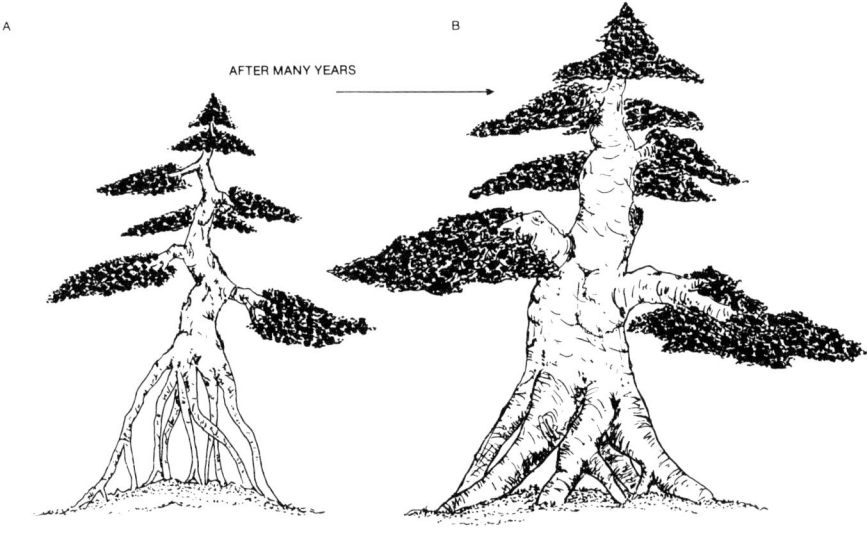

FIGURE 148
A. This tree seems to be planted on top of some roots, where the tree does not belong.
B. This tree forms a unit with its exposed roots, as opposed to the tree in Figure 148A.

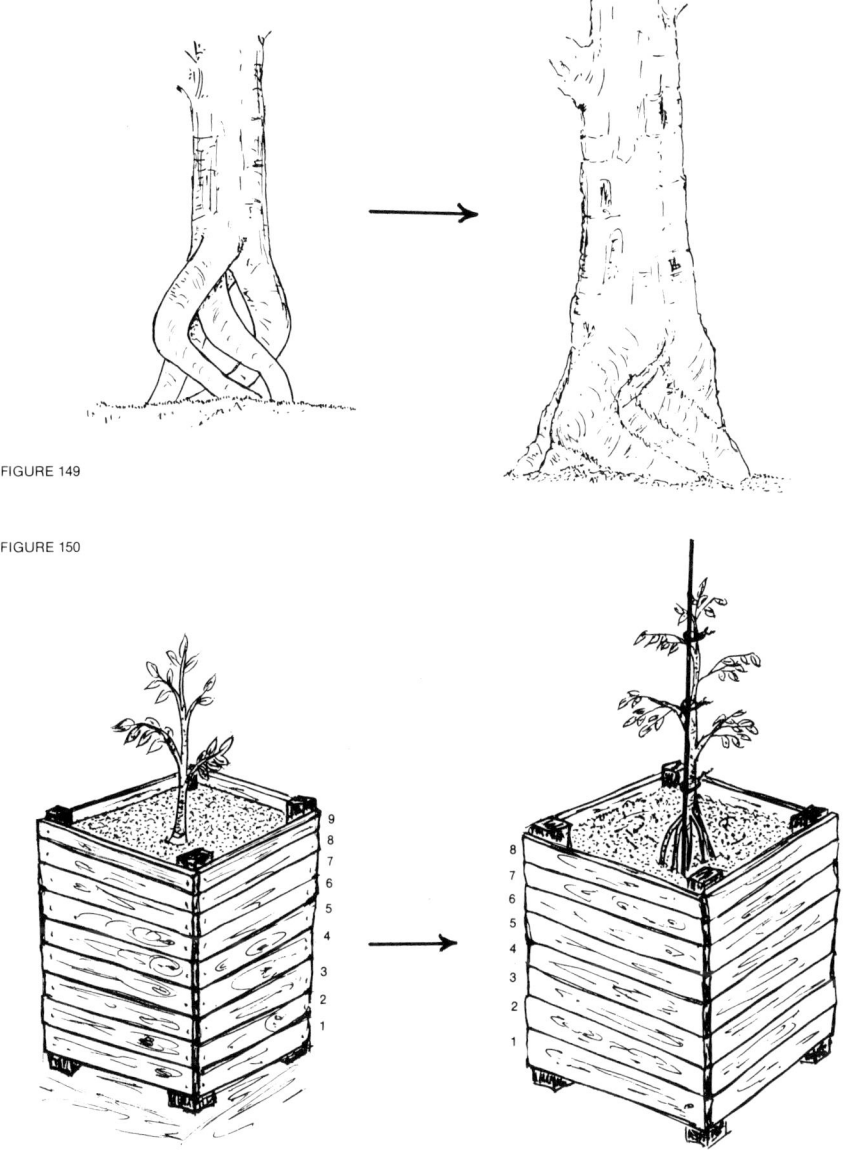

FIGURE 149

FIGURE 149 This way of plaiting the roots looks, in most cases, artificial, although the end result will look like a tree that has aged quite naturally.

FIGURE 150

FIGURE 150 Plant the tree in a wooden box with horizontal slats, and as the roots develop the slats are removed to expose the roots. The tree will need support.

underneath and between the roots. Repeat the procedure until the desired root length has been reached. Even then the tree will need support for some time before it can stand on its own, while the roots gradually thicken.

(b) The second method entails using a plastic tube which is filled with sandy soil. The tree is positioned so that its roots hang into the tube. The tube is then carefully filled with a sandy soil mixture. The advantage of this method is that it seems to make it easier to support the tree; in other respects both methods are virtually the same. The tube is supported to enable it to stand in some sort of container. The tube can be cut away at the top every few months to gradually expose the lengthening roots; less risky than doing it all at once. This is similar to the method of developing roots in the root-over-rock style, where a wooden box with horizontal slats is used. In fact the same method can be used here. As the roots are exposed, the tree is going to need support, and when they have grown to an adequate length and thickness, the process is terminated.

FIGURE 151 Plant the tree in a plastic cylinder and as the roots develop the plastic is reduced.

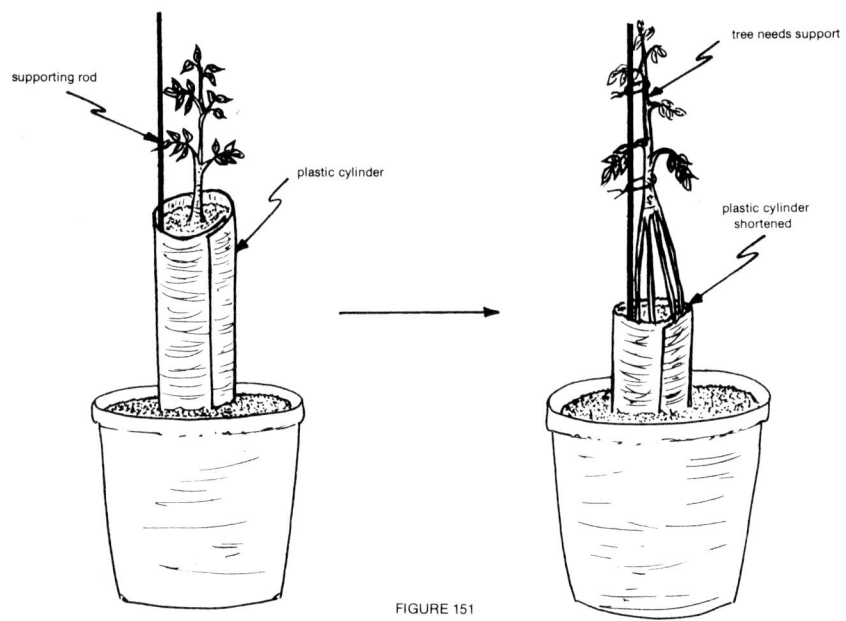

FIGURE 151

With both methods you should allow the foliage to grow profusely, as this promotes root development. Continuous cutting back of the foliage impedes the development of a large root system — the rule of supply and demand! Even once the roots have reached the required length and have been bent, shaped and positioned in the shallower training container, it may still take some months of training before they will support the tree without help.

You need to bend and plait the roots while they are still young and flexible. As years go by and the roots thicken these curves will even out to a degree, simply because the roots are thicker. You will find that the plaited roots grow together completely, so much so that it even becomes impossible to see that they were plaited. The roots appear to be the trunk, and have a beautiful craggy, uneven surface; gradually they will become covered with bark. This happens because they are exposed to the dry air. (Underground the bark also forms, but it is continuously absorbed!)

The shape of pot to be used depends on the overall height, the thickness of the roots, whether the roots have fused and, to a degree, on the crown shape.

RAFT AND SINUOUS STYLES — IKADA-BUKI AND NETSU-RANARI

The two styles are virtually the same but differ in the manner in which they are created. Both styles represent a group of seemingly individual trees, which somehow share the same root-system. The raft style has all the trees in a nearly straight line and is the result of a tree having fallen on its side, with the upward-facing branches having grown into individual trees. The sinuous style may develop in the same way, but with a tree which did not have a straight trunk; or it may happen that branches which are now lying horizontally also give rise to new trees from their upward-growing branchlets. Generally however one finds a wandering surface root, sprouting trees in a haphazard way.

Well-grown raft and sinuous styles are difficult to distinguish from one another.

A very interesting tree is the wild fig near Pretoria (*F. salicifolia*) which is an incredible size, and although it seems to be many trees, is one original tree, which became so large that its branches, due to their weight, touched the ground and sprouted roots there. The result is a variation of the sinuous style with the mother tree in the middle and surrounding it, concentric rings of offspring — all one tree!

One advantage is that you can use a tree with one-sided branching to create a raft style. This kind of tree would otherwise have to be used in a group planting or you would have to apply difficult techniques to either twist the tree to rearrange its branches, or improve its appearance by grafting.

One of the benefits of raft or sinuous style planting is that seemingly individual trees have the same properties. These trees will, if they are deciduous, sprout their leafbuds at the same time, develop the same autumn colours at the same time, and they will shed their leaves as a unit.

The same rules for basic styling or appearance apply as for any bonsai — especially group plantings. The overall shape must be in the form of a triangle, the group could have one dominant tree, no trunks may cross one another and there must be a three-dimensional appearance (not a row of trees with no depth).

It is reasonably easy to create the raft or sinuous style from a tree lying on its side. Choose a tree which has more or less one-sided branching. Do this at any time except during winter. A tree still in its plastic container, acquired from a nursery, is placed on its side and the container kept in its original state with the roots intact. The branches must be pointing upwards and the unnecessary branches, for instance the very short ones and the ones growing downwards, must be removed. The curve of the trunk should be towards the back for a better three-dimensional effect.

A strong, thick wire is now attached to the tree with thinner tie-wires. This wire is then bent into the required shape, along with the trunk of the mother tree. The free ends of the tie-wires should be long enough to project above the surface of the soil, once the tree has been placed into the soil of the training container. These free ends serve as markers when the wires need to be removed. The thick wire must be on the upper surface of the horizontal trunk, to facilitate removal. If this is not done, the wire will become entangled in the new root system. The present vertically growing branches (future trunks) may need support or anchorage, and this is achieved by using wire which is anchored to the thick horizontal wire or to the trunk.

The next step is to induce root-formation in the trunk from its under-surface. These roots need to replace the roots which are still growing and functioning in the original plastic bag. Cut flaps into the trunk on its under-surface. The cuts must be

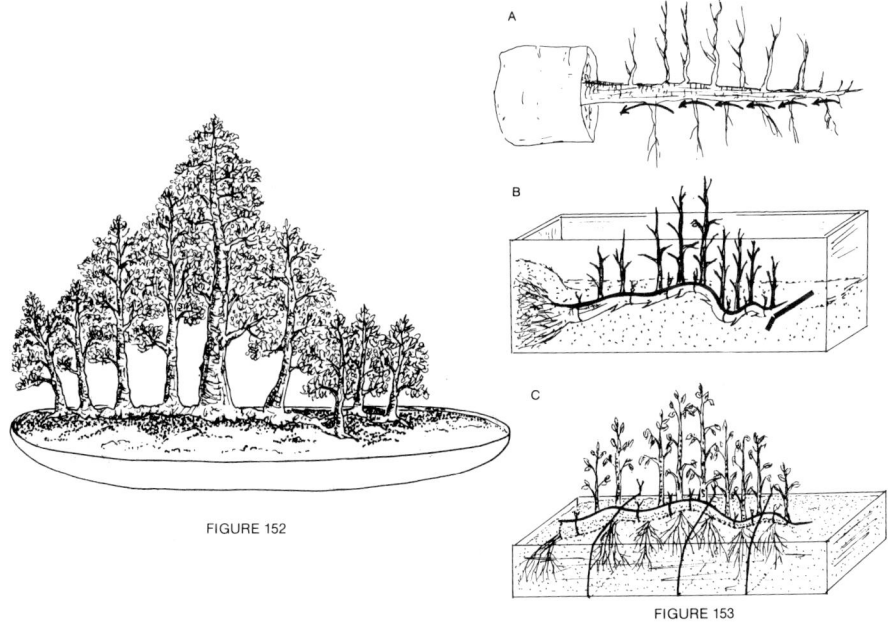

FIGURE 152 The raft style.

FIGURE 153
A. The lower branches, as the tree is lying on its side, are removed.
B. The whole tree in a wooden box, with the trunk buried. The trunk is tied to a thick training wire which lies on top of the trunk. Cuts, to ensure root-formation, are made on the underside.
C. The tree is placed in a training container. The original root ball is cut off and the wound sealed. The foliage is allowed to grow.

FIGURE 154 Better dimension is created by the vertical deviation as well as horizontal contouring.

FIGURE 155 A bird's eye view of the raft style. For a three-dimensional appearance the side branches are used.

FIGURE 154

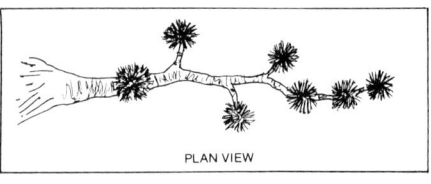

PLAN VIEW

FIGURE 155

in the direction of the growing tip and must be about a third of the diameter of the trunk in depth. If the cuts are done this way, the sap returning from the leaves accumulates in the flap and promotes root-formation. Wet the flaps and apply a rooting compound. To prevent the flaps from closing and healing over, a small pebble can be squeezed into the cut. The whole plastic bag is now removed and the tree is planted into a large training container. A wooden box is ideal for this purpose as it can be taken apart when the roots have developed after about a year or two. Pine trees are slower to respond. The soil mixture should be on the sandy side to promote root development and also to ensure easier uprooting of the trees when the roots have developed. The horizontal trunk must be covered with approximately 5 cm of soil. In the first place, if it is less than 5 cm, the soil may dry out and kill the new tender roots — a very real possibility because the soil is sandy; in the second place it must be remembered that the closer the trunk is to the surface, the more light will penetrate, and it is known that roots develop better in the dark. On the other hand, if the trunk is too deep, roots might develop from the upright branches instead of the cuts! The original rootball must be completely covered with soil, even if it means building a small compartment to have the soil at a higher level.

Once the new roots have developed and are able to nourish the trees, the original rootball is cut off and the cut sealed. Apart from doing whatever is necessary for the purposes of general design, the new trunks must be allowed to develop unhindered, as this promotes root growth. When the new roots have established themselves, the raft is planted in a shallower container, but with the trunk now only partially embedded. Only when it has completely recovered and new foliage has started developing, should further pruning be attempted.

A note of caution. It is true that once a tree is established, any movement of the trunk, for instance due to wind, will help to increase the girth of the trunk and also encourage root development which will serve to better anchor the tree, but if any movement is allowed before the roots have developed, this will retard or completely prevent formation of roots. This means that the newly planted tree, which has to develop into the raft, must also be anchored to the container in which it is growing.

It is very important that this group of trees presents a natural appearance. Even if they are in a reasonably straight line (*ikada-buki* = raft style from fallen trunk) you should create depth in the forward-backward dimension by having forward and backward growing branches. Remember to have the ones at the back project somewhat further to the back than the forward ones project forwards. It is an interesting variation to have curves in the trunk in a vertical direction as well. The daughter trunks must sprout from the convexity of each curve.

Another possibility is to employ horizontally growing branches to develop trees to the side of the main horizontal trunk. This helps to create a natural three-dimensional arrangement. It is easy enough to accomplish, because you simply include a few horizontal branches in your design. They are staked out horizontally and if they have vertical branchlets, the branch is severed behind the branchlet, the cut is sealed and the branchlet is anchored vertically. For root-formation, a cut is also made on the underside of the branch. If, however, the branch does not have a

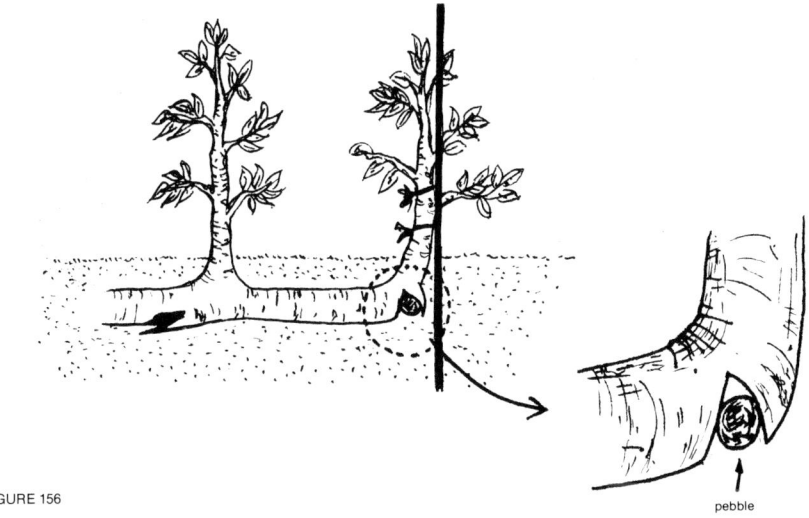

FIGURE 156

FIGURE 156 Nick the growing tip and tie it upwards.

branchlet, its tip can be bent upwards after having been wired. If it won't bend well enough, it can be nicked on the outside of the bend, which will have the added benefit of forming roots at the neck.

Different methods employed in ground-layering can be used to induce the formation of roots.

THE CLUMP OR SPROUT STYLE — KABUDACHI

The stump or turtle-back style is very similar to the clump or sprout style, and the two styles will be discussed together. Both are a group of trunks growing from one base. In the case of the sprout style, the division into individual trunks happens at or around soil level, while with the turtle-back style, the trees grow from a hump which has its own root system. In the sprout style each tree will still have its own roots, although the roots seem to be shared.

In nature the sprout style develops in different ways. It may be the result of a few seeds germinating close to each other, with the trunks then gradually fusing at soil level. It can easily be artificially reproduced by tying a few trees together at soil level and waiting for them to develop. Another method is to drill a few holes through a thin piece of wood and thread a sapling through each hole. The holes must be about four millimetres in diameter. The saplings must be positioned so that their roots are just under the wooden board and then the whole unit is planted in the garden with the board about two centimetres under the soil. The saplings will increase in size and soon the openings in the board will be acting like a tourniquet forcing the small trunks to swell out above the holes. In time these swellings will fuse together to form a sprout style tree. Roots will also develop above the board and, once this has happened, the original roots under the board can be cut off and the sprout group can be separated from the wood and planted in a training container.

A common way of forming a sprout or the turtle-back style is when suckers develop from the base of a tree or from the roots next to the original trunk. The wild olive, flowering quince and serissa species like doing this.

A special occurrence is where a pine cone falls on the ground and some of the seeds in the cone germinate at the same time. These develop and merge into a multi-trunked tree. This is called *yama-yori*.

You may be lucky enough to come across a natural sprout or turtle-back style group of trees which you are allowed to uproot, but a reasonably easy way to acquire tree material for this purpose is to air-layer a tree which has branches sprouting on the same level. (See Figure 159)

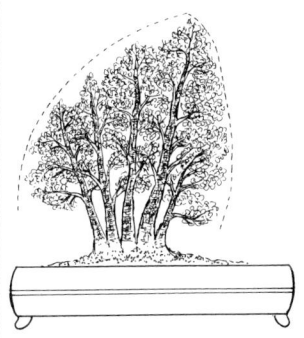

FIGURE 157 The clump or sprout style. The bases of the trees have joined, but they will still have individual root systems. In this instance the foliage forms a rounded-off triangle and the pot is in harmony with the soft lines of the foliage.

FIGURE 158 The humpback style.

89

FIGURE 159 Air-layering just below a cluster of branches.

FIGURE 160 New growth in the right direction — that is, outwards.

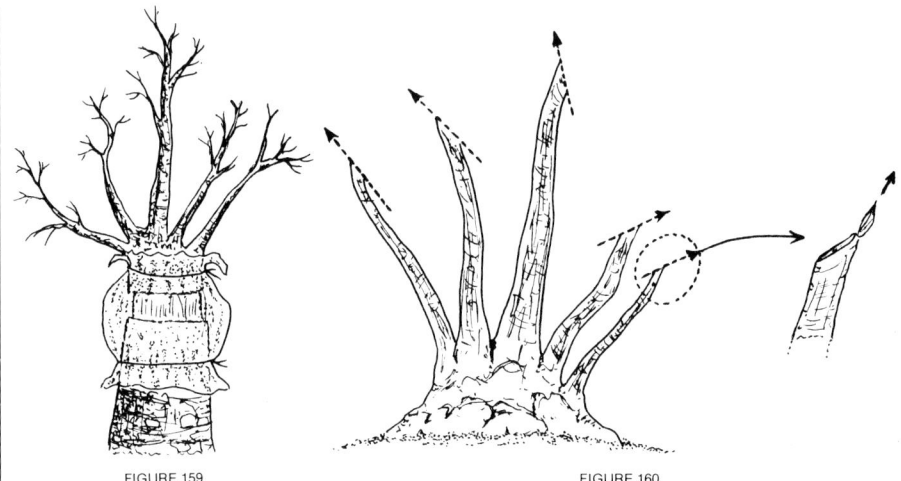

Another technique, although more risky, is to severely trim back a trunk or simply to cut it off above soil-level, and in so doing create a severe imbalance between demand and supply of nutrients. This sometimes results in development of new trunks from the edges of the cut, or around the base of the trunk.

When pruning the trunks, or branches, the cut surface must face inwards, to cause the growing tip to grow outwards, as shown in Figure 160.

Whatever the shape of the foliage, triangular or umbrella, just stick to the rules applied to a group-planting.

BROOM STYLE — HOKI-ZUKURI

This is a crown in the shape of a broom — not the usual triangular shape. I have come across the term *besom* style, which refers to a broom made out of a bundle of twigs, and because the broom style is especially appreciated during winter when it is leafless, this term is quite appropriate.

The tree resembles an upturned broom, a fairly common shape in nature. The trunk is reasonably straight and without branches for about one third to half of its length. The bristle part of the broom, in other words the branches and leaves, can be grown in two ways.
(a) The branches all sprout from the trunk at approximately the same level, and only about three or five primary branches are used.
(b) The branches sprout in an alternate way, close to each other, for some way up the trunk until only the apex continues.

If you want to grow a tree in the broom style you can use one of the trees bought at a nursery, of which the lower branches have been removed and which has a bare trunk for some distance before the branches start. Try to get one with a tapering trunk, so that it doesn't look like a pole planted in the ground. Here are two methods of creating a broom style.
(a) Using a seedling, plant it in a training container and ensure that the trunk will grow straight upwards, by tying it to a stake if necessary. When it is about 20–30 cm tall the tree must be pruned during spring to leave only three or perhaps five buds or young branches, if they grow close enough to each other. They should face in the normal left, right and backward directions. Be sure to leave the main trunk in the middle, although you may have to shorten it. Let the buds or branches develop until you judge them to have the required diameter. They are then pruned back to a length equal to half or two thirds of the length of the main trunk. From then on pruning is done to create smaller branching to form a compact crown. Branches

FIGURE 161 The broom style.

FIGURE 162 The broom style with the branches growing in the usual left, right, back spiral.

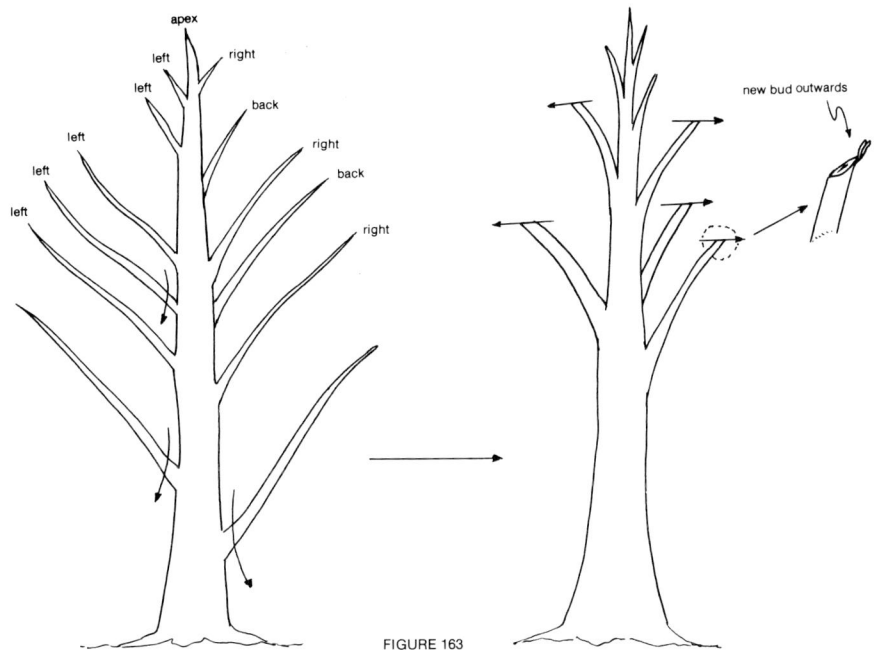

FIGURE 163 The branches are cut at about half their length, with the cut surface facing inwards to force growth outwards.

may need wire-training to correct their positions, as the ideal broom-bonsai has no branches crossing each other. When cutting a branch, the wound must face inwards to have the new branch growing outwards.

(b) Using nursery stock with a straight tapering trunk, no lower branches and good rootage, cut the trunk off at a point approximately three times the diameter of the trunk. (See Fig. 164) Cut the trunk in a 'V' shape which is slightly off-centre to avoid the new branches forming symmetrically. With a larger trunk, hollow out some of the heart-wood, without damaging the cambium. With a thinner trunk, drill a shallow hole in the 'V'. This should be done when the tree is still dormant. Once this has been done, tie tape or string around the 'V' to prevent the healing callus tissue forming bulges when the branches start to develop at the cut edge. As soon as the new shoots have established themselves, the tape or string has to be removed,

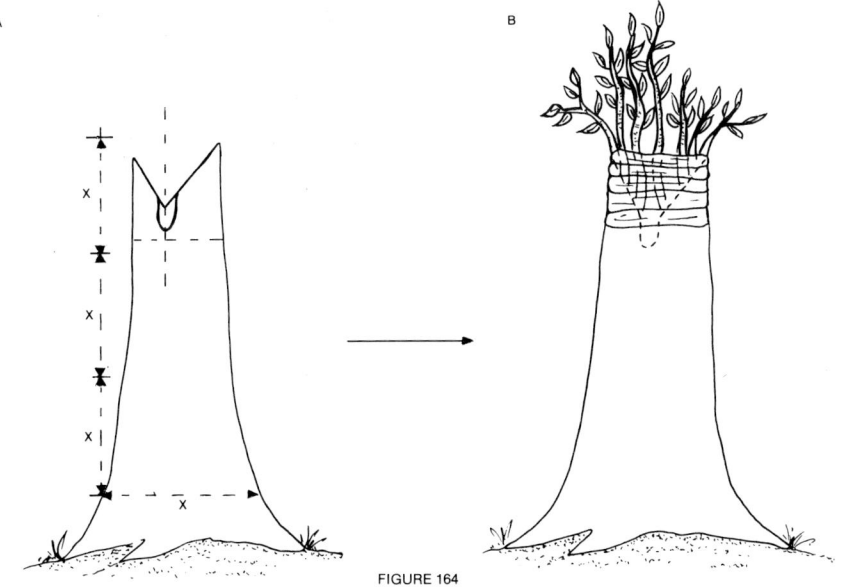

FIGURE 164
A. The 'V' is slightly offcentre. A small hole is drilled down the centre of the 'V'. The total length of the trunk is three times the diameter of the trunk at the base.
B. Tape is tied around the trunk to prevent bulges forming as the cambium starts forming new branches.

otherwise it works like a tourniquet, and a bulge will develop above it. Another method is to tie pieces of cut garden hose around it. Shape and tie a plastic funnel around the cut end and fill it with sphagnum or peatmoss to keep it wet. The whole tree could be kept under a plastic transparent covering — a kind of hothouse — till the tree starts developing.

In autumn all the twigs needed are cut back to a length equal to one third or half the length of the original trunk, and the others removed completely. When the twigs develop it will be with a good taper. The rest of the procedure is the same as for the first method.

Trees that style easily as broom-bonsai are trident maples, zelkovas and Chinese elms. Deciduous trees are preferred, because when the trees are in leaf, the beautiful pattern of branch development is obscured and these bonsai are therefore most appreciated during winter.

BALL OR SPHERE SHAPE — TAMA-ZUKURI

There is little to say about this style aside from the fact that the tree should have a reasonably straight trunk from which the branches then form a round, ball-like shape. There are many examples of this style in nature. It is an exception (like the flame style) in that it could have lower branches that are smaller than the higher ones.

FLAME SHAPE — ROSOKU-ZUKURI

The flame-shaped tree is often seen. Ginkgo trees are popularly trained in this shape. The flame's shape varies from narrow to wide. The trunk has to be straight.

UMBRELLA STYLE — KASA-ZUKURI

In the umbrella-shaped style there are two variations. The first has almost no apex at all, while the second has a definite apex, albeit not as prominent as in the traditional triangle. The trunk is curved and branchless in the lower portions. This variety is typical of the acacias, where a group of branches sprout close to each other and in fact a central trunk cannot be discerned. There are no secondary branches till high up, where the leaves are carried. The acacias even tend to have this umbrella shape as a group of trees.

The umbrella shape crown is popular in the *bunjin* style.

WEEPING BRANCHES STYLE — SHIDARE-ZUKURI

The weeping-branch style is self-explanatory. It is important to have only the branches weeping — not the trunk or leaves or flowers. The branches should

FIGURE 165 As with the broom style, the round and flame-shaped styles look very beautiful during winter when they have shed their leaves and are appreciated for their branches.

FIGURE 166 The flame shape.

FIGURE 167 The umbrella shape with a definite apex. The apex is situated formally over the base of the trunk.

FIGURE 168 Here the umbrella looks like an upside-down triangle. It is virtually flat-topped.

FIGURE 169 The *bunjin* umbrella.

FIGURE 170 The weeping style.

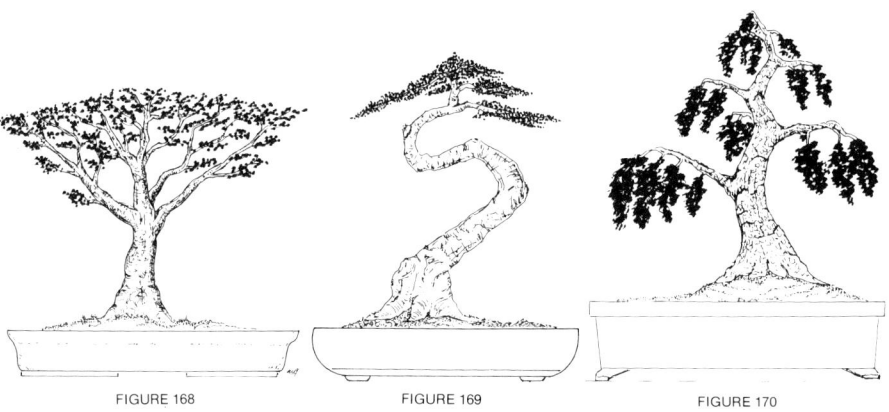

preferably even grow slightly upwards before bending down to weep. The trunk could be in virtually any style, but must be strong and impart the impression of sturdiness to counteract the fragility of the thin weeping branches. The willow is an obvious choice but is difficult to handle. The *Ficus benjamina* also has a weeping tendency and you could try the bougainvillea which has masses of flowers, or rather leaves which look like flowers.

OCTOPUS STYLE — TAKO-ZUKURI

The octopus style seems slightly chaotic in that it has long spindly branches, which have severe curves and resemble the multi-directional arms of an octopus.

SPIDER STYLE — KUMO

In this style the exposed roots are spread to look like the legs of a spider. The base of the trunk from which the roots develop is at the same time the apex, for the branches grow from about the same level and are spread horizontally, wider than the roots.

LITERATI STYLE — BUNJIN

This is an abstract style for which only guidelines can be given. No specific rules govern this style, as in the case of *chokkan* or *kengai* and others. It seems, in many instances, that *bunjin* ignores the rules applied to other styles. An important feature of *bunjin* is its simplicity. This is also why it is called the *literati* style, referring to the group of Literati who did not want to be restricted by the complicated rules of society. In China, many years ago, there were three ways in which a person could become part of the higher class in society, namely: (i) being born into it, (ii) being a leader of a powerful gang of crooks, and (iii) through studying, writing government exams and so becoming a literate person. This last group of people was called the *literati*. It is reported that the literati grew and tended to trees in pots, in places like the court yards, and that these trees were shaped as we know *bunjin* today.

Bunjin is expressive; it conveys feeling and is highly symbolic. It tries to portray the effects of wind, rain, snow and drought dramatically, but with simplicity.

The most important element of *bunjin* is the trunk. The trunk must be visible for 60–75% of its total length. The foliage should be unobtrusive but in a way which is complementary to the trunk. The foliage is there to show that the tree has survived the onslaught of nature and is alive. It also helps to balance the trunk in an aesthetic sense. If the foliage is abundant, it tends to contradict the rough texture of the trunk (in many instances), and the angular, sometimes harsh curves thereof. The trunk of

FIGURE 171 The arms of the octopus are spread in all directions — somewhat chaotic.

FIGURE 172 A very contrived style. The spider.

FIGURE 173 The very simple and plain *bunjin*.

FIGURE 174

FIGURE 175

FIGURE 174 A tree which has been warped by weather extremes and is only left with a few branches and little foliage.

FIGURE 175 By reducing the excessive foliage, the whole picture is more pleasing and relaxed.

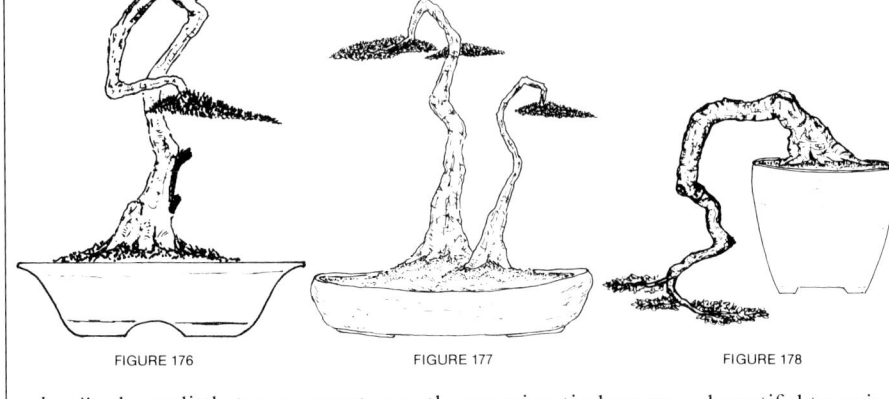

FIGURE 176 A *bunjin* with only the barest foliage but interesting curves in the trunk.

FIGURE 177 Twin trees as *bunjin*.

FIGURE 178 A *bunjin* cascade.

a *bunjin* shows little taper except near the growing tip because a beautiful tapering trunk will lead your eyes away from the trunk towards the foliage. The same applies to an obvious branch lower down on the trunk, where the eyes would be led along the branch and away from the all-important trunk.

The branches, few as there are, may cross the trunk — a violation of the general rules. The trunk may even cross in front or behind itself.

Bunjin are planted in relatively small and shallow pots with shapes varying from round to somewhat unusual.

Bunjin can be grown as a style on its own, but it can also be incorporated in the double trunk, cascade, slanting and group planting styles. The *Acacia erioloba* has a natural *bunjin* trunk tendency, especially in groups.

WINDSWEPT STYLE — FUKI-NAGASHI

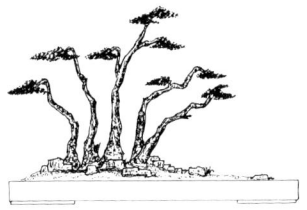

FIGURE 179 A *bunjin* group.

The windswept style is described as though it is a style of its own, but it is in reality only a description of the branch positions of one of the other styles, like slanting, literati, semi-cascade, informal upright and even group plantings. It is a style which allows the imagination excellent scope. The branches are alive, there is movement.

Two effects can be simulated: the effect of branches being blown in a particular direction at that particular moment, or the effect of years of winds which have permanently warped the tree. To make it seem as though the wind is blowing at that particular moment, only the smaller branches are bent in the wind's direction. When all the branches and even the trunk are bent in the wind's direction it shows that the wind has permanently deformed the tree over a long span of time.

FIGURE 180 A windswept tree with only the smaller branches and leaves being blown sideways.

The normal stylistic rules apply, although one would use less branches to prevent crowding and the resultant loss of visual impact. Always keep a triangle in mind and use back branches to create depth. The sturdy trunk must be anchored by strong roots, applying the same rule as for cascades, or else the tree will seem in danger of falling over. Once again, the tree should be positioned towards the so-called windward side of the pot, in other words, with the branches blowing over the empty part of the pot.

Jin and *shari* fit into the windblown picture. Smaller branches in particular, which are *jinned*, create a natural appearance.

Use trees with thicker trunks because if the trunk is thin you will get the impression that the tree will break under the force of the wind.

FIGURE 181 The effect of continuous wind with the branches permanently bent.

Large-leaved trees are not suited to this style, but small-leaved and in particular needle-foliaged trees are ideal. Be sure to have sparse foliage especially closer to the trunk, as this is indicative of a tree being exposed to the harsh winds which have stripped some of the leaves off the branches. The foliage should be as far away from the wind as possible (whilst still being visually pleasing), as if the wind has lessened by the time it reaches the foliage. As the wind blows from a certain direction it will strip the leaves from the branches where the wind first contacts the leaves and because these first leaves and branches act as a windbreak or obstruction, the effect is less on the parts further away from the wind. The shape of the foliage unit on each branch will be similar to the wing of an aeroplane (as seen on cross-section) to lessen the effect of the wind. It can also be seen as a triangle or rather diamond shape (refer to Chapter 2) of which the sharp corners have been rounded by the abrasion of the wind.

GROUP PLANTING — YOSE-UYE

The group planting could be anything from five to about forty trees. It presents one with a chance to use young trees with good effect. It is also the place where trees with shortcomings, which cannot be used as single trees, may be utilised. In mentioning the use of defective trees the point is stressed that in a group planting, it is the group that counts and *not* the individual trees. The total impact is what matters and single trees with their faults are just part of the whole. A tree with a defect such as one-sided branching finds an excellent spot on the edge of the group as this is exactly what is wanted there. Defects which take the form of ugly scars due to bad pruning are not acceptable. Trees with few or no lower branches are grouped together with great success.

The following general approach should be followed:
- The group as a whole should form a triangle or whichever overall shape is required.
- Choose an uneven number of trees, unless there are so many that the eye cannot easily discern how many trees are used.
- In a small group, no tree may be seen to be in front of another from *any* direction. No trunk may cross another, unless it occurs in a very dense grouping.
- Generally trees of the same species are used, and even then one tries to use trees which have the same characteristics, such as shedding leaves at the same time or having the same autumn colours. When using different species of trees, try to get trees with the same soil and moisture requirements.
- Plant the trees at varying distances from each other, as in nature, and not as if this were a man-made plantation. Do not place every tree on a little mound of soil because it looks artificial and trees simply do not grow that way in nature. Have the soil surface undulating in a natural irregular fashion, varying the level, usually with the taller trees also at the highest places.
- Plant the trees so that the distance from the edge of the container to the smallest tree on the side of the group is greater than the distance from the edge of the container to the larger tree on the side. (See Figure 188) This guideline does not apply if the container is virtually filled with trees.
- The area which is without trees is of extreme importance and should appear absolutely natural. If this effect is not achieved, the whole scene will be spoiled. Carefully select the area where the trees are going to stand in the pot. Do not simply

FIGURE 182 On the windward side the trunk shows signs of dead wood in the form of *jin* and *shari*. The bark is weathered on the rest of the tree and the foliage is not abundant — all showing the hardship the tree is experiencing.

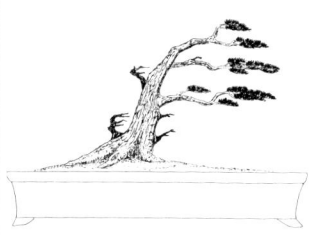

FIGURE 183 The windswept tree, with every branch as well as the apex bent over to one side.

FIGURE 184 A group of five trees forming one unit.

FIGURE 185 A group of twenty-three trees forming the unit, although made up of two triangles.

FIGURE 186 The outline forms a triangle and here you are concerned only with the branches on the outside of the group. There are three variations in the angles the trunks can assume. In this case it is in a fan shape with the trees slanting towards both sides.

FIGURE 187 The second variation of the fan shape, with the trees slanting towards two sides — slanting from the left over to the right — always towards the smaller trees.

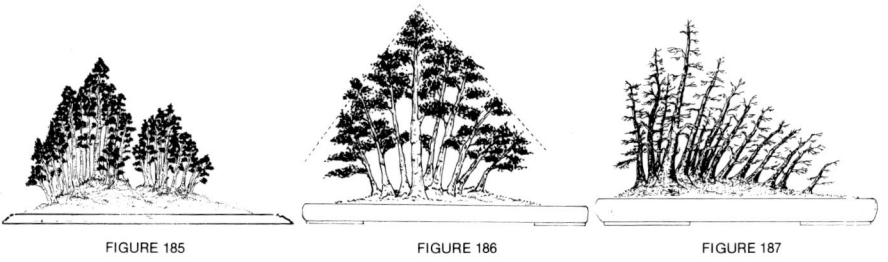

FIGURE 185   FIGURE 186   FIGURE 187

FIGURE 188 The third variation of the fan shape has all the trees growing upright.

FIGURE 189 Trees slanting in the direction of the taller tree are incorrect.

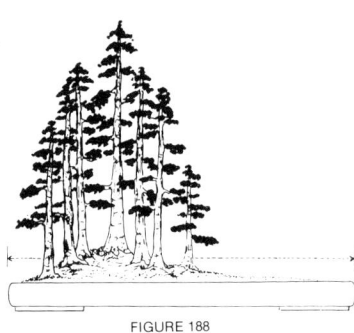

FIGURE 188

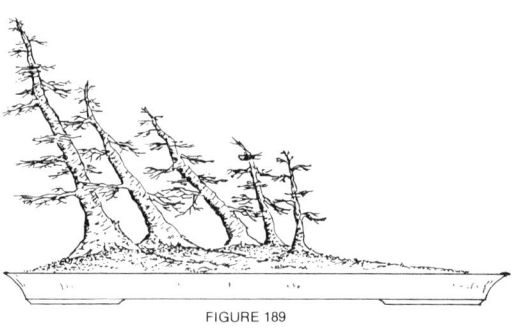

FIGURE 189

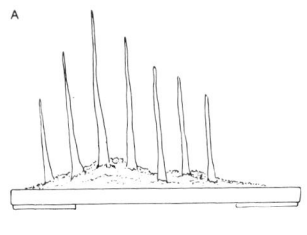

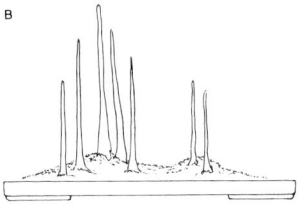

FIGURE 190
A. With all the trees upright and evenly spaced the impression is that of artificiality.
B. In this example all the trees are still upright but due to the uneven spacing it looks natural.

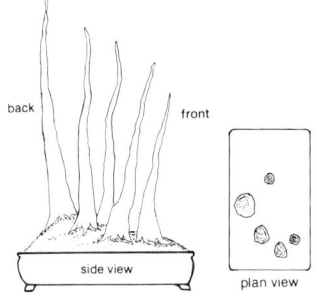

FIGURE 191 A sideview of a group planting to show that no trunks cross each other. This is a so-called distant view with all the smaller trees closer to the viewer (but seen from the side!)

FIGURE 192 A view from above of a group planting. The diameter of the trunks should also give an indication of height. The thicker trunks will belong to taller trees. The direction of the branches should in general be towards open spaces. This means that branches must not grow into one another, as they would naturally grow away from each other to reach towards the light.

splash the trees all over the container.
- Retain the branches which point sidewards and backwards. Remove the branches pointing towards other trees, or shorten them, else they will be growing into the neighbouring trees which is not natural.
- Trees in a forest tend to grow upright, away from each other to gain access to sunlight, which means that they tend to have branches higher up, with long bare trunks. This is especially true where they grow close together.
- There are two perspectives of a group planting: a close-up view and a view from far-off. These are easy enough to create. For a close-up view, the front trees are taller and for a distant view, the trees at the back must be the taller ones. It is a matter of perspective that the closer you get to an object like a tree or a building the larger it seems while those far away seem small. The overall scene you are going to depict is your own choice and there is a wide variety of different moods and views: standing close to the group, standing further away, looking up at them or looking downwards, standing between them, with flat terrain or an undulating surface, rocky or marshy appearance, trees growing undisturbed and abundantly or under strenuous conditions, and more. Even the container you use has an effect on the impression you create: for example where a slab of slate will seem to give the scene no boundaries, a square shallow container will look like a section of a forest having been cut out.

The Method of Planting a *Yose-ue*

Select trees and remember that ones which have branches to one side only can be utilised as well as younger trees. Do not use trees with ugly scars unless these scars can be 'beautified' to look natural and complement the total impression.

Study the trees and decide on their positions in the group. While they are still in their present containers, place them in their approximate relation to each other and,

FIGURE 192

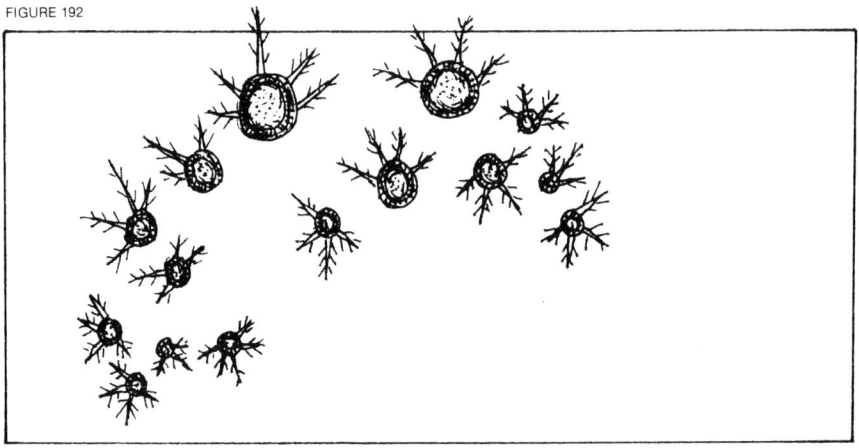

FAR LEFT
Ulmus parvifolia
Chinese elm
Height: 65 cm
Owner: Eddie van der Westhuizen

LEFT
Juniperus
Height: 32 cm
Owner: Eddie van der Westhuizen

BELOW LEFT
Pyracantha
Fire thorn
Height: 40 cm
Owner: Eddie van der Westhuizen

RIGHT
Ligustrum
English privet
Height: 33 cm
Width: 40 cm
Owner: Alf Jones

BELOW RIGHT
Celtis africana and *Celtis sinensis*
White stinkwood and Hackberry
Height: 70 cm
Width: 85 cm
Owner: Alf Jones

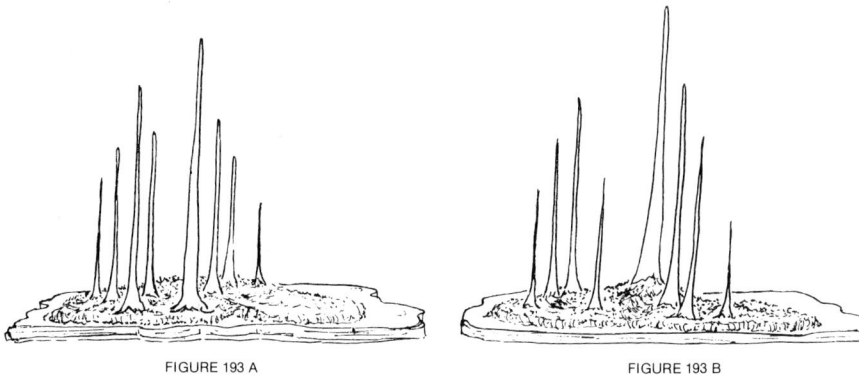

FIGURE 193
A. A close-up view of the group — the taller trees at the front.
B. A far-off view — the smaller trees at the front.

while imagining their final positions, roughly prune them. Detailed pruning follows after all the trees have been finally positioned.

After the pruning they are removed from their containers, roots are pruned and they are placed in their final positions. The reason for not removing them from their containers at an earlier stage is because the process might take a long time and there is a risk of the roots drying out.

The roots underneath the pruned and removed branches are generally removed. If two or more trees stand close together, drastic rootpruning is necessary on the sides facing each other to enable you to place the trees close to each other. Whilst positioning the trees you may have to use various means to hold them steady, until the growing medium has been added, and in many cases even afterwards. Wooden pegs can be used as temporary support, as well as stiff wire and wooden wedges.

It may be necessary to support some trees till the roots have developed sufficiently to prevent them falling over.

The same initial care must be taken as with any other transplanting or repotting. However, a problem will arise when the soil needs replacing. Here are two approaches to this problem.

- Make a sketch of the exact positions of the trees. Separate them and remove them from the soil. The roots can then be trimmed, the soil replaced and the trees put back in their original positions.
- With a sharp bladed instrument the soil is removed between trees in the form of wedges, like slices of a pie, and replaced. The position from which the wedge was removed should be noted on a sketch of the planting. The following year a wedge is removed next to the previous one. Repeat this process so that the soil is completely replaced every three to four years.

It is interesting to note that using nine trees in a group is considered uninteresting. A Japanese word with the same pronunciation as nine, *ku*, means pain or suffering and superstitiously *ku* should be avoided, having similar connotations as the number thirteen for the Westerner.

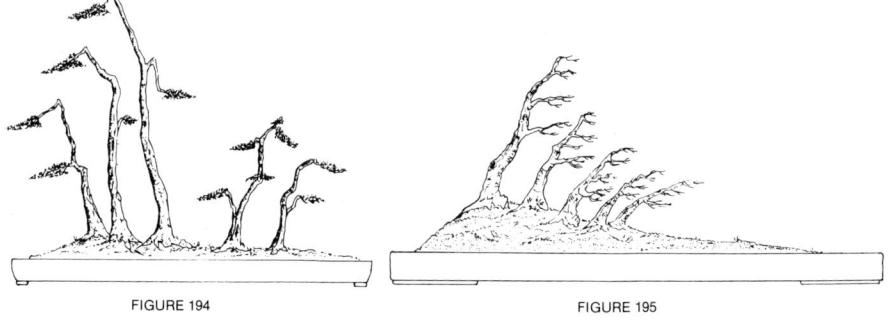

FIGURE 194 A group planting but with the trees in the *bunjin* style.

FIGURE 195 The apparent movement of the windswept style is over the container, but could also be in the opposite direction, i.e. over the short side.

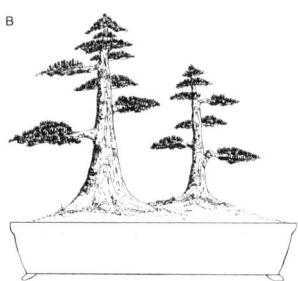

FIGURE 196
A. The larger tree is in front, but with the smaller tree close to it as though supporting the taller tree. It is called '*Fu-lao*'.
B. The smaller tree stands further away and it seems as though the taller tree is leading the smaller one. It is called '*Hsieh yo*'.

FIGURE 197 Two trees in a deep pot.

FIGURE 198 Two trees in a shallow pot.

FIGURE 199 A double trunk with a sharp 'V' notch between the two trunks at soil level.

There are three variations to the sidewards angle at which the trunks can slope. Figure 188 shows all the trunks upright and Figure 187 shows all the trunks at a slant (windswept?), but still all in the same direction. Figure 186 is a fan shape, which mixes upright and slanted trees — in this case both to the left and the right. As shown in Figure 189 the slant is also in one direction, but now towards the taller trees and this is visually wrong.

An unusual approach to *yose-ue* is to arrange the branches in a windswept position or alternatively as *bunjin*. In the case of the windswept group, be sure that the trees are all bending their branches in the same direction, and do not have too many trees as the larger quantity of foliage would obscure the effect of the wind on the individual branches. With *bunjin*, also have only a few trees and keep foliage and branches to a minimum.

TWO TREES AND DOUBLE TRUNK STYLES — SOJU AND SOKAN

The double trunk and twin tree planting are very similar to each other and both are in a sense group plantings, the only difference between the two being whether they share the same roots or not, i.e. shared roots would be twin trunk and individual roots systems give a two tree setting. In pines they are often referred to as *aioi-no-matsu* or *meoto-matsu*, that is 'Mr and Mrs Pine' and they are like two companions who will go through life's hardships or pleasures together.

The height and diameter of the two trees should be different and perhaps seen in a 'mother and child' relationship. The thicker tree must be the taller of the two and with the same ratio as the widths of the trunks. A very interesting variation on this theme is where the younger tree may be the taller one, as this would indicate the younger child supporting the aged mother, and perhaps even leading the older woman.

When pruning the trees the cut surface should face inwards to promote outward direction of new growth, or the two cuts should be in the same direction. If the cuts both face outwards, the new growth will force the new branches or apices to cross each other. (See Figure 160).

The two trees should be positioned in such a way that one stands slightly behind and to the side of the other to create a feeling of depth. Never have one tree directly in front of the other, or standing right next to it. The container can be deep or shallow.

When you are working with a double trunk the division between the trunks should be no higher than the base and in a 'V' shape not a 'U'.

Usually the two trunks and apex follow the same direction. Exceptions are where one trunk is upright and the other cascades, or where two trunks separate but the branches are windswept in the same direction.

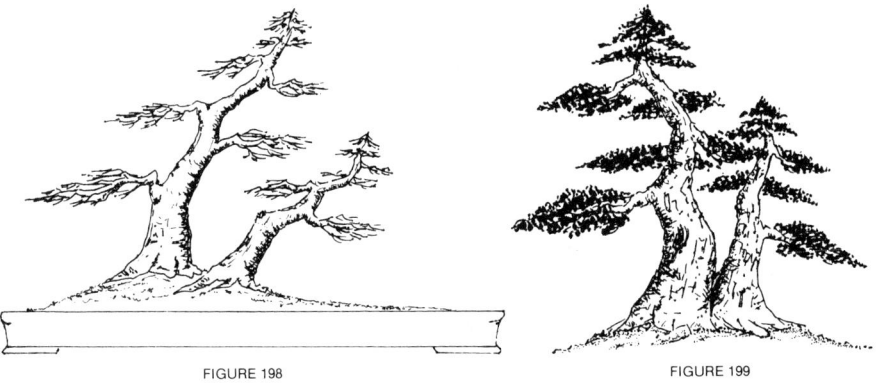

FIGURE 198 FIGURE 199

FIGURE 200

FIGURE 201

FIGURE 200 the notch between the two trunks is a 'U' shape and this should be changed to a 'V'. The notch should be at soil level.

FIGURE 201 The two trunks follow about the same directions in their curves and the apices point in the same direction. The branches are shared with the two trees forming one unit. The same principle is followed with a double trunk. The two apices may diverge as long as approximately 2/3 to 3/4 of the trunks follow the same direction.

An undesirable situation is where trunks separate, then grow towards each other and separate again.

Ensure that the texture of the two trunks is the same. It would be wrong to have one trunk with *jin* and *shari* while the other is without any signs of weathering. Do not have one trunk with a smooth bark while its partner is rough and full of knobs and scars, because you will not find this contradiction in nature — two trunks next to each other would be exposed to the same conditions.

With two trunks close together, the branches are treated as belonging to a single tree:

- Don't have branches at the same level.
- The first branch should belong to the smaller tree.
- Branches should not cross the trunks in the front.

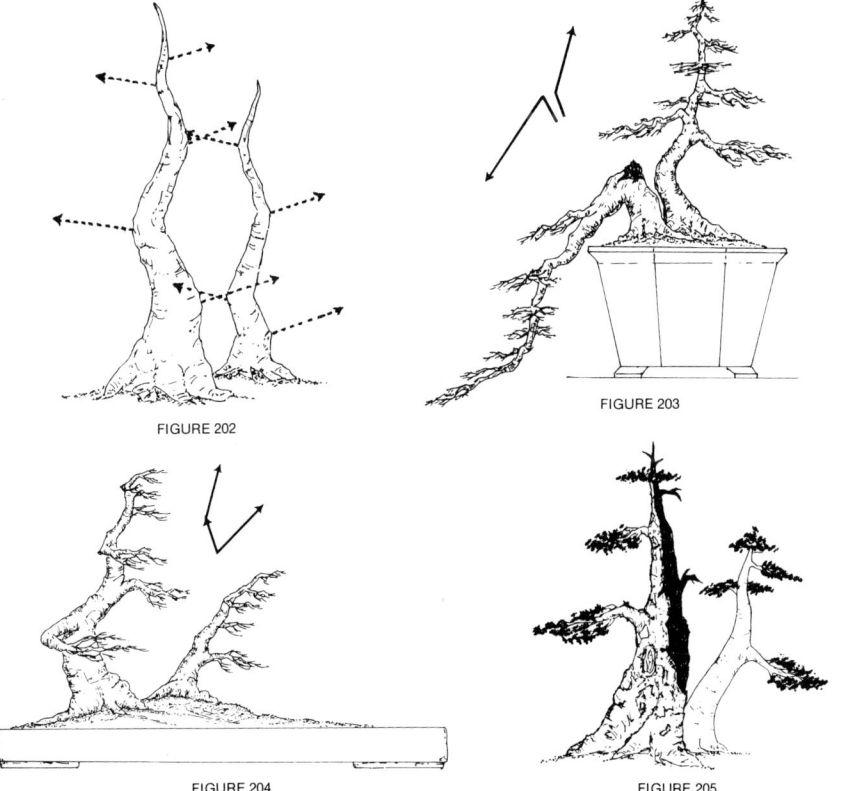

FIGURE 202

FIGURE 203

FIGURE 204

FIGURE 205

FIGURE 202 These two trunks show exactly opposite movements. They are not in harmony. Placing of the branches becomes virtually impossible, because you want the branches on the outside of the trunk curves, even if the curves had been in the opposite direction as shown.

FIGURE 203 With two trunks (or trees) and one cascading, the upright tree acts as the balancing 'head', while the cascading tree is the 'tail'.

FIGURE 204 In this instance the trees are separating from each other in direction but the overall slant is towards the same side, and the branches which portray the windswept atmosphere, combine the two trees into one unit.

FIGURE 205 The two trunks (or trees) do not form a matching couple, due to the difference in bark texture and aged appearance. On the other hand, it symbolises the aged being supported by the younger. (See also Figure 196)

- There must not be a branch of the taller tree directly over the apex of the shorter tree, because normally the smaller tree would be growing away from this shadow-causing obstruction above it.

The oft mentioned principle of foliage in the shape of a triangle or ball, etc. applies as ever, but with the two trees considered as one unit.

TRADITIONAL PINE SHAPE — MATSU-ZUKURI

From approximately 1800 to 1830 the taste in Japan for growing plants particularly for their flowers was replaced by a taste for trees to be appreciated for their foliage and branches. During that time writings were published to delineate the standards for these trees, among them the 'Somoku Kinyoshu' in 1829. In this work was a description of the classic pine bonsai: 'The classic pine bonsai is a tree in which neither the trunk of the tree, the roots, nor the balance of the right and left branches has any front or back, and which has no taboo branches from whichever side it is viewed ... From base to top, it should show no cut-off branches; it should be free of faults such as bent branches or uneven curves in the trunk. And it should present convincingly the appearance of an aged pine, with no sign of artifice remaining, from every viewpoint.'

So strict were these rules that an expert in growing pines (a *matsushi*) was considered very fortunate if he accomplished more than one in his lifetime. There was even a show at the Maruyama-no-ryo in the Kyoto district for these particular pines.

In this 'style' the classical triangular shape is used, but the trunk need not be straight. Presently it need not even be a pine specimen as long as the rules for branch arrangement are strictly adhered to, along with the other specifications as mentioned.

BAOBAB STYLE

The most impressive feature of this style is the massive trunk, with sparse and simple branching only high up on the trunk. The trunk dwarfs the rest of the tree.

The baobab (*Adansonia digitata*) is also called the 'upsidedown tree', because of a legend which gives an indication of what the tree looks like. According to the folklore, the devil uprooted the baobab and then thrust the branches of the tree into the earth, with the roots taking the place of the branches. The trunk is formally

FIGURE 206 The very traditional triangular shape.

FIGURE 207 The smaller branches and leaves (when in season) are of less importance. They are entirely overpowered (visually) by the massive trunk. In fact the branches seem diminutive. Looking carefully the trunk gives off branches in the usual left, right and back sequence and the main branches are uneven in number.

FIGURE 206

FIGURE 207

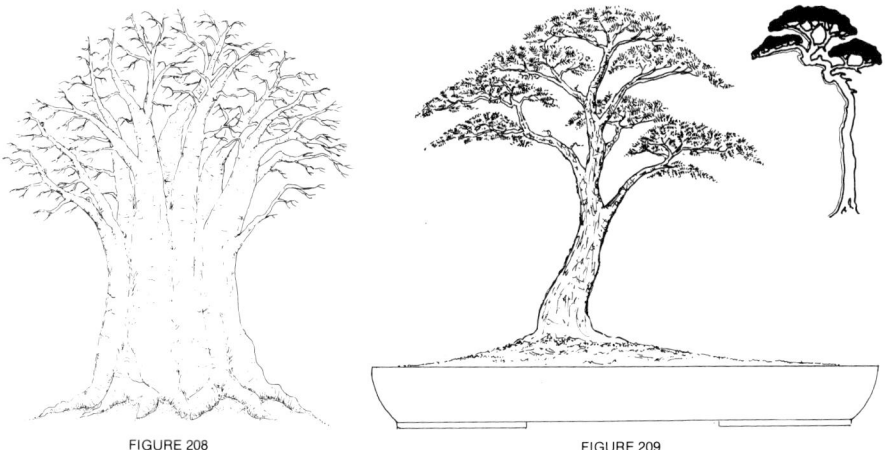

FIGURE 208 The baobab with seven trunks.

FIGURE 209 Placing this tree in a shallow pot with a lot of space around the trunk gives one the impression of a tree standing in a vast plain.

upright with the branches arranged in a fashion which is a variation of the broom style. The trunk must give the impression of sturdiness and stability and must show roots at the base to prevent it looking like a thick post in the ground. The trunk gives one the impression of many trunks fused together and this is in fact the way to create a trunk with this appearance. A few trees (any kind) are grown tightly against each other, with the bark removed in the approximating areas to facilitate their fusing together. It is also helpful to tie the trees together temporarily. The resulting trunk is uneven on the surface. This is a longterm project. Exactly the same technique is followed as is described under Thickening of the Trunk, on page 37.

The branches are not straight and pointing upwards as in the case of the formal broom style, but they are angularly twisted and could even curve downwards. The leaves are not plentiful and form a canopy on the ends of the branches, very like the Pierneef style. The smaller branches are mostly outward growing. The leaves are of less importance and should not detract from the tree due to their profusion.

The pots to be used should be on the deep side, but in diameter not much wider than the massive trunk, so as to emphasise the latter.

PIERNEEF STYLE

The Pierneef style is a variation of the umbrella style, based on the paintings of the renowned South African, J H Pierneef, and created by using especially the *Acacia tortilis* as subject matter. The trees consist of a main trunk which is bare of branches for approximately 80% of its height. Even where branches are given off at a lower level, they are once again void of secondary branching till just before the ends of the branches. The trunk and branches should be grown in the clip-and-grow manner to ensure angular bends, instead of gentle smooth curves. From the main trunk the branches sprout upwards and sidewards as a framework to form the 'spokes' of a wheel or umbrella. The finer branches grow upwards, and near the edge of the umbrella they spread horizontally and even bend downwards. The smallest branches grow in all directions to form the canvas section of the umbrella. The leaves make up a small portion of the total, and are only present to fill in the outer section or edge of the umbrella. The tree may have more than one umbrella, and the style can also be used in a group planting. In nature one also notices trees which split up into a few trunks with no single one dominating and all the trunks together form either a few umbrellas or one large umbrella.

Because this is an elegant style the pots must not be dominant, sturdy, strong or rugged looking; they should rather be dainty with soft outlines.

The acacia species lend themselves to this style naturally. In fact the acacias were

FIGURE 210 A group of trees on a rocky outcrop. The overall shape of the foliage is still roughly a triangle, but divided up into individual 'Pierneef canopies'.

FIGURE 211
A. 'Pierneef' with many trunks but only one canopy of foliage.
B. Note how a different container improves the appearance.

FIGURE 211 A

FIGURE 211 B

the trees which Pierneef portrayed in this unique style.

Trees are allowed more than one trunk, each with its own smaller canopy of leaves.

FLAT-CROWN STYLE

In nature the *Acacia sieberana* (paperbark) and *Albizia adianthifolia* (flat-crown false thorn) typically form these flat crowns, which could be likened to an umbrella which has been opened too far, or perhaps to a funnel.

The stronger branches grow outwards in a fan shape. They may originate close together on the trunk. The smaller branches grow inwards which prevents an apex forming.

FIGURE 212 The flat-crown style.

FIGURE 212

SPECIAL TECHNIQUES OF CHARACTERISATION

6

The following descriptions could perhaps come under the heading 'styles', but I prefer to call them modifications of the trunk, as they could all be incorporated in the aforementioned styles. One could say that they are used to create a more natural appearance, although with the plainted trunk *pien-tshu* and perhaps also the twisted trunks in *horai* and *nejikan*, this would be stretching the point somewhat.

HOLLOW TRUNK — SABA-MIKI OR SABAKAN

Saba-miki means a 'hollow trunk'. It might be the effect of the damage caused by lightning, or a branch ripped off by strong wind. This scar on the trunk may face forwards, without detracting from the value of the tree; in fact it enhances the appearance. It is a way of disguising the scar left by removing a thick branch. The trunk is hollowed out by means of a chisel, taking care to shape the hollow so as to allow any water to flow out to prevent the area from rotting. Do not create *saba-miki* all the way down to ground level as the moisture from the soil will also start a rotting process on the scar. Today the hollowing out of the trunk is easily accomplished using power tools like drills with special bits.

When the tree has been chiselled away, allow the wood to dry out and then apply undiluted lime-sulphur (about two to three months later), to the dry wood. Be sure that the wood on the surface is dry or dead or else the lime-sulphur is going to detrimentally affect the tree. The lime-sulphur is called *jin* liquid by bonsai enthusiasts. If you do not like the white colour produced by the lime-sulphur, a few drops of black India ink could be added or even a few drops of any colour PVA paint as this is water soluble. Repeat this twice a year for three years or whenever the effect of the lime-sulphur has worn off, because the duration is going to vary according to the climate and exposure of the tree. Before applying subsequent coatings of lime-sulphur, the previous application should be sanded down. Always protect the nearby trunk and soil from exposure to the lime-sulphur by covering these surfaces with some protective cloth or plastic, as lime-sulphur will kill off healthy leaves, branches, roots or moss. Soon after the application, the exposed trunk will look white in colour, but this slowly disappears to leave the natural colour of the wood. The lime-sulphur acts as a preservative and prevents rotting of the exposed wood as well as closing the scar through healing growth, with the sulphur acting to prevent the rotting action of fungi and the lime to act as preservative. December, January and February are the most favourable months to apply the lime-sulphur treatment (in the southern hemisphere). Repeat this treatment a month later. Apply it at midday on a hot, dry day to enable the lime-sulphur to dry as quickly as possible.

The scar should be big enough to prevent the cambium from simply healing over the edges and closing the *saba-miki*. This is especially true in the case of deciduous trees or trees which heal easily, e.g. figs. Not all trees can be enhanced with *jin* or

Why does a bonsai grow old handsomely? Because it lives off as little as possible, uses the little as best possible and grows old little by little.

FIGURE 213 The *saba-miki* enhances the overall appearance of the tree, causing it to appear aged. The hollow trunk is so wide that it cannot be closed by reparative growth. In fact the 'rolling' of the cambium edges only improves the naturalness of the *saba-miki*.

FIGURE 214 *Saba-miki* and *jin* on a younger tree.

shari due to the softness of their wood, and especially so with *saba-miki*.

Saba-miki can be used in conjunction with *jin* or *shari* and the tree need not necessarily have a rugged appearance for the technique to be effective.

JIN AND SHARI

Jin is the dead *tip* of a branch or a trunk, while *shari* is a dead *strip* on a live branch, trunk or even exposed root. A *jin* may even include a whole branch along with its branchlets.

Jin and *shari,* and for that matter *saba-miki*, should only be used on trees with hardwood, like conifers, old acacias and olea. *Jin* and *shari* do not suit a young tree, or a tree with lush foliage, as they tend to impart a feeling of age or weathering, which must not contradict the general appearance of the tree.

Jin

Apart from the fact that a *jin* is used to make a tree look aged, it has a practical application where an apex or thick branch has to be shortened. Instead of trying to disguise it by growing other branches over the scar, the *jinned* portion is left as the apex or branch. When a *jin* appears as an apex of a tree, it is usual to have the *jin* in front of any live portion of a branch — the *jin* should not appear from behind some healthy foliage as if out of nowhere, although this rule is debatable.

There are two refinements which give the *jins* a different aesthetic appeal. In smooth *jin* the surface is smoothed with sandpaper. It has the appearance of having been weathered to a smooth finish. There should be no sharp points, ridges or grooves.

Rough *jin* has a rough, uneven surface and seems as though it is a more recent incident than in the case of the smooth *jin*.

The method of creating a *jin* is simple. Cut through the bark and cambium layer in a circular cut at the level where the *jin* must end. This is a precaution to prevent the bark from tearing off further than planned. The trunk or branch is cut off at the height at which the trunk or branch must end. The trunk or branch could be sawn

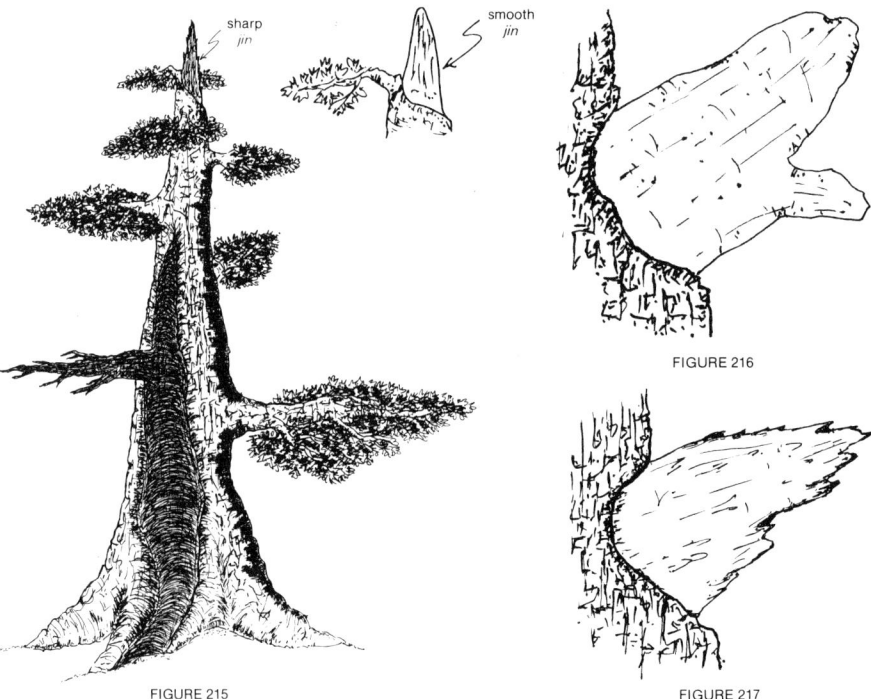

FIGURE 215 *Jin* and *shari* on one tree.

FIGURE 216 Smooth *jin*.

FIGURE 217 Rough *jin*.

through halfway (the trunk from any side and the branch from above) and the intact half gripped with pliers and pulled downwards. The remaining portion is then pulled down bit by bit till a tapering point is left. A trunk could also be split vertically a few times with sharp knife and the pieces then pulled downwards till they tear off.

Alternatively the tip may be crushed with pliers and then pieces ripped off till the desired shape has been reached. This usually leaves a rough *jin*. With the help of chisels and files the *jin* is refined as needed.

If the *jin* must be smooth, pliers are used to gently crush the bark just enough to loosen it from the cambium, whereafter it is stripped from the hardwood. Do not leave the tip sharp — it should be rounded off.

When considering *jin* on a bonsai, remember that it is easy enough to create *jin* on green wood because of its softness and controllable breakage, but is very difficult on dead wood that has already hardened. In the soft green wood, detail can be created easily, but nowadays, with power tools the hard, old wood is shaped quite readily.

In both cases, if the branch, or trunk, is alive while it is being *jinned*, it can be wired and bent to the desired shape as soon as the *jin* has been formed. After about three weeks, the *jin* will not contain any more sap and the wires can be removed. If the *jin* already consists of dead wood, it can be softened by steaming the *jin*, or by applying a cloth which has been soaked in boiling water for a few minutes.

Apply lime-sulphur as described with *saba-miki* to preserve the *jin*. Remember to apply it only after the *jin* has died completely.

Where a trunk is too thick to have a nice taper, it could be chiselled and whittled to look as if the trunk has been divided at the apex. These separated tips could be wired and shaped as required, while they are still alive, and when the tips have settled into their new positions the wire must be removed. Similarly, if a jin has formed but needs adjustment in position, the wood could be softened by wrapping towelling soaked in boiling water around the dead section for a while and thereafter wiring it and bending it. The wiring could be done beforehand because the wood will not stay soft for long.

Shari

Perhaps the *shari* could be seen as the lesser variation of the *jin*, because it does not involve the whole circumference of a trunk or branch. It is a longitudinal stripping of bark on a trunk, branch or root. It is similar to *saba-miki*, but not as severe, and could also be the result of a branch having been torn off by wind. The *shari* could even be in the form of a spiral up the trunk. *Shari* looks very good where it is the continuation of a *jin* going further down the trunk or branch.

Keep the *shari* from reaching soil level because the wet soil may cause it to rot. Also, do not have little pockets in the *shari* which are able to hold water. Rotting may be retarded or prevented if the dead wood is well preserved through the use of lime-sulphur. It is also advisable to have the top of the soil mixture very sandy to improve drainage of the surface soil. Try not to have moss growing against the dead area of the trunk, as it keeps the area moist. After many years you may, however, have to convert the *shari* into a hollow trunk due to the decaying wood. *Uro* is the extension of the hollow or split trunk to the ground level.

Shari is created by cutting a flap of bark loose and pulling it downwards, as far as required. Follow the grain of the wood. Do not end directly above the branch, as the branch may die back due to lack of sapflow from above.

If a *shari* is small, it should be temporarily sealed off to prevent the cambium growing over it again. It is a good idea to seal a *jin* and *shari* in any case, until the wood is dry, to prevent it from dying back further than intended. When applying lime-sulphur later on, be extremely careful not to drip it onto live tissue like leaves or the roots of the tree.

A somewhat drastic and even risky method of creating the dramatic appearance of a coiled trunk with *shari*, is the following: Use only a young and hardy tree like juniper, pine, cedar or cypress, and select one that has many small branches — in fact if they are more or less on one side it is even easier. With a sharp knife, start a cut at a point a little distance from the apex and split the trunk downwards, at a depth of about half the trunk diameter, to somewhere above the soil (in the case of one-sided branches, obviously, you remove the side without branches). Do not seal the wound or if you want to be very careful only use a sealant on the cut edge of the cambium. The trunk — not the branches — can be wrapped with raffia for protection against the wiring which follows. Then anchor a long thickish wire at the base of the trunk. Work upwards with the wire and as you twist the trunk, wire it to hold it in the twisted position. It will not hold as well if you twist the tree first and then wire it. It is often difficult to twist the tree with the wire around it, for a variety of reasons; one being the difficulty in gripping the trunk without injuring the bark. A method to help you is to bend the trunk (with wire around it) to about 90°, and then use this piece of wire as a handle to twist the lower section of the tree. When this has been accomplished, that section is simply straightened again. The tree is then left to grow, even if the wire cuts into the bark as these marks, in this case, only add to the rugged look and coiled appearance. As soon as the wire cuts in, loosen it, and if the trunk holds its shape it need not be rewired.

A variation of the above technique is to wrap a few wires around the trunk in a spiral form, with the wires being wrapped lying next to one another to form a wide band spiralling upwards. It must be wide enough to prevent the bark from healing over it. The wire must fit tightly and the spiral must be irregular to have a natural

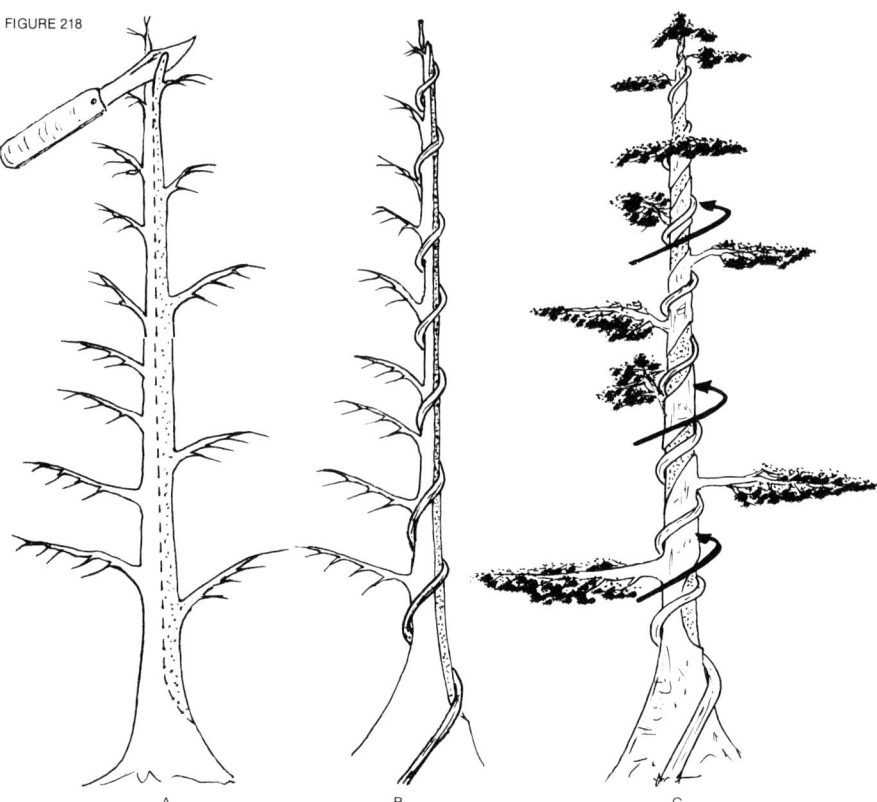

FIGURE 218
A + B Technique to create a twisted trunk with a strip or coil of dead wood right up to the apex. It is very easy on the more elastic trees, for instance cedarwood.
C. The twisting must be done so that the debarked portion is twisted at irregular distances apart.

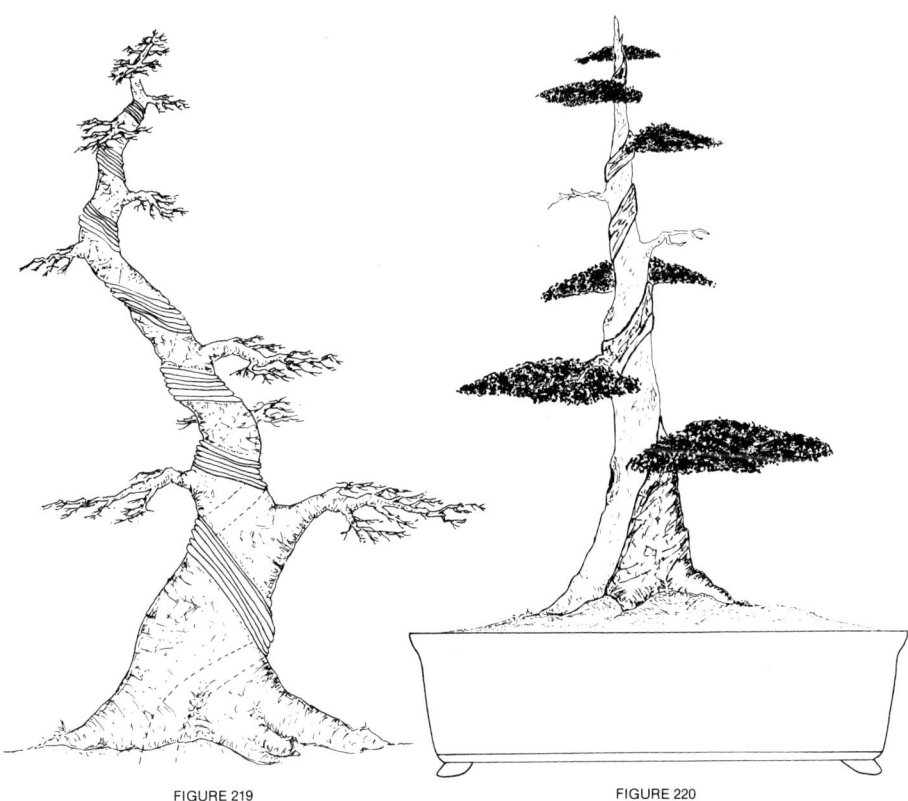

FIGURE 219   FIGURE 220

FIGURE 219 Creating the twisted appearance by wrapping wire around the trunk.

FIGURE 220 Some branches can be jinned to emphasise the dead strip on the trunk. Note that the apex must be either the live tip or a *jin*, but never the two at the same height. The live portion is usually behind the *jinned* apex.

appearance. As the tree grows the wire cuts into the bark and eventually the bark under the wire dies. The tree doesn't die, because the sap-flow finds a new route down the trunk. Once the bark is dead the wires are removed, leaving a spiralling *shari*. The dead bark — and it must be completely dead — is then carved out. If the bark is not completely dead, the sap-flow might not have developed an alternative route yet.

The creation of the *jin*, driftwood or *shari* is best done while the tree is dormant, because such drastic work on live portions of the tree, while it is actively growing and functioning, could cause unnecessary damage and weaken the tree and its root system. Never create any dead wood or branches on a tree that has not properly established its root system. In any case, once the dead wood has formed, the tree should be protected against severe sun and wind for the first few weeks.

PLAITED TRUNK — PIEN-TSHU

This style gives the appearance of great age, with the trunk twisted and warped by the elements.

To create the style you need young pliable trees with long trunks. Trees with no lower branches can be used, as the plaiting will shorten the trunks, and available branches will be shared. The trees should be planted as close together as possible, then tied together at the base and plaited. There is no need to strip bark off the adjoining surfaces, as the young trees will soon merge. Be careful when handling the branches as they are pulled through the plaiting. The trunks must be plaited so that they are held tightly against each other, after which they must be tied together. If wire is used, it must be checked regularly to see whether it isn't cutting into the bark. To hasten the merging of the trunks as well as their thickening, the trees could be planted in the garden or in a larger container.

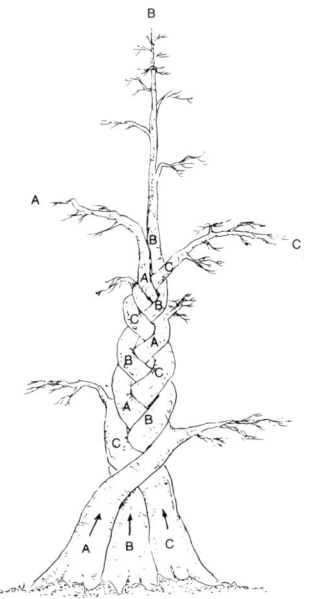

FIGURE 221 The initial stage of a plaited trunk.

TWISTED AND COILED TRUNK — HORAI

As explained in the chapter on the history of bonsai, the *horai* style is of Chinese origin. The tree is bent or grown into extreme curves and angles, with an overall rugged and gnarled appearance.

During the Muromachi period (1335–1573) one fashionable style of bonsai was called *tako*, the usual subject being the Japanese white pine (*Pinus parviflora*). The trunk was contorted several times, forming tiers at equal intervals and resulting in a pyramid shape. In later times, smaller bonsai trained in this same style were called *horai*, evidently inspired by *Horai* mountain, one of the three holy islands of Buddhism. *Horai* is the legendary mountain island of perpetual youth. On occasions of feasting and blessing it is customary for the symbolised Mount Horai, made from artificial pine and apricot trees, bamboos and carved creatures, to be decorated. It follows that this happy, natural idea made the inhabitants of that village call the beautiful style they had developed the *horai* style.

The other name for this style is *Honai*. This method was developed by the commercial growers of the hamlet Honai, in Echigo province, North-Western Japan. Honai is a small hamlet with an area of about 15 acres of rice fields and 130 acres of land which is used to grow various woody ornamental plants. 75 of the 130 acres are used solely for the purpose of growing several hundred thousand *honai*-trained Japanese white pines. Honai hamlet is one of many typical, small nursery centres found throughout Japan, situated and developed on fertile land not too far from a castle town, during the Tokugawa period (1603–1867). Some two hundred years ago, a group of Honai farmers learned the training of bonsai at Edo. When they returned, they encouraged the cultivation of bonsai on the hill, to afford the village security during those times when the periodic flooding of the River Shinano destroyed the rice fields. They refined the popular *Horai* or *Honai* style for bonsai.

FIGURE 222 Shaping the *horai* style through wooden rods in the soil. This stage is at least three years in development.

The method of creating the *horai* style is tedious and time-consuming: it takes a few years for the tree to acquire its basic shape and a further period of waiting for the trunk to develop its rugged appearance. Growing the tree in a deep container, or even in the ground will speed up the development.

Use a young tree which still has a flexible trunk and also one which will develop a rugged bark. Trees with smooth bark, like *Celtis*, are not suited to this style. A wooden rod is anchored in the soil and the tree is then coiled around it and tied to the rod. The coiling might have to be done in steps, gradually bending the tree from the base. The distance between the coils must vary, so as to give a natural appearance. Only in two or three years' time can the crown of the tree be shaped, and when that has been completed, the trunk will have developed a more rugged appearance. Remove the wooden rod carefully. If a length of cane is used instead of wood, removal of the cane rod will be easier, because it can simply be crushed and pulled out of the coils.

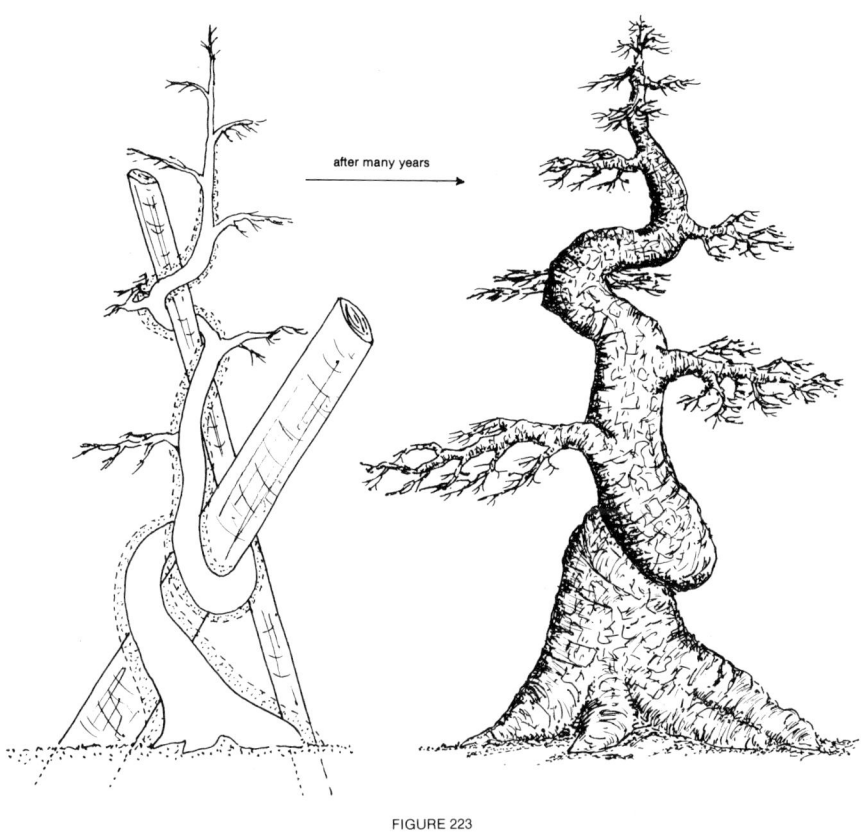

FIGURE 223

FIGURE 223 In creating the *horai* style, two wooden rods are used at the same time to form curves or coils at different places — varying distances between the coils to ensure a natural appearance. Before bending the trunk, the soil must dry out to cause the tree to wilt somewhat and make it more flexible.

DRIFTWOOD — SHARIMIKI

The tree has the appearance of having been battered by the forces of nature with branches dead and the trunk debarked and bent. It must really look weathered. It will contain *jin*, *shari* and *saba-miki* to varying degrees.

There are many variations of what could have happened to the trunk, and creating any of these requires the use of your imagination, while always remembering that it must look natural. Examples are the gnarled trunk (*bankan*), split trunk (*sogu-ki*), struck-by-lightning (*kaminari*), knobby trunk (*kobukan*) and peeled bark (*sharikan*).

FIGURE 224 *Sharikan*

FIGURE 225 Here you are showing off the dead portion of the tree. Only a small part of the living tree is showing at the base and the apex to 'prove' that the tree is alive, although most of it is dead.

FIGURE 226 The gnarled trunk.

FIGURE 227 The split trunk — *sogu-ku*.

FIGURE 228 *Kaminari*: Struck by lightning, only one branch has survived. Now most of the tree is made up of dead trunk and branches, but it still has to form a triangle in its outline. The live section may not compete with the dead trunk in terms of height — only one may be the apex.

FIGURE 229 A knobby trunk.

MAINTENANCE AND DAILY CARE

7

Climate is what is predicted.
Weather is what you experience.
This means that climate refers to a
longer period and weather is short term.

THE BONSAI CALENDAR

The bonsai calendar refers to the chores one has to attend to during the run of the year. This is only a general approach, because for example, what happens during September in the interior of the country is entirely different to what happens at the sub-tropic coast or in the Mediterranean areas, or wherever one may be growing bonsai. It means that you must adjust the monthly grouping as it fits into the year according to where you live. You might find that you have a winter of five months, while I describe a winter which lasts three months. In any case, the duration and severity of seasons differ from year to year. You will have to watch your bonsai and learn from their changes exactly where you are in terms of seasons, as well as keeping an eye on the weather.

Spring

SEPTEMBER (March in northern hemisphere) This month heralds the start of the growing season and it is a very busy month for the bonsai grower. Frost may still occur, although it is not common. Some pretty cold weather can be experienced, especially in areas near mountains, where heavy snowfalls may occur. Nonetheless, buds will be sprouting and tender light green leaves will be a common sight. Trees which have been protected for the winter should be brought into the open and exposed to sunlight. Keep in mind that unexpected cold or heat may be experienced.

Watering The bonsai now need more water, if only for the mass of new growth. It is time to apply the technique of spartan watering, if you so wish. Too much water in this period can cause dead branches in summer.

Trimming Start pinching back the new growth as it starts to elongate, in order to force compact growth, unless you want it to grow in length. Some flowering bonsai will be in bloom by now. Allow the bonsai to develop 70–80% of its flowers, and then remove all the flowers as well as the remaining buds to prevent the tree from using too much of its reserve energy. In the case of fruiting varieties, allow only a few fruits to develop, for the same reason. Berries which are a form of fruit may be left on the bonsai. Too long needles on pine must be pulled out.

Fertilising Newly repotted bonsai do not need any fertiliser now. Use organic fertilisers for trees which have not been repotted. Fertilisers with high nitrogen content are not advised. Apply boneneal to flowering, fruiting and conifer bonsai. Give deciduous trees superphosphate when they are budding and 2:3:2 when the leaves have hardened. Flowering trees should receive some seaweed derivative. Evergreen trees can be given either 2:3:2, chicken manure or superphosphate. This feeding regime is good for the spring period.

Spring, the low prelude of a
lordlier song;
Summer, a music without
hint of death;
Autumn, a cadence,
lingeringly long;
Winter, a pause; the
Minstrel-Year takes breath

WILLIAM WATSON
From *The Year's Minstrelsy*

Transplanting It is a good time to transplant bonsai, and no problems should be experienced with bonsai which are transplanted only to change pots. Where root-pruning is done, restrict this to trees which have not yet sprouted. Do not transplant trees which are healthy and growing well.

Grafting It is the best time to graft deciduous trees.

Propagation It is a good time for taking cuttings.

Pests may appear. Attention to the trees will enable you to pick up these problems quickly. It is likely that aphids will be attacking the young growing tips.

OCTOBER (April in northern hemisphere) For practical purposes this month does not differ greatly from the previous one. The days may become very hot and care should be taken in this regard. Rotate the bonsai in relation to the sun.

Watering is the same as in the previous month. If pines need to be restricted in growth, they must be kept on the dry side: in other words apply spartan watering. Because of the different stages of development of different species, trees will be using varying amounts of water and this means taking care of trees individually.

Trimming Trim back the long shoots as needed. Pinch back candles on pines if necessary.

Fertilising It is a good month to start the fertilising program. No high nitrogen content fertilisers must be used. Bonemeal or superphosphate is good to prevent fruit and berries being shed. Use the same fertilisers as mentioned under the previous month.

Transplanting It is still a good time to transplant, in fact some varieties such as serissa, figs, Chinese elms, junipers, azaleas and gardenias prefer to be transplanted now or the following month.

Grafting A very good time to graft, especially on the species which start developing a little later.

Pests Aphids will be very active.

Shaping It is an excellent time for making *jin* and *shari* because the healing ability of the trees is very good now due to the high sap-flow.

Summer

NOVEMBER (May in northern hemisphere)

Watering It is helpful if the trees are watered in the morning. The wet surroundings keep the temperatures down. Beware of late afternoon watering, for fear of mildew developing. Broad-leaf and most deciduous species need a lot of water, compared to pines and cedars which prefer a dryer soil. Spray the underside of the leaves, as this helps to kill red spider-mites. Too much water will cause excessive foliage growth and lengthening of internodal distances, as well as weak growth.

Trimming Long shoots must be cut back, especially if they spoil the shape of the tree. Conifers require pinching back to ensure compact growth; do not use scissors, as this will cause browning of cut tips. Start removing candles on young pines and vigorously growing older pines, in the lower parts of the trees.

Fertilising Continue the program, but it may be a good time to change the type of fertiliser. Deciduous trees can receive Seagrow, 2:3:2 and L.A.N., alternated each month. Flowering species may be given 3:1:5 slow release or 2:3:2. Conifers like 3:1:1 or seaweed extract. Continue with these fertilisers, alternating them as recommended and at half-strength, for the entire summer.

Transplanting Only bonsai which start developing later can be transplanted, for instance cotoneaster, pyracantha, pomegranate and conifers.

Grafting is still possible.

Pests Keep a lookout for fungal diseases and as a preventative measure, dust with lime-sulphur.

Sing a song of seasons!
Something bright in all!
Flowers in the summer,
Fires in the fall.

R L STEVENSON
From *Autumn Fires*

Shaping Wiring can be done, as the young growing tips will have hardened. Do not wire tightly, as the branches are thickening quickly and the wire will cut in soon. The bark is also soft and may be damaged easily. Keep a watch on the older wiring to see that it does not cut into the bark.

DECEMBER (June in northern hemisphere) In general this is a quiet time, because trimming and pruning are minimal. Just enjoy your bonsai, as the growth will have become established. Keep rotating the trees.

Watering Water as in the previous month but perhaps slightly more due to the heat. Keep the surroundings wet and cool.

Trimming It is a good month for defoliation. If at all possible, try to bend vertically growing branches down to a horizontal position, even if you have to tie them to the pot. Wiring is difficult due to the compact foliage. Conifers may need pruning back.

Fertilising Fertilise all quick-growing deciduous trees, except the fruiting, flowering and berry-carrying ones. Conifers require only a small amount of fertiliser.

Transplanting Pines and azaleas in particular do not mind transplanting, but after-care is important.

Pests Watch for fungal diseases.

JANUARY (July in northern hemisphere) This is a very hot month.

Watering As in the previous month.

Trimming Finish trimming in this month especially flowering bonsai which should only be trimmed again after their next flowering session in spring. Remove all flowers, as well as buds. It is the last month for defoliation of deciduous trees.

Fertilising Remember to switch the type of fertiliser.

Transplanting This is very risky now, although if it is done without root-pruning, the worst you need expect is the dropping off of a few leaves.

Pests It is a very active time for pests. Watch for scale.

Propagation Air-layering and ground-layering can be done, because the trees are very active.

FEBRUARY (August in northern hemisphere) The growing cycle has slowed down. Trunks and branches are thickening as the trees store food for the coming winter. In some areas this is the hottest month of the year.

Watering As in the previous month.

Trimming No trimming should be necessary. Defoliation is very risky. Keep a watch on the wiring because of the thickening of the trunks and branches which will cause the wire to cut into the bark. Wiring can still be done but take care because the new growth will have hardened. Remove any flowers that may remain.

Fertilising Carry on with the programme. Rather use fertilisers with more potassium and phosphates.

Transplanting Do not try it.

Pests They are still very active. Watch for scale.

Propagation Air- and ground-layering can still be attempted.

Autumn

Autumn may herald the start of beautiful changes in the colour of the foliage. Temperatures will start dropping, but this is unpredictable and a few very hot days may be encountered.

MARCH (September in the northern hemisphere)

Watering A tricky time for watering because the growth is slowing down at varying rates in different species.

Trimming Because winter die-back is unpredictable, do not cut young growth back too far.

> *O be less beautiful,*
> *or be less brief!*
>
> **WILLIAM WATSON**
> From *Autumn*

Fertilising Only fertilise young bonsai that still show signs of growth. Do not use fertilisers with a high nitrogen content. Use 2:3:2 on deciduous trees and 3:1:5 or 2:3:2 on flowering trees. Evergreens can receive 2:3:2, superphosphate or chicken manure, while conifers can get 2:3:2 or seaweed extract. This fertilising programme is used the whole autumn.

Transplanting Towards the end of this month and into the next month, conifers and most deciduous trees can be transplanted, but no serious root-pruning must be attempted. Rapid growers, like willow and tamarix, may now have their second annual transplant, because even if the portion above the soil may seem to have ceased growing, the roots will still be growing, albeit at a slower rate.

APRIL (October in northern hemisphere) This is the month during which the trees show their splendid autumn colours. Temperatures during the day will generally be mild, but days of unusual heat or even frost may occur. Try to keep deciduous trees cool, as heat may stimulate an unseasonable spurt of growth which will not stand the winter cold. Protect your frost-sensitive trees.

Watering This has to be decreased and trees need individual care, because of their individual requirements.

Trimming Deciduous trees can be trimmed back on the previous year's growth. Wiring can be done on smaller branches, but take care because the branches may still be thickening in which case they will not wire easily. Pines can be trimmed fairly drastically, and all dead needles must be removed.

Fertilising Use potassium and phosphate-rich fertilisers which will not promote new growth.

Transplanting The last month this can be done safely, but you must look after the tree in terms of watering.

MAY (November in northern hemisphere). May signals the end of autumn. Many trees are still covered in their autumn clothes. Many leaves will be falling, and they need to be picked up, because insects will breed under them. Moss will start becoming active in winter-rainfall areas due to the dropping temperatures. Guard against frost. Remove leaves still remaining on deciduous trees. If any fruit, berries or seeds remain, they must be removed as well. Remove needles which show brown tips or are too long after two years' growth. Wire with care.

Watering Reduce watering.
Fertilizing None.
Transplanting None.

Winter

JUNE (December in northern hemisphere) All bonsai should be dormant. In winter-rainfall areas, moss, which is now growing well, should be collected.

Watering Very little is given. Do not water frozen soil!

Trimming Now that the branches are bare of leaves, the shape of the tree can be studied and pruning can be done with care. Do not cut big branches, as the healing process is virtually at a standstill.

Fertilising None is given to deciduous trees, but evergreens can receive 2:3:2 or superphosphate and conifers some diluted seaweed extract.

Transplanting Only hardy trees which haven't matured as bonsai.

Propagation Pines can be grafted (as well as other conifers) because they are dormant and the pitch will not isolate the scion from the understock.

Pests Apply lime-sulphur to mildew-susceptible trees.

JULY (January in northern hemisphere) July is a quiet month, because all trees will be dormant. Like June (December), however, this is a very cold month. Be extremely wary of 'black frost' which will kill any tree which is not very hardy. Both June and July might be very wet months in the winter-rainfall areas and it may not

---

The flowers withered,
Their colour faded away,
While meaninglessly
I spent my days in the world
And the long rains were falling

ONO NO KOMACHI
From *Kokinshu* (905 AD)

be necessary to do any watering at all. Cold-sensitive trees may have to be kept indoors or in cold-frames.

Trimming It is a good time to trim the trees because they are without leaves.
Fertilising None.
Transplanting None.
Pests Spray the trees with lime-sulphur.
Grafting It is time to graft pines and other conifers.

Now is a good time to care for your tools. Sharpen them, treat any rust, oil them and disinfect them. Study your own trees as well as pictures of trees. Get your soil mixtures ready, because August is a repotting month.

AUGUST (February in northern hemisphere) In the summer-rainfall areas the days become warmer, but frost may still occur, which means you have to be careful in exposing sensitive trees. Trees which show signs of flowers or buds developing must be brought into the sun to ensure good colours in the flowers and to prevent the new shoots becoming too long.

Watering Individual watering is needed, because some trees will start their growth earlier, especially towards the end of August.

Trimming It is a good time for trimming, especially fruit-bearing bonsai. If repotting and root-pruning are done, trimming of the twigs and branches is recommended.

Fertilising None as yet. If the tree is transplanted, it should not need any fertilising, because the new soil will supply all that is necessary for at least a few months. In the winter-rainfall areas the heavy rain may have affected the condition of the soil and this must be adjusted by using gypsum (lime) or wood ash to sweeten the soil.

Transplanting The end of August is a popular time to transplant bonsai. The exact time is important, however, and it must be done as the leaf buds start swelling. When the leaves have started unfolding and you can see the green, it is too late. Some trees prefer to be transplanted later, for instance cotoneaster, pomegranate and figs.

Propagation It is a very good time to start cuttings.
Grafting It can be started on deciduous trees.

THE BONSAI-EN

When discussing the care of bonsai, the first question that arises is where to keep them. A bonsai needs to be kept outdoors where it is exposed to rain, sun, wind, dew and fresh air. This is not as simple as it may sound, because bonsai are susceptible to the exhaust fumes from motorcars and toxic gases from factories. The danger of hailstorms or heavy downpours is a reality in many areas. The severity of the sun is also a factor to be reckoned with, as well as the frost and even snow during winter.

If you feel like taking your bonsai indoors, it should not be for more than two or three days at a time. The indoor climate is not conducive to healthy bonsai growing because the air inside is too dry and the sunshine and fresh air are lacking. The dry air causes the breathing pores (stomata) to close, thus preserving the moisture in the trees, but in doing so it also prevents the tree from 'breathing'. You may find, as an example, that acacias will start shedding leaves in a day or two. The sun is very beneficial, in that it causes smaller leaves to be formed and the internodal distance to be shorter. Sunlight is necessary for flower and fruit-formation. A plant receiving enough sunlight is less susceptible to disease.

The amount of sunlight to which a bonsai is exposed has a direct influence on the water evaporation from the soil and the loss of moisture through the leaves, and different trees will react in different ways: one need only observe, for example, the reaction of a broad-leaf tree as opposed to a needle-leaf tree. The particular soil mixture (growing medium) and the shape and make of the pot will affect water loss. A pot made out of terracotta is more prone to water loss than a stoneware pot. Experience gained throughout practice and experiment is the key to success.

In general it is better to subject the bonsai to morning sun with shade in the afternoon. Do not keep the bonsai in the shade of a garden tree for fear of bird droppings falling on the bonsai, and insects or diseases affecting it in that position. Another problem lies in birds getting at the moss or tender shoots. Trees secrete a substance called lye, and this substance may be injurious to the particular bonsai. Lye might drip on the bonsai with detrimental results, if it is positioned under a tree.

It is convenient to keep your bonsai on some form of bench or table, a so-called *bonsai-tana*, for a variety of reasons. Firstly the bonsai is kept out of reach of animals, such as dogs, that think nothing of uprooting a tree. Secondly, the trees are kept at a convenient height to view and work on them. Thirdly, it is more difficult for ants, earthworms and other pests to reach the trees — in fact insecticides can be applied on the floor around the *bonsai-tana* with no fear of injuring the bonsai. Lastly, the trees are some distance above the ground, which may freeze, with the resultant cold affecting the trees. The reverse may also happen during a heatwave.

The *bonsai-tana* may be made from bricks, wood, railway sleepers and many other materials. Probably one of the best methods is to support a corrugated sheet of asbestos on pillars and then cover the asbestos with gravel. This has several advantages, one being that the gravel will retain the excess water if overhead spraying is applied, and that will ensure a good humidity around the trees. The gravel also does not contain seeds of weeds, which ensures a neat surrounding. The constant moistness of the gravel keeps the area around the trees cool as it evaporates — a great help in summer. After some time you will notice a special microclimate system develop in the area in which your bonsai are kept.

Avoid keeping the bonsai near glass windows or doors and white walls as these reflect the sunrays onto the trees. The reflected sunrays are very dangerous. Shadecloth of varying filtering degrees is available. It is absolutely necessary during the summer in most parts of the country. Apart from filtering the sunrays, it also keeps hailstones and heavy rain from injuring the trees or washing away the soil from the pots. Under cover of the shadecloth, moss has a better chance of taking and surviving. Do not keep bonsai under an awning or roof-overhang where they won't receive direct sunlight. Neither should the bonsai be exposed to severe windy conditions. The extremes of summer and winter are your biggest problem. Summer is easier to cope with than winter; as described previously, with the use of shadecloth the tree will be adequately protected. The freezing conditions of winter and the feared 'black-frost' are headaches. It is easy enough to tell you not to keep bonsai which are not adapted to your particular climate, but it can be such a pleasure to have a fig tree or bougainvillea or any other frost-sensitive tree, as an exception. Where frost is a problem, the sensitive trees must be protected in some manner. A cold frame is a solution. If you have only one or two problem trees, they can be taken indoors at night, but remember that it is still extremely cold till about 9 a.m. and the trees could be damaged by taking them out too early in the morning. Frost is not only dangerous to the foliage of trees, as it damages the cells through ice-crystals, but the pots which are barrel-shaped may crack through the expansion of the ice. The frozen soil takes a long time to defrost and presents difficulties when watering the trees.

Whatever position the trees are standing in, they need to be turned in relation to the sun to ensure even development of the foliage. If one side of the tree permanently faces north, the foliage on the side facing the sun develops better and more compactly. In fact a tree becomes so accustomed to facing in a particular direction, that when you acquire such a tree it should initially be trained facing the same direction. Gradually it can be turned as described.

If a tree has been kept under some form of protection during winter, it must be exposed to the sun gradually during spring, as the sudden exposure to too much sun would be dangerous.

WATERING BONSAI

The watering of bonsai should be read in conjunction with the section on soil (page 131).

Rainwater is best: it is not polluted, it has a slightly acid pH and it contains trace-elements and nitrogen in the form of ammonia. If possible, collect rainwater in a wooden or pottery container. The problem is that rainwater is not available throughout the year. Also if you have many trees, it is very tedious to wet the bonsai in this manner, as it means that you have to use a sprinkling can and water each tree individually. That is the ideal way, but often does not fit into the busy daily program of the modern person. Water from boreholes can be used but it often has a high lime content. Tap-water on the other hand contains chlorine which is harmful. It does however help to keep tapwater in a large container for 24 hours. Chlorine stains the leaves as well as being toxic. Tap-water can be passed through carbon filters to purify the water. A bicarbonate of sorts is also responsible for staining leaves.

Willow water

When a young willow tree branch is cut into small pieces and these pieces are submerged in water for 24 to 48 hours, a chemical is released into the water. When this water is administered to a tree which has been repotted or transplanted, the 'chemical' in the water encourages root growth. This water is called 'willow-water'.

When to water Bonsai

In general it is best to water the bonsai at about 11 a.m., thus ensuring that the bonsai have enough water available to see them through the extreme midday heat. During winter, this prevents the water in the pots from freezing overnight. If by any chance this does happen, be sure to wait till the ice has thawed out completely. If the foliage has been sprayed in the morning, any humidity will have dried up by nightfall — it is a precaution against mildew which is likely to develop in humid conditions.

I prefer to set my automatic spraying system to spray the trees during the morning. Although this means that, during summer, some trees may need water again in the afternoon, that suits me because after work when I get home, I attend to the trees and water them by hand as and when necessary. This almost amounts to spartan watering, but at least I know my trees are not drowning.

Amount of water

If you should notice that a tree's leaves develop dry margins, this quite possibly means that the roots are not able to supply adequate water to the foliage. It rarely indicates insufficient watering. In most cases this is due to excess foliage as compared to the root system, and the solution is simply to remove some of the leaves randomly over the entire crown of the tree.

I cannot tell you how much water to give to your trees as there are too many variables affecting drainage, water-use, evaporation and transpiration. Probably the most important factor is the reigning weather conditions, with the soil quality in close second place. A very important weather condition is wind. Be sure to give special attention to the soil's water content during windy days. I must remind you

Haiku
An old pond
A frog leaping in
The sound of water

MATSUO BASHO

here, to beware of moss covering too large a portion of the soil surface, as described on page 25. Water is essential and comprises an extremely high percentage of the weight of a plant. A shortage of water will cause a tree to die, but as surely, an excess of water will do the same. Remember that a 25% (per volume) water content of the soil is the optimal moisture for a tree's health.

The tree must never stand in soggy or wet soil for as long as six weeks, because the roots will suffocate and the tree will die. When watering a tree, it is good practice to wet the soil up to a point where the water runs from the drainage holes. Then the water must be withheld till the soil on the surface becomes dry, when it must be watered again. The saturation of the soil, followed by drying out means that fresh air is sucked in repeatedly to replace stale air. If the soil is saturated completely when watering, it causes the roots to spread through the whole volume of soil. When the soil is only partially wet, the roots grow along the surface portion of the soil, and should even a short period of drought be experienced, the tree might die.

Wilting

In general, if the soil gets dry enough for the tree to wilt, the soil should not be saturated immediately. First of all the foliage should be sprayed wet and the tree kept in a shady place protected from the wind; alternatively a plastic bag can be used to cover the tree overnight (after spraying). The next day the soil can be wetted thoroughly. Deciduous trees and large-leaved evergreens recover better than needle-leaf trees due to a 'tube' system in the trunk and branches, which enables them to suck water up to the leaves more quickly than the slow process in other trees.

Spartan watering

The so-called 'spartan watering technique' is applied to reduce the spurt of growth during springtime. This technique is effective but very risky. It boils down to reducing the frequency of watering, but not the quantity of water at a time. You must thoroughly wet the soil and then wait till the soil dries out again, before the next watering. If not, you run the risk of allowing the soil to dry out too much, with consequent damage to the tree. Because it is done in spring when the young leaves and buds are developing, the dry conditions retard their growth. Exactly the same technique can be applied to restrict growth in mature trees. You will also notice that the flowering varieties produce better flowers under dry conditions, because the tree is fighting for survival and needs to produce fruit and seeds to ensure its reproduction.

Methods of watering

Automatic spraying or misting is very handy and very reliable, but it estranges you from your trees. You don't get to know their likes and dislikes. You can also overwater your trees this way and that is why I use it as described under 'When to water bonsai' on page 117. When you go away on holiday, this method is indispensable.

Watering by hand using a watering-can is, perhaps, the ideal way, as each tree gets individual attention. Because it is impossible to thoroughly wet the soil in one session (the water runs off the surface of the soil), you should wet the tree, wait a few minutes for the water to be drawn into the soil, and wet it again. Repeat this till water runs from the drainage holes. With this method you can use stored rainwater, tap-water or borehole water. Do not wet the soil again before the surface of the soil is dry.

A drip-system can be installed. The system affords better control over the quantity of water than the spraying system, as it can be adjusted from one to a few drips per tree, but you won't have the advantage of wetting the foliage.

For a rock planting an interesting variation of the drip can be used: A plastic cooldrink bottle is filled with water and suspended over the rock. A small hole is made in the plastic and the constant dripping on the rock creates a very realistic situation, with the spray wetting a large area, the rock staying wet and moss growing well.

PESTS AND DISEASES

A brief description of some of the common diseases and pests encountered will suffice, as complete coverage of this aspect is available in horticultural publications. Because a bonsai gets more attention than the average garden tree or plant, any pest or disease should be noticed before it has assumed monstrous proportions. I advocate a non-chemical approach as far as possible, because I believe that a healthy tree kept in airy, sunlit conditions will not be very prone to disease, and if it should contract some disease it has a better chance of surviving. Thus it is imperative to supply adequate nutrients, to expose your bonsai to enough sunlight, to allow sufficient fresh air to circulate (which also means foliage which is not too compact!) and to attend to your trees.

A chemical with overall preventative application is lime-sulphur. This is applied to *shari* and *jin* and to leafless deciduous trees winter, to prevent rotting and fungal growth.

If pests, like mealy bug, slugs, snails and scale are noticed, they must be removed by hand. Only when the outbreak is massive may you resort to some of the many pesticides available. With pesticides always apply the law of 'minimum violence' although you must realise that the pest is not less harmful on bonsai and the pesticide must be used at full strength.

Tiny black ants are a giveaway that your trees are harbouring aphids or scale, because both these organisms secrete a sweet, sticky substance which attracts ants. Ants can also damage the bonsai, especially when they create tunnels in the soil. The ants can only be treated chemically.

Aphids attack the young leaves and growing tips of the trees. It is impossible to remove them by hand, but they may be forced off with a forceful stream of water, or otherwise killed by chemicals.

Mealy bugs are sucking insects. They are not easily killed by chemicals, as they are protected by a waxlike covering. It is easy enough to remove them by hand.

Scale insects are also sucking insects. They are readily killed with chemicals, especially in summer when the young insects are not protected by their wax covering. If the attack is not severe they can be removed by hand.

Australian bug is a form of scale insect. The female carries a sac of eggs beneath and behind her, which looks like a white cottony ribbed sac. These insects are also easily removed by hand.

Mildew comes in many forms, varying in colour from white to black. In this case prevention is better than cure. A winter spray of lime-sulphur, repeated two or three times on susceptible trees, is an excellent preventative measure. Other chemicals work well to cure the disease. Hot humid conditions encourage the growth of mildew.

Red spider is a mite of minute proportions and becomes visible if the tree is shaken while being held over white paper, when the tiny mites fall off and can be seen moving on the paper. Signs of the infection are leaves which lose colour, usually becoming lighter. The mite is found on the underside of the leaves, where they spin a fine reddish-brown web over themselves as protection. They can be detected through a magnifying glass. By spraying the underside of the leaves with water once or twice a week the incidence of red spider-mite is drastically reduced.

Rust is also a form of fungus which causes spots of discolouring on the leaves.

These spots are permanent and the leaves have to be removed. A fungicide will kill the fungus and spores.

There is an interesting story about the 'ingenuity' of the red spider-mite. The red spider-mite lives on the dry underside of a leaf, where it damages the leaf causing it to curl its edges around, and so form a protective covering for the mite. In an orchid nursery mist sprayers were used, but were placed in a position so as to wet the leaves on the underside. The red spider-mite promptly started living on the dry upper side of the leaf and caused these leaves to curl their edges upwards.

What to do if something goes wrong

The colour and conditions of the leaves act as indicators of the health of the tree, and experience will soon teach you to read the signs.

Wilting leaves are a sign of lack of water or, in other words, that more water is being lost from the growing medium than is reaching the leaves. The leaves may also be losing more water than they are being supplied with via the roots. The method for dealing with a tree which is wilting has been described under 'Watering bonsai' on page 118.

If you find that a tree is suffocating due to a soggy growing medium, this must be replaced by a more sandy mixture, and if the condition is severe the tree must be planted in sand. The roots should be inspected and if found to be rotting, they should be cut back into live tissue before planting again.

Leaves can change colour, and here you look for spots, a general dulling or greying and yellowing. When there are spots of discolouration it may indicate rust, mite or scale on the underside of the leaves. With rust, the affected leaves must be removed immediately and the rest of the tree and soil sprayed with fungicide. Remember to spray the underside of the leaves. The scale can be removed individually or treated with Oleum or Malathion as indicated. A general dulling or greying in colour is probably red spider-mite. Treat with Karbadust, Malathion, Metasystox or Kelthane.

If leaves turn yellow, the tree is probably not receiving enough sunlight. The solution is to move the tree to a sunnier spot. The yellow leaves may, however, be due to a shortage of magnesium which is solved by adding magnesium-sulphate to the soil (Epsom salts). Yellowing can also be caused by a lack of nitrogen.

If the root system or trunk need development, the tree can be planted in the garden for a year or two before it needs to go back to its container for training.

One problem with any pesticide is that it will not stick to the leaves or trunk, due to the presence of a waxlike covering. This can be overcome by using a wetting agent along with the pesticide. These are commercially available under different names. However, a teaspoon of liquid soap added to a litre of prepared pesticide will suffice.

A final word about pests and diseases is that to some extent pests can be controlled by natural enemies like Vendalia ladybirds, praying mantis and spiders.

FERTILISING

Perhaps the biggest single mistake you can make in bonsai training is being in a hurry to get results. This attitude boils down to being greedy and then overdoing things. Linnaeus warned us generations ago that 'Nature does not proceed in leaps!' You cannot speed up nature without causing harm. If you think you are doing good by giving the tree more fertiliser than prescribed, or more water, or more pruning, or whatever, the tree will suffer harm or even die. Treat the tree like a baby by first of all looking after its basic growth, and secondly feeding it a little at a time, but regularly.

Read the part on soil on page 129, along with this section, to understand how the roots function. It is important to keep in mind that fertilisers are additional sources of nutrients, and you cannot rely only on them to keep your bonsai healthy. A little knowledge of which nutrients plants need, and why they need them is helpful to achieve the hoped for results.

Nutrients are divided into two main groups: macro-nutrients, needed in large quantities, and micro-nutrients, which are needed in small quantities, but are just as important as the macro-nutrients.

Carbon, oxygen and hydrogen are freely available out of the air and water and need not be given to the bonsai specifically. Of the other elements nitrogen, phosphorus and potassium — hereafter also referred to by their chemical symbols. N, P and K — are very important and have to be supplied, because of the large quantities needed to sustain plant life. They must be added firstly in the way of new, fresh soil and secondly as fertilisers. Trees need a total of 16 different elements to grow normally.

- Nitrogen (N) is necessary for healthy foliage and its presence is manifest in strong leaves of a deep green colour. It is required in the manufacture of chlorophyll and is an important element in proteins. When there is a shortage of nitrogen, the leaves grow slowly, they are fewer and smaller and are pale in colour. The opposite effect occurs when too much nitrogen is administered and this is seen as an unbalanced growth with exceptionally large leaves which are soft and limp.
- Phosphorus (P) forms part of the protein molecule and thus helps to strengthen the tree. It also encourages the development of a strong root system. To a degree it lessens the effect of an excess of nitrogen. Phosphorus is not leached out through an abundance of water and, although most soil contains enough phosphorus, the problem lies in its inaccessibility to the tree's roots. Even when it is applied through fertilisers, the phosphorus is soon bonded into inaccessible forms.
- Potassium (K) does not have as obvious an effect as nitrogen and phosphorus, but it plays an important part in the overall resistance a tree has to disease. It reacts in conjunction with nitrogen and also has a limiting effect on the activities of nitrogen. Potassium acts as a catalyst for the reaction of many other elements. It helps in the formation of a strong root system and aids in the process of photosynthesis.
- Calcium is an important element in the construction of the cell walls. It also acts as a catalyst to enable the tree to utilise phosphorus and potassium. Calcium has a beneficial influence on overall growth — including roots and branches. Where calcium is lacking, it could cause young shoots to die. Superphosphate contains about 50% calcium-sulphate (gypsum), and because superphosphate is the main ingredient in most combination fertilisers, trees usually get enough calcium without any trouble.
- Magnesium forms an integral part of the chlorophyll molecule. If the supply of magnesium is depleted, the leaves will turn yellow.
- Sulphur forms part of the plant protein-molecule and it helps to ensure strong root development.
- Trace-elements have a wide variety of effects, and can cause deficiency diseases but are also poisonous when present in excess.

The following two incidents will suffice to show in what minute quantities trace-elements will have an effect:
- In Australia it was observed that the natural grass grew longer and more abundantly directly underneath the telephone lines in the rural areas in grasslands. This was particularly noticeable from the air, and was found to be the effect of copper being washed off the lines through rain, thus 'fertilising' the soil.

- In South Africa the maize farmers simply pull a naked copper wire along the soil whilst ploughing or tilling. This supplies the necessary copper element for the maize crop.

Perhaps iron is the more important one, and its importance lies in its help in forming chlorophyll, so that its absence leads to pale leaves (chlorosis) especially in young trees. This form of chlorosis differs from nitrogen deficiency in that the veins on the leaves stay green.

From this information it is clear that you can fertilise a tree for different purposes. To improve the foliage you need a fertiliser with a high nitrogen content, for instance urea or limestone-ammonium-nitrate (L.A.N.). Potassium sulphate will improve the root system and branches. For young trees to thrive, a fertiliser which is richer in nitrogen is necessary, but if you want good flowers and berries or fruit, a fertiliser with a high nitrogen content should not be given till after early summer. These trees will need potassium and phosphorus. Trees carrying flowers and fruit may receive bonemeal during late autumn. Do not fertilise them while they are full of flowers, as the fruit will fall off when it starts forming, because the tree will give preference to new vegetative growth. As soon as the fruit has set (ripened), the trees can receive fertiliser with a low nitrogen and a high phosphate content.

Fertilisers must only be applied during the growing season. Never fertilise a sick or weak tree, and do not fertilise directly before or within about two months of a transplanting. In any case, if you have a fresh soil mixture, the tree shouldn't need any fertiliser for the first year. Most conifers do not need as much fertiliser as deciduous trees do. It is preferable to fertilise a tree with a large quantity of weaker solution, than to give small but highly concentrated doses. Should you be concerned about the newly transplanted tree's ability to form new roots and finer branches, you can first of all mix some superphosphate with the new soil mixture, and secondly water the tree with willow water for the first few days after transplanting. After about a month you should treat the tree to its first foliar feeding of seaweed extract, to induce the formation of finer branching, new leaves and finer roots. The seaweed extract application can be repeated on a weekly basis.

Plants get their nutrients from fertilisers and manures apart from those nutrients already available in the virgin soil. The mineral fertilisers (inorganic fertilisers) have a very quick action, as they supply their nutrients directly to the plants. They do not improve the quality of the soil in any way because they lack the humus-forming organic materials found in animal manures or compost from vegetative sources. Fertilisers are either organic or inorganic. The organic fertilisers are carbon compounds from animal or vegetative sources, and although many gardeners claim they are superior to the synthetically manufactured inorganic fertilisers, there is no scientific evidence to support this claim. The inorganic fertilisers are manufactured or derived from mineral deposits and are partially or completely soluble. They usually have a high percentage of nitrogen, which can be absorbed very quickly by the plants. However, due to the concentrations in which they dissolve, they can prevent the roots from absorbing water (so-called reverse osmosis, see page 128).

Fertilisers are supplied in the form of liquids, crystalline powders, pellets, granules and rods or cones. They are usually acquired in set mixes, containing different ratios of nitrogen, phosphorus and potash, and are then considered to be complete fertilisers. When one or two of the elements are absent it is not a complete fertiliser. These ratios are required to be indicated on the packaging and it is always in the sequence of nitrogen, phosphorus and potassium (N,P,K), for example 2:3:2 (22). The first three figures indicate the ratio in which the N, P and K occur, while the figure in brackets indicates the percentage N, P plus K. In the formula of 2:3:2

the fertiliser contains 2 parts nitrogen (N), 3 parts phosphorus (P) and two parts potassium (K) — that is 6,28% nitrogen, 9,44% phosphorus and 6,28% potassium, totalling 22%.

Liquid fertilisers are particularly easy to apply. They are supplied in concentrated solutions or in a soluble form to be mixed with water. The mixture can then be sprayed onto the trees or onto the soil, or simply poured onto the soil. Some automatic watering systems have special devices through which the liquid fertiliser can be administered, but this tends to be wasteful in the case of bonsai trees, as the spray is not restricted to the potted trees only. Whichever method is applied, the big advantage is the immediate availability of the nutrients to the roots. One additional benefit of the liquid fertilisers is the fact that they can be used on foliage. The liquid fertiliser — in diluted form, to prevent leaf-burn — is readily absorbed by the leaves. Within an hour of application, the fertiliser is already detectable in the plant sap. To improve leaf growth, a spray containing urea (15 g to 10 litres water) will have the desired effect. When the stems and leaves are soft and sappy and require hardening without restricting the growth, applications of potassium nitrate (15 g to 10 litres of water) will harden the soft growth. Potassium and phosphorus are not easily absorbed through the leaves and may in fact be washed off before they are utilised. To a lesser degree this also applies to nitrogen and with this problem in mind you can see why it is necessary to spray on a day when it is not expected to rain. Be sure to spray both sides of the leaves and to use a fine mist spray.

Although fertilisers containing the NPK trio are considered to be 'complete' fertilisers, this is in fact not true, because they lack the trace-elements, as will be mentioned a little further on.

To grow and survive a plant needs certain elements. These are divided into two groups according to the quantities in which they are required by the plants: (see page 121)

- Main elements (macro-nutrients) carbon (C), oxygen (O), nitrogen (N), hydrogen (H), phosphorus (P), potassium (K), calcium (Ca), magnesium (Mg), sulphur (S).
- Trace-elements (micronutrients) manganese (Mn), copper (Cu), boron (Bo), zinc (Zn), molybdenum (Mo), cobalt (Co) and iron (Fe).

This grouping is only based on the quantities required and has nothing to do

TABLE OF FERTILISERS (INORGANIC!)

Fertiliser	Nitrogenous N			Nitrogenous N				Potassic K		Mixtures N.P.K.		
Properties	Promotes better growth of whole plant. Promotes better leaf colour			Improves root development. Improves flower and fruit formation				Improves resistance against disease. Improves general growth		Improves general growth		
Type	Ammonium-Sulphate	LAN	Ureum	Super-Phosphate	Raw rock phosphate	Super-plus raw rock phosphate	Basic slag	Potassium- Chloride	Potassium- Sulphate	2:3:2 (22)	2:3:4 (24)	2:3:2 (14)
Chemical content	21% N	28% N	46% N	10,5% P	9,2% P	10% P	7% P	50% K_2O	4% K_2O	6,3% N 9,4% P 6,3% K	5,3% N 8,0% P 10,7% K	4% N 6% P 4% K
Uses	1. To improve leaf condition 2. As additional fertiliser when still un-decomposed materials are contained in the soil			1. Before seedlings are sown or planted 2. Promotes root growth when needed				1. Seldom used alone, but when chicken manure is used it balances the effect of the manure 2. Prevents flowers and fruit dropping by strengthening plant		Basic fertiliser together with organic fertilisers		
General	1. Is slow 2. Regular use tends to increase acidity of the soil	Probably the best of the group. It has no effect on acidity of the soil	Cheapest. Could be used as foliage fertiliser	Works the fastest in the group	Slowest effect	A blend of the previous two	Works slowly but for a long period. It improves soil acidity (makes it more alkaline)	Beware of excess.		Should always be used in conjunction with compost and manure.		

with the degree of dependability on the particular element.

Fertilisers are divided into four groups according to their content:

1. Nitrogenous fertilisers

Sulphate of ammonia (21% N) is a common form in which nitrogen is applied. It must however be changed into the nitrate form before it can be utilised, and in summer this takes 5 to 7 days after application and even longer in winter. It tends to make the soil more acid and should therefore be used on alkaline soils to reduce this effect. Sulphate of ammonia can be dissolved as 1.5 g into 5 litres of water.

Limestone ammonium nitrate (28% N) (L.A.N.) is a mixture of nitrogen in the nitrate and ammonium forms, along with lime so that it does not affect the acidity (pH) of the soil. L.A.N. should be applied in the dry granular form, because when it is dissolved the ammonium nitrate dissolves and the lime is left as a sediment in the container. The effect of L.A.N. is seen in five to seven days.

Urea (46% N) is a highly concentrated form of nitrogen. Although it is chemically manufactured, the nitrogen is in the amide or organic form. Its nitrogen is quickly available to the trees. Urea may be used as liquid, produced by dissolving 15 g urea in 15 litres water. If used repeatedly it will also acidify the soil.

2. Phosphatic fertilisers

Superphosphate The content is indicated as the amount of phosphate which will dissolve in water, and this is in the region of 10%. It contains about 50% calcium sulphate, which prevents it from affecting the pH of the soil. It is the most popular form of phosphate.

Raw ground phosphate rock is not a fertiliser, it is simply crushed phosphatic rock. It is used as a long term treatment of the soil, because although it contains a high quantity of phosphorus, this is not in a form that can be utilised by plants.

A mixture of superphosphate and ground phosphate which combines the properties of the two.

Basic slag is a by-product of the steel industry. It is finely ground and contains 7% phosphorus, as well as some calcium compounds and trace elements magnesium and manganese.

3. Potassic fertilisers

Potassic fertilisers are seldom used on their own because the combination fertilisers usually contain enough potassium to cover the needs of most plants. However when chicken manure is used, additional potassium is needed.

Sulphate of potash (40% K)

Muriate of potash (50% K) is usually applied but care should be taken not to use it in excess.

Potash contains potassium as well as lime, but when it is exposed to rain the potassium salts are leached out.

4. Fertiliser combinations

These are the combinations of the nitrogen, phosphorus and potassium elements mentioned earlier on page 122.

Lime

Lime is mainly applied to the soil to correct the acicity (pH) and not to supplement any calcium deficiency in the plants. The lime itself is not a fertiliser, but through its action on the pH, it enables plants to utilise other nutrients such as phosphates which cannot be taken up in very acid soil. Be very careful when applying lime and never do so before the soil has been tested for acidity. If through the application of lime the soil becomes too alkaline, it will not be able to absorb such elements as manganese and iron.

Lime not only affects the acidity of the soil, but it also changes the physical condition by binding very sandy soil and breaking up clay. By correcting the acidity, lime also enables micro-organisms to live under more acceptable conditions for their own effectiveness.

Two types of lime are recommended for use, namely calcium carbonate and calcium hydroxide (agricultural lime and slaked lime).

SOIL

The soil consists of five components:
- minerals (inorganic)
- plant and animal deposits in varying degrees of decomposition (organic)
- water in which different materials have dissolved
- air
- numerous living organisms, from the smallest fungi and bacteria to insects like earthworms and crickets.

These listed components form the living soil mixture — with every one of the components necessary to nourish the plants living in the soil. When a hole is dug in the soil, three different layers will be noticed. This is known as the soil profile.

The three layers are as follows:

(a) Topsoil — the uppermost layer. It contains the plant and animal deposits. It is home to many micro-organisms. Topsoil is exposed to the rain which washes out some of the salts and nutrients. This is called leaching out. The rainwater and humus humus increase the acidity of the soil, which in turn enables the water to react chemically with the minerals.

(b) Subsoil — the middle layer. It contains more clay, as this is washed out of the topsoil. This is a hard layer which is not penetrated easily by plant roots.

(c) Geological base — the bottom layer. It is the layer of mineral materials of geological origin, and it may be solid rock or porous or loose soil to a great depth. It is very poor in humus and living organisms.

Soil is in fact a framework of solid inorganic particles with spaces in between. The solid particles occupy 50% of the total dry soil volume — the rest is air. These solid particles are the remnants of rocks from which soil was formed eons ago and it means that they have resisted the erosion process over many thousands of years, which again means that they are nearly inert, and act only as framework to contain the water and nutrients.

Kinds of soil

According to texture, soil is divided into sand, loam and clay.

SAND These particles barely cling to each other, even when wet. This means soil with a high sand content can be handled easily, and contains a lot of air. The disadvantage is its inability to retain water and its low nutrient value.

LOAM These particles are finer than sand and cling together better, leaving fewer air spaces. Loam has a good water retention ability and a higher nutrient content.

CLAY Clay particles are extremely small — in fact at least one thousand times smaller than sand. The particles are called colloids, which are flat, irregularly shaped discs. They are formed from potassium and aluminium silicates, and are still able to react chemically and to participate in the release of nutrients to the plants' roots. Because the colloids are so small and flat, they compact tightly, which causes the inter-particle water to be released slowly and vice versa, that is, when clay becomes dry it does not absorb water easily. The advantage of clay is that due to its water retention, it holds the nutrients available for absorption through the hair roots.

A good general soil mix should be such that you can compress it into a ball in your hand when it is optimally wet, but should you tap the same ball with a finger, it must crumble to pieces.

The organic components of soil

The organic components are derived from plant, animal and insect deposits and debris. Plants take whatever they need from the soil, but add to soil again in the form of dead leaves, branches and roots. Very little soil has adequate organic content unless it has been deliberately added. This is then the reason for working compost, animal manure and other organic products into the soil.

COMPOST The word compost is derived from the Latin verb *componere* which means: 'To put together'. Compost is the end product resulting from the breakdown of organic matter by bacteria and other micro-organisms, with help from insects such as earthworms. Organic matter is of plant, animal or insect origin — in fact, the remains thereof. It is all some kind of carbon compound. Material to make compost could be nearly any plant components cut up into small pieces. Materials to avoid are high carbon-low nitrogen wastes like mature grass, straw, paper, sawdust and wood shavings, woody stems of shrubs and coarse hedge clippings. Avoid plants containing oils or resins, for example leaves of the eucalyptus trees or pine needles, because they are slow to decompose. Nitrogen is the major element required by micro-organisms as they decompose organic matter to acquire carbon products for their energy uses. A nitrogen deficiency will limit the process. Nitrogen can be lost, as ammonia gas, if the compost heap is too loose, or it could be leached out as nitrate, through rain. Loss of nitrogen can be compensated for by adding animal manure, blood and bone and inorganic nitrogen fertilisers.

For ordinary plants, add small quantities of agricultural lime, because slightly acid or neutral conditions in the compost heap will promote the activities of micro-organisms and earthworms. For acid-loving plants, like azaleas or camellias, lime should be omitted. In their case, gypsum, which is an alternative source of calcium, can be added to advantage.

There are many millions of tiny living organisms in the soil. These organisms help to break down the soil, but also form antibiotics, which protect the plants against diseases. The organisms need the nutrients and energy derived from the organic material. The organic material also improves the physical condition of the soil by breaking up heavy soil into smaller pieces. This means that it granulates the soil and makes it porous, enabling the roots to spread better. It also aerates the soil. When soil is not aerated it becomes solid and sour (acid) and does not allow natural decomposition to occur.

There are good reasons for adding compost to soil instead of raw organic materials. First, decomposed compost has a balance of carbon and nitrogen compounds which produce a nitrogen-rich residue. Raw materials are low in nitrogen content and the micro-organisms use what little nitrogen there is in the soil to break down the raw organic materials. Second, with large quantities of raw organic compounds to be broken up the plant roots may well suffer from an excess of carbon dioxide, which is a by-product of decomposition. Even traces of ammonia may be liberated and this has a detrimental effect on germination of some seeds and on the early growth of seedlings.

HUMUS It is very important to note that organic material is the main source of nitrogen supply. Most of the compost does not decompose immediately when it is mixed with the soil, but only over a period of months to years. The portion of compost which breaks down to simple chemicals consists mostly of carbohydrates (starches) and proteins. The remainder consists of fragments which join together into small particles to form a dark brown substance (sometimes called black earth). This substance is humus. Humus particles act as colloids and are able to attract and hold plant nutrients on their surfaces. They also improve the drainage and aeration of heavy soils. Humus improves the physical quality of the soil by binding sand, loam and clay particles into crumbs or aggregates. Humus is the vital centre of chemical and biological activity. It acts as a reservoir for storing nutrients and moisture. Humus also acts as a space-filler and as the humus is used, spaces develop in the soil not only to accommodate root growth but also to allow air and water exchange.

It is mainly through bacterial action that nitrogen is released from the humus in a usable form for plants. Interesting is the fact that 70% of the air consists of nitrogen, but in an inactive (inert) form. It is thus clear that the bacteria must be kept alive in the soil and it is wrong in principle to sterilise soil used for bonsai, whether through chemicals or heat. Some chemicals like Jeyes fluid and methylbromide, however, kill only harmful bacteria. Methylbromide should be used where large volumes of soil need to be treated. Jeyes fluid could be used as 50 ml in 10 litres water for each square metre of garden soil. It penetrates the soil for about 1/2 metre, which would mean 50 ml Jeyes fluid per 0,5 cubic metre of soil. It must be stated that Jeyes fluid has not been registered as being safe for plants and it is cumulative in effect, which means it stays in the soil for a long time and, if used repeatedly in the same soil mass, the effect is intensified. I contend that by using fresh soil and good compost a healthy bonsai will result. Refrain from using chemicals in the war against pests and diseases as far as possible.

PEAT Peat is a brown fibrous organic material formed by the decay of vegetation, but where the process has been checked by extremely wet and usually very acid conditions. The plants from which peat is derived are commonly mosses, especially sphagnum, and other bog species. Peatmoss is poor as a supplier of plant nutrients. It is strongly acid, and lime should be added (apart from fertilisers) unless acid loving plants are to be grown. Peat should mostly be used as soil conditioner because its nutrients are released so slowly. It contains, for example, twice as much nitrogen as cattle manure, but very little of it can be utilised. Peat loosens the soil and aerates it. It has the same properties as clay in that it holds moisture for a long time but once dry, does not wet easily.

MANURE Animal manure, including cattle, horse and pig manures, is mixed with soil mainly for its humus forming property. It is also a good source of nutrients. One ton of cattle manure produces approximately 5 kg phosphorus and 4 kg potassium. The advantage of cattle manure is that it stays active over a long period and releases the nutrients slowly, preventing root-burn.

The effect of fertilisers in the soil

Fertilisers are chemicals manufactured in factories. They are supplied in the ratios of 2:3:1, 3:2:1 as well as other mixtures such as limestone ammonium nitrate. They contain different forms of potassium, nitrates, nitrogen, ammonium, calcium and other elements. Fertilisers should be considered as supplements for the nutrition of a bonsai. Soil quickly deteriorates as the humus is consumed and the application of fertilisers is then indicated. One big problem is the possibility of root-burn through concentrated fertilisers. Excellent combinations of nutrients are supplied, however, in varying ratios to reach different results and in concentrations that cannot burn the roots. Very important is the inclusion of trace-elements which may be lacking in the natural nutrients. Excellent products which are available are the seaweed derivations. The first variety contains cytokinins and is a plant growth stimulant that increases the number of flowers and shoot and root masses. The second variety also includes trace-elements. Somehow both these products keep insects off the plants as well as certain other pests.

Osmosis is the process whereby solutions intermix through a semi-permeable membrane, depending on the concentration on the two sides of the membrane. If you have a high concentration of, for instance salt, on side A of a membrane, you would find that the concentration tries to even out by the salt (in solution) moving through the membrane to side B or, conversely, water would move to the high concentration to dilute it. This explanation is needed to understand how the roots absorb fertilisers, or for that matter, water.

Roots prefer to absorb water that is as close to a distilled condition (pure water) as possible. If the water contains fertilisers or salts in a high concentration, the roots will not be able to absorb them or the water in which they are dissolved. (And please note that to be able to absorb any fertiliser, it must be dissolved!) In fact, the reverse may happen in that the high concentration of fertiliser might even draw water from the roots back to the soil — that is, it will burn the roots! (reverse osmosis). When applying fertilisers, it is better if it is done frequently, but in reduced concentrations. With a high concentration of fertiliser you could even find your bonsai wilting, as it cannot absorb the water from the 'wet' soil.

Soil water

The soil is permeated with tiny spaces containing either water or air. Too little water is the obvious problem, but too much water is a problem on its own. It is the bonsai grower's responsibility to control the water content of the soil with judicious use of his knowledge of the water needs of a particular tree, as well as the soil's ability to retain water in the container and the existing climatic conditions.

Water is extremely important in the health and growth of a tree as it determines the eventual growth in different ways, for instance it acts as a carrier for all the nutrients as they are dissolved in the water. If too much water is given, it can wash the nutrients out of the soil (leaching out!). It may also happen that the concentration of fertilisers in the water is so high that through osmosis the water is drawn out of the tree (to dilute the high concentration), and although the tree may be receiving a lot of water it will wilt.

By whichever method a bonsai is watered, some of the water is going to run off the soil surface, while the rest enters the soil by filling up the existing spaces. If a bonsai container does not have large enough drainage holes, the water will collect in the pot and the roots will suffocate. The soil mixture should be of a kind to retain enough water between watering sessions. When the water is absorbed and the surplus drains through the holes in the pot, fresh air is literally sucked into the soil. This should occur repeatedly. If there is a small ridge around the drainage hole, the bottom section of the soil will stay soggy and wet, because it cannot drain away.

Water is retained in the soil in two ways. Firstly, water is present as capillary water which is free to be absorbed. secondly, water is present as hygroscopic water which surrounds soil particles and clings tightly to them due to surface tension. The optimal moisture content of the soil is 25% — that means half of the spaces between the soil particles are filled with water.

It is obvious that individual watering of trees compared to a general system is preferable by far.

Acidity of the soil

Soil can be either acid, neutral or alkaline. The scientific abbreviation, pH, is used when referring to the soil's acid or alkaline content. pH is expressed on a scale from 0 to 12, with pH = 7 as neutral. When the pH is below 7, the soil is acid, and above 7 it is alkaline (or as some people say, it is basic). pH refers to the proportional presence of hydrogen (H^+) ions. The more hydrogen ions present, the more acid the soil, and the more hydroxyl ions (OH^-) present the more alkaline.

Where there is a higher rainfall, the soil is more acid. This is not the case with tapwater or borehole water.

A tree normally prefers a pH from 4,5 to 6,5. Exceptions are trees like leptospermums, azaleas and camellias which prefer a very acid soil. It is rare to need

LEFT
Acer beurgerianum
Trident maple
Height: 66 cm
Width: 80 cm
Owner: Alf Jones

BELOW LEFT
Celtis africana
White stinkwood
Height: 20 cm
Owner: Derry Ralph

RIGHT
Juniperus sabina tamariscifolia
Spanish juniper
Height: 75 cm
Owner: Alf Jones

FAR RIGHT
Ulmus parvifolia
Chinese elm
Height: 65 cm
Owner: Eddie van der Westhuizen

BELOW RIGHT
Celtis africana
White stinkwood
Height: 63 cm
Owner: Derry Ralph

a very alkaline soil.

Chemicals, and more importantly, nutrients are broken down for absorption at a better rate and quantity in an acid soil. The pH also influences the activity of bacteria and fungi such as mycorrhiza, which prefer a more acid soil.

Leaching

Leaching refers to the washing out from the soil of soluble plant nutrients. The degree to which this happens depends on two factors, namely the type of soil and the amount of water the soil receives. Yellow or grey soil often suggests leaching.

Good drainage of the soil is essential to leach out excess fertilisers and salts. If this is inadequate, the salts will cause a white deposit on the soil at the base of the trunk or at the edges of the container. However, these deposits could also be the result of a too highly concentrated fertiliser being applied, with the result that the bonsai cannot utilise it all.

ROOTS

Roots have two functions, namely to anchor the tree to the soil and to absorb nutrients and water.

The growing portion of the root is a white flexible tip. The tip is hollow and contains a tiny loose ball of starch, the position of which is influenced by gravity. This little ball helps the root to determine how to grow downwards. Special cells on this tip form a protective thimble-like sheath. As the root progresses through the soil, these cells are worn off and this results in the root-tip being slimy and smooth, which helps it to move between soil particles. The worn-off cells are replaced from the inside of the root tip.

Behind the root-tip is a smooth shiny part where cells increase in length, and in so doing, push the root tip forwards. Directly behind this part is the area where root-hairs develop. Root-hairs represent the mouth of the tree, through which water and nutrients are absorbed. To thoroughly utilise the soil, an enormous root system is formed. It has been shown through experimental calculation that a single sunflower plant has a total root length of 440 metres.

Normally roots are very easily formed when needed; for instance after a root pruning and repotting session.

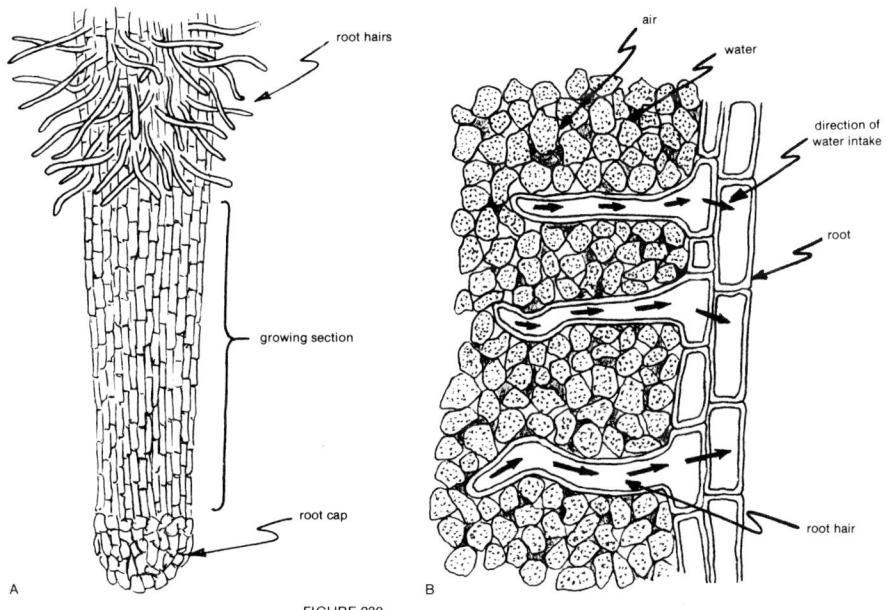

FIGURE 230
A. A root-tip enlarged.
B. Root-hairs growing between soil particles.

It is interesting to notice that roots have the ability, through contraction, to maintain a tree's level in the soil.

When a tree is growing unrestricted in open soil, which is poor or barren, the roots will spread out wide and be sparse as they search for water and nutrients. With a rich, fertile soil the tree will have a compact root-spread as the roots do not need to search for nutrients.

In a restricting container, as in the case of a bonsai, a poor soil mixture will result in a sparse root system, and the tree will deteriorate rapidly. With a rich soil mixture the roots will grow quickly and start off in a more or less horizontal direction towards the vertical sides of the container. As soon as they reach this obstruction, they will grow downwards. When they reach the bottom of the pot they will grow horizontally and inwards. This means that the ball of soil beneath the trunk is not used.

The bonsai grower needs to find an average soil mixture which prevents either of the above conditions.

Another difference to be observed in a container-grown tree, is that as the roots grow, the space in the container is gradually filled and a situation is reached where no spaces are left to contain water or air. This once again stresses the need for organic materials to create space.

Mycorrhiza

On some trees a fungus grows within or surrounding the smaller roots. It is called mycorrhiza. It is a symbiotic parasite, which means that although it lives on and uses the host (the tree), it is also beneficial to the host. With some trees like pines, firs, cedars, spruce, beech and oak, the mycorrhiza grows on the outside of the roots. Other trees, like junipers, maples and casuarina, actually have the mycorrhiza growing inside the roots and it is invisible to the naked eye. Mycorrhiza is species specific. The mycorrhiza of a pine will only grow on a pine and not for instance on a beech or oak.

To show how important mycorrhiza is, it was placed in water, and this solution was used to water young trees. Their growth was compared to trees which did not receive this suspension. The trees receiving mycorrhiza suspension showed a much better growth.

Apparently mycorrhiza functions through enlarging the root surface, and although it uses carbohydrates and vitamins from the tree, it gives the tree a better absorption ability. Apart from this, mycorrhiza produces acids which break down the soil around the roots as well as the organic nutrients, thus improving the tree's ability to absorb nutrients and minerals. Mycorrhiza also absorbs ions which it makes available to the tree (ions being electrically unbalanced elements — thus actually ready to combine with another oppositely loaded ion).

When, for instance, a pine is repotted, the white fluffy substance among the roots, namely mycorrhiza, must be repotted along with the tree. Collect the mycorrhiza, mix it with some of the new soil mixture and line the bottom of the new container with it. Never remove the mycorrhiza from the roots.

PRACTICAL TIPS

When clay or sand is used, it should be washed to remove the dust, otherwise the dust will clog up all the spaces in the soil.

Preferably use a sharp or angular sand, as opposed to sand that has been washed smooth. Sharp sand will cause the roots to divide and form a denser, more fibrous root system. Sand in the upper course of a river is still sharp, whilst sand near the estuaries is weathered and thus smooth. Sand with a smaller grain is used to develop a more finely divided root system, although it retards root growth to a degree.

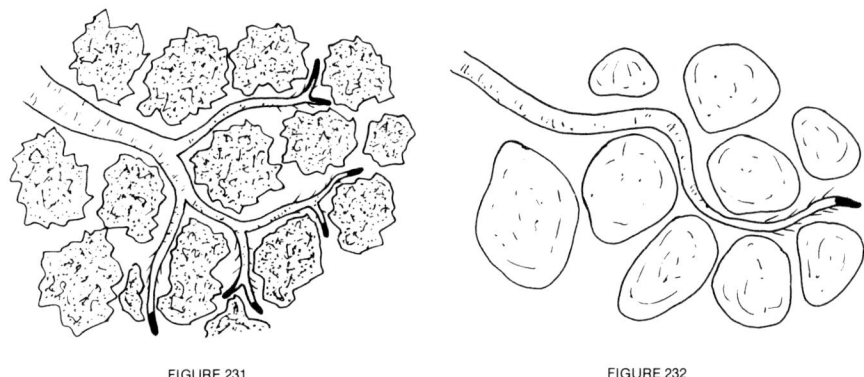

FIGURE 231 The sharp (rough) soil particles cause the roots to split up and divide many times.

FIGURE 232 Rounded soil particles cause the root-tip to slide between the individual particles instead of dividing.

Coarse sand speeds up development of roots but also improves drainage. With coarse sand, the roots are not so finely divided.

Soil mixture

To say that a particular species of bonsai needs a specific soil mixture (as growing medium) is only true in a general sense. Different factors influence the tree's reaction to the soil mixture in the container, from the quality of the pot to the reigning climate. The humidity of the air is going to affect the transpiration (loss of water through leaves). The temperature, the wind conditions and the area where the trees are kept all matter.

The bonsai grower will have to adjust the soil mixture to compensate for the above-mentioned conditions. Experiment with different mixtures and seek advice from experienced growers and nurseries in the area.

Possibly the most important feature of a bonsai soil mix is the soil's ability to allow water to drain off, soon after having received it. Any water that enters the soil must drain through the drainage holes (after having drained through the soil!) within a day or two, or else the roots will be immersed in water for too long. Being surrounded by water will mean that normal transfer of gases at root level cannot take place and the roots will deteriorate. The *akadama* clay soil used in Japan has as its main advantage exactly this capacity for excellent drainage. In the United States of America a similar although synthetically prepared material is used, namely calcined clay. Another alternative to ensure good drainage is making use of sand particles of different sizes, mixed with a material which will retain some water, as is detailed a little further on. Some degree of water retention is necessary otherwise the water flows through the soil mix in too short a time and the roots dry out. This is, however, where the problem lies, in that a balance has to be achieved between drainage and water retention.

The soil has to retain water at least for a short period of time. This statement does not contradict the previous one, because if you only take care of the drainage you could have a soil mix which does not hold water at all, and may dry out in a matter of a few hours — not what you would want at all. This means that if a pure sand mix is used some material which will retain water has to be added. This could be in the form of washed crushed clinker, peat moss or compost, for example. Each one of these has some merits as well as demerits. For instance, the clinker has a good water retention capacity but little nutrient value, as opposed to compost which has good water retention as well as nutrient value. In addition, compost aerates the soil, and, as it is utilised, it allows spaces to be formed into which roots can develop. This effect is temporary and the compost needs to be replenished as soon as it is depleted. Peat only conditions the soil, and contributes very little towards the nutrient value, as well as being slightly acid, although the acidity depends on the origin of the peat. Also the acidity can easily be counteracted by adding lime to the soil. Unless a lot of peat is used, it will not have a practical effect on an ordinarily basic (alkaline) soil, due to the fact that most plants grow well in a pH range and not a specific acidity or alkalinity.

You can allow the soil mix to be devoid of nutrients or have a very low cation exchange capacity (CEC), i.e. a low rate of nutrient release, for the simple reason that many different formulations of fertilisers are available, or may be made up, that could be applied to the soil mix. In so doing, trees can be nourished at will and in a controlled manner. This method is in fact gaining in popularity throughout the world. If a so-called soilless mix is used, this has the additional advantage that it is also weedless and is removed from the roots exceptionally easily when it is time for the tree to be repotted. The same mixture can also be re-used after adding some peat or compost. It may thus be more appropriate to speak of a growing medium, rather than a soil mix.

By using sand of different size gradings and degrees of sharpness, a better root system is developed. It also means that the same soil mix can be made up every time due to the fact that sand is *supplied* in different size gradings or you can make up your own sand gradings by using sieves (screens).

Be sure to use a soil mix which is heavy enough to stabilise or anchor the tree. A case in point is the use of vermiculite which, although it is able to absorb water, is too light in weight to support the tree.

You have to take the colour of the soil into account, although this only matters for the soil at the surface, as this is the only soil you can see after the bonsai has been potted. I use a kind of brittle rock which is abundant in the area where I live, and I crush this rock which is then screened according to size and used in the soil mix. After having sieved the crushed rock, a very fine sand remains (the particles from 0,2 to 0,5 mm in size) and this is used to cover the surface sand (crushed rock). It has an acceptable soil colour and is of such a nature that moss will grow on it. In the case of larger or more rugged looking trees, I simply use a larger sized grit, in the areas where moss will not be growing. I have come across different shades of brown in this same rocky material and can thus change the colour to match the tree and pot. A simple and effective solution is to use silica sand (supplied by the manufacturers of sand for swimming pool filters) which is supplied in different size gradings.

I do think that you have to use different soil mixes for trees of different sizes and ages. In general it is so that larger trees will prefer a soil mix containing large and medium sand particles, while smaller trees prefer medium and small particles. These sizes are explained in the next paragraph. It is also necessary to distinguish between younger and older trees or, to be precise, between recently potted and more established trees. Large bonsai are trees somewhere in the order of more than 650 mm in height, and older trees are those that have been trained in pots for longer than five years. This distinction is only for the purpose of mixing the growing medium. There are simple, practical reasons for using different sized sand particles as these examples will show:

- If a bonsai is small and is thus grown in a small pot, there simply is not enough space for large sand particles, whereas in the case of a large pot, larger particles are more suitable.
- Smaller sand particles will cause the roots to divide and establish a finer root system, which is so necessary for any bonsai and this process should be started when the trees are still in the initial stages of training — thus with young bonsai.
- Trees which cannot stand a very wet soil mix need larger sand particles to ensure good drainage.

The following is a guide to the size groupings of sand particles:
- Large particles will pass through a 6 mm screen, but not through a 3 mm one.
- Medium sized particles will pass through a 3 mm screen, but not through a 1,5 mm one.
- Small particles will pass through a 1,5 mm screen, but not through a 0,5 mm one.

The details of what makes up naturally occurring soil are discussed earlier on page 125, but this soil cannot be used as the growing medium for bonsai, for the reasons mentioned above. Some adaptations have to be made for bonsai soil mixes, with specific reasons for doing so each time. Possibly the first choice you have to make is whether you are going to use any garden soil at all, that is, using a 'soilless' growing medium or not. The merits of not using garden soil include having no weeds appearing in the mix, having complete control over the supply of nutrients and being able to make up a mix which has the same ingredients every time. One problem with the soilless mix is that you have to make provision for water retention in some manner and this is usually achieved by including compost or peat moss in the mix, with calcined clay, clinker and fir bark sometimes used for the same purpose. When including garden soil in the mix be sure that it is of a loamy nature and that it does not make up more than one third of the volume of the mix. Clinker has to be washed, to clean it and rid it of poisonous chemicals, of which sulphur is but one.

In order to mix the ingredients properly it is best to use them in a dry state and, once mixed, they should be of such a nature that, if you pick up a handful of the mix and then open your hand, the soil mix should sift through the fingers.

If you decide to place the different grade sizes of soil mix separately in layers in the bonsai container, the large particles must be at the bottom to ensure drainage, followed by the medium-sized particles with the small particles on top. In time however, through the washing action of the water, the small particles will sift down between the others and start clogging up the air spaces which spoils what was originally intended to be a loose, aerated soil mix. It is also found that water has some difficulty moving from one layer to the next, which could complicate the watering of the tree and the eventual spread of the roots. I prefer to have a definite layer of coarse sand in the bottom of the container for drainage purposes and then mix the particles for whichever tree is grown, to form the bulk in the middle, with a very thin layer of crushed rock on top to round off the planting.

A very general mix is the following: one part soil; one part compost or peat; one part large sand particles; one part medium sized sand particles — all measured by volume. This mix is then changed for particular trees; for instance, for smaller or younger trees the large sand particles will have to be replaced by small particles. Trial and error, the experience of friends and information from other sources will all influence the mix you are going to use in the end.

HOW PLANTS LIVE

The roots

The root system anchors the tree in the soil and extracts the nutrients needed for growth. The tiny little root hairs on the root tips absorb moisture and dissolved nutrients and they keep a constant flow of sap going through the whole plant. A single wheat plant may need 2,5 litres of water a day.

Both the roots and stem grow from a single cell, but the roots grow downwards and the stem upwards towards the light (positive phototropic). Once the seedling's stem is exposed to light, a pigment called chlorophyll forms. From this moment on the plant can take in its own nutrients and in this manner feed its growing tissues.

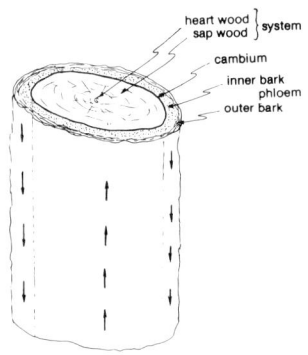

FIGURE 233 A section of a trunk to show the direction of sap-flow.

The trunk

The stem (or trunk) has two functions: first, it has to support the branches with leaves and flowers for the purpose of food manufacture and reproduction; second, it contains channels which distribute the water and dissolved nutrients (which have been absorbed by the roots) to the leaves, and distribute food produced by the leaves back to the other sections of the plant.

The stem (trunk) is divided into three sections. The inner layer is the xylem or sapwood. This layer is responsible for the transport of water, minerals and nutrients up towards the leaves. In the very middle of the sapwood mature wood is formed, this being the wood that is eventually used for the manufacture of all kinds of products.

The inner layer is surrounded by the only living layer of the trunk, which is called the cambium. It is the layer of cells from which growth takes place. You will find that I often refer to this cambium layer, because if it is damaged, the results could be fatal to the tree, but it is also the cambium which enables you to do grafting as well as any repair work on a tree.

On the outside of the cambium is the phloem, which is the bark of the tree. The phloem has two sections, namely an outer bark which can be pulled off easily and an inner bark, which is responsible for the transportation of food products from the leaves to the rest of the tree.

The leaves

Their main function is the production of food through the process of photosynthesis (manufacturing through light). The leaves use the energy of sunlight to manufacture sugars and other complex foods from the simple raw materials and water absorbed by the roots, as well as the carbon dioxide 'breathed' in through the stomata of the leaves. A key in the process is chlorophyll, the substance which makes leaves green. Chlorophyll absorbs the sun's light rays and converts them into a form of energy for the manufacture of the plant's food (carbohydrates — which are sugars and starches).

The lower surface of the leaf, as well as the upper surface, is covered by a transparent wax-like layer of cells, but the lower surface contains many openings (valves), known as stomata (Greek for mouths). When the plant has absorbed sufficient water, the stomata open up to allow water vapour to escape and more air to enter the leaves. With plentiful supply of water available, the food production in the leaves is increased. When the water supply diminishes, the reverse happens. The activity of stomata is affected by light as folows: the two kidney-shaped cells forming the lips of the stomata contain chloroplasts which become active in light, the sugar content of the cells increases and more water is required. The water entering the cells makes them swell and that action opens the stomata. When light diminishes, as in the darkness of night, the sugar turns to starch, the cells lose water and the stomata close up.

Water and other dissolved chemicals move up the trunk and branches through the xylem into the leaves. Here they come into contact with the carbon-dioxide breathed in by the leaves. Where this happens in cells containing chlorophyll and in the presence of light, the light energy sets off a series of reactions, from which glucose (a sugar or carbohydrate) is formed. A by-product is oxygen which is released into the atmosphere through the stomata — a process which is responsible for the maintenance of life as we know it. As the glucose accumulates in the leaf, it is converted into other sugars and starches which are redistributed throughout the tree by means of the phloem.

The greener the leaf, the more chlorophyll it contains. Some trees are grown for their coloured leaves, the colour of which is formed through pigments which mask the chlorophyll. Green leaves, photosynthesis and light go together. Without light, leaves turn pale and eventually white, and growth ceases. All light-loving plants have mechanisms, usually in their leaf stalks and growing tips, whereby they can turn their leaves so as to allow the greatest amount of leaf surface to face towards the source of light.

Added to this you will find that the side of the plant directed towards the light is the side that flourishes. For this reason bonsai have to be turned repeatedly so as to present all sides in turn to the sun.

The respiration of the plant must not be confused with the use and release of carbon-dioxide and oxygen through the process of photosynthesis. Plant cells also 'breathe' to take in oxygen for the manufacture of food, liberating carbon-dioxide in the process.

AUTUMN

Deciduous trees are now preparing to shed their leaves. Some degree of change in leaf colour is going to occur, which will vary from a fading in the green to the prettiest oranges, reds and purples. The tranquillity of the greens is replaced by the warmth and liveliness of the autumn colours — a delight to the eye.

Remember that the shape of the bonsai tree is of greater importance than the presence of flowers and fruits. At all times the correct shape must be your prime concern, even if it is at the expense of flowers and fruit. Once the right shape has been achieved, you can concentrate on producing good flowers and fruit. The foliage of a bonsai can be enjoyed and appreciated all year round — with perhaps a little more enjoyment during autumn. As a matter of fact the shape of a tree can also be appreciated during winter!

What happens to change the colours in the leaves? The green colour of a leaf is dependent on the presence of a chemical called chlorophyll. Cholorophyll is not stable and is continuously being broken down and rebuilt. During the active growth period, enough chlorophyll is formed to make up for the loss, which results in the leaf staying green. There are two ways of forming autumn colours:

- As soon as the temperatures start falling, the production of chlorophyll is retarded up to a point where the production is less than the breakdown. When this happens, pigments which are there, but were masked by the presence of chlorophyll, become visible. These pigments are formed by chemicals called carotenoids (carotene) and anthoxanthina (xantophyll). Carotene is orange-yellow and xantophyll is light yellow. Trees like *Ulmus, Betula, Ginkgo, Larix, Celtis* and acacias change colour in the above-mentioned way. This change in colour is seen mainly in deciduous trees, but can also be seen to a lesser degree in some evergreen trees, which revert back to normal in spring. Examples of 'evergreens' that change colour are *Cryptomeria japonica, Citharexillum quadrangulare* and *Buxus*.
- During autumn, sugars are trapped in the leaves as the day temperatures are still reasonably high, but night temperatures are too cold to allow the tree to move the sugars down into the trunk. If these sugars were to collect in the leaves, a high pressure would develop which would rupture the cell walls and destroy them. To prevent this happening, the sugars are transformed into flavinoid pigment: flavones and anthocyanins, which are red, purple or blue. These pigments therefore, were not present during summer, but are produced specifically during autumn. Examples of trees are *Acer, Rhus, Liquidambar, Quercus* and *Fraxinus*.

In the end the leaves all turn brown because of the tannins present in the yellow leaves. In the case of the flavinoid pigments, the tannins produce the purple colours, but when all the pigments have broken down the tannin is left, giving it the brown colour.

HAIKU
A harvest moon!
And on the mats
Shadows of pine boughs

KIKAKU
From Harvest Moon

The leaves then fall off because of the action of a special little group of cells where the leaf stalk joins the branch, called the abscission layer. These special cells die and the leaf is 'shed', leaving a small scar which is sealed off. In the case of for instance the *Fagus* (beech), the new leaves push the old ones off in spring, which means that the leaves are shed at a much later date than most deciduous trees.

Practical applications

If the sap movement in the tree is very active, the colours will not be so bright and intense. That is why heavy rain or excessive watering, just when the leaves start changing colour, spoils the colours.

The trees must be free of disease and healthy for the colours to be as beautiful as they can be. Give the tree enough nutrients and do not allow it to experience drought. Keep fungal diseases and red spider-mite off the leaves.

Defoliation halfway through summer produces good autumn colours, because with the coming of autumn, the new set of leaves still contains a lot of chlorophyll and also more carotenoids and anthoxanthins.

Night temperatures of between 7 and 9 degrees Celcius are necessary to induce the formation of autumn colours. It also helps to expose the trees to sunlight, and to have five consecutive nights of cold — even frost.

Water only when necessary, and definitely not late in the day, to reduce sap-flow and trap the sugars in the leaves.

Anthoxanthin is better produced where there is less nitrogen and phosphates.

Older trees have better autumn colours, as well as trees in containers, and this may be because of reduced sap-flow.

TOOLS AND THEIR CARE

Certain tools make life a lot easier when creating bonsai. I have divided them into essential and handy.

Essential tools and equipment

- Ordinary pruning shears for cutting larger branches and roots.
- Pointed scissors to prune smaller branches and leaves.
- Wire cutter to cut wire lengths needed to train branches.
- Nylon mesh to cover drainage holes.
- Tweezer to remove weeds, dead leaves, and for other small jobs.
- Water spray or misting pump to spray roots and trees.
- Knob cutter to hollow out scar where branch is cut.
- Branch cutter for cutting smaller branches flush with the trunk or other branch.

Handy tools and equipment

- Medium-sized shears with pointed blades — for general pruning.
- *Kuikiri* trimmer to cut branch off without leaving stub, or to nip out a branch in the V-branching. A large trimmer could be used to cut large branches or roots.
- Small saw (perhaps with folding blade) — to saw thick branches, trunks or roots that cannot be pruned otherwise.
- Sharp pocket knife for grafting, budding, *shari*, etc.
- Pliers with long pointed nose for bending or removing wire. The type with only the point of the beaks touching is nice to have, as it cannot pinch branches caught between the beaks.
- Levers for bending large thick trunks or branches.
- Chopsticks to remove or compact soil between roots.
- Some form of hooked instrument to remove soil between roots.
- Small broom or brush to tidy up soil surface.
- Turntable on which to place bonsai when working on it. A stopper to lock the table into position would be ideal.

- Triangular wooden block with one side cut off at a slope, to support the bonsai pot at an angle, whilst designing.
- Carving tools to create *saba-miki* for instance.

Have a toolbox to carry the tools in, and to prevent them from getting lost.

The following items are also essential

- tree sealant;
- rooting hormone;
- vitamin B_1 and B_{12} for preventing transplant-shock;
- twine, raffia, rubber (old bicycle tube);
- epoxy glue to hold roots in *ishi-zuke* style;
- when necessary, willow twigs, to make willow water for transplanting.

Copper or aluminium wire is absolutely essential. Get a stock of different sizes (gauges).

With the right care and maintenance, the tools will last many years. Always keep all cutting instruments very sharp. After being used the blades need to be disinfected with alcohol to prevent diseases being spread. Oil moving parts regularly. It is good practice to empty a water sprayer after use and leave it open to dry, otherwise mould will form on the inside.

A few tips on using cutting instruments

- Do not cut branches or trunks thicker than the width of the blade.
- Cut with the base of the blade and not the tip, with the exception of very soft tissue.
- Do not cut a root when it still has soil covering it — soil damages the sharp cutting edges.
- Beware of cutting branches that have wire around them. Never cut wire with anything but a wire cutter.
- Keep the instruments in a dry place to prevent rust forming. Spraying them with a silicone oil will prevent rust forming.

Sharpening of cutting instruments

The bonsai cutting instruments work in two ways, namely:

- cutting in a similar fashion to scissors, which means two sharp blades sliding past each other in close proximity; and
- two sharp blades meeting each other with their edges opposing, and thus pinching off the branch or leaf.

Whichever blade is encountered, it will always have one flat surface and another bevelled surface. This bevelled surface is the one which needs to be kept sharp, and which must be kept at the same angle as when new. Before filing the blade, wipe it clean with a rag wet with a disinfectant. This must also be done after every use. At times the blade may be contaminated with a sticky substance, or it may not have been cleaned properly after use; when this is the case, the substance can be removed with steelwool. For the actual sharpening, a very fine grit sharpening oilstone should be used. The blade should be given two or three gentle rubs with the stone on the angled surface, and then one gentle rub on the back to remove any furring. When the blade is convex (lengthwise), a stone which is half round should be used, because the angled surface is in fact on the inside of the curve, that is, on the concave aspect.

Of interest is the way the instruments which do not work like scissors do in fact function. These instruments do not have their two opposing blades meeting edge to edge, although it looks like that on the surface. When looking at them closely, it can be seen that the one blade slides over the other for a very small distance. The two blades meet at a very acute angle with the one inside the other. If these blades are sharpened to meet exactly edge to edge it will jeopardise the function and quickly damage the blade.

A blade which is severely damaged needs to be tended to by a professional, who can use the appropriate tools, as long as this person has experience with bonsai tools, otherwise you can write off your instrument!

When an instrument is not being used, the blades should be protected, especially the sharp points, by slipping a rubber or plastic covering over the blades, for instance a short length of hosepipe. At all times the instruments should be handled carefully by not throwing them onto a surface or dropping them. If at all possible, design a toolbox which has special inlets in a spongy lining to house the individual instruments, or at least keep them in a container with separate sachets to prevent them bumping against one another.

POTS, POTTING AND REPOTTING

8

> *No handycraft can with our art compare*
> *For pots are made of what we potters are*
>
> A motto of 18th century potters, often used on glazed ware.

Pottery is made from naturally occurring, common clay, subjected to intense heat in a furnace. The word 'ceramic' is derived from the Greek '*Keramikos*', which means earthen; or you could think of it as 'coming from clay'. Clay does not become pottery until all the water it contains, both in free and chemically bonded form, has been removed by heat. When this is achieved by firing in a kiln, the hard permanent result is in a stable state and is more permanent than many kinds of rock. If the ceramic is covered on the surface by a glaze (glassy surface), it is even more impregnable. The atomic bonds in a ceramic crystal have both a covalent and ionic character, which are responsible for the great stability of ceramics and impart very useful properties, such as hardness and resistance to heat and chemical attack. The bonding, however, causes ceramic materials to be brittle.

The moist clay is pliant to command,
Unwrought, and easy to the potter's hand:
Now take the mould; now bend thy mind to feel
The first sharp motions of the forming wheel

DRYDEN
From *Third Satire of Persius*

HISTORY OF CERAMICS AND POTS

Ceramics are the earliest group of inorganic materials to be structurally modified by man, and his early history is principally traced by dating these materials. Ceramics did not become an everyday reality until the neolithic period (± 4000 to 2000 BC). Objects, usually containers, were made for domestic purposes. These have been found in tombs, where they were buried to accompany the dead. This ancient pottery was discovered in countries such as Spain, Scandinavia and areas surrounding the Danube River. The earliest glazing was a Sumerian invention, made famous around 4000 BC as Egyptian blue faience. This process is still in use today in Iran. From this early work all the developments in ceramic technology grew.

Clay is weathered decomposed granite, and consists mainly of alumina and silica. Where clay lies in deep beds near its origin it is likely to be fairly pure or uncontaminated. China clay or kaolin is the real mother clay, consisting of only silica, alumina and water. All other clays contain impurities and, interestingly enough, it is the impurities which give clays their character and value. For instance, clays containing iron turn a rusty pink colour once they have been fired in the kiln. The more impure a clay, the better working qualities it may have. This does not however refer to organic matter such as old dead roots, leaves or shells. These have to be removed before the clay is used.

Earthenware and stoneware form the two main groups in pottery. The difference between the two is the result of their being fired at different temperatures, during the second firing in the kiln. Earthenware is also called terracotta and it is fired at between 950 degrees Celsius and 1 100 degrees Celsius — enough to melt the glaze, but not high enough to change the body inside. At about 1 150 degrees Celsius, the clay itself begins to vitrify or to cause the particles to become fused together as a solid nonporous mass. When vitrification has taken place, it becomes stoneware. Vitrification in ceramic terms is the development of a liquid phase, by reaction or melting, which on cooling provides the glassy phase.

Stoneware firings occur at 1 250 degrees Celsius, because it is at this temperature that the glaze takes on its best character. Earthenware is the least vitrified of all ceramics, which means it is the most porous, not very dense and not very heavy. For bonsai purposes this poses a problem, because although it allows exchange of gases through the pot, the water in the soil is also lost at an alarming rate. Stoneware produces pots that are ideal for bonsai purposes. It is porous enough to allow exchange of gases through the sides of the pot, but it also absorbs water and retains it for some time before drying out. Stoneware is denser than earthenware, for the clay has fused together and it is therefore heavier than similarly sized earthenware pots.

Porcelain is a well-known branch of stoneware. It is often translucent and is light in weight. It needs a special pure clay and glaze, and is fired at between 1 350 and 1 400 degrees Celsius. Porcelain is too nonporous to be used for bonsai.

Neolithic pottery first made its appearance in the Yellow River basin in China during the third millenium BC. The first glazed surface probably dates from the Han dynasty (206 BC to 220 AD) or perhaps even earlier, from the Warring States period (403 – 206 BC). The T'ang dynasty (618 – 907 AD) and Five dynasties (907 – 960 AD) were great eras for Chinese ceramics. The first 'bonsai pots' were from the Sung dynasty (960 to 1280 AD) and thereafter.

Japanese ceramics have been so closely linked to the tea-ceremony, which has been performed since the 13th century, as well as to the techniques imported by Korean potters, that the originality of earlier pottery tends to be forgotten. History has also been strongly coloured by folklore which at times is contradictory. There are records of cord-decorated *Jomon* pottery from the third millenium to the second century BC. Due to cultural exchanges with the Chinese mainland, technical improvements were introduced to Japan. One of the stories has it that during the Kamakura period (1180 – 1330 AD) a Buddhist monk, Toshiro, who was a potter went to China and learned the techniques from the Chinese potters. He returned to Japan with large quantities of raw materials, before he started searching for similar raw materials in Japan. The Japanese had been making primitive pots since the introduction of Buddhism in the Yamato era ($\pm$ 538 AD).

The first Japanese *porcelain*, according to tradition, was manufactured by Gorodayo go Shonzui, who travelled to Ch'ing-te Chen in 1510 to study pottery. He returned after five years, also bringing along raw materials, to Arita in Hizen province, in order to manufacture 'Blue and White' porcelain. When his materials were depleted, production waned. When, in 1598, General Hideyoshi brought home among his prisoners a number of Korean potters, porcelain manufacture became popular again. Porcelains of interest to the collector thus belong almost entirely to the Edo period (1603 to 1853), when Japan was ruled by the Tokugawa shogunate at Edo, present-day Tokyo. A Korean discovered deposits of *petuntse* near Arita at the beginning of the 17th century, initiating the first major phase of porcelain production in Japan.

During the Meiji period (1869 – 1911) the Japanese imported their pottery from the Yixing kilns in China, and continued doing so until the Second World War (1938). Recently the Japanese had some of the antique pots taken back to the Yixing kilns to be duplicated. These are now called *shinsin-to* or 'the new Chinese pot'.

In the middle of the Edo period (1703 – 1800) the number of porcelain factories in Japan greatly increased, of which two deserve special mention, namely at Okawichi and Mikawachi. Six centres were well known for their ceramics, and they are known as the 'six ancient kilns of Japan' — Tokanabe, Shigaraki, Tamba,

Bizen, Echizen and Seto. Hoever, for the purposes of bonsai pots, because of the increased demand, the Japanese also started making their own pots, for instance in Tokoname, Shigaraki, Yokkaichi, and Seto areas, where many different potteries exist.

At present there is little difference between Japanese and Chinese pots. Bonsai pots are now made all over the world, to varying standards, and quality is rapidly improving.

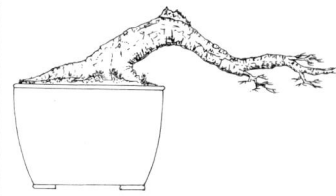

FIGURE 234 The semi-cascade in a pot which is about as high as its diameter.

About reduction firing in a kiln

An old Chinese legend tells of a potter many centuries ago who, one day, was having trouble firing his kiln. The kiln wouldn't burn properly, the chimney wouldn't draw, the area was full of smoke and filled with a terrible smell. When the potter opened the kiln his fears were justified and all his pottery with a lovely green copper glaze was ruined — all his pieces were blistered, blackened and dulled — with one exception. In the middle of the kiln was a vase which had the most beautiful blood red colour, never before seen. Every potter marvelled at it. He sent it to the Emperor as a gift, who in turn admired it so much that he had it broken up into smaller pieces which were set in rings, as though they were precious stones. Along with this came an order for a dozen more of the same vases, to the potter's despair, because try as he would he could not reproduce the vase. He tried to duplicate the formula of the glaze along with the conditions of that particular day, all to no avail. The Emperor grew impatient and as the poor potter loaded the kiln in a last attempt, his courage deserted him and he jumped into the kiln.

The kiln fire was suddenly smoky, filthy, smelly, putrid. The assistants shut down the flames and allowed the kiln to cool down. When they could open the door there was no sign of the poor potter, but lo and behold, the kiln was full of beautiful red pieces of pottery.

FIGURE 235 The full cascade in a deep round pot.

The potters thought that by substituting a dead pig in place of the potter they might achieve the same results, which indeed happened. Later they had the same results with ordinary wood and straw. The explanation, as we know today, is that the organic material causes the fire to be overloaded with carbon and the green copper oxide loses some of its oxygen (it is 'reduced') and becomes a red oxide — the *sang-de-boeuf* or ox-blood colour. The same happens to other oxides like iron, with different results!

CHOICE OF POTS

The choice of the correct pot is so important that you should never pot a tree before the tree has been shaped. In any case, you might find that the tree develops differently with time, and the pot may have to be changed again some time later. Always remember that a pot should be selected for a trained tree; never select the pot first and then train the tree to match the pot, as this would be nearly impossible.

First a few words about the colours of the pots. Most of the time the more common brown, grey and terracotta pots can be used. The surface of the pots could be glazed or dull (matte). Dull surfaces, in colours that are not too bright are suited to evergreen trees, while glazed pots are best for deciduous trees. The colour chosen should compliment the tree and its flowers or berries and fruits. A colour conveys a mood and has a psychological effect. It would be wrong, for instance, to have a rugged trunk on a rock and plant it in a white glazed pot — to give an extreme example. Glazed pots are used with azaleas and other heavily flowering species to show off the flowers. A non-glazed surface will dull your vision and prevent you from seeing the fine detail in the tree and its flowers.

FIGURE 236 A *bunjin* in a small shallow pot.

Some pots have beautiful artistic patterns or designs, either painted on or moulded into the ceramic. Be careful with these beautiful pots, for as beautiful as

FIGURE 237 The group planting in a shallow pot.

FIGURE 238 A squat short tree. The depth of the pot is equal to the diameter of the base of the trunk. The width of the pot is approximately 3/4 of the width of the tree. X = the diameter of the base and height of the pot.

FIGURE 239 A tall tree. The width of the pot is slightly more than 2/3 of the height of the tree.

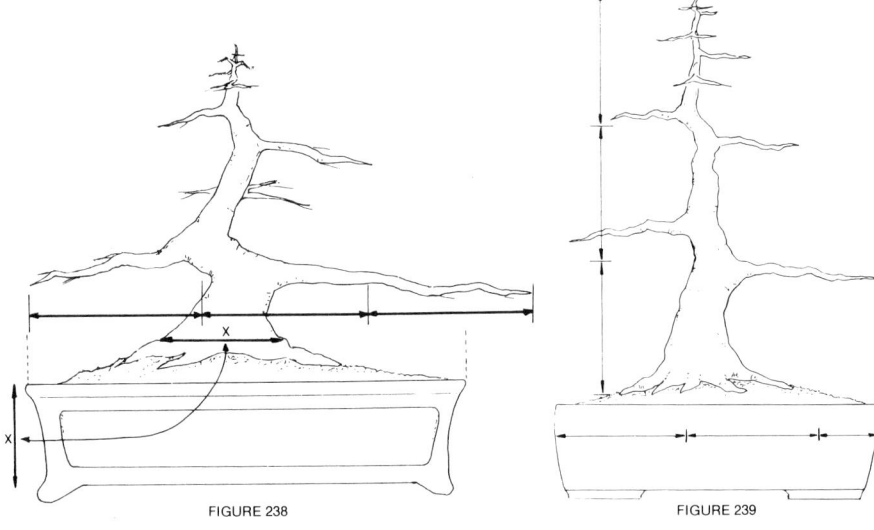

FIGURE 238

FIGURE 239

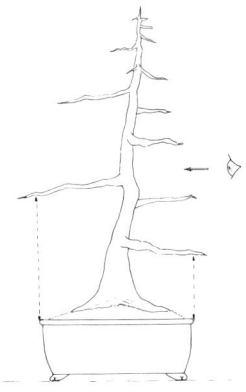

FIGURE 240 A side-view of a pot to show that the pot should be slightly narrower than the width of the tree.

they may be, they could detract from the impact the tree should have. The same applies to pots which have intricate designs. It really is an art to choose a pot which, in all aspects, compliments the tree. It is therefore wise to have a supply of pots to choose from — then you can choose a pot for a tree, and need not try to get the tree to suit the pot.

The pots that suit cascade styles, *bunjin*, multi-trunk and multiple tree styles are different from those for single trees in the various upright or slanted styles. The semi-cascade style should have a pot that is as high to about twice as high as its diameter. The cascase has a pot that is also about two or three times as high as its diameter to enable the tree to cascade. *Bunjin*, on the other hand, are grown in pots that are relatively small and usually of a round or hexagonal shape. Multiple trunk and multiple tree styles are grown in shallow pots that are oval or rectangular. With the upright and slanted styles, the shapes of the pots vary according to the appearance of the tree, its trunk diameter and texture, the style of the crown, etc. A general rule is that the depth of the pot should range from approximately the same as the diameter of the trunk at its base, to about twice the diameter. The width of the pot, as seen from the front, depends on whether the tree has its accent on the height or on the width. If the tree is tall, the width of the pot should be slightly more than two thirds (2/3) the height of the tree. If the tree is squat, where the width is more than the height, the width of the pot should be slightly more than two thirds (2/3) the width of the tree. The third dimension to consider is the width as seen from the side. Here the pot should be slightly narrower than the side width of the tree. This last dimension is not so easy to control, as the potmaker has already built this into the design of the pot.

The visual effect of a pot is also determined by the lip, the concavity or convexity of the sides and the design of the legs. If a dozen people should choose a pot for a particular tree, as many different pots may be selected, and every choice could be acceptable. It is wrong to make a fixed set of rules for the choice of a pot, but one piece of advice should be followed, and that is that it is preferable to have a pot with a subdued colour and less obtrusive shape than otherwise.

The glaze is impervious to water and should thus only be applied to the outside of the pot, extending over the lip to the inside, and ending just below the lip. If the glaze covers the whole pot, it will be detrimental to the roots of the tree, as it influences drainage and exchange of vital gases. The soil used in unglazed pots cannot be the same as the soil used in glazed pots where the glaze is overall.

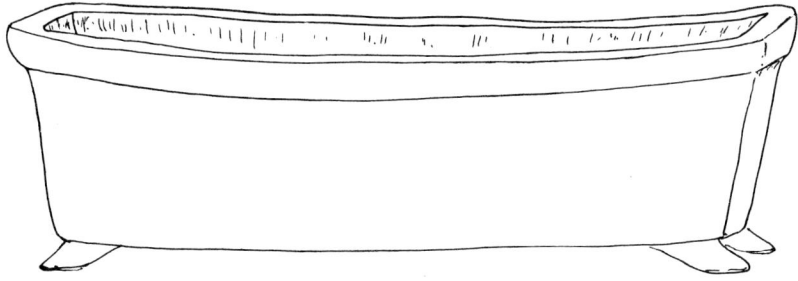

FIGURE 241 The anatomy of a pot.

THE ANATOMY OF A BONSAI POT

A bonsai pot has four parts: the lip or rim, the body, the corners and feet.

The lip could be an outer lip (directed away from the body) or an inner lip which is folded inwards towards the cavity of the pot. The lip can be with lines and angular, or soft and rounded. It could be wide or narrow. The lip can also be shaped with indentations and markings. At the other extreme, the lip could be absent and the side of the pot could end as a straight rim.

The sides of the body can be concave or convex (hollow or bulging), or straight. When straight, the sides can be nearly parallel or tapering, downwards. Sometimes the side looks like a picture frame with a ridge on the upper, lower and side edges. The pot may be decorated with a band or double band around the belly. The drum-shaped pots often have nodules like rivets all the way around. It is fairly rare to find designs like the lotus on the sides, or calligraphy, or even handpainted designs. When these designs and decorations are present, you must take great care that they do not detract from the tree. With calligraphy, the words have to match the tree's style or spirit. Chinese pots are more apt to be decorated with calligraphy and drawings of branches and flowers.

The corners can be rounded, sharp and angular or indented. The foot of a pot comes in many shapes. A very popular shape is the cloud. also seen very often is a leg with straight cut lines, which is sometimes curved in part. In some instances the foot is actually a continuation of the body of the pot and it only seems as if the lower rim has been cut out or notched. It is also possible for the pot to have no feet, but to actually rest on a ridge (or rim) which is the total circumference of the pot, to allow drainage to take place, as the base of the pot, with the drainage hole, is at a higher level than the ridge on which it is resting.

Pots come in a variety of shapes: rectangular, round, octagonal, hexagonal, quince flower shape, flower shape, bag-shaped. They can differ in depth, from shallow (about 25 mm) to deep (20 cm or more), and can be either upright or rather flat. The size of the pot could be anything from thimble size to something like one meter in diameter.

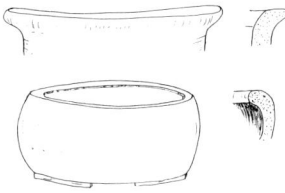

FIGURE 242 An outer and inner-projecting lip.

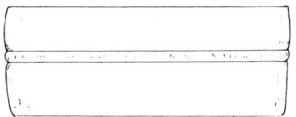

FIGURE 243 Ridging around the pot.

FIGURE 244 The side is convex.

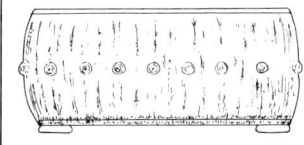

FIGURE 245 A drum-shaped pot with nodules on the sides.

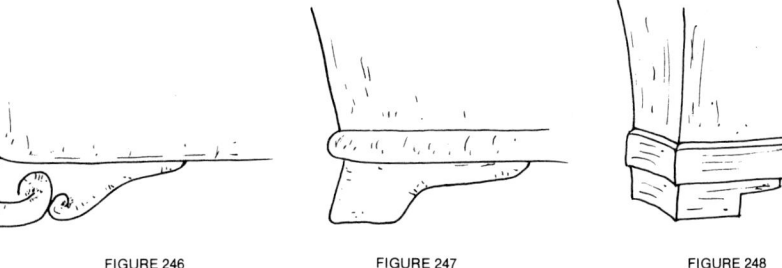

FIGURE 246   FIGURE 247   FIGURE 248

FIGURE 246 A cloud foot.

FIGURE 247 A simple foot with straight lines.

FIGURE 248 The side is slightly concave.

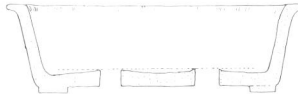

FIGURE 249 The drainage holes are higher than the base of the pot which will cause waterlogging.

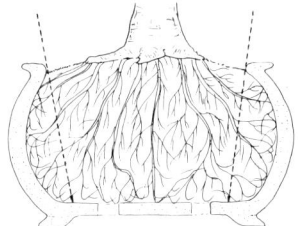

FIGURE 250 Cut along the dotted lines to ease out the trapped root-ball.

FIGURE 251 A round pot with one foot facing forwards.

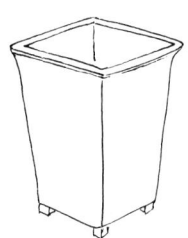

FIGURE 252 A rectangular pot with a corner facing forwards.

FIGURE 253 The opening between the legs faces forwards.

FIGURE 254 A foot facing forwards is also correct.

FIGURE 255 A notch facing forwards.

FIGURE 256 A foot facing forwards is also correct.

FIGURE 257 A shallow hexagonal pot with a side facing forwards.

FIGURE 258 A deep hexagonal pot with a corner facing forwards.

HANDLING A POT

A new pot should be soaked in water till it is saturated to prevent water absorption when the first tree is planted in it. Check whether the drainage holes don't have little ridges surrounding them, or if the floor of the pot isn't at a lower level than the drainage holes. If there is a little ridge, it can be filed down, but if the floor of the pot is the problem, it is not easy to solve. The alternatives are to either not use the pot or to drill holes in the hollow section for extra drainage.

If the pot has a folded-in lip or rim (and usually this is combined with a barrel shape), a problem arises during winter, when the soil could freeze, and, because it is trapped, the expansion might crack the pot. These pots must therefore be protected from extremely low temperatures. Another problem arises when it becomes time to repot, because the soil and root-ball will not lift out of the pot. A sharp knife will have to be used to sever the roots in the soil in order to lift the tree out of the pot.

The best side of the pot *must* face forwards!

When in doubt about the colour to use, make use of the colour wheel to help you. Choose the colour opposing the colour of the flower or berries of the bonsai or choose the colour next to the opposing one.

MATCHING POTS WITH TREES

Here follows a list of possible pots for some trees:

TREES	CONTAINERS
Strong, rugged upright, large trunk (also old tree)	Rectangular or square, straight sides, definite lip, deep, obvious legs, darker subdued colour.
Dainty upright, thin trunk	Rectangular, but more often oval or round, shallow, wide with slight or gentle curve, legs inconspicuous, light colours.
Dense heavy foliage	Rectangular or square, heavy, obvious size.
Tall tree	Pot opening towards rim and with outer lip smaller.
Short squat tree	Vertical sides, inner-lipped, bigger.
Small leaves	Simple lines, dainty.
Large leaves	Overall larger feeling, sturdy, deeper.
Informal but strong, rugged	Any shape, convex or concave or tapering to bottom, outer-lipped but not wide, or rolled lip, legs obvious and even ornamental.
Informal but dainty	Oval, round or petal-shaped, sides tapering downwards or concave but wider at top, legs inconspicuous and small, dainty.

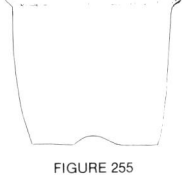

FIGURE 255

FIGURE 256

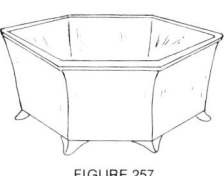

FIGURE 257

FIGURE 258

FAR LEFT
Bougainvillea
Height: 95 cm
Owner: Alf Jones

LEFT
Cedrus atlantica
Atlas cedar
Height: 55 cm
Width: 73 cm
Owner: Derry Ralph

BELOW LEFT
Juniperus
Height: 46 cm
Owner: Alf Jones

RIGHT
Pyracantha
Fire thorn
Height: 40 cm
Owner: Eddie van der Westhuizen

BELOW RIGHT
Acacia caffra
Cat thorn
Height: 46 cm
Owner: Pieter Loubser

PLACEMENT OF POT

The overall shape of the pot and its legs determines which side of the pot must face the viewer. Rectangular pots have a longer side and this is always turned towards the viewer. Square pots usually have a side facing forwards, but it is permissible to have a corner facing the viewer. With round pots the position of the feet matters, as well as it does if the pot has only notches in its lower rim — here either a notch or opening between the feet, or a foot must face forwards. As far as hexagonal pots are concerned, the shallow pot will have a side facing forwards and in the case of the deep pot a corner will face forwards.

PLACEMENT OF BONSAI IN A POT

Apart from selecting an appropriate pot, the placement of the bonsai in the pot is of ultimate importance.

Only in the case of round and even-sided pots is the bonsai placed slightly behind the exact centre of the pot. In rectangular or oval pots the bonsai is positioned off-centre, as shown in Figure 259.

The tree is placed on the mound or cone of soil, as described, so that the base of the trunk is about as high above the rim of the pot as is the depth of the pot. Obviously this does not apply when an exceptionally deep pot is used, as with cascade styles, or in certain other cases.

When repotting is done the same procedure is followed as described in the following section. The only difference is that it is nearly always accompanied by root-pruning.

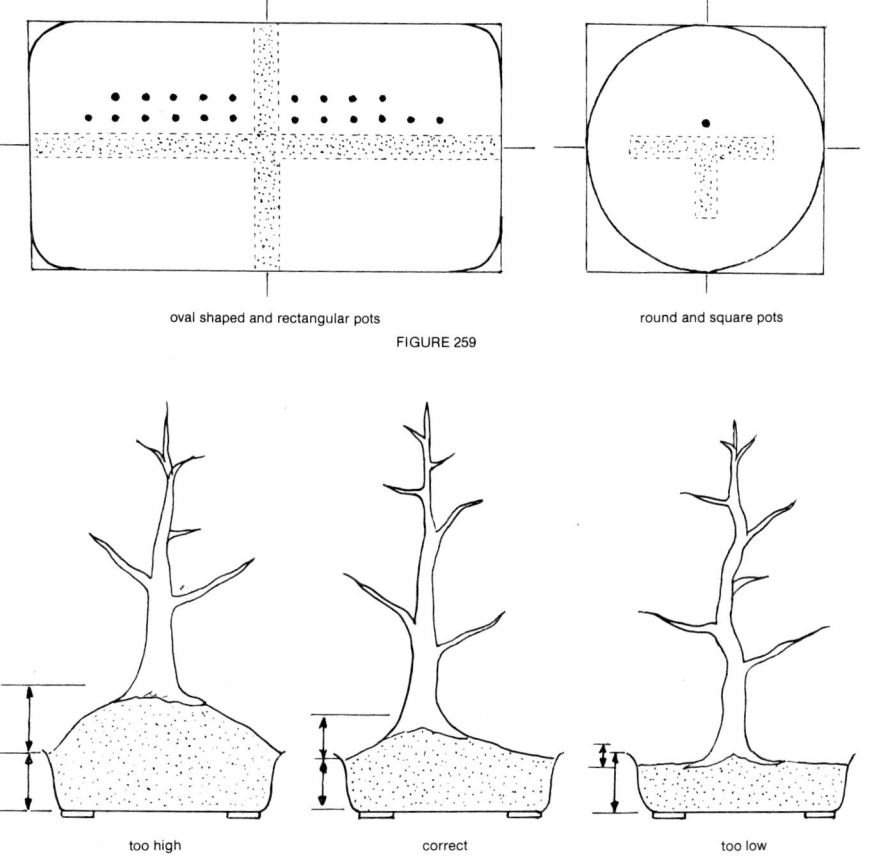

oval shaped and rectangular pots   round and square pots
FIGURE 259

FIGURE 259 The tree should be planted on the dots, depending on its shape, but never on the shaded areas.

too high   correct   too low
FIGURE 260

FIGURE 260 Height of the tree above the rim of the pot.

ROOT-PRUNING AND REPOTTING

As time goes by, the roots of a tree will gradually fill up the space available in the container. The soil will be depleted of nutrients — in fact as the roots start filling the air space, exchanging gases will become more and more difficult. Now you have a choice of either placing the tree in a bigger container, or reducing the amount of roots and giving them new soil.

A good time for root-pruning and repotting is during the end of winter and early spring, although it can also be done in summer. The disadvantage of doing it before the new buds have started developing is that the tree is dormant, and once pruned and repotted will recover quickly in the spring growth spurt. If you do the root-pruning when the buds have started opening up, the buds will not survive. In any case it is advisable to combine root-pruning with foliage trimming to *keep a balance between supply and demand*, which means that the newly formed leaves will be cut off, depleting the reserves of the tree unnecessarily, because they are now not available to form new leaves.

It is a fallacy that root-pruning is in any way harmful to the tree. Old roots cannot absorb water and minerals — this work is done by the young roots. When root-pruning is done the old roots are removed and within a few weeks they are replaced by young healthy roots which can utilise the fresh soil mixture.

A tree which needs to grow in size, could have the soil replaced every year, but once the tree has reached its mature size, the soil only needs to be replaced from once a year to about every seven years. Deciduous trees should have their soil changed more often than conifers, and you can remove more soil from the deciduous trees than from the conifers and old trees. Pines require a well drained soil. Broadleaf trees (elm, *Celtis*, maples, *Liquidambar* and others) require soil which contains a higher quantity of compost.

Method

First, remove the soil surrounding the tree, but only the outside 1/3 to 1/2. Loosen the next 1/3 and leave the inner 1/3 of the rootball undisturbed. This method works well for trees which have a fibrous root system. Cutting out wedges of soil and roots between the larger roots works well for trees which tend to form only a few, but larger roots.

When the outer portion of soil is removed, you should also remove some soil directly underneath the trunk. If you have removed all the soil between the roots of a tree and are afraid of trapping air bubbles between the roots when replanting the tree, you should turn the tree upside down and work the new soil in between the roots in the area which is going to be directly underneath the trunk when the tree is

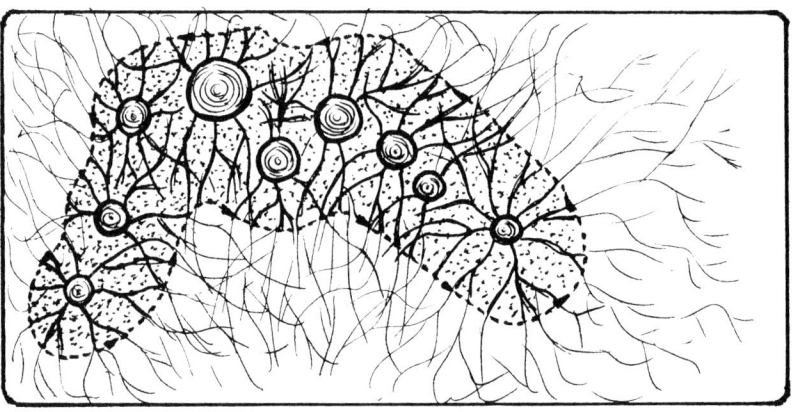

FIGURE 261 Cut roots along the dotted line on the circumference of the group.

FIGURE 261

FIGURE 262

FIGURE 262 Cut wedges out along the dotted lines.

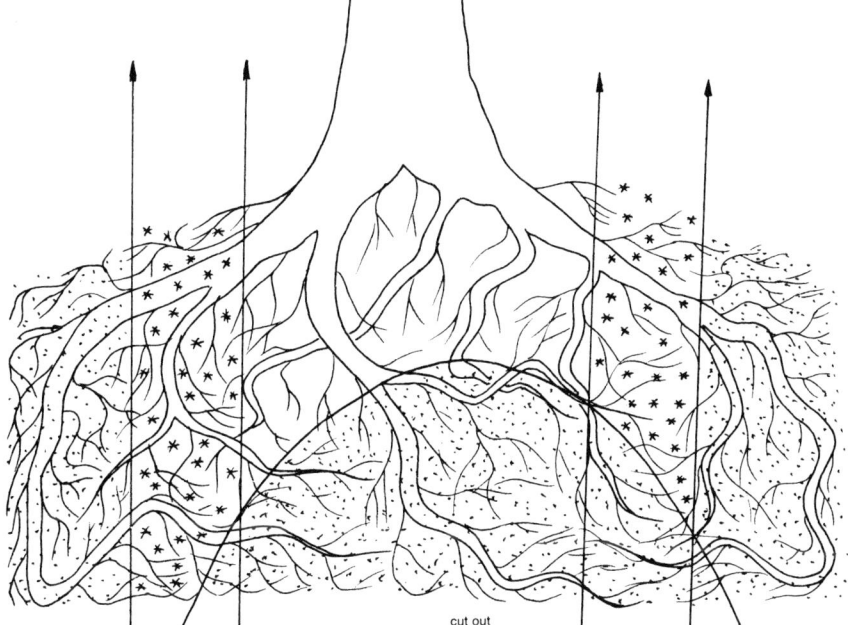

FIGURE 263

FIGURE 263 Side-view of a root-bound tree. Cut off outer 1/3. Loosen next 1/3.

upright. You will probably need somebody to help you do this. The soil should be damp to prevent it from simply falling off when you turn the tree upright again.

If you do not remove soil when repotting, at least loosen the soil on the outside of the root-ball, as the roots tend to stay in the old soil when repotted, unless they are teased out a bit.

Your aim when root-pruning is to end up with three or five root systems radiating out from three or five main roots. By using the wedges method you can achieve this. You can still remove the outside 1/3 of the soil as well as cutting or combing out the wedges. When you cut off the outside 1/3 you can do it with a saw, sawing through dry soil. Then wet the soil and comb out the roots gently. If you simply hack out the soil you will damage too many roots. If larger roots are encountered they may be cut off, while retaining the finer more fibrous

FIGURE 264 View from above, of a root-bount tree. Cut out between large roots and loosen around them.

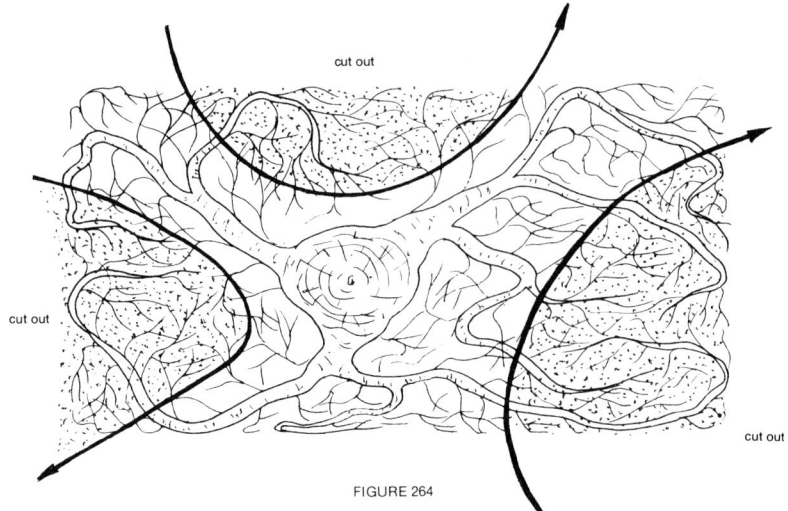

roots. When a larger root is cut, the cut should be at an angle facing downwards. Larger roots are cut to a shorter length than smaller roots, to enable the smaller ones to develop and then have a more balanced root structure in the whole circumference of the tree.

What happens if your forest or group planting needs repotting? The problem is to place the trees back in the same position! Make a sketch of their positions and replant them as they were. Alternatively you have to cut out wedges between the trees, like slices out of a pie. Make a note of exactly where the slices have been taken out so that you can cut slices out in a different position the following year. In about three years the soil mass should be completely replaced. A third method entails removing soil in the circumference of the group. You will have to lift the group up and remove some soil underneath as well.

The act of root-pruning rejuvenates any tree, and this procedure, more than anything else, is responsible for the longevity of bonsai. Quite soon after a bonsai has been repotted after a root-pruning, the foliage responds with renewed growth and vigour. This serves to confirm the value of root-pruning, but also shows the danger of root-pruning a mature tree which will respond by forming juvenile foliage, or simply growing so strong that the new growth ruins the shape of the tree. A mature tree should be repotted less frequently.

Directly after transplanting a tree the surface of the soil should be covered with some mulch to prevent not only the surface drying out, but possibly also the finer roots just under the soil surface. This is a severe threat to the survival of the tree.

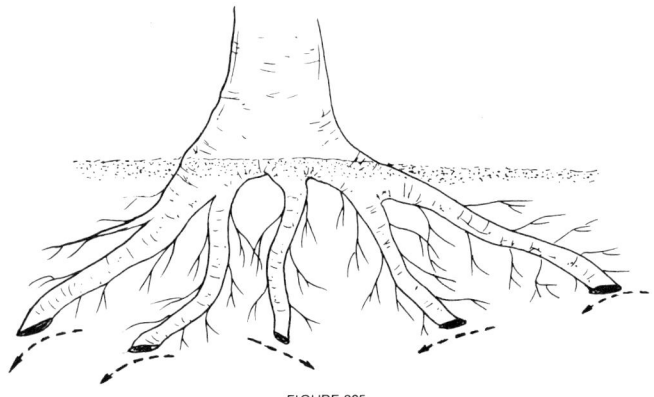

FIGURE 265 Cuts on roots should face downwards.

DISPLAYING BONSAI

9

The purpose of displaying bonsai is simply to show off your tree, not only for your own enjoyment, but also for any other viewers. Of course you are not going to keep your specimen bonsai hidden in the backyard. The time will come when you will wish to put your bonsai on show, if only in your own home. The manner in which a bonsai is exhibited contributes to its beauty, but it could also have the opposite effect, in fact spoil it. That is why it is important to know something about how bonsai are displayed.

You could either display on your own, where it would be a single exhibition (a single tree, twin trunk, group setting or any other), or it could be a display of a selection of trees grown, for instance, by the members of a bonsai society, and displayed in an exhibition centre of some kind.

Originally in ancient Japan displays were for the purpose of entertaining the 'literary men' (the *bun jin*), the 'sophisticated men' (the *cha jin*) and the 'men of leisure' (the *kan jin*). In these displays, bonsai were used along with other objects like antiques, scrolls, and pieces of art. This gave rise to the three ways of displaying bonsai today — formal, informal and casual, which will be described in more detail a little further on.

PLACES TO EXHIBIT BONSAI

- In a western type room — *Yoma-kazari*
- In a Japanese type room — *Tokonoma-kazari*
- In a garden or patio — *Niwa-kazari*
- At an exhibition — *Seki-kazari*

Kazari is the Japanese word for display.

A warning which needs to be heeded is that in whichever place it may be on show, you should always see to it that the pot or stand does not visually overshadow the tree and that the background and surroundings do not distract from the tree.

This is quite important, because you would like your bonsai to be seen and it should be the eyecatching item in any display, especially so when the tree is displayed on its own, and even more important when it is being photographed.

There are three ways of displaying bonsai in terms of the mood it conveys to the viewer: formal, informal and casual.

- the formal display (*shin*): The composition is very solemn, rigid and prescribed. The trees are usually in the formal upright or sometimes the slanting and informal upright styles, and are mostly conifers. A scroll is usually used as accessory, but *suiseki*, complementary plants and an incense burner are not inappropriate. These may be used in combination and should be the bonsai, scroll and one of the other items.
- The informal display (*gyo*): This arrangement is less rigid but should not be *carte blanche* or unconstrained. Trees used include conifers, deciduous, flowering and

fruiting trees grown in the informal upright, slanted, broom, group and exposed root styles. Accessories that suit this display are scrolls, household items, *suiseki*, grasses, figures of birds and animals and works of art.

- The casual display (*so*): A lot of freedom and flexibility is allowed in this method of display. Any kind of tree may be used and popular styles are *bunjin*, cascades and windswept. In some instances the main piece of the display is a *suiseki* accompanied by accessories like grasses, bamboo, palms, wild flowers and reeds.

Every item displayed must be on a stand of some kind. These may be a slab of slate, a reed mat, a wooden table and others, as is described in the section on stands. The purpose of the stand is to separate the item on it from its surroundings and present it to the viewer. The accessory items should be on flatter stands to enable you to create the scalene triangle, and not to be more dominant than the main exhibit.

Tokonoma

In a Japanese home which is traditional or modern with traditional touches, there is an area or alcove — the *tokonoma* — which is reserved for displaying works of art. It is a sort of platform, slightly higher than the floor, against the wall and about 1 metre deep by 2 metres wide. Against the wall, behind the *tokonoma*, paintings, scrolls or calligraphy are hung. In the *tokonoma*, the work of art is displayed, which may be bonsai.

In the Western world, houses are not built containing *tokonomas*, which for the wester-minded bonsai enthusiast has this disadvantage, that one has to learn how to choose and arrange bonsai and its accessories in a restricted space, according to the size and dimensions of the available space, unlike the Japanese who grow up with the perception. The problem lies in using very little material to create a pleasing composition, which in the end has more meaning than the sum of its individual components. Consider these statements: 'Less is more' and 'I don't want to read the novel, just tell me the story.' This is exactly what an individual bonsai — as well as a bonsai composition — should portray.

COMPLEMENTARY ITEMS

A bonsai is not always displayed on its own, but is often part of a composition, although it may be, and usually is, the principal piece. Items that are displayed along with bonsai include paintings, scrolls or calligraphy against a wall, with plantings of small weeds, palms, reeds and grass, as complementary plants in small containers on their own stands, or figures of humans, birds and animals and a *suiseki*.

The first step is to take into account the size of the area available and according to this, the main exhibition piece is chosen and then the accessory pieces, if any. Never choose two pieces of the same visual value to be exhibited together, as they would be competing for attention — this usually refers to size but may also be in terms of colour, when flowering material or an autumn display is used. It also follows that the different items may not contradict each other — for instance a scroll showing a winter scene along with a bonsai showing young spring growth. It is possible to create a scene which has more total impact than the sum of the individual pieces would give, and this is achieved by carefully selecting the pieces on display and arranging them in a manner which would suggest a story or incident. As an example a group planting could be positioned close to a scroll which depicts a mountain, and to the side one could have an accessory planting of low-growing grass which would suggest a meadow — this arrangement would lead you from the meadow up through the forest to the mountain peaks, from where you would have a view over this landscape below. The variations are endless. Also take into consideration what kind of surface the display will be positioned on, for instance a tatami mat, woven material of some colour, wooden boards, etcetera — for it will also influence the mood of the display. The same applies to the background of the display.

A scroll is only used in a *tokonoma*. If the scroll shows calligraphy, it must be in harmony with the rest of the display.

SUISEKI

A *suiseki* is a viewing stone or a group of stones which is displayed on its own stand or in its own container. In most cases, the *suiseki* is used as a complementary item in a bonsai display, with the bonsai as the main focus point. Sometimes, however, the roles are exchanged and the *suiseki* is the primary object and the bonsai complementary. At other times, *suiseki* is the only item on display.

Suiseki is of Chinese origin. The Chinese have for centuries attached great value to mountains. These were brought into their gardens in the form of rocks. These rocks were called *san-sui-sek* — literally translated as 'stones used for landscaping'. *San-sui* means 'mountain and water'. Over many years the word was shortened to *sui-sek* which means 'waterstone'.

Some pots have no holes and are meant to contain water — they are called *sui-poon* or *sui-bon* (*sui-ban*), and are used to display rock landscapes or *suiseki*, standing in water or in gravel.

The Chinese used the rocks mainly to symbolise mountains. The art form reached Japan, but from the outset the stones represented a wider range of images for the Japanese. I think the viewing of stones could rightly be called a hobby because, as seen during the T'ang Dynasty, the Chinese people were quite obsessed with their rock collections.

Rocks offer much to please the eye and stimulate the imagination:

- *Yamagati-ishi*: The physical shape of the rock can be seen as a mountain or an island in miniature. When the stone is displayed on its own stand, it represents a mountain but when it is displayed in a *sui-bon* it symbolises an island.
- *Keisho-seki*: The rock can look like an animal or bird, or any object close to nature. The rock can vary in colour and take on for instance the aspect of jade or it may have an interesting shape.
- *Tamari-ishi*: The lake stone, which has a hollow in which water collects.
- *Taki-ishi*: A stone which contains a white or light colour vertical streak, which resembles a waterfall in a rocky area. It may be of the variation where the waterfall seems to be dry and then it is called *karedaki-ishi*.
- *Dan-ishi*: The stone looks like a mountain peak with a plateau next to it, with the plateau making out about seventy per cent of the stone. The flat surface of the plateau must not have any slope.
- *Doha-ishi*: This is the slope stone which has a rounded form, suggesting sloping hills but it is similar in shape to the *dan-ishi*.
- *Kuzuya-ishi*: Thatched-house or hut stone. It looks like a small house or bungalow with a thatched roof.
- *Shimagata-ishi*: Island stone. It is similar to the mountain stone but is displayed in a *sui-bon* with sand or water, representing an island.
- *Isogata-ishi*: This is the shore stone which represents rocks near the edge of the sea which have been weathered and shaped by the waves. It should have a rough and jagged appearance. It is always displayed in a *sui-bon*.
- *Sugata-ishi*: The figure stone looks like the torso or head of a person, as examples.
- *Iwagati-ishi*: The craggy cliff stone which looks like cliffs along a shoreline. This

sui-seki can be displayed on either a wooden stand, a pottery stand or in a shallow tray.
- *Amaya-dori-ishi*: This stone has a shape which shows an overhang under which you would be able to shelter during a rain storm.

These are some of the variations in which stones could appear. There are more, but the selection will give the reader an idea of what to look for.

The difference between *suiseki* and bonsai lies in the fact that the *suiseki* was formed by nature, without the intervention of man, and it will and must stay as it is, without being changed. It is the viewer who has to read into the rock what it has to say. The viewer may be helped by the display which conveys a message. There are two ways of displaying *suiseki*, namely:
- in shallow bonsai containers filled with water or sand, depending on whether it symbolises an island or a mountain;
- on a special little stand which has been shaped to contain the *suiseki*.

If the shallow tray is filled with white pebbles, it may also symbolise water. The wooden stands are made to the shape of the base of the rock. Ideally the wood should be hollowed out to accommodate the rock, but if this is too difficult the base of the rock can be ground flat to rest on the wood. Pottery stands can also be made to support the rock.

The individual rocks or stones are treated over a period of many years, by rubbing them with one's hands once they have been wiped on the forehead for instance, to pick up the natural body oils. These oils give the stones a beautiful hue or tone, but this takes many years to achieve. One could rush the treatment by using white olive oil or glycerine which is painted over the stone. The stone is then left to dry in the sun for a month or two. Thereafter, body oil can be rubbed in regularly, alternated with olive oil or glycerine which should be buffed on with a brush and soft cloth at least once a month.

INHERENT MOVEMENT IN A DISPLAY

Another consideration is the potential or inherent movement in the bonsai, which should be in harmony with the movement in the complementary item. When looking at a bonsai, you should try and see the movement in the tree. A tree isn't visually dead or immobile — it contains an inherent movement. This movement is generated by the direction in the trunk, branches and to a lesser degree, by the leaves. It may be upwards, downwards, from one side to another or a combination of one or the other, but it will always be there. The movement is called *gei*. In close relation to *gei* is the *aji* or 'Zest for life' which is portrayed by the tree. A diseased tree would not have zest, but even old trees or ravaged trees will still display zest for life in their living portions. When two trees are displayed together the *gei* (movement) of the individual trees may not contradict one another. The same applies to a complementary exhibit along with the bonsai.

FIGURE 266 The complementary display points towards the main display and thus draws the attention to the right item.

FIGURE 267 The complementary exhibit's movement contradicts that of the main display — they flow in different directions.

FIGURE 266   FIGURE 267

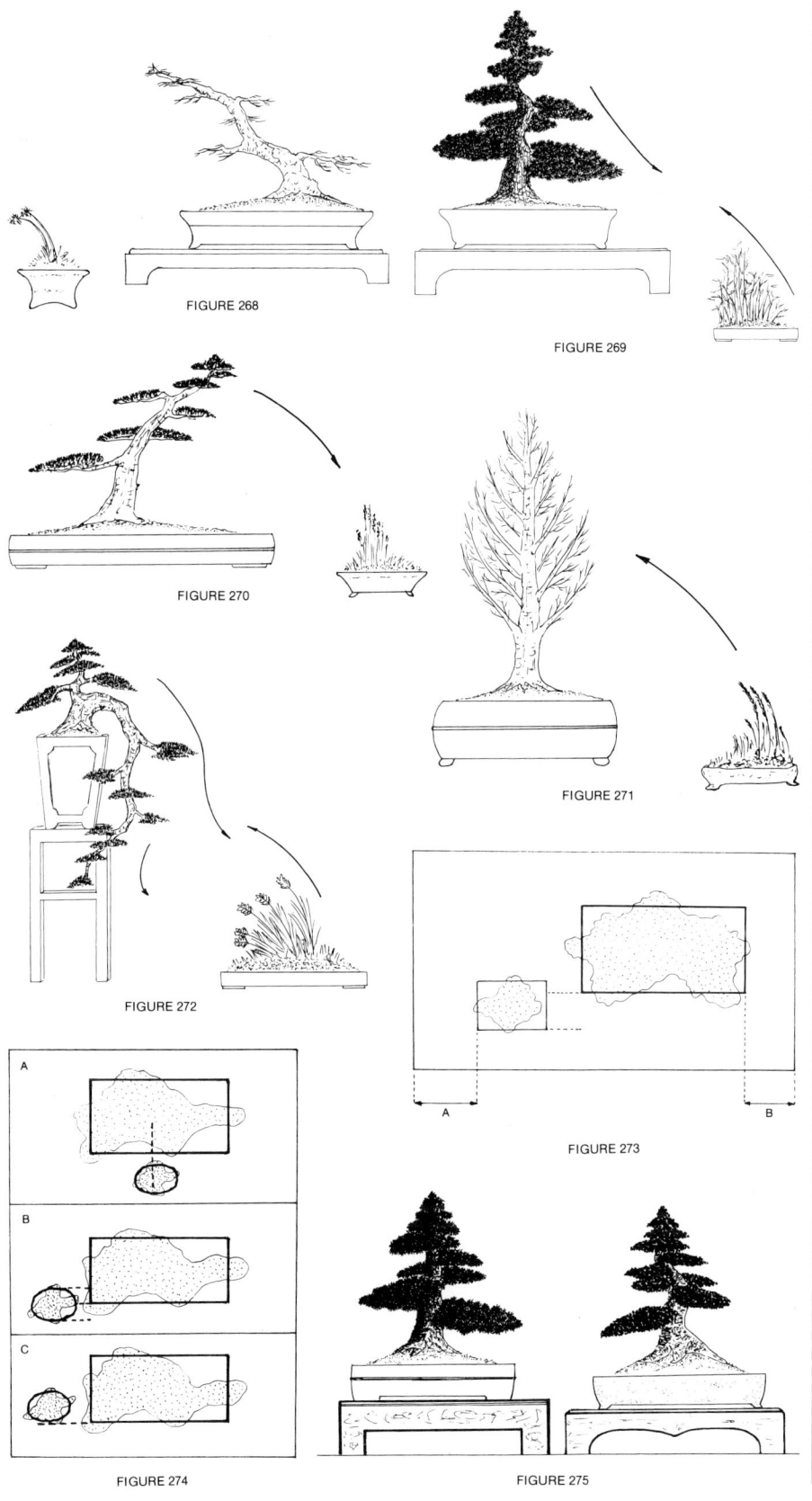

FIGURE 268 The direction of the complementary exhibit is away from the main tree. This is wrong because the complementary exhibit should be focusing the attention on the main tree.

FIGURE 269 If both complementary and main exhibit are upright, that is, if both have upward movement or direction, their movements don't clash. When this is the case, be careful so as not to have a display that is monotonous. Allow more space on the side of the stand between the two exhibits, because if this space is small, the display will seem crowded. Have the complementary item on the same side as the first branch of the main tree.

FIGURE 270 When only one of the two items displayed has any inherent sideways movement, this movement should be in the direction of the other exhibit. Whether it is the main tree or the complementary plant does not matter.

FIGURE 271 The complementary display points to the upright main display.

FIGURE 272 Even with the cascade, the flow direction should be the same as with non-cascading trees.

FIGURE 273 The diagram shows a view from above, of a whole display. Note that the complementary item is not in front of the main tree, neither is it exactly in line with it as seen from the side. The distances A and B may not be the same either.

FIGURE 274 In A, the complementary item is wrongly placed directly in front of the main tree. In B, the complementary item is to the side of the main tree and not directly alongside it, which is correct. In C, the complementary item is next to the main tree but their front surfaces are in line, which is wrong.

FIGURE 275 Never display two trees which are visually equally important and similar in size next to each other as one exhibit. They should be displayed separately, perhaps with smaller side items like *suiseki*.

FIGURE 276 Different stands.

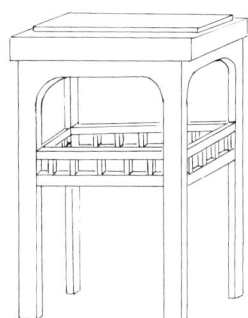

FIGURE 277 A tall stand for a cascade.

FIGURE 278 The movement in the tree necessitates the tree being placed slightly to the right of the centre of the stand.

FIGURE 279 Shifting the tree in Figure 278 towards the right improves the overall appearance.

POSITION OF PIECES ON DISPLAY

When more than one item is used in the display, the main unit must be positioned off-centre. The position in which the complementary item is placed in relation to the bonsai is of importance. As usual keep asymmetry in mind! If three objects are used, they must be different distances apart. The front edges of the complementary plant must be placed either slightly forward or further back. If the display is on a surface like in a *tokonoma* or in a booth at an exhibition, the complementary plant and the bonsai must not be equidistant from the sides of the surface. Never place the complementary item directly in front of the bonsai or exactly in line next to any other item on display. The more dainty or smaller bonsai look good with complementary items, but a large, gugged bonsai must be displayed on its own, in most instances.

As is the case in bonsai styling, use is made of the scalene triangle when viewing the composition from the front as well as from above. This last dimension will give depth to the display. Never have the two items on display right next to each other in a straight line. This looks even worse when three items are used. When a scroll is used as accessory it will be the highest point of the triangle. The sides of the triangle will be from the highest point down to the two corners at the base of the triangle. The corners at the base could be any of the following: the outside edge of the bonsai stand or container, the front corner of the surface on which the display is positioned or the outer side of any accessory item on display. Whilst the outline of the triangle may not consist of absolutely straight lines, the shape is suggested to the imagination of the viewer.

STANDS

A bonsai is never displayed without a stand of some kind, even if it is only a bamboo mat. Dainty bonsai can be displayed on a bamboo mat or thin plank; the latter is especially effective if it has been weathered — called *jiban*. A tree trunk can be sawn in slices or slabs (*shizen-ban*) which are polished and used as tands. They are used for different bonsai, depending on how thick or robust they are on the one hand, or how delicate they appear on the other hand. The bonsai trunk and overall appearance must be in harmony with the wooden slab. To further complicate things, the design of the pot must also fit into the picture. Wooden stands are also made in the form of small to relatively large tables or as rolled stands. The higher stands are used to display cascade style bonsai.

A bonsai must be on the stand to lift it up from its surroundings and have the attention focused on it. Stands are called *shaku* or *taku*. The stand must not detract from the bonsai, as its purpose is quite the opposite. The stand also serves to give an eye-level view of the bonsai, and as the tree must be viewed from about 2 metres away, it is obvious that a tall bonsai should not be displayed on a tall stand. The

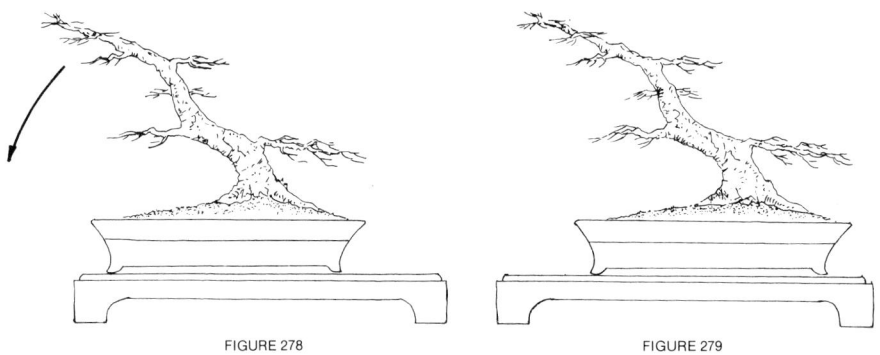

FIGURE 278   FIGURE 279

stand should not be as tall as the bonsai itself; it is usually about as tall as the pot is deep, but not exactly so.

The bonsai must be positioned on the stand according to the movement in the bonsai. This means, for example, that a slanting bonsai would appear unbalanced if it were positioned in the centre of the stand.

BACKGROUND

The last important point relates to the background against which the bonsai is viewed. Once again of prime consideration is the fact that it must not detract from the tree. It must not be multi-coloured, it must not be bright in colour, it must not be lower than the height of the tree and it must be large enough in width and height to show off the whole display. This means that pastel colours are good, but especially the dull light brown shades.

I must mention a few points about the containers (mostly ceramic pots), in which bonsai are displayed. It goes without saying that the pot must be immaculately clean and cared for when the bonsai unit is on display. All blemishes and stains must be removed, and the pot must be lightly oiled — I prefer furniture oil — as this brings out the colour.

The lime deposit you often find on the edges of pots can be removed by gently rubbing it with steel wool and some mild domestic abrasive. It is very risky, but effective to remove this deposit by treating it with hydrochloric acid. Be extremely careful to apply this acid only on the affected areas with a cotton pellet held in a tweezer, so as not to spill it on the soil. Thereafter it needs to be rinsed off with copious amounts of water. If it is possible to lift the tree out of the container, with the rootball intact, the procedure is obviously much easier.

JUDGING BONSAI

The following criteria could be used (as an example):

(a)	Trunk	shape	15%
		taper	
		bark	
		marks or blemishes	
(b)	Branches	position	20%
		shape	
		marks or blemishes	
(c)	Foliage	density	15%
		blemishes	
		position	
		size	
(d)	Roots	distribution	10%
		visibility	
(e)	Soil	surface	5%
(f)	Container	cleanliness	10%
		proportion to tree	
		position of tree	
		suitability	
(g)	Overall artistic quality		20%
(h)	Health		5%
			100

These points cover all aspects of the tree, but it must be realized that a *bunjin* or a

FIGURE 280 The delicate *bunjin* is dwarfed by the massive clumsy stand.

FIGURE 281 A heavy thickset tree, albeit with rounded curves, needs a pot which is large enough, perhaps with gently curving sides and a stand which is sturdy enough to support it.

FIGURE 282 This twin tree bonsai is too large for the delicate stand.

FIGURE 283 The delicate *bunjin* should be displayed on a similarly delicate stand.

FIGURE 284 The tree is too robust and large for the delicate stand.

seki-joju, to give two examples, should be judged slightly differently, due to the different emphasis in the styling.

It used to be popular to have a description of every bonsai on exhibit next to the display, with the following information: scientific name of the tree, common name, name of owner, estimated age, and length of period grown as a potted tree. Presently only the scientific and common names are given and the rest omitted, as the name of the owner brings the idea of competition to the fore and the age is not really of importance because the tree should look old even though it may not really be very old.

I have mentioned the criteria to be used in judging bonsai, but in fact to see bonsai as being in competition with one another is contradictory to the principles of *wabi* and *sabi*, according to which you should be content with what you have, and enjoy your simple earthy possessions without show. When bonsai are on display it is for the purpose of satisfying viewers; giving them a chance to enjoy and appreciate the little wonders. The criteria for judging may however help you to decide whether a bonsai has some quality or not — to decide whether the bonsai is *shibui!*

SOURCES OF BONSAI MATERIAL 10

The question is often asked by novices: 'How do I decide which tree is suitable to be grown as a bonsai?' or 'Where do I get a potensai?' (A tree which has the potential of becoming a bonsai is popularly called a 'potensai'). The problem you, as beginner, face, is that you have become interested in the fascinating hobby and would like to get a collection started, but how? I know this feeling because I had the same frustration when I started! Do you go to a bonsai grower and try to buy an existing bonsai? Sure, that is fantastic if you can do that, but if you do not know how to care for the bonsai, you may regretfully find the tree dying on you — not that all bonsai growers do not have their own bonsai graveyards. On the other hand you may have bought a tree at an ordinary nursery, or have uprooted a specimen from somebody's garden and you find after a while that your choice of material simply cannot be developed into a bonsai. How do you then acquire material, a potensai, to create your own bonsai? Below, five methods are mentioned, but you need a trained eye and some knowledge of bonsai to enable you to select a tree with bonsai potential, from a nursery, from the garden or nature, or even to grow through layering.

Of foremost importance is to get as much knowledge as possible about what a bonsai should look like. Start by knowing what an informal upright bonsai consists of. Do not attempt fancy styles before you can handle an informal upright comfortably. Study photographs of bonsai and actual trees in gardens and in nature. If possible, get a knowledgeable person to assist you in your choice of tree, and to explain why a particular tree is chosen. Join a bonsai club!

When searching for potensai in a nursery, look for healthy trees with small compact foliage. Do not choose a tree without branches in the lower portion of the trunk. Do not choose a tree on which the branches are few and far between. It may well be that the tree is going to form branches lower down or in places other than the existing ones, but the problem, understandably, is that you don't have the patience as a novice to wait a few years for the branches to develop. A similar problem is that nurseries tend to have trees with few lower branches, as their trees are intended for gardens and they have been pruned to grow in height as soon as possible. If you like one of those you will have a tree which, when you reduce it to a length of eight times its diameter, may have no branches on the remaining trunk. At times, however, you come across trees in nurseries which other people don't want because of stunted growth or awkwardly shaped trunks, and these may well be just the material you need. Always try and get trees with enough branches so you can select which ones to keep and which ones to cut off without leaving ugly pruning scars in the wrong positions. Try and visualise what the tree might look like in a few years, imagine how branches will develop, how the tree could look (for instance in the slanting or windswept style), where the apex should be, which branches may look better *jinned* and so forth.

'For there is hope for a tree – if it's cut down it sprouts again, and grows tender, new branches. Though its roots have grown old in the earth, and its stump decays, it may sprout and bud again, at the touch of water, like a new seedling.'

LIVING BIBLE
Job 14:7-9

Try and dig into the soil around the trunk, using your fingers to feel for roots if you can't see roots above or at the soil surface. With a tree having no major roots or a single root, it is going to be far more difficult to develop a visually pleasing root system. In the case of a tree with nice roots, but with these roots in the wrong positions in relation to the branches, the problem will not be so difficult to overcome.

From the above it can be seen that with a little knowledge and maybe some help, the bonsai-grower can acquire good tree material to start a collection. There are five ways of acquiring bonsai material:
- grown from seed
- from a cutting
- layering techniques — either air or ground layering
- in nature
- from a nursery — either ordinary garden stock or partially trained bonsai.

The methods are all horticulturally acknowledged techniques, and only occasionally is the technique adapted in a minor way to suit the bonsai requirements. For more detail, horticultural books should be consulted.

FROM SEED

This is a slow method and it will take a few years before you have a bonsai, but training the seedling over this period into a bonsai can be most enjoyable. This method does not require major pruning, because small twigs and buds are nipped off from where they are not wanted, while the rest of the tree is allowed to develop. Wiring may be necessary on occasion.

Growing a bonsai from seed results in a well-tapered shape with compact growth in fine leaves and branches. In fact the bonsai can be grown into any shape, without major problems. It is an excellent way to grow *mame* bonsai.

When the seedling can be transplanted, the taproot is cut and the seedling planted over a flattish pebble with the roots spread over it to ensure the right rootage in the future. To have a thick trunk and well developed base in a short time, a wire tourniquet can be tied round the base of the trunk, and this area kept underground. With a little bit of luck, roots may even sprout from just above the tourniquet giving you beautiful *nebari*. This is actually essential and a manner to ensure this, is to make a ringbarking cut below the wire to a width of about one and a half times the diameter of the trunk.

FROM CUTTINGS

With cuttings, quicker results are achieved than with seedlings, with the added advantage that the characteristics of the parent tree are reproduced exactly in the 'offspring' cuttings. This is particularly important if a group planting is intended, or if you like the autumn colour of a particular tree, because you are, in essence, cloning from that tree.

The best time of the year to take a cutting is during early spring, before the buds start developing into leaves, or even during autumn, when the trees are dormant.

Cuttings can be made from different parts of the tree:
- leaves and buds — called leaf- and bud- (eye) cuttings
- trunks and branches — referred to as stem-cuttings
- roots which give root-cuttings.

The cuttings most often used are those from the trunks and branches (or stems) and roots.

Tools required are a sharp knife or razor blade mounted on a handle, a good pair of secateurs (pruning shears), dibbers (pegs to make holes in the rooting medium)

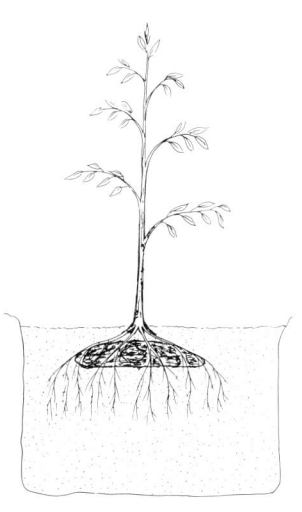

FIGURE 285 The young tree is planted in a large container with its roots spread over a flat slab. Because of the large amount of soil available, the tree will develop quickly.

and, if possible, a propagating frame in which to grow the cuttings.

The propagating frame is made of wood, with a glass or polythene cover. The frame can be any size. Its purpose is to provide a controlled atmosphere, in which the temperature and humidity remain close to constant. A miniature propagation frame can be made by covering the plastic container in which the cuttings are planted with polythene bag on a wire frame, or with a glass fishbowl.

It helps to have an automatic misting system installed to keep the humidity high enough to supply more water than the cuttings can lose through transpiration. Just be sure that the drainage of the rooting medium is adequate; for that purpose, sharp sand mixed with peat (1:2) is excellent. Using sand makes it easy to take the rooted cutting out of the rooting medium to grow in a nourishing soil. To encourage the roots to develop, rooting compound (hormones) is applied: these are available from shops selling horticultural products.

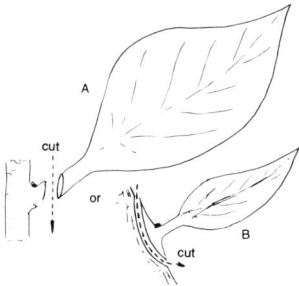

FIGURE 286 A represents cutting off the leaf and stalk. B represents cutting off the leaf including the dormant bud.

The stems from which cuttings are taken will be at different stages of maturity and are divided into softwood, semi-hardwood and hardwood. Depending on which kind you want, the cuttings are taken at different times of the year, for instance softwood in late spring, et cetera.

Leaf-cuttings

Leaf-cuttings are taken from semi-hardwood. This is wood that has grown somewhat after spring, and the cutting is taken in early summer. It entails cutting off a leaf along with its stalk, and placing it in the rooting medium at an angle of 45 degrees. Very similar to this is where the leaf and stalk are cut off, but also the dormant bud at the point where the leaf-stalk joins the stem.

Bud-cutting

A bud-cutting is similar to the leaf-bud cutting but with no leaf attached. It is taken from dormant wood in autumn or winter.

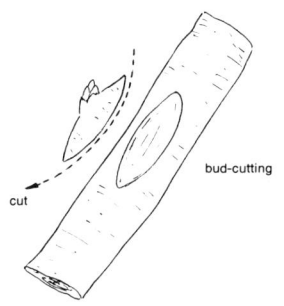

FIGURE 287 A bud-cutting including the dormant bud, before it starts sprouting.

Stem-cutting

They can be taken from soft, semi or hardwood. Softwood cuttings are taken from young growth in spring, that is growth that is still flexible, but will break if sharply bent. Semi-hardwood cuttings come from stems that have grown a bit longer and have formed more wood, which means they are less flexible and break more easily. They are taken towards the middle of that summer's growth. Hardwood cuttings come from stems that are woody.

Softwood and semi-hardwood cuttings need more care in the form of misting and must be prevented from drying out. These cuttings send out roots reasonably easily when the stem is cut off just below a leaf node. They are cut to a length of 7,5 to 12,5 cm, with leaves removed from the lower half.

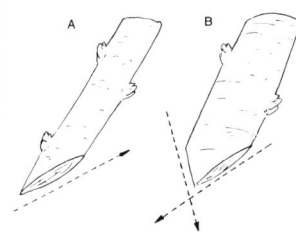

FIGURE 288 Stem-cuttings showing the straight cutting in A and the doubleedged cutting in B.

Hardwood cuttings take longer to develop roots, but they do not need as much care in terms of misting. You are able to have a reasonably thick trunk in a short time, because in the species that form roots easily (for example pomegranate), they could be as thick as 7,5 cm.

There are many ways in which the cut is made when severing the cutting from the parent tree or shrub, as shown in the drawings. The bonsai grower must try to use the method which will encourage the best spread of roots when they develop and, in this regard the following three methods can be tried:

(a) The tapering point, which means the cut is tapered from two sides, to expose more cambium and to absorb more water. Thicker stems work well with this method. See Figure 288B)

(b) A notch can be cut into the cut end, and this can then be forced open even more by wedging a small pebble into the notch. This is similar to the method used to create a thicker trunk base, and results in a tree with a nice taper. (See Figure 289)

(c) Very much the same as the notch method: flaps of bark are cut and separated

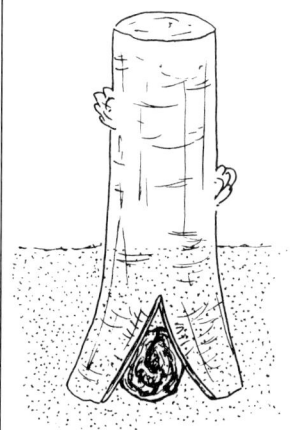

FIGURE 289 The wedge.

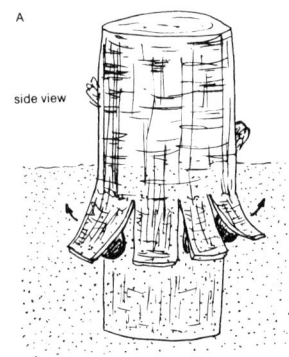

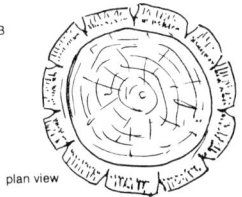

FIGURE 290 Using flaps in the circumference of the stem. The flaps are kept open with pebbles as shown in A. A crosscut is shown in B.

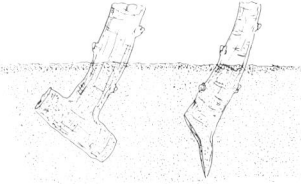

FIGURE 291 This figure shows two variations of the stem-cuttings In A it shows the 'mallet' cutting and in b it shows a cutting with a heel of the bark of the 'mother-stem'.

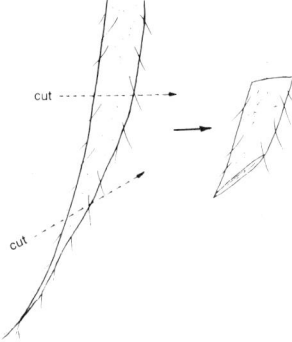

FIGURE 292 A root can be cut into sections and these are placed in a sandy soil and cultivated in the same way as stem-cuttings are.

from the sapwood by small pebbles. This is not an easy method, but it gives a good spreading of roots right around the circumference of the trunk. (Figure 290)

After cutting off the stem, the cut end must be dipped in water and then into rooting hormone powder. If you cannot do this quickly after the stem has been cut, you will need to cut it a second time, slightly closer to the growing tip, to remove the section where tiny air locks may have blocked the tiny tubules transporting water. With a dibber, a hole is made in the rooting medium, the cutting is placed in the hole and the soil is compacted around it. After about six months roots should have started forming. If uncertain, wait till new leaf growth is noticed before transplanting.

Root-cuttings

Roots can be cut and grown into trees as shown in Figure 292.

> If we compare bonsai which have been grown from seedlings, cuttings or graftings, we notice the following differences:
> - Seedlings require many years before they produce fruit, but they have more delicate foliage than grafted trees;
> - The specimen from a cutting may initially grow at a slower rate, but this contributes to its compactness later;
> - A grafted specimen will grow quite fast, but, in the beginning at least, it is not very compact.

FROM LAYERING

Layering is a method through which the 'cutting' or future tree is induced to form roots, before it is severed from the parent tree. The layering is done either in the ground, or in a special medium which is kept around the trunk at the level where the roots are required, so that you have ground-layering and air-layering respectively. Layering has advantages over other methods in that, for instance, the branch or trunk is not severed completely and it gets its moisture supply from the parent tree, giving it a better chance of survival, while developing roots. This alone is a major reason for using layering. It also works well on quite large diameter stock, which gives you a thick trunk to start with. It also allows you to choose the exact position in which you want the roots to develop in relation to the position of the already existing branches. It boils down to your being able to literally select a bonsai on a mature tree, and by waiting perhaps one or two years end up with an instant bonsai. You may also come across a tree at a nursery which has all the qualities you want, but the branches only sprout from a tall trunk 40 or 50 centimetres from the roots. By air-layering it a few centimetres below the first branch, you virtually have an instant bonsai.

Air-layering

This method is also called marcottage. It is a very old method of propagation. Air-layering is best started in spring, but it can be done at any time; it only means that you may have to wait longer at other times of the year. Trees that send out roots easily, like figs, will give you roots within three months, but pines may take as long as five years.

Air-layering is done by ring-barking a branch or trunk and then applying rooting hormone, followed by packing clay and/or wet sphagnum moss around the area. This is done by tying a piece of clear plastic around the branch or trunk just below the ring-barking, so that it forms a funnel. This funnel is filled about 2/3 with sphagnum or Irish moss which is thoroughly wet. If preferred, a ball of clay can be used to cover the ring-barking. Then the funnel is closed at the top and tied tightly

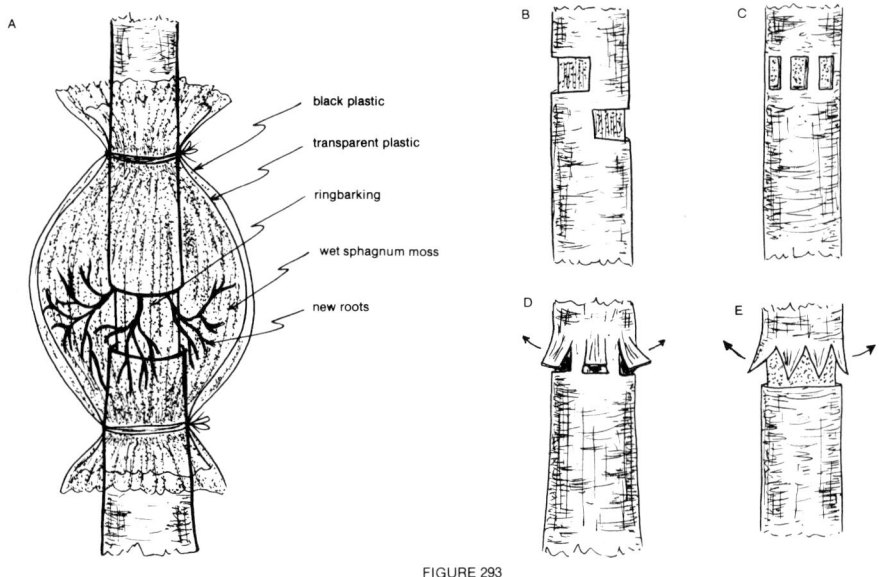

FIGURE 293

FIGURE 293 Air-layering as shown in A with ring barking. In B two half-circle strips are removed a small distance apart. In C little blocks or windows are cut out. In D flaps are lifted up as separate flaps. In E continuous triangular slaps are lifted up.

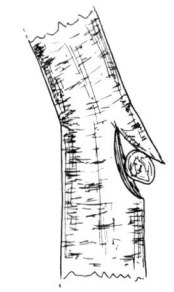

FIGURE 294 A slice is cut into the stem or branch. The stem or branch is bent and the slice is forced open. A pebble keeps it open.

around the branch or trunk, somewhat above the ring-barking. The whole structure is then covered with black plastic: roots form better in the dark (under the ground!). To enable you to see whether anything is developing in the moss, the black plastic is opened and you can see through the clear plastic. If the moss is drying out, the moisture can easily be replenished. As soon as enough roots have developed, the trunk or branch is cut off just below the roots and the new tree is transplanted into a container. Handle it in exactly the same way as any transplanted tree.

RING-BARKING This is a technique whereby a circular cut is made in the whole circumference of the branch or trunk, very definitely through the cambium, and with another cut made in the same manner about 1 to 3 or 4 cm away from the first. If the cut is not made through the cambium, or the two cuts are too close together, healing will take place over the 'ring'. The strip (ring) of bark between the two cuts is gently prised loose and removed to leave the sapwood exposed.

Ringbarking can be done in a variety of ways. If a tree is slow to produce roots, the cuts should not be made right around the trunk or branch. In this case it can be done by making two half-circle cuts on the two opposite sides of the trunk or branch, a little distance apart. It can also be done by cutting tiny blocks through the bark or lifting up small flaps and keeping them open with tiny pebbles.

When the cuts are made in the circumference of the tree, it will result in roots around the trunk, which is ideal for bonsai purposes.

A very simple method is to make a cut into the trunk or branch at an angle. The cut is forced open by means of a pebble.

FIGURE 295 Ring-barking, but with the upper margin cut into wedges and these lifted up.

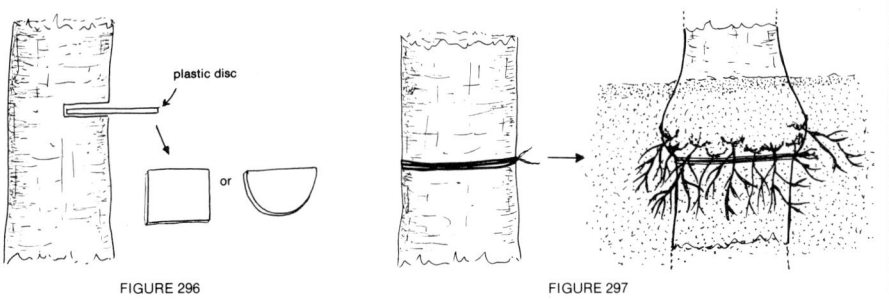

FIGURE 296

FIGURE 297

FIGURE 296 A slit is cut or sawn into the branch and a plastic disc is slipped into the cut to prevent it closing.

FIGURE 297 A wire tourniquet tied tightly around the trunk will initially cause swelling up of the trunk due to nutrients being blocked above it. Thereafter, roots can develop if this area is air-layered or kept underground.

FIGURE 298 If you should come across a branch which has the potential of becoming an 'instant' bonsai, you can air-layer it, and with some care have it growing in its own pot in a short while. Ring-barking is possible, although the first ring-barking will receive less nutrients as it can only be supplied through the potential bonsai! The ring-barking must only go halfway around the branch on its lower side, because you don't want roots on the top section. Instead of ring-barking you can saw out two thin wedges from the underside of the branch. With this method however you have to prevent the branch from breaking under its own weight and you should thus provide it with some form of support. The ring-barking, denuded strips or the wedges must be air-layered. As soon as enough roots have formed, and this could well be within a year, the branch should be cut off at both ring-barked areas. To improve root-formation on the underside of the trunk base notches can be cut into the lower surface of the section between the ring-barking, and these should be kept open with pebbles. Alternatively, the lower surface of the trunk can be scraped away to stimulate root-formation. Be sure to seal off the cut ends on either side of the new trunk base.

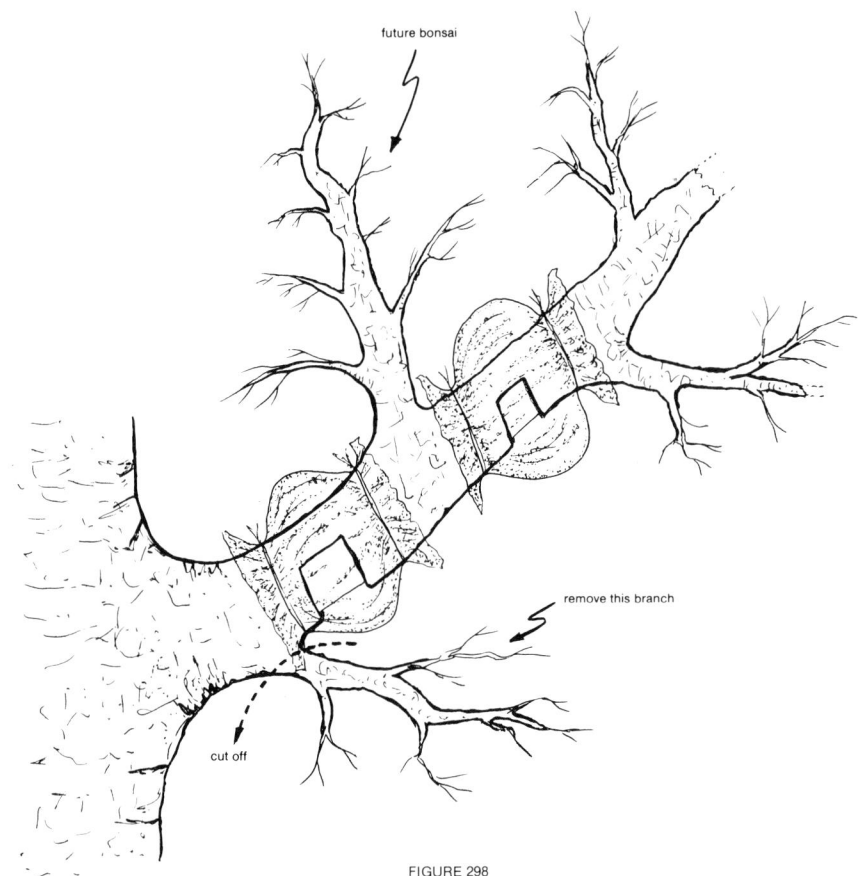

FIGURE 298

Another variation is to make the top circular cut in 'V' shapes, which are lifted up like flaps and kept open by pebbles.

Some people prefer not to close the top portion of the plastic funnel. Although this requires far more attention to keeping the rooting medium wet, roots will form much more quickly due to better circulation of air. This method is applied to pines with considerable success, and may even result in roots within months. When you tie a piece of thick wire tightly around the trunk or branch, the trunk or branch swells up above the tourniquet and roots will appear when this area is kept in a rooting medium.

If you ring-bark on both sides of a branch-base you can develop a bonsai very quickly, as shown in Figure 298.

Ground-layering

In this method, a branch is bent downwards to a point where a section of it can be taken underground, while its growing tip stays above the ground and continues to grow normally. This technique presupposes a supple branch which is close enough

FIGURE 299 Shaving off the underside or notching to create more roots. It results in a tree with a broad base and roots radiating outwards.

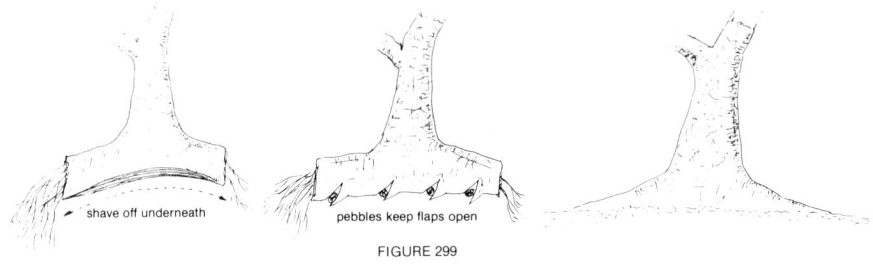

FIGURE 299

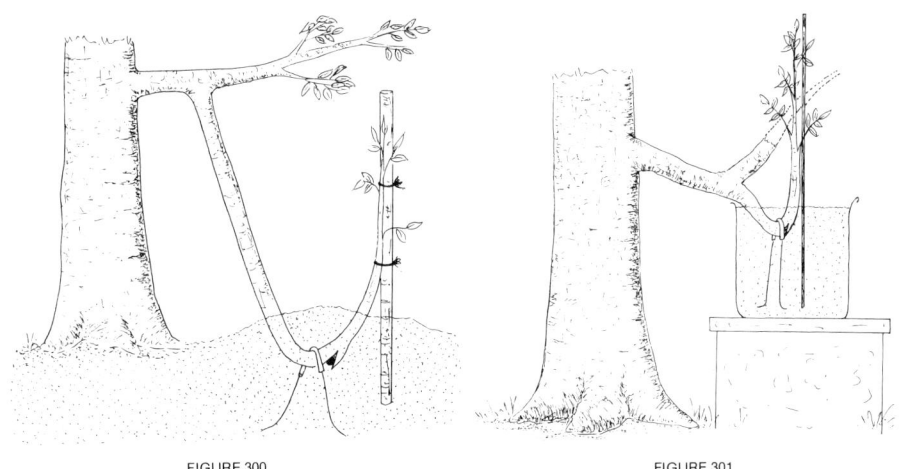

FIGURE 300

FIGURE 301

FIGURE 300 The long branch is first grown upwards and when it is long enough it is anchored in the soil, notched on the underside, and the growing tip is supported by tying it to a post.

FIGURE 301 The branch is ground-layered directly into a training container.

to the ground. If however the branch cannot reach the ground, it can be ground-layered into the future temporary container directly. Layering into the ground presents a problem in the respect that the soil may be hard, and when the roots have formed it may be difficult to get the new tree out of the soil into the future pot. If the branch has been bent down into the soil of the future container, it is easy to separate the new tree from the parent tree and get it to start its life as a bonsai.

As with air-layering, there are various ways in which the cut can be made in the branch, where it is kept under the ground. Whichever way is used, the branch needs to be pinned down to keep it underground, and for this purpose any wire can be used. Bend the stiff wire into a U-shape and pin the branch down. If this is done in a bonsai container, the wire can be passed through the drainage holes and tied to the container from underneath.

The branch can be nicked in a 'V' shape and then bent upwards at the nick, or simply cut into the sap-wood diagonally in the direction of the growing tip and then bent. A pebble could be forced into either of the cuts to keep them open. (See Figure 294).

To create a better distribution of roots in the complete circumference of the branch, the branch could be ring-barked or girdled by tying wire tightly around it. This method is slow but very reliable. (See Figure 297).

Instead of only having a small section of the branch underground, the whole

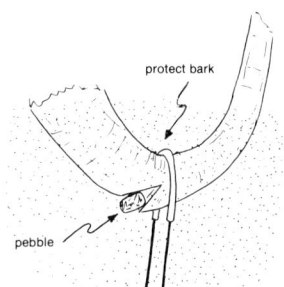

FIGURE 302 The branch is cushioned to prevent the wire cutting into it. This is done by passing the wire through a piece of plastic tubing.

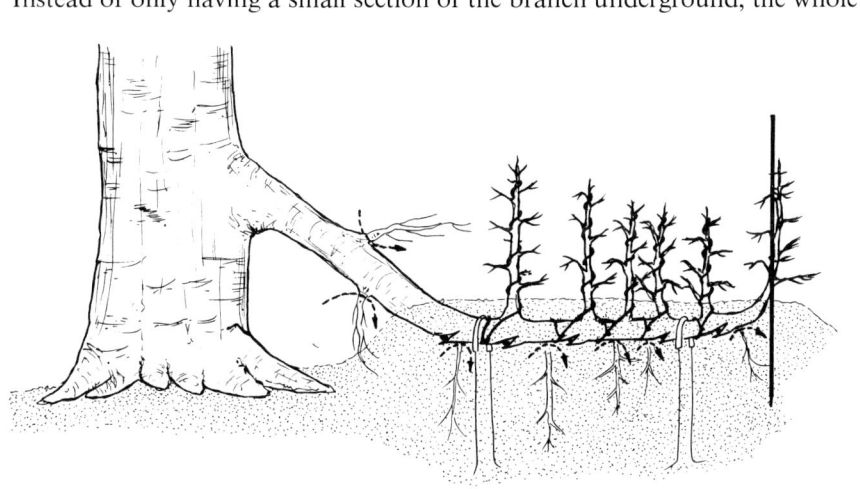

FIGURE 303

FIGURE 303 Ground-layering an entire branch to create a raft style.

163

FIGURE 304 When new roots have formed and the old branchlets are now individual trees joined by the old branch as a base, the raft is cut off from the tree and placed in its own container. It may be left in the soil for a while before it is transplanted, to be sure it has taken. It is a matter of choice whether the soil should cover the trunk completely to start off, or not.

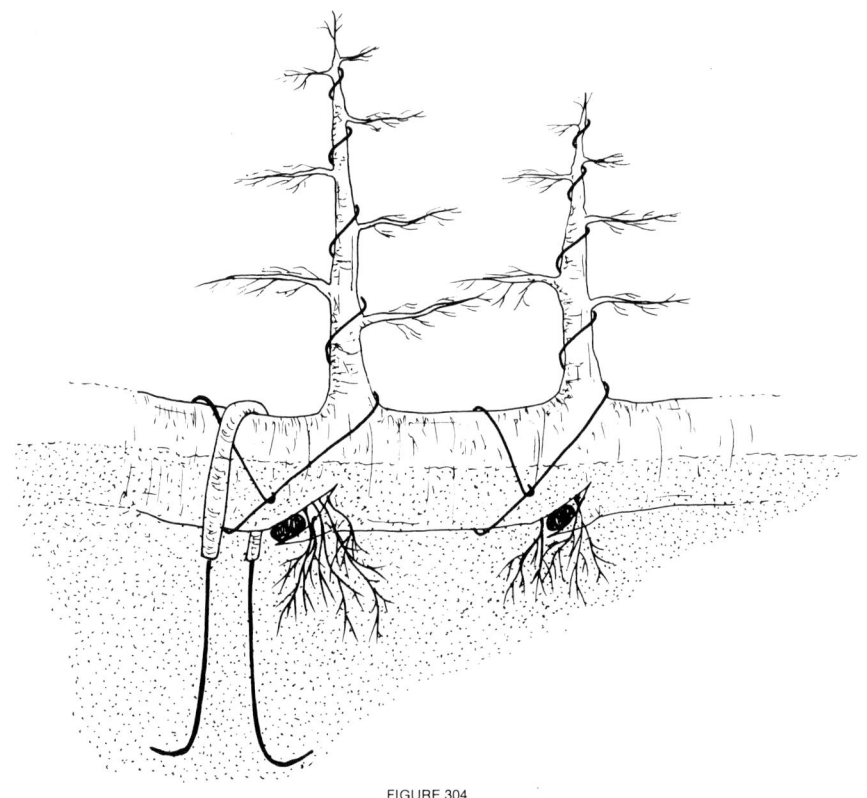

FIGURE 304

branch, barring the tip, could be kept underground. This results in a raft style. Where possible the upward-growing branchlets must be kept (that is, upward-growing once it is underground!). The branches growing into the ground must be removed. Where these branches have been removed, a 'V' is cut into the main branch. If there are not enough downwards-growing branches, 'V' shaped cuts or diagonal cuts can be made in the underside of the branch. These must be kept open to allow roots to develop. The tip of the main branch must be above the soil and be trained upwards. Handle this technique in the same way as a raft-styling.

If you prefer separate trees, the individual upright branches can be separated from one another as soon as enough roots have developed. This would give you a couple of individual trees with similar characteristics.

FROM NATURE OR THE GARDEN

The technique to follow when collecting a bonsai in nature, and when digging one out of a garden is the same. In both instances you will need the permission of the owner of the property to dig out the trees, but in nature you must be very careful not to collect a specimen of a protected species, not only for fear of a severe fine, but also because the authorities have definite reasons for protecting the trees in the wild.

Having decided to go on a tree hunt, you must get all your equipment together. You will need the following: container with water, misting device, wet sphagnum moss if possible, sacking or hessian, large plastic bag or piece of plastic to wrap around roots, saw, secateurs, spade, possibly a small axe, tree sealant, length of string to tie sacking and plastic to the rootball, crowbar and if you are going to spend some time with the tree — refreshments!

The best time of the year to collect trees from nature is during early spring, before the new buds have sprouted. At any other time, the risk of the trees not surviving the shock is too great. During winter the trees are dormant and do not have the resources to start forming new leaves and roots; and during summer they have a lot of leaves to keep alive. Success depends to a great extent on the quantity of soil you can keep on the roots, as well as the amount of live branches and leaves on the tree. before the tree is taken out of the soil, it is wise to reduce the amount of leaves at least by half, and to remove all unwanted branches.

When you start digging out the tree, the first consideration is how big the root-ball must be that you are going to dig out. I cannot think of a golden rule because it depends on the size of the trunk and the amount of smaller roots available. If the tree has only one large taproot, as acacias do, forget about removing the tree from the soil. On the other hand, if the tree has a mass of fibrous roots, it stands a very good chance of surviving the transplanting even if a smaller rootball is kept. A tree like the wild olive (*Olea europaea*) will often survive even if all the roots are cut off. It has enough reserve nutrients to form roots over a long period of time if kept in the right conditions. I have come across rules such as making the diameter of the cut around the tree equal to 1/3 the height of the tree or equal to three times the diameter of the trunk of the tree. Maybe a rule like that could give you some indication of the size of the root-ball.

If possible, dig a furrow around the tree up to the right depth. Thereafter, dig a furrow perpendicular to the circular furrow. This last furrow is necessary to enable you to dig in underneath the tree to cut off the roots and loosen the rootball completely. If this last furrow is impossible, the circular furrow must be sloped in underneath the tree.

Mark the tree as to which side is facing north, and when the tree is in its temporary container, this same side should again face north, for the first few months at least.

As soon as the tree is entirely loose it can be picked up, placed on the hessian or sacking and then the hessian is rolled up around the rootball and tied in place. The hessian should be wet! So as not to cause a mess when transporting the tree, as well as to keep the hessian wet, wrap plastic around the root-ball or, if small enough, put it in a plastic bag which is also tied around the base of the trunk. If the tree is too large to pick up comfortably, the hessian should be rolled up on one side, then the tree must be tilted to a side while the rolled end of the hessian is placed underneath it. The tree is then tilted to the other side so that the hessian can be unrolled underneath it. This will cause little damage to the root-ball. The hessian is now folded up against the trunk and tied around it.

The next step is to place the tree into either a training container or the garden. As a temporary training container, use anything large enough to contain the root-ball, plus a little extra space which should be filled with a more sandy soil mixture to enable the tree to send out new fibrous roots. The container must have adequate drainage holes as well as a sandy layer of soil at the bottom to ensure drainage. If the original ball of soil on the roots is of a very bad clay type, the clay can be removed as far as possible without damaging the roots unduly, and the tree is then grown in a coarse sandy soil mixture. When planting it temporarily into the garden to develop, the same principle should be followed. After having been transferred to its new home, it is important to keep the tree in a shady place and out of wind. Water it regularly to keep the soil wet and even if the soil is wet, the foliage should be sprayed with a misting device quite often for the first few weeks.

If it is at all possible the first few weeks' watering should be in the form of willow water. (See Chapter 7, page 117). Added to this water, or even to ordinary water, vitamin B can be given to reduce the shock of transplanting. Wherever roots of a larger size are cut off, as well as larger branches, or the trunk, these wounds must be

FIGURE 305 Digging is done along the dotted lines, to create a furrow around the tree, as well as to one side to enable one to loosen it completely underneath without disturbing the roots close to the trunk.

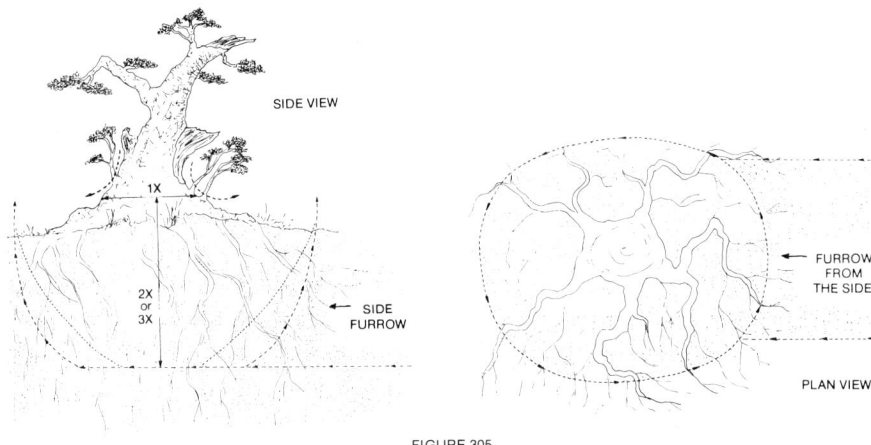

FIGURE 305

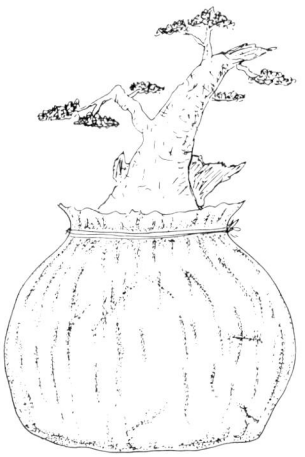

FIGURE 306 Wrap the ball of soil and roots in wet sacking and cover this with a plastic bag.

sealed off. Do not fertilise the tree during the first few months, until some new roots have developed.

The trees should only be moved from the garden soil after a year, whereafter it should go into temporary training container. After another year it can be checked for the development of fibrous roots. In doing so, the original root-ball will be disturbed and the roots are treated in the same fashion as for a repotting, although to a lesser degree during the first year or two, until it can be considered a bonsai. Though it may take a few years to create the final shape of your bonsai, this method of acquiring material will give you bonsai of great character in a much shorter time than is otherwise possible.

When establishing a tree which has been collected from nature or from a garden, the roots closer to the trunk are mostly of a larger size because the finer root system, which is responsible for the intake of water and minerals, is spread out under the drip-line of the tree. This presents a problem, because the tree has to absorb water from the restricted amount of soil in the temporary container — without its essential finer roots. To nurse the tree over this initial period of stress it is good to reduce the foliage to prevent transpiration. If overhead misting devices are used now, this will mean that the leaves receive water directly and this in turn reduces the dependence on the presently inadequate root system to supply the tree with water. When watering is done by means of a watering can or something similar, but directly onto the soil instead, it forces the tree to rapidly form a fibrous root system to supply in the demand from the leaf system. If this last form of watering is applied, it should be done in a 'spartan' manner. (See Chapter 7, page 118)

A sign of a tree's recovery after a transplantation, is when the old leaves start turning yellow and fall off while at the same time new growth is noticed at the growing tips. It shows that the tree is not dependent on the old leaves for its photosynthesis.

When a tree is collected from nature or a garden, and a ball of soil is maintained around the old roots (that is, those that remain after the tree has been removed from the ground), the formation of new fibrous roots is delayed, even if the tree is potted in a reasonably large temporary container. It would be better to remove all the old soil — especially if the roots are thick and old with few smaller, fibrous ones — and regular watering is of utmost importance. This is however a very risky procedure. Rather keep some old soil on the roots and very carefully loosen the soil on the outside of the ball to expose some roots which will then be in contact with the new fresh soil in the training container. Some trees will survive very harsh treatment and it means that you have to know the tree's ability before you attempt to uproot it.

After a year or even two, some new fibrous roots will have formed. If, on inspection, this is found to be the case, the old soil should be removed very carefully so as not to damage the young roots, and the tree should then be repotted in a fresh soil mixture.

The first training (temporary) container should be quite deep. Due to the effect of gravity, the water quickly drains to the bottom, drying out the surface soil, meaning that there is a rapid interchange of water and air (oxygen and carbon-dioxide are of importance in this case), and this whole process is metabolically healthy. The complete process of water and air interchange, and the more constant availability of water in the deeper section of the container, stimulates the tree to rapidly send out new, healthy roots in search of water and dissolved nutrients. In the case of a transplanted tree (or young cutting) this is crucial to the development of the rest of the tree above the soil surface. One should beware of overlooking this fact — the importance of the water and air interchange — and the danger of substituting it with the implementation of fertilisers. It is impossible to have a well-grown, healthy tree without a well-developed, life-giving root system. Attend to the basics until the tree is well-established and then you can concentrate on details. Watering comprises 80% of the tree's needs and is far more important than fertilising, pruning, positioning of branches and leaves — or anything else.

FROM NURSERY STOCK

You will need a temporary training container, plastic gauze, or broken pottery pieces, gravel, soil mixture, groundcover (moss or gravel), willow water, vitamin B_1 and B_{12} (Cytacon tablets or Thiamine hydrochloride injection), tree seal, pruning shears, wire cutter, water spray or misting apparatus, old bent screwdriver, or piece of iron in the shape of a hook.

Look for a tree with the right roots and the right branches, or the potential to have the right branches. If the tree needs drastic pruning, it must not be transplanted into another training pot immediately. After the pruning and wiring have been done, the tree is left in its original container until it has recovered, which will be after about a month or two. Even when it is eventually transplanted, this may have to be into a deeper container than the final pot, to gradually train the roots and reduce them without setting back the tree. In doing it in stages the tree has a chance to develop a fine and fibrous root system.

Before pruning and wiring, allow the tree to wilt somewhat to make the branches flexible.

The water used during the first week or two should be willow water as this reduces the shock and induces root-formation.

Decide on the front of the tree and, if in doubt, decide which side you don't want as the front and the rest will follow. Do the pruning and wiring, and seal off the larger cuts. The most attractive side of the tree is called the '*Omote*' or front. The back is called '*Ura*'.

Remove the tree and the ball of soil from the tin or plastic container — if you think it is safe, because if major pruning was done, this is dangerous. The rest of the steps are followed if the tree is removed. If a major pruning was done the other steps should only follow once the tree has recovered completely. Another viewpoint is to shock the tree only once (prune plus repot) and get this over and done with in one operation!

The soil must now be removed without damaging the roots. If the root-ball is soaked in water, the soil can be washed from the roots with no damage to the finer roots. Tease the roots apart. While doing this and what follows, the roots *must* be kept damp by the water-misting device.

FIGURE 307 The steps to pot a tree from a nursery bag:
Trim and prune completely;
Wire branches if necessary;
Remove the nursery bag or tin;
Remove the excess soil and roots and tease out most of the remaining roots.
Use a slightly deep container to start with;
Fix gauze over the drainage holes;
Place a layer of gravel in the bottom of the pot to ensure drainage;
Build a mound of soil in the position where the tree will stand;
Anchor the tree on the mound of soil;
Work the soil in between the roots with chopsticks and clean up the area around the tree by brushing the excess soil off and placing moss or other groundcover there.

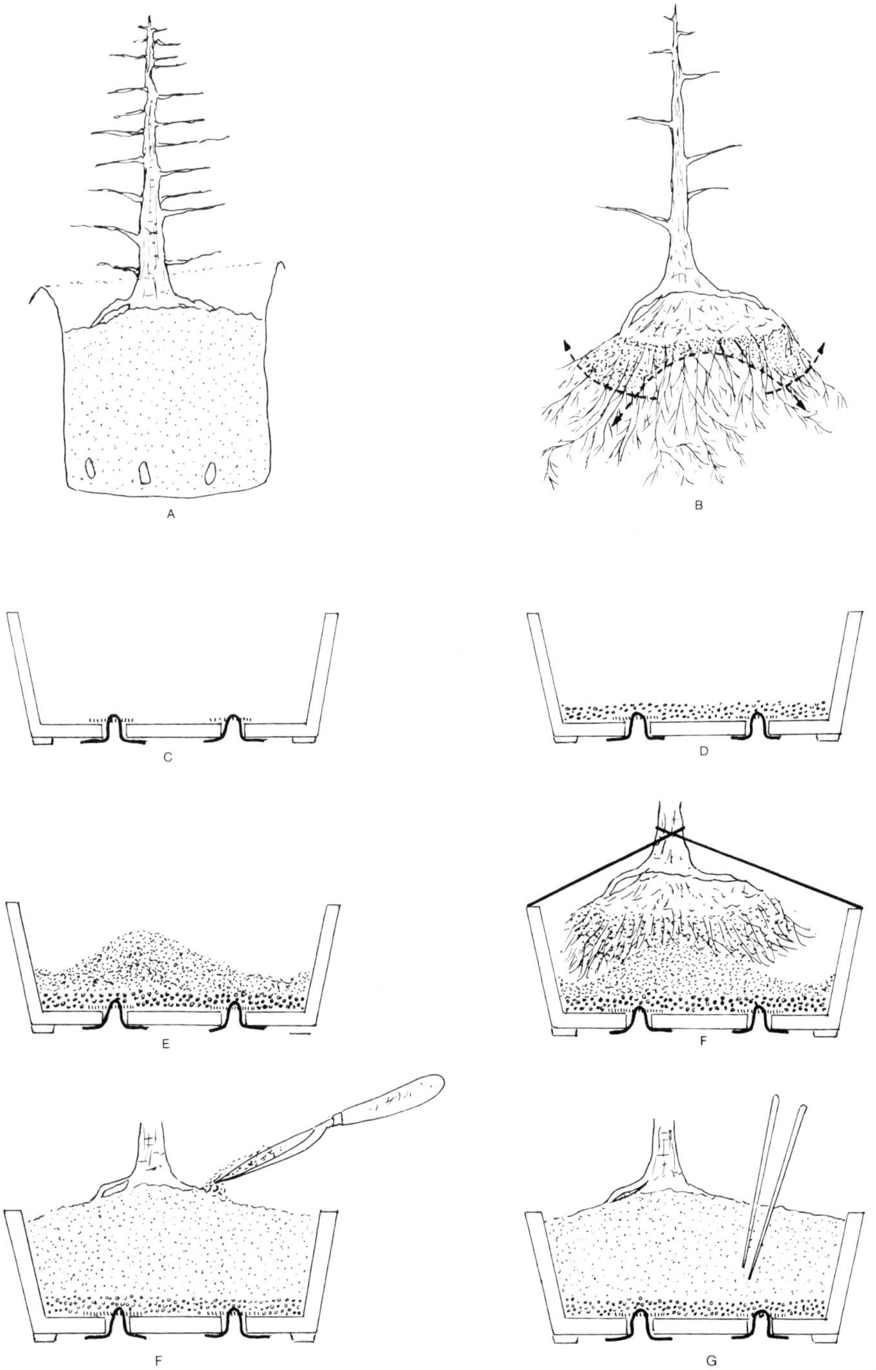

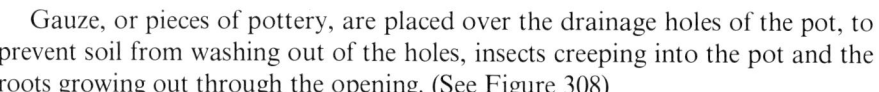

FIGURE 307

Gauze, or pieces of pottery, are placed over the drainage holes of the pot, to prevent soil from washing out of the holes, insects creeping into the pot and the roots growing out through the opening. (See Figure 308)

Cover the bottom of the container with gravel to prevent waterlogging and then build a cone of soil over the spot where you want the tree to stand. Reduce the tree's roots to fit into the container, spread them out and place the tree on top of the cone of soil. If the tree is not stable it can be tied to the container temporarily by means of a piece of wire which is passed through the drainage hole and tied to a small

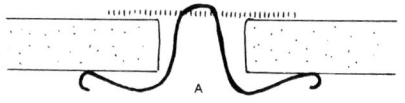 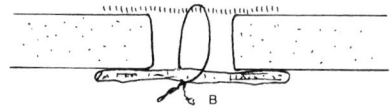

FIGURE 308

FIGURE 308
A. Tie gauze or mesh through the drainage hole with wire.
B. Tie gauze or mesh to a stick or thick wire underneath the drainage hole.

crosswire or stick underneath the pot, or else a piece of string or wire can simply be tied round the outside of the container.

If you have difficulty spreading the roots in the container, the tree can be placed on a flat stone, slate or piece of wood, and the roots can even be tied down to keep them horizontal. (See Figure 309) Fill the container with soil, but see to it that no air is trapped around the roots as this will cause them to rot, when the air is replaced by water. Work the soil in thoroughly by using chopsticks or your fingers.

The whole tree and container is submerged in water (if available, in willow water). When the soil is saturated, powdered vitamin B_1 tablets can be spread over the soil and worked into it. This is to prevent transplant shock.

Complete the surface of the soil by covering it with gravel or moss plantings, whereafter the tree is kept in semi-shade, out of the wnd, for about a month. If possible, keep wetting it during that period with willow water. Water it only when the soil has started drying on the surface.

When transplanting the bonsai into its final pot certain rules have to be followed, but the technique is exactly the same as described for a tree from a nursery. For the rules of tree placement read Chapter 8 on repotting.

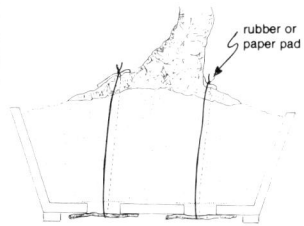

FIGURE 309 Anchor the tree through the drainage holes or tie it to the pot around the outside to prevent movement in the early stages, when new roots need to be formed.

GLOSSARY

Acidity — the degree of acid content, sourness. Expressed as pH.
Air-layering — the technique to create an individual tree out of a branch or trunk of the original tree, by stimulating the branch or trunk to form roots through cutting a ring out of the bark and covering it with wet sphaghnum moss.
Algae — see Fungus.
Antibiotic — substance produced by bacteria (or synthetically) which kills other bacteria.
Apex — the top point of the tree. It could also refer to the tip of a branch.
Aphid — small insect similar to a fly, various colours, attacks young growing tips of branches.
Apical bud — bud on the tip of the shoot.
Axil — the upper angle between branch and leaf.

Bonsai-tana — a bench or table on which a bonsai is kept and trained.
Bud cutting — a bud with a small piece of bark still attached to it. Used for propagation of plant.

Callus — wound repair tissue formed by woody plants to close wound.
Cancer — abnormal, excessive uncontrolled growth, giving rise to tumour formation. A disease — often fatal.
Candle — new growth on pines.
Capillary gauze — synthetic material able to absorb a large quantities of liquid.
Classification — sorting of items into groups that belong together in terms of species, genera etc.
Clip-and-grow method — a very old way of influencing plant growth pattern by severe pruning. Also called *Lingnan* method.
Cold frame — a structure made to protect plants against cold, usually with a transparent lid to allow sunlight in.
Compost — fertiliser and soil conditioner consisting of plant and animal debris, sometimes containing manure of herbivorous animals.
Cone — fruit of a conifer.
Conifer — plant that has cones as fruits, usually evergreen with needle-like or linear leaves.
Cool greenhouse — nursery where temperature does not fall below 4,5 degrees Celsius (40 degrees Fahrenheit).
Coral spot — a fungal disease caused by *Nectria cinnabarina*. It is common on dead branches but could affect live branches through wounds.
Crown — top of tree, total mass of branches and foliage.
Crown gall — parasitic swellings caused by *Bacterium tumefaciens*, on roots of plants.
Cultivar — a variation of a plant, recognised by certain characteristics which are maintained whichever way a plant is propagated.
Cuttings — lengths of branches used for propagation.

Damping off — a fungal infection on seedlings which causes them to collapse.
Deciduous — the leaves drop at end of growing season.
Defoliate — the removal of leaves at approximately midsummer to have smaller leaves with next growth.
Die-back — drying out of branch towards trunk, after having been pruned or through natural causes during winter.
Dormancy — period (winter) during which tree stops growing or grows very little.
Drainage — the ability of soil to let water through without becoming soggy.

Endemic — is confined to a particular area as compared to epidemic which is widespread.
Etiolate — loss of colour due to deficient light. Also refers to lengthening of shoots for same reason.
Evergreen — leaves or needles stay on tree for duration of year.
Eye-level — level opposite eyes. For bonsai purposes the tree should be at such a height that the eyes are at the level of two-thirds of the length of the trunk.

Family — a group of plants of similar nature. Consists of different genera.
Fertiliser — a mixture of chemicals made up of the essential nutrients for plants, for instance phosphates, nitrogen, potash.
Fungicide — chemical which kills fungi.
Fungus — aquatic or sub-aquatic plants which vary in size from microscopic single-celled plants, to enormous sea-algae, some of which are harmful to plants.

Genus — a group of plants of similar nature. Consists of different species.
Germination — the stage when a seed starts developing into a plant.
Grafting — the joining together of branches or trunks and branches of different plants to form new branches, where for instance a branch is needed.

Ground-layering — the formation of roots on a branch by bending this branch to below soil level and then creating a separate tree by separating this branch from the tree.

Growth control — method of controlling growth in tree as a whole or in particular parts by selective pruning or application of fertiliser.

Haiku — Japanese form of poetry. A short verse, usually 17 syllables.

Half-hardy — trees and shrubs that need some degree of protection against frost during winter.

Hardy — trees and shrubs that do not need protection against cold.

Heel — a cutting with a small tag of bark off original branch or trunk.

Humidity — refers to degree of water-vapour in air.

Inarch-grafting — method of grafting a branch onto the same tree or one tree onto another by opposing wounds created in both.

Indole-3-acetic acid — a plant-hormone which suppresses the development of secondary branches.

Lateral — towards the side as opposed to central.

Leader — main trunk, usually in sapling.

Leafmould — partially decomposed dead leaves.

Lime-sulphur — a chemical used to prevent diseases, especially fungal diseases.

Lingnan — a school of bonsai styling which was started by Cantonese growers at the start of the twentieth century.

Literati — a group of scholars in China, also the *bunjin* style of bonsai named after Chinese scholars.

Loam — a fertile soil of good texture.

Micro-climate — the local climatic conditions in immediate vicinity of trees for instance in a greenhouse.

Micro-nutrients — nutrients which are needed in minute quantities by plants, for instance manganese, magnesium, chloride, iron, zinc.

Mineral salts — chemicals found in soil, some of which are used as nutrients by plants.

Moss — very primitive and simple plants which grow in damp, shady areas.

Mould — a kind of fungal disease.

Mycorrhiza — fungi on roots or in roots which are beneficial to plants.

Nanga — a cultural movement to which painters of the Southern School of Chinese landscape artists belonged.

Needles — a leaf shape in for instance pines.

Node — the position on a branch from where leaves sprout.

Parthenogenesis — method of asexual reproduction.

Photosynthesis — method whereby leaves produce starches from carbon-dioxide, oxygen and other nutrients in the presence of light.

Pinching — to pinch off buds or leaves with fingernails or sharp instrument to restrict growth.

Pinnate — a leaf which consists of many smaller leaflets which are located on opposite sides of a divided stalk.

Propagation frame — glass or plastic on raised frame to form a container in which to propagate plants.

Pruning — the method of cutting off leaves and branches to improve shape of plant, to remove unwanted parts and to promote new growth and better fruit and flowers.

Raffia — a kind of palm (*Raphia ruffia*) of which the leaves are used to make a form of tape which is in turn used to plait or tie plants to stakes.

Respiration — the absorption of oxygen and release of carbon-dioxide during the day, reversing the process when it is dark.

Ring-barking — a process whereby a ring of bark is removed around the trunk to get the upper portion of the trunk to die, but it is also used in air-layering to form roots.

Rootbound — the condition when roots have grown to completely fill the container and the tree starts deteriorating.

Root-hormone — a hormone (chemical produced by the plant) which promotes root growth.

Root-pruning — pruning of roots which in bonsai is necessary to help restrict growth of the trees.

Saikei — grouping of trees in a container together with rocks, grasses, gravel etc. to create nature scene.

Scale — small insect within a shell and with sucking mouth parts through which they suck out the plant-sap.

Sealant — a paste which is applied on a pruning wound.

Seedling — young plant just after germination.

Sensei — master in bonsai who teaches bonsai.

Species — grouping of plants which are nearly or exactly the same.

Sphagnum moss — a type of moss growing in marshes.
Stomata — pores on the surface of a leaf through which a plant takes in water vapour and air, and disposes of surplus oxygen and moisture.
Stratification — the overwintering of seeds or hardy plants either outdoors or by making use of a refrigerator to break the dormancy and induce germination.
Sucker — a shoot from a root or trunk which is underground.

Taproot — the main water-seeking roots which also anchor the tree.
Temporary container — a temporary container in which a tree is initially trained. It is usually deeper than the final ceramic pot.
Topiary — the pruning of shrubs and trees into unnatural shapes, for instance animal shapes.
Training pot — see temporary container.
Transpiration — the continuous process of expulsion of moisture by a plant through the pores (stomata) of its leaves.
Turntable — a rotating platform on which bonsai are placed when working on them.

Vestigeal bud — an incompletely developed bud.
Viability — the capacity of seeds to germinate.

Whorl — an arrangement of leaves or flowers in a form like the spokes of a wheel.
Wiring — the technique through which branches and trunks are formed by wrapping wire around them and then bending them into the required shape.
Woolly aphid — an aphid which looks like a tiny ball of fluff.

Zen — regarded as a religion by its followers although without sacred scriptures, fixed canon, rigid dogma, saviour or divine being. Its aims are to bring about a high degree of self-knowledge.

JAPANESE TERMINOLOGY TRANSLATED

Aioi — double trunk or twin tree.
Aioi-no-matsu — Mr and Mrs Pine, as double trunk or twin trees.
Aji — atmosphere presented by tree trunk, literally taste, flavour, or zest.

Bankan — 1. Large curves on a smaller trunk, like a coiled snake. 2. Gnarled trunk. 3. Flat slab of rootage instead of individual roots, typical of olive trees.
Bonju — a bonsai tree.
Bonsai-en — area where bonsai trees are kept and trained.
Bunjin — free style of growing bonsai, abstract, artistic.

Chokkan — formal upright style of bonsai.
Chumono bonsai — medium size bonsai; 40–90 cm tall.
Chu-shakan — tree with medium slant.
Chu-taku — stand of medium height.
Crokan — tree with five trunks.

Dai-bonsai — large bonsai, over 90 cm tall.
Dai-kengai — very vertical, formal cascade.
Dai-shakan — tree with extreme slant.

Fuki-nagashi — windswept style
Fuki-nagashi kengai — cascade with windswept branches and/or trunk.
Funa-ita — board formed from old used wooden structure like boat or door.
Futamata-eda — Y-shaped branch.
Futu-koro — where the two sides of a kimono overlap and form a kind of pocket.
Futu-koro-eda — pocket branch.

Gaito-kengai — cascading from the top of a cliff or dome.
Gei — inherent movement in trunk.

Gohan-yose — group planting of five trees.
Gokan — tree with five trunks.
Goza-kake — raincoat-hanger style.
Gyaku bosori-eda reversed growth branch.
Gyaku-eda — ingrowing branch.
Gyo — a formal display.

Hachi-uye — a large trained tree in a container, but too large to be considered a bonsai: larger than ±1,4 m.
Haiku — Japanese form of verse.
Han-en-eda — half circle branch.
Hankan — gnarled trunk.
Han-kengai — semi-cascade style.
Hiji tsuki-eda — elbow branch.
Hira-dai — a flat stand.
Hoki-zukuri — broom-shaped style.
Honai — 1. A hamlet in Japan. 2. Also earlier style of bonsai as grown in the hamlet.
Honen — a flame-shaped tree.
Horai — 1. The mountain of perpetual youth. 2. A twisted and coiled old-fashioned style of bonsai.

Ichi-no-eda — first or lowest branch.
Ikada — a raft.
Ikada-buki — raft style. A tree that has fallen on its side and the then upright branches have become individual trees.
Ikada-buse — see Ikada-buki
Ikada-uye — see Ikada-buki
Ikada-zukuri — see Ikada-buki
Ippon-uye — a single tree.
Ishi-uye — a rock as a container.
Ishi-zuke — rock-clinging style.
Ito-kengai — cascade in the form of a group of strings.

Jiban — a thin wooden board on which to display medium-sized bonsai.
Jin — dead tip of a branch or apex of a tree.

Kabu-buki — a bonsai with multiple trunks from the same trunk base.
Kabudachi — sprout style.
Kaerumata-eda — U-shaped branch.
Kaminari — trunk struck by lightning.
Kannuki-eda — bar branch.
Karame-miki — entwined trunks.
Kosa-eda — crossed branches.
Kotaku — a tall stand for cascades.
Ku — 1. Nine 2. Pain and suffering.
Kumo — spider style.
Kumo-ashi — cloud-formed leg of container.
Kurume-eda — wheel-spoke branches.
Kusamono — weed or grass for displaying.
Kyuhon-yose — nine trees in a group-planting.
Kyukan — nine trunks on one tree.

Mae-eda — front branch.
Maki-adai — rolled stand.
Mame bonsai — small bonsai. Shorter than 10 cm.
Matsu-zukuri — pine tree shape. Very traditional.
Meoto-matsu — Mr and Mrs Pine, twin trees.
Metsuki-eda — eye-poking branch.
Miki — trunk.
Miki kiri-eda — a branch crossing the trunk.
Mino-kake — raincoat-hanger style.
Moyogi — informal upright growing tree.
Musha-date — see Kabu-buki.

Nagare — tail. Literally 'flowing'.
Nanahan-yose — seven trees in a group-planting.
Nanakan — seven separate trunks on one tree.
Nanban — an area which covers the southern coast of China around Xiamen (Amoy).

Nanga school — Southern School of Painting in China.
Ne-agari — exposed roots style.
Nebari — rootage.
Nejikan — twisted trunk.
Ne-jirekan — twisted trunk.
Ne-joku — a stand made from natural tree roots.
Netsu-ranari — raft style resulting from a long superficial root that has grown sprouts, which have grown into trees.
Ni-no-eda — the second branch.
Niwa-gi — a trained tree in a garden, even if it is smaller than 1,5 m.

O — large.
Omono bonsai — large bonsai: 1,5 m high.
O-Moyogi — excessively curved trunk.

Penjing — Chinese bonsai.
Pen-tsuai — to plant in a pot.
Pien-tshu — a plaited trunk.

Rosoku-zukuri — a flame-shaped tree (candle-flame).

Sabakan — split or hollowed trunk.
Saba-miki — hollowed trunk or split trunk.
Sabi — Buddhist attitude: a graceful form of loneliness and solitude.
Sagari-eda — a dangling branch.
Saikei — a planting of trees, moss, grass and rocks as a landscape scene.
Samon-yose — a group-planting with only three trees.
Sankan — three trunks on one tree.
San-no-eda — the third branch.
San-sui — mountain and water.
San-suiseki — scenery with rocks as the main subject.
Seki — stone.
Seki-joju — root-over-rock style.

Seki-kazari — displaying in individual display booths.
Shakan — slanted style.
Shari — debarked trunk.
Sharikan — debarked, peeled trunk.
Shari-miki — driftwood style or effect.
Shea-tzu-ching — potted trees during the Yuan dynasty (1280–1368)
Shibui — a simple beauty which defies description.
Shickikan — a tree with seven trunks.
Shidare-zukuri — weeping style.
Shin — 1. Apex of tree 2. A very formal display
Shinkire-eda — a stubbed branch.
Shinnashi — no apex.
Shito bonsai — small bonsai, smaller than 7,5 cm tall.
Shizen — natural.
Shizen-ban — a slab of wood formed by sawing a disc of wood out of a trunk. Used to display large bonsai.
Shizen-taku — a stand made from natural roots.
Shizen-zukuri — natural shape.
Shohin bonsai — 1. Small bonsai, *mame bonsai*. 2. Small articles, literally.
Sho-shakan — a tree with a minimal slant.
So — a casual display.
Sogu-ki — a trunk split in two.
Soju — two individual trees but displayed as a unit in a pot.
Sokan — two individual trees but sharing one root system.
Sue-mono — an art item used as complementary display.
Suibon — a flat shallow glazed container for flower arrangements or *ishi-zuke* and *suiseki*.
Sui-poon — see suibon.
Sui-sek — waterstone.
Suiseki — viewing stone.
Sumi-e — a kind of brush painting.

Tachi-agari — base line of a trunk. Literally: standing upwards.
Tachi-agari kengai — upright cascade.
Tachi-eda — upgrowing branch.
Tachiki — informal upright tree (also *tachi-gi*)
Takan-kengai — more than two trunks cascading.
Take-dai — woven bamboo mat to display delicate bonsai.
Taki-kengai — waterfall cascade.
Tako-style — octopus style.
Taku-zukuri — octopus style.
Taku — a stand (also *shoku*).
Tama-zukuri — ball or sphere-shaped tree.
Takan — a single trunk.
Tatami mat — table cloth or floor covering.
Tokonoma — a displaying area, alcove.
Tokonoma-kazari — displaying in a *tokonoma*.
Tsukami-yose — fist planting.

Uke — head. Literally 'to receive'.
Ushiro-eda — back branch.

Wabi — Buddhist attitude comprising absence of superflous material possessions.

Yamahori — a trunk composed of several fused trees due to their developing close together from seeds.
Yama-yori — see Yamahori.
Yama yose — see Yamahori.
Yoko-nagashi kengai — a side-sweeping cascade.
Yoma kazari — a westernised room used for displaying.
Yose-uye — a group-planting similar to a forest.
Yumi-kan — a bow-shaped trunk.

BIBLIOGRAPHY

Kan Yashiroda/*Bonsai: Japanese miniature trees*/Faber and Faber Ltd, 1960
The Encyclopaedia Britannica
Reader's Digest/*Complete Guide to Gardening in South Africa*, 1975
Christine Stewart/*Bonsai*/Orbis Publishing, 1981
Kyuzo Murata/*Bonsai Miniature potted trees: their training and care for beginners*/Shufunomoto Co. Ltd, 1964
Editors of Sunset and Sunset Magazine/*Bonsai: Illustrated guide to an ancient art*/Lone Publishing Co, 1981
John Yoshio Naka/*Bonsai Techniques 1*/Dennis Landman Publishers, 1973
John Yoshio/*BOnsai Techniques 2*/Dennis Landman Publishers, 1982
Deborah R. Koreshoff/*Bonsai, It's Art, Science, History and Philosophy*/Macmillan South Africa, 1984
Anne Swinton/*The Collingridge Handbook of Bonsai*/Collingridge Books, 1982
Doug Hall/*Growing Bonsai in South Africa*/Southern Book Publishers, 1988
Betty Edwards/*Drawing on the Artist Within*/Collins: Johannesburg, 1987

INDEX

adult shape 47
aesthetic impact 12
age
   – actual, of bonsai 2
   – apparent, of bonsai 2, 12, 19
air-layering 180
   – to create sprout style 89
Aji 152
algae 27
apex 34, 48
   – as jin 31
   – of cascade style 79
   – of semi-cascade 77
asymmetry 13
autumn 135
auxin 22, 41, 51
   – effect on leaf size 22
Azaleas
   – flowers 59
   – pruning 59

background to display 155
balance
   – cascade, 79
   – semi-cascade, 76
ball-shape style 92
baobab style 100
bending 59
   – branch 59
   – thick branches 64
bonsai
   – art 11
   – aura 12
   – calendar 111
   – containers 141
   – definition 1
   – displaying 149
   – from cuttings 158
   – from nature 164
   – from nursery stock 167
   – from seed 158
   – harmony 12
   – history of 5
   – individuality 12
   – inherent movement 152
   – judging 155
   – outline of 18, 20
   – planted in garden 32
   – pots 141
   – purpose of 2

   – repotting 146
   – shaping 39, 59
   – size 67
   – styles 71
   – unit 13
   – watering 117
bonsai-en 115
bonsai-tana 116
branches – 15
   – angles of 16, 17
   – bending 64
   – diameter 16
   – elasticity 61
   – faults 34
   – grafting 35
   – position of 16
   – pruning 44
   – sacrificial 31
broad-leaf trees, trimming 56
broom style 90
bud-cuttings 159
Buddhism, influence of 6, 69
bud-nipping, method 22
Bunjin, style 93
   – group-planting 98
   – pots for 94

calendar for bonsai 111
candles on pines 53
cascade style 78
ceramics 139
characterisation 103
charts for fertilisers 123
China
   – map 7
   – bonsai in 5, 9
Chokkan style 72
classification of bonsai 67
clay
   – in growing medium 125
   – in pottery 139
clip-and-grow method 39
clump style 89
collecting bonsai from nature 164
complementary exhibit (piece) 150
compost 126
container (pot) 139
copper wire 60
corded growth 58
cut surface, angle of 56

cuttings 158
cytokinins 22, 41, 51

decaying wood, prevention 103
deciduous trees
   – defoliation 23, 49
   – leaf-cutting 22
defoliation 23, 49
diseases 119
displaying bonsai 149
distribution of vigour 48
divine proportion 14
double trunk style 98
drainage of water 131
driftwood 109
dwarfing, of tree 3

evaluating bonsai 2
exposed roots style 84

fertilising 22, 120
Fibonacci series 14
flame shape style 92
flat-top (crown) style 102
flexing of trunk 30
flowering bonsai 58
formal upright style 72
fruit on bonsai 58
Fuki-nagashi style 94
full cascade 78

garden-growing 32
Gei 152
giberillin 51
gnarled trunk style 109
Golden Section of Division 14
golden rectangle 15
grafting
   – branches 36
   – buds 38
   – general 35
   – roots 36
   – trunks 36
Gravel as groundcover 25
groundcovers 25
   – lichen 26
   – moss 25
ground-layering 162
group-planting
   – as bunjin 94

177

– Pierneef style 101
– style 95
growing medium 131
growing tips, pinching 22, 58
growth, regulation of 51
Gyo (informal display) 149

Haiku 3
Han-kengai 76
head
    – of full cascade 79
    – of semi-cascade 76
healing of wound 45
hollow trunk 103
Honai method 108
Horai style 108
hormones, *see* auxin and cytocinin
humus 126

informal upright style 73
internodal distance 20
Ishi-ue (uye) 84
Ishi-zuke 82

Japan 6
jin 104
    – in semi-cascade style 77
    – liquid 103
judging bonsai 155

Kengai 78
knobby trunk 109

layering
    – air-layering 160
    – ground-layering 162
leaves 20
    – alternating, pruning of 56
    – autumn colour 135
    – compactness 20
    – cuttings 159
    – defoliation 23, 49
    – internodal distance 20
    – leaf-cutting 22
    – nipping out 22
    – paired, pruning of 56
    – small 21
    – spartan training 22
    – wilting 118
Leonardo of Pisa 14

lime 124
lime-sulphur 103
Lingnan
    – method 40
    – school 9
literati
    – scholars 9, 93
    – style 9, 93
liverwort 26

maintenance 111
Mame bonsai 67
manure 127
marcottage *see* air-layering
mealy bugs 119
mildew 119
modelling, method of shaping 39
moss 25
movement
    – inherent 152
    – in complementary display 152
Moyogi style (informal upright style) 73
mycorrhiza 130

Nagare (tail) 79
Nanga school 9
natural style 73
Nebari 24
negative method of shaping 39
nipping out
    – buds 22
    – leaves 22
    – octopus style 93

Ō-moyogi 74
outline of bonsai 18, 20

Pacioli, Lucas 14
peat 127
peeled bark trunk 109
Penjing 9, 10
pests 119
phosphates 124
photosynthesis 134
Pierneef style 101
pinching, new shoots (buds) 57
pines 52
plaited trunk 107
positive technique of shaping 39
pots 139

– choice of 141
– position in display 154
– position of bonsai in pot 145
potting 146
proportion, divine 14
pruning 43
    – broad-leafed trees 56
    – clip-and-grow technique 39
    – cored growth 58
    – effects in general 46
    – effects of during different seasons 48
    – flowering trees 58
    – fruiting trees 58
    – Lingnan technique 40
    – pines 52
    – prevention of scars 45
    – purpose of 43
    – scale-like growth 58
    – timing 43
    – tufted growth 58

raft style 86
raincoat-hanger style 77
reduction method 42
repotting 146
ring-barking 161
rock
    – choice for *ishi-zuke* 82
    – choice for *seki-joju* 80
    – container 84
rock-clinging style 82
roots 24, 129, 133
    – faults 27
    – size of 23
root-over-rock style 80
rules 1, 9

Saikei 3, 9
sand 23
scars, due to wires 61
sculptural method 39
semi-cascade style 76
shape, triangular 13, 20, 47
shari 105
sinuous style 86
slanted style 74
soil 125
    – acidity 128
    – effect of fertilisers 127

– kinds of 125
– leaching 129
– loam 125
– mixture 131
– organic component of 126
– practical tips 130
– sand 125
– water 128
South African styles 69
spartan watering 20, 22, 118
sphere shape 92
spider style 93
split trunk 109
sprout style 89
stands 154
struck-by-lightning style 109
styles
   – ball shape 92
   – baobab 100
   – broom 90
   – bunjin 93
   – clump 89
   – exposed roots 84
   – flat crown 102
   – formal upright 72
   – full cascade 78
   – horai 108

– informal upright 73
– literati 93
– natural style 16
– Pierneef 101
– raft 86
– raincoat-hanger 77
– rock-clinging 82
– root-over-rock 80
– semi-cascade 76
– sinuous 86
– slanted 74
– sphere 92
– sprout 89
– traditional pine 100
– umbrella 92
– twin (two) trees 98
– twin (double) trunks 98
– weeping branches 92
– windswept 94
Suiseki 151
sunlight 21
symmetry 13

tail 76, 79
Tokonoma 150
tools 136
tourniquet 31

traditional pine shape 100
trunk 15, 134
   – apex 15, 31
   – bunjin 93
   – faults 30
   – flexing 30
   – grafting 36
   – increase in diameter 30
twin trees style 98
twisted trunk 108

umbrella style 92
upright cascade 78

vigour distribution 48, 59

water 31, 79
watering 117
weeping branches style 92
willow water 117
wilting 118
windswept style 94
wiring 60
   – removing 66
   – time to 61

Yose-uye 95

NOTES